Digital Holography

Digital Holography

Pascal Picart
Jun-chang Li

First published 2012 in Great Britain and the United States by ISTE Ltd and John Wiley & Sons, Inc.

ISTE Ltd
27-37 St George's Road
London SW19 4EU
UK

www.iste.co.uk

John Wiley & Sons, Inc.
111 River Street
Hoboken, NJ 07030
USA

www.wiley.com

Library of Congress Cataloging-in-Publication Data

Picart, Pascal.
 Digital holography / Pascal Picart, Junchang Li.
   p. cm.
 Includes bibliographical references and index.
 ISBN 978-1-84821-344-9 (hardback)
 1. Holography--Mathematics. 2. Holography--Data processing. 3. Image processing--Digital techniques. I. Li, Junchang, 1945- II. Title.
 QC449.P53 2012
 621.36'750285--dc23
                                                                    2011050552

British Library Cataloguing-in-Publication Data
A CIP record for this book is available from the British Library
ISBN: 978-1-84821-344-9

Printed and bound in Great Britain by CPI Group (UK) Ltd., Croydon, Surrey CR0 4YY

Table of Contents

Introduction

Holography was invented in 1947 by the Hungarian physicist Dennis Gabor during his research into electronic microscopy [GAB 48, GAB 49]. This invention won him the Nobel Prize in physics in 1971. It took until 1962 [LEI 62, LEI 61, DEN 62, DEN 63] for the first lasers used for this technique to find concrete applications [POW 65, COL 71]. Holography is a productive mix of interference and diffraction. Interference encodes the amplitude and relief of a 3D object, and diffraction works as a decoder, reconstructing a wave that seems to come from the object that was originally illuminated [FRA 69]. This encoding contains all the information on a given scene: amplitude and phase – thus relief. Practically, the execution of a "Denisyuk" type [DEN 62, DEN 63] "analog" hologram is carried out in three steps: the first step concerns the recording of the interference pattern on a photosensitive support, typically a plate of silver gelatin; the second step involves the chemical process of development/treatment of the support (which typically lasts around a quarter of an hour with silver gelatin plates); and the last step is the process of the physical reconstruction of the object wave, where the laser is diffracted by the sinusoidal grating encoded in the photosensitive support, making the initial object "magically" appear. The magic of holography is explained by wave optics [GOO 72, BOR 99, COL 71, HAR 02, HAR 06]. Considering the constraints involved in the treatment of holograms (an essential stage of their development), which make their industrial use difficult for quality control in production lines, for example [SMI 94], the replacement of the silver support by a matrix of the discrete values of the hologram was envisaged in 1967 [GOO 67]. The idea was to replace the analog recording/decoding by a digital recording/decoding simulating diffraction by a digital grating. Holography thus became "digital" [HUA 71, KRO 72]. The attempts of the time suffered from a crucial lack of technological means permitting the recording of holograms while respecting sampling conditions and allowing the reconstruction of the diffracted field with a reasonable calculation time. From the 1970s up to the 1990s we witnessed a veritable boom of holography, as much from the point of view of applications [JON 89, RAS 94, SMI 94, KRE 96], as from the holography of art [GEN 00, GEN 08]. Some industrial systems based on dynamic holography are even currently commercialized [OPT 11]. The material used for the recording is a photoreactive crystal [TIZ 82]. Nevertheless, the difficulty of the treatment of the holograms and the relative complexity of the devices have impeded a real industrial penetration of the methods developed in the laboratory in the past 30 years. In parallel, at the same time, we witnessed the development of interferometry techniques (Twyman–Green and Fizeau interferometry) for the control of optical surfaces using phase-shifting methods [WYA 75, CRE 88, DOR 99]. The reader will notice that in the literature several terms have been used to describe "holography", often among which is the term "interferometry". With the advent of image sensors, the rapid development of "digital" interferometry [BRU 74] and of "TV holography" [DOV 00] has blurred the distinction between holography and interferometry. Holography was initially, and foremost, a non-conventional imaging technique permitting a true 3D parallax, whereas interferometry was a useful tool for the analysis and the measurement of wave fronts. With the development of laser sources and the increase in the resolution of image sensors, from which both disciplines have benefited, the frontier between Michelson interferometry, Mach–Zehnder interferometry, Twyman–Green interferometry, and holographic interferometry is henceforth much less marked than previously. The common objective of these methods is to record/reconstruct the smooth or speckled optical wave front. This means that these disciplines are intimately linked by the connectedness of their fundamentals. Thus, in this book, we can use the terms "holography" and "interferometry" interchangeably.

Even though the concepts of the implementation of digital holography had been known for some time, it took until the 1990s for "digital" holography based on array detectors to come about [SCH 94]. In effect, at the end of the 1980s, we witnessed important developments in two sectors of technology: microtechnological procedures have allowed the creation of image sensors with numerous miniaturized pixels, and the rapid computational treatment of images has become accessible with the appearance of powerful processors and an increase in storage capacities. These advances were made possible by the video games industry that boomed in the middle of the 1980s. From 1994, holography found new life in the considerable stimulation of research efforts. Figure I.1 shows graphs demonstrating the number of scientific publications in the domain of digital holography between 1993 and 2011 (keywords "digital holography", source: ISI – Web of Sciences, 2011). The database lists more than 2,300 articles, of which 57 have been cited more than 57 times.

The most cited articles concern the methods of reconstruction, digital holographic microscopy, secure encoding, and metrological applications. The development of digital holographic microscopy from 1999 has led to commercial systems [LYN 11]. Figure I.1 shows that the explosion of digital holography dates from the start of the 2000s. This revival is explained in part by the appearance on the market of numerous laser sources (laser diodes or diode-pumped solid-state lasers), at moderate cost, giving the opportunity to develop compact and versatile systems. Thus, 10 years after this boom, it seems an opportune time to propose an introductory book on digital holography. This book describes the mathematical fundamentals, the numerical calculation of diffraction, and the reconstruction algorithms, and precisely explains a certain number of techniques and applications that use the phase of the reconstructed field.

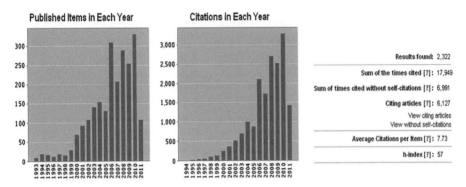

Figure I.1. *Graphs of the number of articles published and of citations since 1993*

Analog or digital holography is closely related to the diffraction of light. However, in practice, it is often difficult to obtain analytical solutions to diffraction calculations, leading to the use of computational methods in order to obtain numerical results. The spectacular development of computational methods in recent years offers everybody the opportunity to calculate the Fourier transform of any image rapidly. Currently, very few works on optics are dedicated specifically to numerical calculations of diffraction, which is fundamental to digital holography. This is why we wish, with this book, to present the fundamentals of diffraction, summarize the different existing techniques of calculation, and give practical examples of applications. This book is for engineers, researchers, and science students at master's level, and will supply them with the basics for entering the vast domain of digital holography.

This book is structured in seven chapters, an appendix, and a list of bibliographical references. The first chapter is a reminder of the mathematical prerequisites necessary for a good understanding of the book. In particular, it describes certain widely used mathematical functions, the theory of two-dimensional linear systems, and the Fourier transform as well as the calculation of the discrete Fourier transform. Chapter 2 introduces the scalar theory of diffraction and describes the propagation of an optical field in a homogeneous medium. The classical approaches are presented and the chapter is concluded with Collins' formula that is used to treat problems of diffraction in waves propagating across an optical system. In Chapter 3, we develop the methods for calculating diffraction integrals using the fast Fourier transform, and we discuss sampling conditions that must be satisfied for the application of each formula. The fundamentals of holography are tackled in Chapter 4; we describe the different types of hologram and the diffraction process that leads to the magic of holography. The fundamentals being outlined, Chapter 5 presents digital Fresnel holography and the algorithms of reconstruction by Fresnel transform or by convolution. We also present methods of digital color holography. This part is illustrated by numerous examples. Chapter 6 is an extension of Chapter 5 in the case where the field propagates across an optical system. The seventh and last chapter considers digital holographic interferometry and its applications. The objective is to propose a synthesis of the methods that exploit the phase of the reconstructed hologram to provide quantitative information on the changes that any object (biological or material) is subjected to.

The Appendix proposes examples of programs for diffraction calculations and digital hologram reconstruction with the methods described in Chapter 5.

Chapter 1

Mathematical Prerequisites

Digital holography is a discipline that associates the techniques of traditional optical holography with current computational methods [GOO 67, HUA 71, KRO 72, LYO 04, SCH 05]. In the framework of the scalar theory of diffraction [BOR 99, GOO 72, GOO 05], digital holography tackles, based on diffraction formulae, the propagation of a light wave in an optical system, the study of interference between coherent light waves, and the reconstruction of surface waves diffracted by objects of various natures. In this context, the propagation of a light wave can be considered as the transformation of a two-dimensional signal by a linear system–the optical system. Various representations of the scalar amplitude of a light wave carrying information use special mathematical functions; the transformation of a light wave across a linear system uses a fundamental mathematical tool: two-dimensional Fourier analysis. The digital treatment of optical information leads us to treat the problems of sampling and discretization, under the restriction given by Shannon's theorem. Thus, the mathematical prerequisites for a good understanding of this book concern the frequently used mathematical functions, the two-dimensional Fourier transform, and the notions of the sampling theorem [GOO 72].

1.1. Frequently used special functions

Many mathematical functions that we will present in this section are frequently used in this book. To understand their properties, we give a brief account of their physical meaning.

1.1.1. *The "rectangle" function*

The one-dimensional rectangle function is defined by:

$$\text{rect}(x) = \begin{cases} 1 & (|x| \leq 1/2) \\ 0 & \text{otherwise} \end{cases}$$

[1.1]

This function is represented in Figure 1.1.

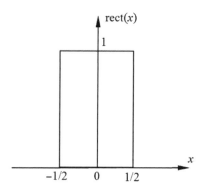

Figure 1.1. *Rectangle function*

Depending on the nature of the variable x, the rectangle function has various meanings. For example, if x is a spatial variable (a spatial coordinate in millimeters), we can use the function to represent the transmittance from a slit pierced in an opaque screen. In this book, we generally use the two-dimensional rectangle function that is obtained by the product of two one-dimensional functions. As an example, the following function is very useful:

$$f(x,y) = \text{rect}\left(\frac{x - x_0}{a}\right)\text{rect}\left(\frac{y - y_0}{b}\right)$$

[1.2]

This function is shown in Figure 1.2. It allows us to simply represent the transmittance from an aperture of a rectangular shape, centered on the point with coordinates (x_0, y_0) and of lengths a and b along the x- and y-axes, respectively.

This binary function is very useful for considering the amplitude of an optical wave limited to a rectangular region, by eliminating the values outside the zone of interest.

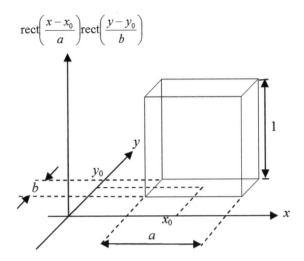

Figure 1.2. *Two-dimensional rectangle function centered on (x_0, y_0)*

1.1.2. *The "sinc" function*

The one-dimensional sinc function is defined by:

$$\mathrm{sinc}(x) = \frac{\sin \pi x}{\pi x} \qquad [1.3]$$

Its curve is presented in Figure 1.3.

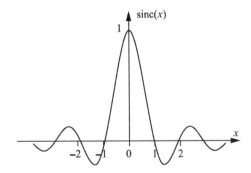

Figure 1.3. *The sinc function*

Also, the two-dimensional sinc function is formed by the product of two functions of independent variables:

$$\text{sinc}(x, y) = \text{sinc}(x)\,\text{sinc}(y) \qquad [1.4]$$

Let us consider two positive values a and b; Figure 1.4 shows the curve of the function $\text{sinc}^2(x/a, y/b)$. In Chapter 2, we will see that such a function represents the intensity distribution of Fraunhofer diffraction from a rectangular aperture illuminated by a coherent wave.

$$\text{sinc}^2(x/a, y/b)$$

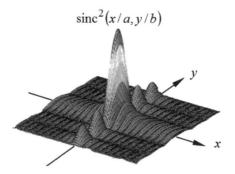

Figure 1.4. *Two-dimensional sinc function*

1.1.3. *The "sign" function*

The one-dimensional sign function is defined as:

$$\text{sgn}(x) = \begin{cases} 1 & x > 0 \\ 0 & x = 0 \\ -1 & x < 0 \end{cases} \qquad [1.5]$$

The curve of this function is given in Figure 1.5.

If a function is multiplied by the function sgn(x–a), for $a < 0$, the sign of the function will be inverted. If a coherent optical field is multiplied by this function, the resulting change corresponds to a phase shift of π. We can also form a two-dimensional sign function by taking the product of two one-dimensional functions.

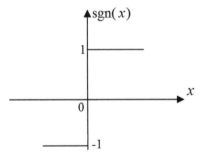

Figure 1.5. *The sign function*

1.1.4. *The "triangle" function*

The triangle function is defined as:

$$\Lambda(x) = \begin{cases} 1 - |x|, & |x| \leq 1 \\ 0, & \text{otherwise} \end{cases} \qquad [1.6]$$

The curve of this function is given in Figure 1.6. Later, we will see that the Fourier transform of the function $\Lambda(x)$ is $\text{sinc}^2(f_x)$ (with the f_x coordinate corresponding to the *spatial* frequency). This function will be very useful in the Fourier analysis of optical diffracting functions (e.g. diffraction grating). As noted earlier, we can form a two-dimensional triangle function by taking the product of two one-dimensional functions.

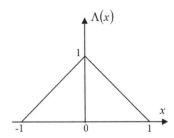

Figure 1.6. *Triangle function*

1.1.5. *The "disk" function*

In practice, an optical system is generally constructed with lenses whose mounts (cylinders) are circular in form. Their pupils are therefore circular and the disk function is often used to model the diffraction of circular elements (iris diaphragms, mounts, etc.). The definition of this function, in polar and Cartesian coordinates, is:

$$\text{circ}(r) = \text{circ}\left(\sqrt{x^2 + y^2}\right) = \begin{cases} 1 & r = \sqrt{x^2 + y^2} \leq 1 \\ 0 & r = \sqrt{x^2 + y^2} > 1 \end{cases} \qquad [1.7]$$

The surface of the disk function is given in Figure 1.7.

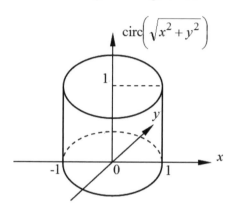

Figure 1.7. *The disk function*

1.1.6. *The Dirac δ function*

1.1.6.1. *Definition*

In the field of optical treatment of information, the Dirac δ distribution (henceforth called the δ "function") in two dimensions is very widely used. Strictly speaking, δ is a distribution but for convenience we will hereafter call it a function. According to the Huygens–Fresnel principle of the propagation of light, a wave front can be considered as the sum of spherical "secondary" sources [BOR 99, GOO 72, GOO 05]. The two-dimensional δ function is often used to individually describe point sources. The fundamental property of the δ function is that, as for an infinitely narrow pulse of infinite height, the sum $\int_{-\infty}^{\infty}\int_{-\infty}^{\infty} \delta(x,y)\,dxdy$ is equivalent to one (x and y being Cartesian coordinates). The δ function can be defined by various mathematical expressions, one of which is presented here.

Let us consider a series of the function $f_N(x) = N\,\text{rect}(Nx)$ ($N = 1, 2, 3,...$). Figure 1.8 shows the curves corresponding to the number $N = 1, 2, 4$. It is evident that the greater the value of N, the narrower the non-zero zone of the function. It is not difficult to imagine that if N tends to infinity, the value of the function $f_N(x) = N \operatorname{rect}(Nx)$ will be infinite as well. On the other hand, the surface enclosed by the curve of the function and the x-axis stays unchanged, and equals one. Thus, by using the rectangular function, the one-dimensional δ function can also be defined as:

$$\delta(x) = \lim_{N \to \infty} N \operatorname{rect}(Nx) \tag{1.8}$$

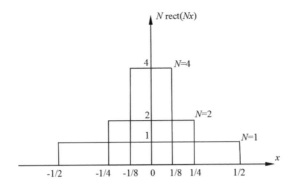

Figure 1.8. *Graph of $f_N(x)$ for $N=1, 2, 4$*

Evidently, we can also define the two-dimensional δ function as:

$$\delta(x,y) = \lim_{N \to \infty} N^2 \operatorname{rect}(Nx)\operatorname{rect}(Ny) \tag{1.9}$$

To facilitate the use of the δ function, we give some equivalent definitions:

$$\delta(x,y) = \lim_{N \to \infty} N^2 \exp\left[-N^2\pi\left(x^2 + y^2\right)\right] \tag{1.10}$$

$$\delta(x,y) = \lim_{N \to \infty} N^2 \operatorname{sinc}(Nx)\operatorname{sinc}(Ny) \tag{1.11}$$

$$\delta(x,y) = \lim_{N \to \infty} \frac{N^2}{\pi}\operatorname{circ}\left(N\sqrt{x^2 + y^2}\right) \tag{1.12}$$

$$\delta(x,y) = \lim_{N \to \infty} N\frac{J_1\left(2\pi N\sqrt{x^2 + y^2}\right)}{\sqrt{x^2 + y^2}} \tag{1.13}$$

In the last expression, J_1 is a first-order Bessel function of the first kind. Depending on the problem being studied, these definitions can be more or less appropriate and we can also choose which definition to apply in each case.

1.1.6.2. *Fundamental properties*

We will now consider some of the mathematical properties of the δ function. These properties will be used frequently in this book.

1.1.6.2.1. Contraction–dilation of coordinates

If a is any constant, we have:

$$\delta(ax) = \frac{1}{|a|}\delta(x)$$ [1.14]

1.1.6.2.2. Product

If the function $\varphi(x)$ is continuous at the point x_0, we have:

$$\varphi(x)\delta(x-x_0) = \varphi(x_0)\delta(x-x_0)$$ [1.15]

1.1.6.2.3. Convolution

Let us consider the convolution of two functions δ and φ:

$$\delta(x) * \varphi(x) = \int_{-\infty}^{\infty} \delta(x_0)\varphi(x-x_0)\,dx_0$$ [1.16]

Then we have:

$$\delta(x) * \varphi(x) = \varphi(x) * \delta(x) = \varphi(x)$$ [1.17]

The δ function is the unity of the convolution product.

1.1.6.2.4. Translation

The property of translation of the δ function is often used for theoretical analyses and proofs. Here we present this property and the corresponding proof. If $\varphi(x)$ is continuous at the point x_0, then we have:

$$\int_{-\infty}^{\infty} \delta(x-x_0)\varphi(x)\,dx = \varphi(x_0)$$ [1.18]

PROOF.– Let $x - x_0 = x'$, on the left of the previous expression we can write:

$$\int_{-\infty}^{\infty} \delta(x)\varphi(x + x_0) dx =$$

$$\int_{-\infty}^{-\varepsilon} \delta(x)\varphi(x + x_0) dx + \int_{-\varepsilon}^{+\varepsilon} \delta(x)\varphi(x + x_0) dx + \int_{+\varepsilon}^{\infty} \delta(x)\varphi(x + x_0) dx$$

[1.19]

If $\varepsilon \to 0$, the first and third terms on the right will be zero, therefore:

$$\int_{-\infty}^{\infty} \delta(x - x_0)\varphi(x) dx = \lim_{\varepsilon \to 0} \int_{-\varepsilon}^{+\varepsilon} \delta(x)\varphi(x + x_0) dx$$

$$= \varphi(x_0) \int_{-\varepsilon}^{+\varepsilon} \delta(x) dx = \varphi(x_0)$$

[1.20]

In the same way, we can show that the two-dimensional δ function possesses the same property of translation.

$$\int_{-\infty}^{\infty} \int_{-\infty}^{\infty} \delta(x - x_0, y - y_0)\varphi(x, y) dx dy = \varphi(x_0, y_0)$$

[1.21]

1.1.7. The "comb" function

The comb function is a periodic series of δ functions. It is frequently used to model the sample of continuous functions. The definition of the one-dimensional comb function is:

$$\text{comb}(x) = \sum_{n=-\infty}^{\infty} \delta(x - n) \qquad (n = 1, 2, 3, \ldots) \qquad [1.22]$$

Figure 1.9 shows the curves of $\delta(x)$ and comb(x). The two-dimensional comb function can be defined by the product of two one-dimensional comb functions:

$$\text{comb}(x, y) = \sum_{n=-\infty}^{\infty} \delta(x - n) \sum_{m=-\infty}^{\infty} \delta(y - m) \qquad (n, m = 1, 2, 3, \ldots) \qquad [1.23]$$

Since the comb function is a periodic series of δ functions, it has analogous properties and is used in numerous analyses of optical signals.

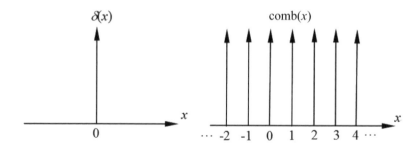

Figure 1.9. *The δ(x) and comb(x) functions*

1.2. Two-dimensional Fourier transform

The Fourier transform is a very useful mathematical tool for the study of both linear and nonlinear phenomena. As the propagation of the optical field can be considered as a process of linear transformation of the "object" field to the "image" field, we are immediately interested in the two-dimensional Fourier transform [BOR 99, GOO 72].

1.2.1. *Definition and existence conditions*

The Fourier transform of a complex function $g(x, y)$ of two independent variables, which we write here as $F\{g(x,y)\}$, is defined as ($j = \sqrt{-1}$):

$$F\{g(x,y)\} = G(f_x, f_y) = \int\limits_{-\infty}^{\infty} \int g(x,y) \exp\left[-j2\pi\left(f_x x + f_y y\right)\right] dx\,dy \quad [1.24]$$

Thus defined, the transform is itself a complex-valued function of the two independent variables $G(f_x, f_y)$, called the spectral function, or spectrum, of the original function $g(x, y)$. The two variables f_x and f_y are considered, without loss of generality, as frequencies. In optics, (x, y) are spatial variables and (f_x, f_y) are *spatial frequencies* (mm^{-1}). Similarly, the inverse Fourier transform of the function $G(f_x, f_y)$, which we write as $F^{-1}\{G(f_x, f_y)\}$, is defined as:

$$F^{-1}\{G(f_x, f_y)\} = \int\limits_{-\infty}^{\infty} \int G(f_x, f_y) \exp\left[j2\pi\left(f_x x + f_y y\right)\right] df_x\,df_y \quad [1.25]$$

We note that the direct and inverse transformations are completely analogous mathematical operations. They differ only by the sign of the exponent in the double integral. However, for some functions, these two integrals cannot exist in a mathematical sense. Therefore, we will briefly discuss the conditions of their existence. Among the various conditions, we concern ourselves with the following:

– $g(x, y)$ must be absolutely integrable in the xy-plane;

– $g(x, y)$ must have a finite number of discontinuities and a finite number of maxima and minima in any rectangle of finite area;

– $g(x, y)$ cannot have any infinite discontinuities.

In general, one of these three conditions can be ignored if we can guarantee strict adherence to the other conditions, but this is beyond the scope of discussions in this book.

For the representation of real physical waves by ideal mathematical functions, in the analysis of tools, one or more of the existing conditions presented above may be more or less unsatisfied [GOO 72]. However, as Bracelet [BRA 65] remarked, "the physical possibility is a sufficient condition of validity to justify the existence of a transformation". Furthermore, the functions of interest to us are included in the scope of Fourier analysis, and it is evidently necessary to generalize definition [1.24] somewhat. Thus, it is possible to find a transformation that has meaning for functions that do not strictly satisfy the existing conditions, provided that these functions can be defined as the limit of a sequence of transformable functions. In transforming each term of this sequence, we generate a new sequence whose limit is called the generalized Fourier transform of the original function. These generalized transforms can be handled in the same way as the ordinary transforms, and the distinction between the two is often ignored. For a more detailed discussion of this generalization, the reader may refer to the work of Lighthill [LIG 60].

To simplify the study of Fourier analysis, including this generalization, Table 1.1 shows the Fourier transforms of some functions expressed in Cartesian coordinates.

1.2.2. Theorems related to the Fourier transform

We now present some important mathematical theorems followed by a brief account of their physical meaning [GOO 72]. The theorems mentioned below will be used frequently as they constitute fundamental tools for the use of Fourier transforms; they allow us to simplify the calculation of solutions to problems in Fourier analysis.

Original function	Fourier transform
$f(x,y) * g(x,y)$	$\tilde{f}(f_x,f_y) \times \tilde{g}(f_x,f_y)$
$f(x,y)\exp\left[2j\pi(xf_0 + yf_0)\right]$	$\tilde{f}(f_x - f_0, f_y - f_0)$
1	$\delta(f_x,f_y)$
$\delta(x,y)$	1
$\delta(x - x_0, y - y_0)$	$\exp\left[-j2\pi(f_x x_0 + f_y y_0)\right]$
$\mathrm{rect}(x)\mathrm{rect}(y)$	$\sin c(f_x)\sin c(f_y)$
$\Lambda(x)\Lambda(y)$	$\sin c^2(f_x)\sin c^2(f_y)$
$\mathrm{sgn}(x)\mathrm{sgn}(y)$	$\dfrac{1}{j\pi f_x} \times \dfrac{1}{j\pi f_y}$
$\exp\left[-\pi(x^2 + y^2)\right]$	$\exp\left[-\pi(f_x^2 + f_y^2)\right]$
$\exp\left[-j2\pi(ax + by)\right]$	$\delta(f_x - a, f_y - b)$
$\mathrm{circ}\left(\sqrt{x^2 + y^2}\right)$	$J_1\left(2\pi\sqrt{f_x^2 + f_y^2}\right) / \sqrt{f_x^2 + f_y^2}$
$\cos(2\pi f_0 x)$	$\dfrac{1}{2}\left[\delta(f_x - f_0) + \delta(f_x + f_0)\right]$
$\dfrac{1}{2}\left[\delta(x - x_0) + \delta(x + x_0)\right]$	$\cos(2\pi f_x x_0)$
$\sin(2\pi f_0 x)$	$\dfrac{1}{2j}\left[\delta(f_x - f_0) - \delta(f_x + f_0)\right]$
$\dfrac{j}{2}\left[\delta(x - x_0) - \delta(x + x_0)\right]$	$\sin(2\pi f_x x_0)$
$\mathrm{comb}(x)\mathrm{comb}(y)$	$\mathrm{comb}(f_x)\mathrm{comb}(f_y)$
$\exp\left[j\pi(a^2 x^2 + b^2 y^2)\right]$	$\dfrac{j}{|ab|}\exp\left[-j\pi(f_x^2/a^2 + f_y^2/b^2)\right]$
$\exp\left[-j\pi(a^2 x^2 + b^2 y^2)\right]$	$-\dfrac{j}{|ab|}\exp\left[j\pi(f_x^2/a^2 + f_y^2/b^2)\right]$
$\exp(-(a|x| + b|y|))$	$\dfrac{4ab}{\left(a^2 + 4\pi^2 f_x^2\right)\left(b^2 + 4\pi^2 f_y^2\right)}$

Table 1.1. *Fourier transforms of some functions expressed in Cartesian coordinates*

1.2.2.1. *Linearity*

The transform of the sum of two functions is simply the sum of their respective transforms:

$$F\{\alpha g(x,y)+\beta h(x,y)\}=\alpha F\{g(x,y)\}+\beta F\{h(x,y)\} \qquad [1.26]$$

Where α and β are complex constants.

1.2.2.2. *Similarity*

If $F\{g(x,y)\}=G(f_x,f_y)$, and a and b are two real constants (different from 0), then:

$$F\{g(ax,by)\}=\frac{1}{|ab|}G\left(\frac{f_x}{a},\frac{f_y}{b}\right) \qquad [1.27]$$

This theorem is also known as the "contraction/dilation" theorem. It means that a "dilation" of the coordinates of the spatial domain (x, y) is expressed as a "contraction" of the coordinates in the frequency domain (f_x, f_y) and by a change in the amplitude and the width of the spectrum.

1.2.2.3. *Translation*

If $F\{g(x,y)\}=G(f_x,f_y)$, then:

$$F\{g(x-a,y-b)\}=G(f_x,f_y)\exp\left[-j2\pi\left(f_xa+f_yb\right)\right] \qquad [1.28]$$

The translation of a function in the spatial domain introduces a linear phase variation in the frequency domain.

1.2.2.4. *Parseval's theorem*

If $F\{g(x,y)\}=G(f_x,f_y)$, then:

$$\int\limits_{-\infty}^{\infty}\int|g(x,y)|^2\,dxdy=\int\limits_{-\infty}^{\infty}\int|G(f_x,f_y)|^2\,df_xdf_y \qquad [1.29]$$

This theorem is generally interpreted as an expression of the conservation of energy between the spatial domain and the spatial frequency domain.

1.2.2.5. *The convolution theorem*

If $F\{g(x,y)\} = G(f_x, f_y)$ and $F\{h(x,y)\} = H(f_x, f_y)$, then:

$$F\left\{\int\!\!\int_{-\infty}^{\infty} g(\xi,\eta)h(x-\xi,y-\eta)\mathrm{d}\xi\mathrm{d}\eta\right\} = G(f_x, f_y)H(f_x, f_y) \qquad [1.30]$$

The Fourier transform of the convolution of two functions in the spatial domain is equivalent to the multiplication of their respective transformations. We will see in Chapter 3 that the Fourier transform can be calculated by the Fast Fourier Transform (FFT). This theorem offers the opportunity to calculate a convolution using FFT algorithms.

1.2.2.6. *The autocorrelation theorem*

If $F\{g(x,y)\} = G(f_x, f_y)$, then:

$$F\left\{\int\!\!\int_{-\infty}^{\infty} g(\xi,\eta)g*(\xi-x,\eta-y)\mathrm{d}\xi\mathrm{d}\eta\right\} = \left|G(f_x, f_y)\right|^2 \qquad [1.31]$$

$$F\left\{\left|g(\xi,\eta)\right|^2\right\} = \int\!\!\int_{-\infty}^{\infty} G(\xi,\eta)G*(\xi+f_x,\eta+f_y)\mathrm{d}\xi\mathrm{d}\eta \qquad [1.32]$$

This theorem can be considered as a particular case of the convolution theorem.

1.2.2.7. *The duality theorem*

Let us consider two functions f and g linked by the following integral development:

$$g(\alpha,\beta) = \int\!\!\int_{-\infty}^{\infty} f(u,v)\exp\left[-j\,2\pi(u\alpha + v\beta)\right]\mathrm{d}u\mathrm{d}v \qquad [1.33]$$

We pose $(u, v) = (x, y)$ and $(\alpha, \beta) = (f_x, f_y)$, then:

$$F\{f(x,y)\} = g(f_x, f_y) \qquad [1.34]$$

We now pose $(\alpha, \beta) = (x, y)$ and $(u, v) = (f_x, f_y)$, then:

$$g(x,y) = \int\int_{-\infty}^{\infty} f(f_x, f_y) \exp\left[-j2\pi(xf_x + yf_y)\right] du dv \qquad [1.35]$$

being equally:

$$g(x,y) = \int\int_{-\infty}^{\infty} f(-f_x, -f_y) \exp\left[+j2\pi(xf_x + yf_y)\right] du dv \qquad [1.36]$$

giving

$$g(x,y) = F^{-1}\left\{f(-f_x, -f_y)\right\}, \qquad [1.37]$$

and by applying the Fourier transform operator to the left and right,

$$F\{g(x,y)\} = f(-f_x, -f_y). \qquad [1.38]$$

Hence the property of duality of the Fourier transforms:

if

$$F\{f(x,y)\} = g(f_x, f_y) \qquad [1.39]$$

then

$$F\{g(x,y)\} = f(-f_x, -f_y) \qquad [1.40]$$

This property is very useful for determining Fourier transforms as it means that a pair of functions where one is the transform of the other generate a second pair of functions where one is the transform of the other. For example, if we consider the function rect(x)rect(y), whose Fourier transform is sin c(f_x)sin c(f_y) (see Table 1.1), then we can easily deduce that the Fourier transform of sin c(x)sin c(y) is rect($-f_x$)rect($-f_y$) = rect(f_x)rect(f_x) by the parity of the rect function.

1.2.3. Fourier transforms in polar coordinates

For a two-dimensional function with circular symmetry, it is more convenient to use polar coordinates. We consider a plane described by rectangular (x, y) and polar

(r, θ) coordinates and the corresponding spectral coordinates are (f_x, f_y) and (ρ, φ), respectively. We then have:

$$\begin{cases} x = r\cos\theta \\ y = r\sin\theta \end{cases} \qquad\qquad [1.41]$$

$$\begin{cases} f_x = \rho\cos\varphi \\ f_y = \rho\sin\varphi \end{cases} \qquad\qquad [1.42]$$

Let $f(x, y)$ be an original function with spectral function $F(f_x, f_y)$. We can rewrite these as functions of polar coordinates:

$$g(r,\theta) = f(r\cos\theta, r\sin\theta) \qquad\qquad [1.43]$$

$$G(\rho,\varphi) = F(\rho\cos\varphi, \rho\sin\varphi) \qquad\qquad [1.44]$$

By substituting these two relations into [1.23] and [1.25], we obtain direct and inverse Fourier transforms, respectively, in polar coordinates:

$$G(\rho,\varphi) = \int_0^{2\pi} \int_0^{+\infty} rg(r,\theta)\exp\left[-j2\pi r\rho\cos(\theta - \varphi)\right]drd\theta \qquad [1.45]$$

$$g(r,\theta) = \int_0^{2\pi} \int_0^{+\infty} \rho G(\rho,\varphi)\exp\left[j2\pi r\rho\cos(\theta - \varphi)\right]d\rho d\varphi \qquad [1.46]$$

Most optical systems are circularly symmetric, and in this case the function $f(r, \theta)$ depends only on the variable r. We, therefore, have $g(r, \theta) = g_R(r)$. We substitute this relation into [1.45] and, using the identity of the Bessel function:

$$J_0(a) = \frac{1}{2\pi} \int_0^{2\pi} \exp\left[-ja\cos(\theta - \varphi)\right]d\theta \qquad\qquad [1.47]$$

we can deduce the Fourier transform of $g_R(r)$ in polar coordinates:

$$G(\rho,\theta) = G_R(\rho) = 2\pi \int_0^{+\infty} rg_R(r)J_0(2\pi r\rho)dr \qquad\qquad [1.48]$$

where $J_0(a)$ is a zero-order Bessel function of the first kind. Thus, the Fourier transform of a circularly symmetric function is itself circularly symmetric and the expression [1.48] is called a Fourier–Bessel transform or Hankel transform of zero order. In the same way, by substituting $G_R(\rho) = G(\rho, \varphi)$ into [1.46], we determine the expression of inverse Fourier transform in polar coordinates:

$$g(r) = 2\pi \int_0^{+\infty} \rho G_R(\rho) J_0(2\pi r \rho) d\rho \qquad [1.49]$$

We note that the mathematical forms of the direct and inverse transformations are the same.

1.3. Linear systems

An optical system allows the transformation of an input signal into an output signal. The device situated between the two planes ("input" and "output") perpendicular to the direction of propagation will be henceforth called an "optical system". An optical system may have linear or nonlinear properties. In most cases, considering the system to be linear as a first approximation, we are able to obtain sufficiently precise representations of the observed phenomena. Here we will consider only linear systems.

1.3.1. *Definition*

From a mathematical point of view, a linear system corresponds to a transformation operation. We conveniently represent such a system by an operator $L\{\}$, at whose output the two-dimensional function $f(x, y)$ becomes a new function $p(x', y')$. This is expressed as:

$$p(x',y') = L\{f(x,y)\} \qquad [1.50]$$

$f(x, y)$ and $p(x', y')$ are called the input function and the output function of the system, respectively.

Let us consider some input functions $f_1(x, y), f_2(x, y), \ldots, f_n(x, y)$ and some output functions $p_1(x', y'), p_2(x', y'), \ldots, p_n(x', y')$. We then have:

$$p_1(x',y') = L\{f_1(x,y)\}$$
$$p_2(x',y') = L\{f_2(x,y)\}$$
$$\vdots$$
$$p_n(x',y') = L\{f_n(x,y)\} \qquad [1.51]$$

Assuming $a_1, a_2, ..., a_n$ to be complex constants, if the set of a system's input and output functions satisfy:

$$
\begin{aligned}
p(x', y') &= L\{f_1(x, y) + f_2(x, y) + \cdots + f_n(x, y)\} \\
&= L\{f_1(x, y)\} + L\{f_2(x, y)\} + ... + L\{f_n(x, y)\} \\
&= p_1(x', y') + p_2(x', y') + ... + p_n(x', y')
\end{aligned}
\qquad [1.52]
$$

and

$$
\begin{aligned}
p(x', y') &= L\{a_1 f_1(x, y) + a_2 f_2(x, y) + \cdots + a_n f_n(x, y)\} \\
&= a_1 L\{f_1(x, y)\} + a_2 L\{f_2(x, y)\} + ... + a_n L\{f_n(x, y)\} \\
&= a_1 p_1(x', y') + a_2 p_2(x', y') + ... + a_n p_n(x', y')
\end{aligned}
\qquad [1.53]
$$

then this system can be considered linear.

The linear approach presents a considerable advantage: it allows us to express the response of a system to any input function in the form of a response to "elementary" functions into which the input has been decomposed. In conclusion, if we can decompose, by a simple method, the input function into "elementary" functions for which the response of the system is well known, we will obtain the output function by the sum of these responses.

1.3.2. *Impulse response and superposition integrals*

Using the translation property of the two-dimensional δ function, we can express a function $f(x, y)$ describing a light wave in the input plane as:

$$
f(x, y) = \iint_{\infty} f(x_0, y_0)\delta(x - x_0, y - y_0)\mathrm{d}x_0\mathrm{d}y_0
\qquad [1.54]
$$

The physical meaning of this expression is that the distribution of the input optical signal $f(x, y)$ can be considered as the linear combination of δ functions weighted by the value $f(x_0, y_0)$ and shifted with respect to each other, the elementary functions of the decomposition being precisely these δ functions. Since the system is linear, its response to the input signal $f(x, y)$ is determined by:

$$
p(x, y) = L\left\{ \iint_{\infty} f(x_0, y_0)\delta(x - x_0, y - y_0)\mathrm{d}x_0\mathrm{d}y_0 \right\}
\qquad [1.55]
$$

We notice that the number $f(x_0, y_0)$ is a simple weighting factor applied to the elementary function $\delta(x-x_0, y-y_0)$. For any point with coordinates (x_0, y_0), $f(x_0, y_0)$ is constant. According to its property of linearity, the operator $L\{\}$ can move inside the summation (integral) sign, giving:

$$p(x,y) = \iint_{\infty} f(x_0, y_0) L\{ \, \delta(x-x_0, y-y_0) \, \} dx_0 dy_0 \, \}$$ [1.56]

If we consider $h(x, y; x_0, y_0)$ as the response of the system at the point (x, y) of the output space, when the input is a δ function situated at the point (x_0, y_0), we have:

$$h(x, y; x_0, y_0) = L\{\delta(x-x_0, y-y_0)\}$$ [1.57]

The function h is called the impulse response of the system. The magnitude of the input and output of the system can then be related by the following equation:

$$p(x,y) = \iint_{\infty} f(x_0, y_0) h(x, y; x_0, y_0) dx_0 dy_0$$ [1.58]

This fundamental expression goes by the name of the "superposition integral".

To completely determine the output signal, we note that we must know the responses to local impulses at every possible point of the input plane. In general, the determination of the impulse responses is very complex. However, we will see in the following section that for an important subclass of linear systems called invariant linear systems, which are invariant in the space, we can determine the impulse responses in a simple way. In most cases, an optical system can be approximated by a space-invariant linear system.

1.3.3. Definition of a two-dimensional linear shift-invariant system

Two-dimensional invariant linear systems are an important subclass of linear systems. If the impulse response of a system $h(x, y; x_0, y_0)$ depends only on the distances $(x-x_0)$ and $(y-y_0)$, this system is considered as a linear shift-invariant system, that is:

$$h(x, y; x_0, y_0) = h(x-x_0, y-y_0)$$ [1.59]

Thus, the optical system is invariant in space if the output signal of a point in the input plane changes position only but not shape when the source point moves around the input plane. For a shift-invariant optical system, the superposition integral can be rewritten as:

$$p(x,y) = \iint_{\infty} f(x_0, y_0) h(x - x_0; y - y_0) dx_0 dy_0 = f(x,y) * h(x,y) \qquad [1.60]$$

This relation corresponds to the two-dimensional convolution of the input function with the impulse response of the system. Consequently, if an optical system is a linear shift-invariant system, on the condition that we are able to determine the impulse response of a point in the input plane (which is often considered on the axis of the system), whatever the optical input signal $f(x_0, y_0)$, the output signal $p(x, y)$ can be determined using expression [1.60].

1.3.4. Transfer functions

By taking the Fourier transform of both sides of [1.60] and using the convolution theorem, we obtain:

$$P\left(f_x, f_y\right) = F\left(f_x, f_y\right) H\left(f_x, f_y\right) \qquad [1.61]$$

with:

$$F\left(f_x, f_y\right) = \int_{-\infty}^{+\infty} \int f(x,y) \exp\left[-j2\pi\left(f_x x + f_y y\right)\right] dxdy \qquad [1.61a]$$

$$P\left(f_x, f_y\right) = \int_{-\infty}^{+\infty} \int p(x,y) \exp\left[-j2\pi\left(f_x x + f_y y\right)\right] dxdy \qquad [1.61b]$$

$$H\left(f_x, f_y\right) = \int_{-\infty}^{+\infty} \int h(x,y) \exp\left[-j2\pi\left(f_x x + f_y y\right)\right] dxdy \qquad [1.61c]$$

Expression [1.61] shows that the spectral function of the output signal is the product of the spectrum of the input signal with the function $H(f_x, f_y)$. This product is the frequency response to one of the elementary functions of the input signal and the function $H(f_x, f_y)$ is called the transfer function of the system. The transfer function of the system is determined by the Fourier transform of the impulse response [1.61c]. The output signal can be determined by the inverse Fourier transform of the spectrum of the output signal, that is:

$$p(x,y) = F^{-1}\left\{P\left(f_x, f_y\right) H\left(f_x, f_y\right)\right\} \qquad [1.62]$$

The spectrum of the output signal $P(f_x, f_y)$ can be calculated by the Fourier transform [1.61b]. If the transfer function of the system can be determined, the output signal can be obtained by [1.61b].

1.4. The sampling theorem

It is often convenient to represent a continuous function $g(x, y)$ by a table of sampled values taken at a discrete set of points in the xy-plane. Current numerical methods allow the presentation, storage, and propagation of almost all information of a physical nature. It is intuitive that if the samples of the continuous function $g(x, y)$ are taken at points sufficiently close together, the given samples are able to reliably represent the original function using a simple interpolation. However, for a given function, the question is to know the maximum sampling interval that we must respect. The answer is less evident. Yet, for a particular class of functions known as "bandwidth-limited functions", the reconstruction can be carried out exactly, on the condition that the interval between two samples is not larger than a certain limit. A bandwidth-limited function is such that its Fourier transform is only non-zero on a finite region of the frequency space. The sampling theorem was initially proven by Whittaker [WHI 15] and was later revisited by Shannon [SHA 49] during his studies on information theory. This principle, which allows us to determine the maximum sampling interval, is called the Shannon–Whittaker sampling theorem.

The following section states the two-dimensional sampling theorem and refers to the work of Goodman [GOO 72].

1.4.1. Sampling a continuous function

Let us consider a set of samples of the function $g(x, y)$, taken over a rectangular mesh. The sampled function $g_s(x, y)$ is defined as:

$$g_s(x, y) = \text{comb}\left(\frac{x}{X}\right)\text{comb}\left(\frac{y}{Y}\right)g(x, y) \qquad [1.63]$$

This function therefore consists of a set of δ functions separated by intervals of length X along the x-axis and of length Y along the y-axis, as shown in Figure 1.10, whose amplitude is the value of the function $g(x, y)$ at the point being considered.

The volume enclosed by the δ function representation in the space and the xy-plane is proportional to the value of $g(x, y)$ at each point of the sampling mesh.

Applying the convolution theorem, we obtain the spectrum $G_s(f_x, f_y)$ of $g_s(x, y)$ by convoluting the transform of $(x/X)\text{comb}(y/Y)$ with the transform of $g(x, y)$, that is:

$$G_s\left(f_x, f_y\right) = F\left\{\text{comb}\left(\frac{x}{X}\right)\text{comb}\left(\frac{y}{Y}\right)\right\} * G\left(f_x, f_y\right) \qquad [1.64]$$

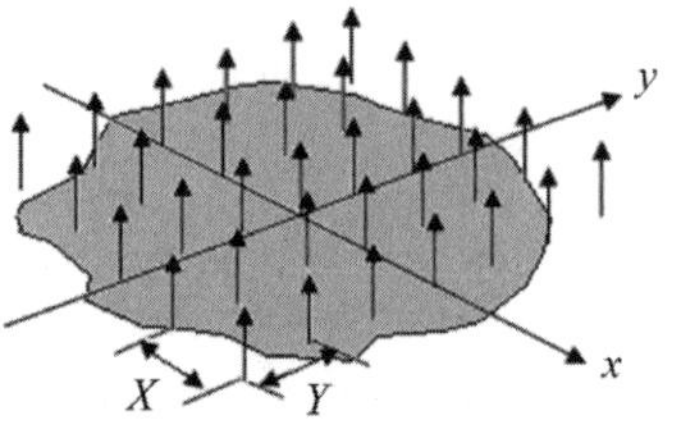

Figure 1.10. *Two-dimensional sampling*

Since:

$$F\left\{\text{comb}\left(\frac{x}{X}\right)\text{comb}\left(\frac{y}{Y}\right)\right\} = XY\text{comb}\left(Xf_x\right)\text{comb}\left(Yf_y\right) \qquad [1.65]$$

$$= \sum_{n=-\infty}^{\infty}\sum_{m=-\infty}^{\infty} \delta\left(f_x - \frac{n}{X}\right)\delta\left(f_y - \frac{m}{Y}\right)$$

then we have:

$$G_s\left(f_x, f_y\right) = \sum_{n=-\infty}^{\infty}\sum_{m=-\infty}^{\infty} G\left(f_x - \frac{n}{X}, f_y - \frac{m}{Y}\right) \qquad [1.66]$$

The spectrum of $g_s(x, y)$ can therefore be simply deduced by considering the spectrum of $g(x, y)$ localized at each point with coordinates $(n/X, m/Y)$ in the $f_x f_y$-plane, as shown in Figure 1.11.

Since we assumed that the function $g(x, y)$ had a spectrum of limited scope, its spectrum $G(f_x, f_y)$ is only non-zero in the corresponding frequency space domain. If X and Y are sufficiently small, in other words, if the samples are taken on points that are sufficiently close to each other, the intervals $1/X$ and $1/Y$ between the various spectral regions will be large enough to ascertain that the neighboring regions do not overlap. To determine the maximum interval between two sampled points, let us suppose $2B_X$ and $2B_Y$ to be the dimensions following the respective directions of the

f_x- and f_y-axes of the smallest rectangle containing the whole spectral domain of $g(x, y)$. As shown in Figure 1.11, if the following two inequalities:

$$X \leq \frac{1}{2B_X}$$

$$Y \leq \frac{1}{2B_y}$$ [1.67]

are satisfied, the different terms of the spectrum [1.66] of the sampled function are separated by the distances $1/X$ and $1/Y$ in the f_x and f_y directions, respectively. The maximum dimensions of the mesh of the sample network, which allow an exact restoration of the original function, are therefore $1/2B_X$ and $1/2B_Y$. Having determined the maximum allowed distances between samples, we now study how to obtain the spectrum of $g(x, y)$ by a filter function, and how to reconstruct the original function $g(x, y)$.

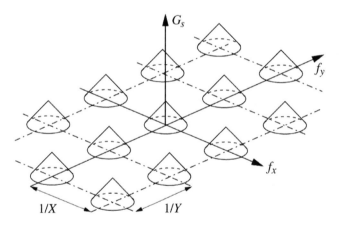

Figure 1.11. *Spectrum of the sampled function*

1.4.2. Reconstruction of the original function

Following Figure 1.11, we consider a two-dimensional rectangular function with sides $2B_X$ and $2B_Y$ along the f_x- and f_y-axes, respectively. The filter function is:

$$H(f_x, f_y) = \text{rect}\left(\frac{f_x}{2B_x}\right) \cdot \text{rect}\left(\frac{f_y}{2B_y}\right)$$ [1.68]

We note that $G(f_x, f_y)$ is obtained from $G_S(f_x, f_y)$ since:

$$G(f_x, f_y) \equiv G_s(f_x, f_y) H(f_x, f_y)$$

[1.69]

This means that, if the sampled function $g_s(x, y)$ is considered as the input signal of a system, the function $g(x, y)$ will be considered as the output signal. Thus, $H(f_x, f_y)$ is the transfer function of the system. In this case, the identity [1.64] translates into the spatial domain by:

$$g_s(x, y) * h(x, y) \equiv g(x, y)$$

[1.70]

where

$$g_s(x, y) = \mathrm{comb}(\frac{x}{X})\mathrm{comb}(\frac{y}{Y})g(x, y)$$

$$= XY \sum_{n=-\infty}^{\infty} \sum_{m=-\infty}^{\infty} g(nX, mY)\delta(x - nX, y - mY)$$

[1.71]

and $h(x, y)$ is the impulse response of the filter, which is written as:

$$h(x, y) = F^{-1}\left\{ \mathrm{rect}\left(\frac{f_x}{2B_x}\right)\mathrm{rect}\left(\frac{f_y}{2B_y}\right) \right\} = 4B_x B_y \mathrm{sinc}(2B_x\ x)\mathrm{sinc}(2B_y y)$$

[1.72]

Consequently:

$$g(x, y) = 4B_X B_Y XY \sum_{n=-\infty}^{\infty} \sum_{m=-\infty}^{\infty}$$

$$g(nX, mY)\mathrm{sinc}\left[2B_X(x - nX) \right]\mathrm{sinc}\left[2B_Y(y - mY) \right]$$

[1.73]

Finally, when we choose the maximum allowed values $1/2B_X$ and $1/2B_Y$ for the sampling intervals X and Y, the identity becomes:

$$g(x, y) = \sum_{n=-\infty}^{\infty} \sum_{m=-\infty}^{\infty} g\left(\frac{n}{2B_X}, \frac{m}{2B_Y}\right) \mathrm{sinc}\left(2B_X\left(x - \frac{n}{2B_X}\right)\right)\mathrm{sinc}\left(2B_Y\left(y - \frac{m}{2B_Y}\right)\right)$$

[1.74]

Expression [1.74] represents a fundamental result that we will henceforth call the Whittaker–Shannon sampling theorem. It states that the exact reconstruction of a bandwidth-limited function can be carried out from the sampled values of the function, taken after a suitable rectangular mesh sampling. The reconstruction is carried out by interpolating each sample point by an interpolation function constituted by the product of two sinc functions.

Note that this result is not the only possible sampling theorem. We chose two rather arbitrary sampling frames in the course of this study; with different assumptions we would have obtained a different sampling theorem. We first arbitrarily chose a rectangular sampling frame. Also, we chose the particular transfer function given by [1.68]. By making different choices we would establish other, equally valid theorems. For more detail, readers may refer to the articles by [BRA 56], [PET 62], and [LIN 59].

1.4.3. *Space-bandwidth product*

For a bandwidth-limited function $g(x, y)$, which is mainly non-zero in a region of the xy-plane bounded by $-L_X \leq x \leq L_X$ and $-L_Y \leq y \leq L_Y$ and whose maximum sampling intervals along the f_x- and f_y-axes are $1/2B_X$ and $1/2B_Y$, respectively, to thus satisfy the sampling theorem, the minimum value of the number of sampling points able to represent the function $g(x, y)$ is therefore:

$$N = (2L_X \times 2L_Y)(2B_X \times 2B_Y) = 16 L_X L_Y B_X B_Y \qquad [1.75]$$

This relation is called the *space-bandwidth* product of the function $g(x, y)$ [GOO 05] and expresses the value of the product of the space and frequency surfaces in which the function $g(x, y)$ and its spectrum $F\{g(x, y)\}$ are bounded. As a result, for a two-dimensional bandwidth-limited function, the space-bandwidth product determines the minimum number of degrees of freedom, N, that correctly represent it. When $g(x, y)$ is real, its number of degrees of freedom is N, since the samples are real; if $g(x, y)$ is a complex function, its number of degrees of freedom becomes $2N$ as each sample must be represented by two real values. Given the theorems of similarity and translation relating to the Fourier transform, the dilation of the coordinates and the translation of the function in the spatial or spectral domain do not affect the space-bandwidth product of the considered function. This means that, for a given function, the number of degrees of freedom is constant. This number can therefore be considered as a significant piece of information expressing the complexity of the function, and as a criterion that allows us to verify whether there is any loss of information during the sampling process.

Chapter 2

The Scalar Theory of Diffraction

The calculation or expression of the propagation of coherent waves, the treatment of the interferences between these waves, and the reconstruction of images based on the different equations describing the diffraction of light are fundamental to the field of digital holography. Light being an electromagnetic wave, optical propagation is the process of diffraction of an electromagnetic wave in a four-dimensional (4D) space (three in space and one in time), which may be of a dielectric nature. In this chapter, we will address the description of the complex functions modeling an optical wave, then, from the electromagnetic theory based on Maxwell's equations, we will introduce the wave equation describing its propagation. It turns out that even though the solution to the wave equation is in vector form, if both the size of diffracting objects and the distance across which the diffraction occurs are much greater than the wavelength, we can neglect the coupling between the electric and magnetic field vectors in the propagation process. Considering the electric field vector as a scalar, the solution to the wave equation can express the physical process of the propagation of light with high reliability. This approach is called the scalar theory of diffraction. In the framework of this theory, the propagation of light is rigorously described by the Kirchhoff and Rayleigh–Sommerfeld equations, and by the angular spectrum method [GOO 72, GOO 05]. The Fresnel diffraction integral, which comes from the Fresnel approximation, is a paraxial (small-angle) expression of these three formulations. These four methods constitute the classic formulation of diffraction, and on the condition that we know the optical field in a plane perpendicular to the direction of propagation, they can be applied to the calculation of optical fields in space, ahead or behind, with excellent reliability.

In this chapter, using the scalar theory of diffraction and the wave equation, we will deduce the angular spectrum and Fresnel diffraction integral methods. Experimentally, the propagation of light is often closely related to an optical system and the classical diffraction formulae are not always useful if we want to deal with a problem of the propagation of light across a structured system with various optical elements. Thus, by associating the matrix method with scalar diffraction, we will propose, at the end of the chapter, a generalized formulation of diffraction, the Collins approach [COL 70], which allows us to express the paraxial propagation of light across an optical system. The presentation of the different formulations of diffraction will be supplemented with examples so as to facilitate the understanding of their physical meaning.

2.1. Representation of an optical wave by a complex function

2.1.1. *Representation of a monochromatic wave*

In a space described by a Cartesian coordinate system *xyz*, a monochromatic wave, at the point P(*x,y,z*) at any instant *t*, can be represented by a trigonometric function of the form [GOO 72, COL 70, YAR 85]:

$$u(x, y, z, t) = U(x, y, z)\cos[\varphi(x, y, z) - 2\pi v t] \qquad [2.1]$$

with amplitude U(*x,y,z*), frequency v, and phase $\varphi(x, y, z)$. The expression is useful for describing a monochromatic optical wave of infinite length. In reality, a perfect monochromatic wave does not exist, as the process that generates it only exists for a finite duration, widening the spectrum of frequencies. However, we may consider the existence of a quasi-monochromatic wave, having a narrow frequency band centered on the average frequency of the wave. Such a wave is produced by a laser. Using Euler's formula, with $j = \sqrt{-1}$, expression [2.1] can be rewritten as:

$$u(x, y, z, t) = \text{Re}\{U(x, y, z)\exp(-j2\pi v t)\exp[j\varphi(x, y, z)]\} \qquad [2.2]$$

where Re{} means the real part of the complex value inside the brackets. It must be noted that, as the cosine is an even function, if we represent optical oscillation by a complex function, then the two functions $\exp(-j2\pi v t)$ and $\exp(j2\pi v t)$ are equivalent for describing the time evolution of a wave of frequency v. Respecting the conventions of the subject [GOO 72, GOO 05, YAR 85], we will always use $\exp(-j2\pi v t)$ in this book. Moreover, to simplify matters, the symbol Re{} will be neglected. Given that the frequency of optical waves is very high (from 375 THz for $\lambda = 800$ nm to 750 THz for $\lambda = 400$ nm, in the visible spectrum), when detecting this type of radiation, the result is generally a mean square value obtained over a very large number of oscillatory periods. It follows from this that time does not play a role in the spatial distribution of the optical field. We can regard the wave as being simply represented by:

$$U(x,y,z) = |U(x,y,z)| \exp[j\varphi(x,y,z)]$$ [2.3]

This equation describes the complex amplitude of the optical wave. It depicts the amplitude and phase of the optical field at each point in space, determining the spatial distribution of the field. In the study of the propagation of light, the intensity distribution is an important physical quantity. The complex representation of a wave considerably simplifies the calculation of this intensity distribution. For example, if we consider the superposition of N waves $U_1(x,y,z), U_2(x,y,z), \cdots, U_N(x,y,z)$, the resulting amplitude is given by the sum of the waves:

$$U(x,y,z) = \sum_{k=1}^{N} U_k(x,y,z)$$ [2.4]

Given that the intensity distribution is proportional to the modulus squared of the amplitude, then:

$$I(x,y,z) = U(x,y,z)U^*(x,y,z) = |U(x,y,z)|^2$$ [2.5]

thus, we have:

$$I(x,y,z) = \sum_{k=1}^{N}\sum_{i=1}^{N} U_k(x,y,z)U_i^*(x,y,z)$$ [2.6]

This expression is the product of the sum of complex exponents. The calculation is considerably simplified compared to the case where the waves are represented by trigonometric functions. Plane waves and spherical waves have pride of place in optics. We discuss their properties and representations in the following sections.

2.1.2. Complex amplitude of the optical field in space

2.1.2.1. Plane waves

The principal property of a plane wave is that its wavefront is a plane. In a homogeneous medium, the wavefront is perpendicular to the direction of propagation. For a plane wave propagating in a direction given by the direction cosines $\cos\alpha, \cos\beta, \cos\gamma$, the complex amplitude is expressed by:

$$U(x,y,z) = u(x,y,z)\exp\left[jk(x\cos\alpha + y\cos\beta + z\cos\gamma)\right] \qquad [2.7]$$

where $k = 2\pi/\lambda$ and λ is the wavelength. This relation shows that for a real number C, the expression $x\cos\alpha + y\cos\beta + z\cos\gamma = C$ describes a phase plane whose normal is in the direction given by the cosines $\cos\alpha, \cos\beta, \cos\gamma$. Since different values of C correspond to different parallel planes, expression [2.7] represents a wave propagating in the direction normal to these planes. Let us consider $\bar{k}$, a unit vector in the direction of propagation, then $\boldsymbol{k} = 2\pi\bar{k}/\lambda$ is called the wave vector. If $\boldsymbol{r}$ is the position vector with coordinates (x,y,z), the complex amplitude of a plane wave can generally be expressed in the following form:

$$U(\boldsymbol{r}) = u(\boldsymbol{r})\exp(j\boldsymbol{k} \cdot \boldsymbol{r}) \qquad [2.8]$$

This expression can be generalized to represent any wave.

2.1.2.2. *Spherical waves*

The wavefront of a spherical wave is spherical. From the generalization of expression [2.8], if the point source of the spherical wave is at the origin of a Cartesian coordinate system, the spherical wave of amplitude U_0 is expressed by a trigonometric function:

$$u(x,y,z,t) = \frac{U_0}{r}\cos(\boldsymbol{k} \cdot \boldsymbol{r} - 2\pi vt) \qquad [2.9]$$

with $|\boldsymbol{r}| = r = \sqrt{x^2 + y^2 + z^2}$. We note that the amplitude is proportional to the inverse of the distance between the point source and r, the observation point. If the spherical wave is divergent, $\boldsymbol{k}$ and $\boldsymbol{r}$ have identical directions and [2.9] can be expressed in the form:

$$u(x,y,z,t) = \frac{U_0}{r}\cos(kr - 2\pi vt) \qquad [2.10]$$

For a convergent spherical wave, the directions of **k** and **r** are opposed, and we then have:

$$u(x,y,z,t) = \frac{U_0}{r}\cos(-kr - 2\pi vt)$$ [2.11]

The complex amplitude of a spherical wave can therefore be expressed by:

$$U(x,y,z) = \begin{cases} \dfrac{U_0}{r}\exp(jkr) & \text{(divergent)} \\ \dfrac{U_0}{r}\exp(-jkr) & \text{(convergent)} \end{cases}$$ [2.12]

When the center of the spherical wave is at the point (x_c, y_c, z_c) instead of the origin, the expressions are identical, with r substituted for:

$$r = \sqrt{(x - x_c)^2 + (y - y_c)^2 + (z - z_c)^2}$$ [2.13]

2.1.3. Complex amplitudes of plane and spherical waves in a front plane

The above analysis conveys the complex amplitudes of plane and spherical waves in a 3D space. However, it is often useful to determine the amplitude in a front plane perpendicular to optical axis or the axis of propagation. For a given plane, the representation of the complex amplitude of different types of wave is therefore necessary. We will analyze two notable examples: plane and spherical waves.

2.1.3.1. Complex amplitude of a plane wave in a front plane

The z-axis being generally considered as the optical axis, a plane wave at $z = z_0$ is expressed by:

$$U(x,y,z_0) = u(x,y,z_0)\exp[jk(x\cos\alpha + y\cos\beta + z_0\cos\gamma)]$$ [2.14]

Since $\cos\gamma = \sqrt{1 - \cos^2\alpha - \cos^2\beta}$ is constant and independent of (x,y), it can be rewritten as:

$$U(x,y,z_0) = U_0(x,y,z_0)\exp[jk(x\cos\alpha + y\cos\beta)]$$ [2.15]

with

$$U_0(x,y,z_0) = u(x,y,z_0)\exp\left(jkz_0\sqrt{1-\cos^2\alpha - \cos^2\beta} \right) \qquad [2.16]$$

If the interference of this wave with other coherent waves is not to be considered, then the constant phase factor $\exp\left(jkz_0\sqrt{1-\cos^2\alpha - \cos^2\beta} \right)$ is generally neglected and [2.15] is the usual representation of the complex amplitude of a plane wave.

2.1.3.2. Complex amplitude of a spherical wave in a front plane

If the point source coincides with the origin, considering z as a constant z_0, expression [2.12] is also a representation of a spherical wave in the plane $z = z_0$. As the study of propagation is often carried out in the neighborhood of the z-axis, for a given value z_0, the studied zone corresponds, in general, to the condition $z_0^2 \gg x^2 + y^2$. Under this condition, the denominator r in expression [2.12] can be replaced by z_0. However, in the exponential in [2.12], since the wavelength is very small with respect to the size of the zone considered, a small variation in r results in a large change in phase, which may be greater than π. To sidestep this problem, by carrying out a binomial expansion of r and keeping only the first two terms, we obtain:

$$|r| = |z_0|\sqrt{1 + \frac{x^2 + y^2}{z_0^2}} \approx |z_0| + \frac{x^2 + y^2}{2|z_0|} \qquad [2.17]$$

Thus, the complex amplitude of a spherical wave in the plane $z = z_0$ can be approximated by:

$$U(x,y,z_0) = \begin{cases} \dfrac{U_0}{|z_0|}\exp(jk|z_0|)\exp\left(jk\dfrac{x^2 + y^2}{2|z_0|} \right) & \text{(divergent)} \\[4mm] \dfrac{U_0}{|z_0|}\exp(jk|z_0|)\exp\left(-jk\dfrac{x^2 + y^2}{2|z_0|} \right) & \text{(convergent)} \end{cases} \qquad [2.18]$$

This expression means that the spherical wave surface is approximated by a parabolic surface, symmetrical with respect to the z-axis. It is called a parabolic approximation of spherical waves. For the case of a point source at position (x_c, y_c, z_c), we can rewrite the previous equation as:

$$U(x,y,z_0)=\begin{cases} \dfrac{U_0}{|z_c-z_0|}\exp\left(jk|z_c-z_0|\right)\exp\left(jk\dfrac{(x-x_c)^2+(y-y_c)^2}{2|z_c-z_0|}\right) & \text{(divergent)} \\[3ex] \dfrac{U_0}{|z_c-z_0|}\exp\left(jk|z_c-z_0|\right)\exp\left(-jk\dfrac{(x-x_c)^2+(y-y_c)^2}{2|z_c-z_0|}\right) & \text{(convergent)} \end{cases}$$

[2.19]

In this expression, the constant phase factor $\exp\left(jk|z-z_0|\right)$ does not influence the associated phase distribution. If we are not considering interference with other coherent sources, it is generally neglected.

2.2. Scalar theory of diffraction

2.2.1. Wave equation

The wave aspect of light is described by the classical theory of electromagnetism, which is described by Maxwell's equations [BOR 99, GOO 72, LAU 10, YAR 85]. In a homogeneous medium, Maxwell's equations are of the following form:

$$\text{div } D = \rho$$
$$\text{div } B = 0$$
$$\text{curl } E = -\frac{\partial B}{\partial t}$$
$$\text{curl } H = j + \frac{\partial D}{\partial t}$$

[2.20]

where D, E, B, and H are the electric displacement field vector, the electric field vector, the magnetic induction vector, and the magnetic field vector, respectively, ρ is the volume charge density, and j is the current density vector. The propagation of the electromagnetic field must also take into account the surrounding medium. The constituent relations describing the interaction between matter and the electromagnetic field must be added to [2.20]. These relations are called "field equations". In a homogeneous medium, they take the following form:

$$j = \sigma E$$
$$D = \varepsilon E$$
$$B = \mu H$$

[2.21]

where σ, ε, and μ are the electrical conductivity, dielectric constant (permittivity), and magnetic permeability, respectively. In a homogeneous insulator medium, $\sigma = 0$ and ε and μ are constants; in the vacuum, $\varepsilon = \varepsilon_0 = 8.8542 \times 10^{-12}$ C^2/N·m^2 and $\mu = \mu_0 = 4\pi \times 10^{-7}$ NS^2/C^2; for non-magnetic materials, $\mu = \mu_0$. The constituent equations represent the magnetic and electric characteristics of the surrounding medium. By combining them with Maxwell's equations, we can describe the fundamental properties of the propagation of the electromagnetic field in a homogeneous medium. To simplify matters, we restrict ourselves to the study of an infinite 3D medium and we consider the region of interest to be far from the optical source. With $\rho = 0$ and $\boldsymbol{j} = 0$, Maxwell's equations are simplified:

$$\text{div } \boldsymbol{E} = 0$$

$$\text{div } \boldsymbol{B} = 0$$

$$\text{curl } \boldsymbol{E} = -\frac{\partial \boldsymbol{B}}{\partial t}$$

$$\text{curl } \boldsymbol{B} = \varepsilon\mu\frac{\partial \boldsymbol{E}}{\partial t} \qquad [2.22]$$

Applying the rotational (curl) operator to the last two equations and substituting $\upsilon = 1/\sqrt{\varepsilon\mu}$, we obtain [BOR 99, GOO 05]:

$$\nabla^2 \boldsymbol{E} - \frac{1}{\upsilon^2}\frac{\partial^2 \boldsymbol{E}}{\partial t^2} = 0 \qquad [2.23]$$

$$\nabla^2 \boldsymbol{B} - \frac{1}{\upsilon^2}\frac{\partial^2 \boldsymbol{B}}{\partial t^2} = 0 \qquad [2.24]$$

where $\nabla^2 = \partial^2/\partial x^2 + \partial^2/\partial y^2 + \partial^2/\partial z^2$ is the Laplacian operator. These two expressions have the same form and are called wave equations.

2.2.2. Harmonic plane wave solutions to the wave equation

The harmonic plane wave solution to the wave equation is of great import, and we will study it in more detail. We imagine a plane wave propagating in the z direction of a Cartesian coordinate system, such that $\boldsymbol{E}$ and $\boldsymbol{B}$ depend only on z and t. Equations [2.23] and [2.24] then simplify to:

$$\frac{\partial^2 \boldsymbol{E}}{\partial z^2} - \frac{1}{\upsilon^2}\frac{\partial^2 \boldsymbol{E}}{\partial t^2} = 0 \qquad [2.25]$$

$$\frac{\partial^2 \boldsymbol{B}}{\partial z^2} - \frac{1}{\upsilon^2}\frac{\partial^2 \boldsymbol{B}}{\partial t^2} = 0 \qquad\qquad [2.26]$$

It is easy to prove that these two equations have solutions of the type:

$$\boldsymbol{E} = f_1\!\left(\frac{z}{\upsilon} - t\right) + f_1\!\left(\frac{z}{\upsilon} + t\right) \qquad\qquad [2.27]$$

$$\boldsymbol{B} = f_2\!\left(\frac{z}{\upsilon} - t\right) + f_2\!\left(\frac{z}{\upsilon} + t\right) \qquad\qquad [2.28]$$

where f_1 and f_2 are any functions representing two waves propagating in opposite directions along the z-axis with speed υ. Consequently, the speed of the propagation of light is given by $\upsilon = 1/\sqrt{\varepsilon\mu}$. The propagation speed in vacuum is generally represented by c. Using the measured values $\varepsilon_0 = 8.8542 \times 10^{-12}\ \mathrm{C^2/N{\cdot}m^2}$ and $\mu_0 = 4\pi \times 10^{-7}\ \mathrm{N{\cdot}S^2/C^2}$, we obtain $c = 1/\sqrt{\varepsilon_0\mu_0} = 2.99794458\times 10^8$ m/s. Introducing the relative permittivity $\varepsilon_r = \varepsilon/\varepsilon_0$ and the relative magnetic permeability $\mu_r = \mu/\mu_0$, the speed of light in a medium is expressed by:

$$\upsilon = c/\sqrt{\varepsilon_r\mu_r} \qquad\qquad [2.29]$$

The refractive index of the medium n is defined by the ratio of the speed in the void and in the medium, i.e.

$$n = c/\upsilon = \sqrt{\varepsilon_r\mu_r} \qquad\qquad [2.30]$$

2.2.3. Angular spectrum

Let us consider a homogeneous plane wave propagating in the z direction. In this case, $\boldsymbol{E}$ and $\boldsymbol{B}$ are functions of z and t. The wave equations simplify to:

$$\frac{\partial^2 \boldsymbol{E}}{\partial z^2} - \frac{1}{\upsilon^2}\frac{\partial^2 \boldsymbol{E}}{\partial t^2} = 0 \qquad\qquad [2.31]$$

$$\frac{\partial^2 \boldsymbol{B}}{\partial z^2} - \frac{1}{\upsilon^2}\frac{\partial^2 \boldsymbol{B}}{\partial t^2} = 0 \qquad\qquad [2.32]$$

As was previously discussed at the beginning of this chapter, if the size of diffracting objects and the propagation distance are much larger than the wavelength, the vector, E, can be considered as a scalar function $u(x,y,z,t)$, and [2.31] and [2.32] can be rewritten in a single form:

$$\nabla^2 u - \frac{1}{v^2}\frac{\partial^2 u}{\partial t^2} = 0 \qquad [2.33]$$

We will see that from [2.33] we are able to deduce the scalar formulation of diffraction by the *angular spectrum*. So as to make the calculation as simple as possible, we take, as an example, a scalar monochromatic wave in vacuum, propagating at speed c. We assume that the field satisfying equation [2.33] is written in the form:

$$u(P,t) = U(P)\exp(-j2\pi vt) \qquad [2.34]$$

where $U(P)$ is the complex amplitude at the observation point $P(x, y, z)$ and v is the frequency of the light wave.

Substituting [2.34] into [2.33], we obtain an equation which is independent of time t, known as the Helmholtz equation:

$$\left(\nabla^2 + k^2\right)U(P) = 0 \qquad [2.35]$$

where

$$k = \frac{2\pi v}{c} = \frac{2\pi}{\lambda} \qquad [2.36]$$

is the so-called wave vector and λ is the wavelength. We suppose that z is the distance between the initial and observation planes, and that $U(x,y,0)$ and $U(x,y,z)$ are the respective complex amplitudes of these two planes. Moreover, in frequency space, their spectral functions are $G_0(f_x,f_y)$ and $G_z(f_x,f_y)$, respectively. Following our discussion of the Fourier transform in Chapter 1, if, from $U(x,y,0)$, we are able to obtain the spectrum $G_z(f_x,f_y)$ in the observation plane, we can obtain the complex amplitude $U(x,y,z)$ by the inverse Fourier transform of $G_z(f_x,f_y)$. This point is now explored. Since $G_0(f_x,f_y)$ and

$G_z(f_x, f_y)$ are the Fourier transforms of the amplitudes $U(x, y, 0)$ and $U(x, y, z)$, respectively, we have:

$$G_0(f_x, f_y) = \int\limits_{-\infty}^{\infty} \int\limits_{-\infty}^{\infty} U(x, y, 0) \exp\left[-j2\pi(f_x x + f_y y)\right] dx dy \qquad [2.37]$$

$$G_z(f_x, f_y) = \int\limits_{-\infty}^{\infty} \int\limits_{-\infty}^{\infty} U(x, y, z) \exp\left[-j2\pi(f_x x + f_y y)\right] dx dy \qquad [2.38]$$

and $U(x, y, z)$ is the inverse Fourier transform of $G_z(f_x, f_y)$:

$$U(x, y, z) = \int\limits_{-\infty}^{\infty} \int\limits_{-\infty}^{\infty} G_z(f_x, f_y) \exp\left[j2\pi(f_x x + f_y y)\right] df_x df_y \qquad [2.39]$$

Equation [2.39] shows the field as the superposition of waves of the form:

$$G_z(f_x, f_y) \exp\left[j2\pi(f_x x + f_y y)\right] \qquad [2.40]$$

Let us substitute [2.40] into the Helmholtz equation [2.35], which represents a light wave. Then, at every point where there is no source, we have:

$$\left(\nabla^2 + k^2\right)\left\{G_z(f_x, f_y) \exp\left[j2\pi(f_x x + f_y y)\right]\right\} = 0 \qquad [2.41]$$

which leads to:

$$\frac{d^2}{d^2 z} G_z(f_x, f_y) + \left(\frac{2\pi}{\lambda}\sqrt{1 - (\lambda f_x)^2 - (\lambda f_y)^2}\right)^2 G_z(f_x, f_y) = 0 \qquad [2.42]$$

To deduce [2.42], some complementary equations were used. These are explained below. For the spatial coordinates, $G_z(f_x, f_y)$ is a function of z alone. We then have:

$$\frac{\partial}{\partial x} G_z(f_x, f_y) = \frac{\partial}{\partial y} G_z(f_x, f_y) = 0$$

$$\frac{\partial}{\partial z} G_z(f_x, f_y) = \frac{d}{dz} G_z(f_x, f_y) \qquad [2.43]$$

Moreover,

$$\frac{\partial}{\partial x}\exp\left[j\,2\pi\left(f_x x + f_y y\right)\right] = \left(j\,2\pi f_x\right)\exp\left[j\,2\pi\left(f_x x + f_y y\right)\right]$$

$$\frac{\partial}{\partial y}\exp\left[j\,2\pi\left(f_x x + f_y y\right)\right] = \left(j\,2\pi f_y\right)\exp\left[j\,2\pi\left(f_x x + f_y y\right)\right]$$

$$\frac{\partial}{\partial z}\exp\left[j\,2\pi\left(f_x x + f_y y\right)\right] = 0 \qquad\qquad [2.44]$$

We note that [2.42] is again a Helmholtz equation of $G_z\left(f_x, f_y\right)$. As $G_0\left(f_x, f_y\right)$ is a solution to the equation when $z = 0$, the general solution to differential equation [2.42] can be expressed by:

$$G_z\left(f_x, f_y\right) = G_0\left(f_x, f_y\right)\exp\left[j\frac{2\pi}{\lambda}z\sqrt{1 - \left(\lambda f_x\right)^2 - \left(\lambda f_y\right)^2}\right] \qquad [2.45]$$

Consequently, we have a relation between the spectrum of the wave in the initial plane which we obtain in the observation plane. This relation shows that, in frequency space, the spectral variation in complex amplitude caused by the propagation of light over the distance z is represented by its multiplication by a phase-delay factor $\exp\left[j2\pi z/\lambda\sqrt{1 - \left(\lambda f_x\right)^2 - \left(\lambda f_y\right)^2}\right]$. According to the theory of linear systems, the process of diffraction is a transformation of the light field across an optical system, as the phase-delay factor can be interpreted as a transfer function in frequency space. To facilitate the understanding of the physical meaning of the previous result, we consider the field written in the form of an inverse Fourier transform:

$$U(x, y, z) = \int_{-\infty}^{\infty}\int_{-\infty}^{\infty} G_z\left(f_x, f_y\right)\exp\left[j\frac{2\pi}{\lambda}\left(\lambda f_x x + \lambda f_y y\right)\right]df_x df_y \qquad [2.46]$$

Coming back to the elements describing a plane wave, we notice that the field $U(x, y, z)$ can be considered as a superposition of plane waves of amplitude $\left|G_z\left(f_x, f_y\right)df_x df_y\right|$ propagating in a direction whose cosines are $\lambda f_x, \lambda f_y, \sqrt{1 - \left(\lambda f_x\right)^2 - \left(\lambda f_y\right)^2}$. Moreover, the propagation of the plane wave can be described in any direction. Given that $G_z\left(f_x, f_y\right)$ is the spectrum of the field $U(x, y, z)$, this physical interpretation of the propagation of light is called *the propagation of the angular spectrum*. Figure 2.1 illustrates this approach.

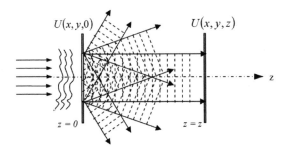

Figure 2.1. *Diagram of diffraction by angular spectrum*

From the diffraction of the angular spectrum, [2.45] means that the elementary waves satisfying $1-(\lambda f_x)^2-(\lambda f_y)^2<0$ are attenuated by the propagation, i.e. all the components satisfying this relation only exist in a zone very close to the initial plane. These components of the angular spectrum are therefore called "evanescent waves". As the components of the observation plane must satisfy the relation $1-(\lambda f_x)^2-(\lambda f_y)^2>0$ or equally $f_x^2+f_y^2<1/\lambda^2$, propagation in free space can be considered as an ideal low-pass filter of radius $1/\lambda$ in frequency space. Consequently, on the condition that we can obtain the spectrum of $U(x,y,0)$, the spectrum in the observation plane, $U(x,y,z)$ can be expressed by relation [2.46].

Using the direct and the inverse Fourier transforms $F\{\ \}$ and $F^{-1}\{\ \}$, the diffraction calculation process can be described in the Fourier way as:

$$U(x,y,z)=F^{-1}\left\{F\{U(x,y,0)\}\exp\left[j\frac{2\pi}{\lambda}z\sqrt{1-(\lambda f_x)^2-(\lambda f_y)^2}\right]\right\}$$

[2.47]

2.2.4. Kirchhoff and Rayleigh–Sommerfeld formulae

In this section, we are going to demonstrate the existence of two more solutions to the Helmholtz equation: Kirchhoff's formula and that of Rayleigh–Sommerfeld. Using the coordinates shown in Figure 2.2, which represents the relationship between the initial and observation planes, these two formulae are written in the same mathematical form [GOO 72, GOO 05]:

$$U(x,y,d)=\frac{1}{j\lambda}\int_{-\infty}^{\infty}\int_{-\infty}^{\infty}U(x_0,y_0,0)\frac{\exp(jkr)}{r}K(\theta)\mathrm{d}x_0\mathrm{d}y_0$$

[2.48]

where $r = \sqrt{(x-x_0)^2 + (y-y_0)^2 + d^2}$, θ is the angle between the normal at the point $(x_0, y_0, 0)$ and vector r from the point $(x_0, y_0, 0)$ to the point (x, y, d), $K(\theta)$ is called the obliquity factor and its three different expressions correspond to following three different formulations [GOO 72, GOO 05]:

- $K(\theta) = \dfrac{\cos\theta + 1}{2}$ Kirchhoff's formula.

- $K(\theta) = \cos\theta$ First Rayleigh–Sommerfeld solution.

- $K(\theta) = 1$ Second Rayleigh–Sommerfeld solution.

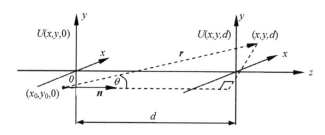

Figure 2.2. *Relation between the initial diffraction plane and the observation plane*

Among the solutions to the scalar theory of diffraction, Kirchhoff's formula is one of the oldest. Even though there exist certain inconsistencies [GOO 72, GOO 05, BOR 99], Kirchhoff's formula gives results in remarkable agreement with experiment, and it is for this reason that it is widely applied in practice. Furthermore, since the angle θ is often small in experimental configurations, the obliquity factors of the three formulations are roughly equal to unity. Thus, the Kirchhoff, Rayleigh–Sommerfeld, and angular spectrum formulae are considered as equivalent representations of diffraction. The derivations of the Kirchhoff and Rayleigh–Sommerfeld approaches are presented in detail in the book of Goodman [GOO 72, GOO 05]. Readers who would like to go into these aspects in greater detail are invited to familiarize themselves with this work.

Until now, we have presented the different formulations of diffraction that rigorously satisfy Helmholtz's equation. Nevertheless, the proposed equations are complex due to the presence of a square root in the complex exponentials. In practice, problems of diffraction quite often concern paraxial propagation, and to simplify the theoretical analysis, we use Fresnel's approximation. When the divergence angle is small, or the size of the observation zone is much less than the propagation distance, the Fresnel approximation allows us to considerably simplify the calculations. We tackle this point in the following section.

2.2.5. *Fresnel approximation and Fresnel diffraction integral*

Let d be the diffraction distance. We define the transfer function of the angular spectrum by:

$$H(f_x, f_y) = \exp\left[j\frac{2\pi}{\lambda} d \sqrt{1 - \lambda^2 (f_x^2 + f_y^2)} \right] \qquad [2.49]$$

Equation [2.47] simplifies to:

$$U(x, y, d) = F^{-1}\left\{ F\{U(x, y, 0)\} H(f_x, f_y) \right\} \qquad [2.50]$$

Expanding the square root in [2.49] to first order, we have:

$$\sqrt{1 - \lambda^2 (f_x^2 + f_y^2)} = 1 - \frac{1}{2}\lambda^2 (f_x^2 + f_y^2) + \frac{1}{8}\lambda^4 (f_x^2 + f_y^2)^2 + \cdots \qquad [2.51]$$

Let us now suppose that the first two terms of the expression are sufficient to represent the square root in [2.51]. This means that we can approximate the transfer function of the angular spectrum by:

$$H(f_x, f_y) \approx \exp\left[jkd \left(1 - \frac{\lambda^2}{2}(f_x^2 + f_y^2) \right) \right] \qquad [2.52]$$

Given that expression [2.50] can be written in the form of a convolution:

$$U(x, y, d) = U(x, y, 0) * F^{-1}\left\{ H(f_x, f_y) \right\} \qquad [2.53]$$

we substitute [2.52] into this expression knowing that the inverse Fourier transform $F^{-1}\left\{ H(f_x, f_y) \right\}$ is an analytic solution (see Table 1.1), and we have:

$$U(x, y, d) = U(x, y, 0) * \frac{\exp(jkd)}{j\lambda d} \exp\left[\frac{jk}{2d}(x^2 + y^2) \right] \qquad [2.54]$$

where

$$U(x, y, d) = \frac{\exp(jkd)}{j\lambda d} \int_{-\infty}^{\infty} \int_{-\infty}^{\infty} U(x_0, y_0, 0) \exp\left\{ \frac{jk}{2d}\left[(x - x_0)^2 + (y - y_0)^2 \right] \right\} dx_0 dy_0 \qquad [2.55]$$

which constitutes *Fresnel's diffraction integral*. Before the discovery of Maxwell's equations, Fresnel established this relation based on an intuitive understanding of Huygens' model of propagation and on the notion of interference between secondary sources of the Huygens principle [GOO 72, MAY 96]. Note that this approximation consists of replacing spherical wavelets by quadratic waves (parabolic surface approximation). Developing the quadratic terms in the exponent, leads us to:

$$U(x,y,d) = \frac{\exp(jkd)}{j\lambda d}\exp\left[\frac{jk}{2d}(x^2 + y^2)\right] \times$$

$$\int_{-\infty}^{\infty}\int_{-\infty}^{\infty}\left\{U(x_0,y_0,0)\exp\left[\frac{jk}{2d}(x_0^2 + y_0^2)\right]\right\}\exp\left[-j2\pi\left(\frac{x}{\lambda d}x_0 + \frac{y}{\lambda d}y_0\right)\right]dx_0 dy_0$$

[2.56]

Thus, with the exception of multiplicative phase and amplitude factors that are independent of x_0 and y_0, we can calculate the function $U(x,y,d)$ by carrying out a Fourier transform:

$$U(x_0,y_0,0)\exp\left[\frac{jk}{2d}(x_0^2 + y_0^2)\right]$$

[2.57]

This transformation must be evaluated at the frequencies ($f_x = x/\lambda d$, $f_y = y/\lambda d$) to guarantee a correct spatial scale in the observation plane. The calculation of the two Fresnel diffraction integrals is relatively simple compared to the formulae that rigorously satisfy the Helmholtz equation. In the regime of paraxial propagation, this approximation is relatively precise. By defining the Fresnel transfer function [GOO 72, GOO 05, LI 07b] as:

$$H_F(f_x,f_y) = \exp\left[jkd\left(1 - \frac{\lambda^2}{2}(f_x^2 + f_y^2)\right)\right]$$

[2.58]

the Fresnel approximation can be expressed by:

$$U(x,y,d) = F^{-1}\{F\{U(x,y,0)\}H_F(f_x,f_y)\}$$

[2.59]

This expression is analogous to the angular spectrum formulation [2.50], but the difference comes from the different transfer functions of the two formulations.

We now examine the paraxial forms of the Kirchhoff and Rayleigh–Sommerfeld formulae. As the observation domain is close to the optical axis, for any observation point, the obliquity factor is $K(\theta) \cong 1$, the formulae are similar and [2.48] simplifies to:

$$U(x,y,d) = \frac{1}{j\lambda} \int\limits_{-\infty}^{\infty} \int\limits_{-\infty}^{\infty} U(x_0,y_0,0) \frac{\exp(jkr)}{r} dx_0 dy_0 \qquad [2.60]$$

For paraxial propagation, the quantity r in the denominator can be replaced by d, as this change does not lead to much modification of the field amplitude. However, the r in the exponent cannot follow this rule as the wavelength λ is so small that the wave vector k is large, so a weak change in r can introduce a change in phase much larger than 2π. If, in the exponent, we replace r by d, the calculation is no longer correct. In order to sidestep this difficulty, we carry out a binomial expansion of r and keep the first two terms as an approximation [GOO 72, GOO 05]:

$$r = d \left\{ 1 + \frac{(x-x_0)^2 + (y-y_0)^2}{2d^2} - \frac{\left[(x-x_0)^2 + (y-y_0)^2 \right]^2}{8d^4} + \ldots \right\}$$

$$\approx d + \frac{(x-x_0)^2 + (y-y_0)^2}{2d} \qquad [2.61]$$

Substituting this approximation into expression [2.60], we obtain an identical formula to [2.55]. Consequently, the paraxial approximations of the Kirchhoff and Rayleigh–Sommerfeld formulae and the angular spectrum method all have the same form as that of the Fresnel approximation. In practice, the Fresnel diffraction integral, the Kirchhoff and Rayleigh–Sommerfeld formulae, and the angular spectrum method are extremely useful tools for the calculation of diffraction. The methods of the numerical calculation of diffraction, based on fast Fourier transform (FFT) algorithms, will be presented in the next chapter.

2.2.6. The Fraunhofer approximation

In expression [2.56], the Fresnel diffraction integral is the direct Fourier transform of the initial field on the condition that:

$$d \gg \frac{k\left(x_0^2 + y_0^2 \right)_{\max}}{2} \qquad [2.62]$$

The quadratic phase term in the integral is almost equal to unity. The diffraction field is written as the Fourier transform of $U(x_0, y_0, 0)$:

$$U(x, y, d) = \frac{\exp(jkd)}{j\lambda d} \exp\left[\frac{jk}{2d}(x^2 + y^2)\right]$$
$$\times \int\int_{-\infty}^{\infty} U(x_0, y_0, 0) \exp\left[-j\frac{2\pi}{\lambda d}(x_0 x + y_0 y)\right] dx_0 dy_0 \qquad [2.63]$$

The image of a given intensity on the observation plane is called a Fraunhofer diffraction pattern. The conditions on which the Fraunhofer approximation [2.62] may be used are very strict. For example (from [GOO 72] and [GOO 05]), for a wavelength 0.6 μm and an aperture of width 25 mm (1 inch), the observation distance d must satisfy $d \gg 1,600$ m. These observation conditions being strict, the practical observation of these figures is delicate. However, they can be observed in the case where the light wave coming from the initial plane is convergent with a focus at the distance d'. Let $u_0(x_0, y_0)$ be a complex function. The optical field of the initial plane is therefore expressed by:

$$U(x_0, y_0, 0) = u_0(x_0, y_0) \exp\left[-\frac{jk}{2d'}(x_0^2 + y_0^2)\right] \qquad [2.64]$$

We substitute this relation into [2.60]:

$$U(x, y, d) = \frac{\exp(jkd)}{j\lambda d} \exp\left[\frac{jk}{2d}(x^2 + y^2)\right]$$
$$\times \int\int_{-\infty}^{\infty}\int_{-\infty}^{\infty} \left\{ u_0(x_0, y_0) \exp\left[\frac{jk}{2d''}(x_0^2 + y_0^2)\right]\right\} \exp\left[-j\frac{2\pi}{\lambda d}(x_0 x + y_0 y)\right] dx_0 dy_0$$

$$[2.65]$$

with,

$$d'' = \frac{d'd}{d - d'} \qquad [2.66]$$

We note that if $d' \to d$, we have $d'' \to \infty$ and the condition for the Fraunhofer approximation is easily satisfied. Given that, in practice, the creation of a convergent wave can be simply executed using a thin lens, Fraunhofer diffraction patterns can often be observed at the focus of a lens. The Fraunhofer approximation is therefore extremely useful, in particular for tackling the problem of resolution optical systems caused by diffraction. The application of the Fraunhofer and Fresnel approximations leads to simplified calculations. In the following section, we give some examples concerning these two approximations.

2.3. Examples of Fraunhofer diffraction patterns

2.3.1. *Fraunhofer diffraction pattern from a rectangular aperture*

Let us consider a diaphragm with a rectangular aperture centered at the origin. Let w_x and w_y be the half-widths of the aperture in the x_0 and y_0 directions, respectively. If the aperture is illuminated along the normal by a monochromatic plane wave of unit amplitude, the distribution of the optical field in the aperture is modeled by $\text{rect}(x_0/2w_x)\text{rect}(y_0/2w_y)$. If there is a convergent lens of focal distance f adjoined to the diaphragm, the light wave crossing the lens becomes spherical and converges toward the focus. Then, we have:

$$U_0(x_0,y_0) = \text{rect}\left(\frac{x_0}{2w_x}\right)\text{rect}\left(\frac{y_0}{2w_y}\right)\exp\left[-\frac{jk}{2f}\left(x_0^2 + y_0^2\right)\right] \tag{2.67}$$

From [2.66], if $d = d' = f$, the field in the observation plane will be the Fraunhofer diffraction field, i.e.

$$U(x,y) = \frac{\exp(jkd)}{j\lambda d}\exp\left[\frac{jk}{2d}\left(x^2 + y^2\right)\right] \tag{2.68}$$

$$\times \int_{-w_y}^{w_y}\int_{-w_x}^{w_x}\exp\left[-j\frac{2\pi}{\lambda d}\left(x_0 x + y_0 y\right)\right]dx_0 dy_0$$

After integration, we obtain:

$$U(x,y) = 4w_x w_y \frac{\exp(jkd)}{j\lambda d}\exp\left[\frac{jk}{2d}\left(x^2 + y^2\right)\right]\text{sinc}\left(\frac{2w_x x}{\lambda d}\right)\text{sinc}\left(\frac{2w_y y}{\lambda d}\right) \tag{2.69}$$

The intensity distribution of the Fraunhofer pattern is therefore:

$$I(x,y) = \frac{16w_x^2 w_y^2}{\lambda^2 d^2}\text{sinc}^2\left(\frac{2w_x x}{\lambda d}\right)\text{sinc}^2\left(\frac{2w_y y}{\lambda d}\right) \tag{2.70}$$

We note that, along both the axes, the distances between the two neighboring zeros are $T_x = \lambda d / 2w_x$ and $T_y = \lambda d / 2w_y$, respectively. Considering $w_x = w_y = 2$ mm and $\lambda = 0.532$ µm, from [2.70], the intensity distribution of the Fraunhofer diffraction pattern for the diffraction distance $d = 200$ mm is shown in Figure 2.3(a). Figure 2.3(b) shows the variation in intensity along the x-axis.

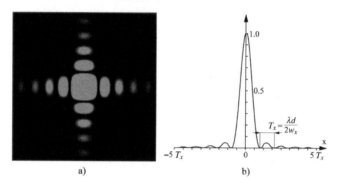

Figure 2.3. *Fraunhofer diffraction image given by a rectangular aperture*
($w_x = w_y = 2$ mm, $d = 200$ mm): a) image (0.266 mm × 0.266 mm);
b) normalized intensity curve along the x-axis

When a collimated laser beam crosses a convergent (convex) lens, we easily observe the Fraunhofer pattern in the focus plane. Furthermore, we will also see in the study of the reconstruction of images in digital holography that the reconstructed image of a point source is a Fraunhofer pattern corresponding to the outline of the pixel matrix of the recording detector.

2.3.2. Fraunhofer diffraction pattern from a circular aperture

Let us now consider a circular aperture of radius w, whose center is at the origin. If, in the plane of the aperture, r_0 is the radial coordinate and x_0 and y_0 are the Cartesian coordinates, we have $r_0 = \sqrt{x_0^2 + y_0^2}$. If a convergent lens of focal length f is adjoined to this aperture, and illuminated by a monochromatic plane wave, the wave crossing the lens becomes spherical and converges toward the focus, i.e.

$$U_0(r_0) = \mathrm{circ}\left(\frac{r_0}{w}\right)\exp\left(-\frac{jk}{2f}r_0^2\right)$$

[2.71]

The circular symmetry of the problem suggests that we rewrite the Fourier transform in expression [2.63] in the form of a Fourier–Bessel transform. We consider $d = f$. Substituting [2.71] into [2.63], we then have:

$$U(r_0) = \frac{\exp(jkd)}{j\lambda d}\exp\left(j\frac{kr_0^2}{2d}\right)F\{U_0(r_0)\}\bigg|_{\rho=\frac{r_0}{\lambda d}} \qquad [2.72]$$

where $\rho = \sqrt{f_x^2 + f_y^2}$ is the radial coordinate in the frequency plane. Since:

$$F\{U_0(r_0)\} = F\left\{\text{circ}\left(\frac{r_0}{w}\right)\right\} = \pi w^2 \frac{J_1(2\pi w\rho)}{\pi w\rho} \qquad [2.73]$$

J_1 being the first-order Bessel function, expression [2.72] can, therefore, be rewritten as:

$$U(r_0) = \frac{\exp(jkd)}{j\lambda d}\exp\left(j\frac{kr_0^2}{2d}\right)\pi w^2 \frac{2J_1(kwr_0/d)}{kwr_0/d} \qquad [2.74]$$

Thus, we obtain the intensity distribution of the diffracted field, under the Fraunhofer conditions, for a circular aperture:

$$I(r) = \left(\frac{\pi w^2}{\lambda d}\right)^2\left[\frac{2J_1(kwr_0/d)}{kwr_0/d}\right]^2 \qquad [2.75]$$

This intensity distribution is called the Airy pattern, from G.B. Airy, who was the first to explain it [BOR 99, GOO 72, GOO 05]. A Bessel function can be represented by different mathematical expressions. For example, the nth-order Bessel function (where n is an integer) can be expressed by:

$$J_n(z) = \frac{1}{2\pi}\int_{-\pi}^{\pi}\cos(z\sin\theta - n\theta)d\theta \qquad [2.76]$$

Using numerical integration methods, we can determine the numerical value of the Bessel function. Table 2.1 shows the successive maxima and minima of the Airy disk.

Z (rad)	$\left\|\dfrac{2J_1[Z]}{Z}\right\|^2$	Max/min
0	1	Max
3.832	0	Min
5.136	0.0175	Max
7.015	0	Min
8.416	0.0042	Max
10.172	0	Min
11.620	0.0016	Max

Table 2.1. *Some maxima and minima of the Airy disk*

The zeros of the Airy pattern are not equidistant. The first is obtained for $Z = kwr_0 = 3.832$, which corresponds to a disk diameter given by:

$$D = 1.22 \frac{\lambda d}{w} \qquad [2.77]$$

Considering w = 2 mm, λ = 0.532 μm, using [2.75] and [2.76], Figure 2.4(a) shows the intensity distribution of the Airy pattern diffracted along the distance d = 200 mm and Figure 2.4(b) shows a normalized intensity curve along the x-axis.

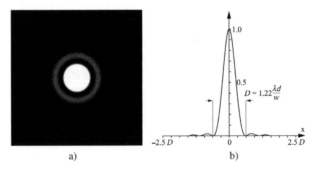

a)   b)

Figure 2.4. *Fraunhofer diffraction pattern given by a circular aperture: a) Airy disk (0.325 mm × 0.325 mm); b) normalized intensity curve along the x-axis*

If a convergent lens with a circular pupil is illuminated by a monochromatic plane wave, the preceding calculation shows that the field in the focal plane is an Airy pattern. Since the circular lens is a widely used element, the distribution in the image of a point source formed by a circular system can be considered as the Airy pattern of a circular pupil [GOO 72, GOO 05]. The spatial resolution of an optical apparatus is therefore given by the Airy pattern of its circular aperture.

2.3.3. Fraunhofer diffraction pattern from a sinusoidal-amplitude grating

The transmission function of a sinusoidal amplitude grating is expressed by:

$$t(x_0,y_0) = \frac{1}{2}[1 + m\cos(2\pi f_0 x_0)]\text{rect}\left(\frac{x_0}{2w}\right)\text{rect}\left(\frac{y_0}{2w}\right)$$ [2.78]

where f_0 is the frequency of the grating whose lines are parallel to the y_0-axis, m is a positive number less than or equal to 1, and the grating is bounded by a square aperture of sides $2w$. If the grating is illuminated at normal incidence by a monochromatic plane wave of unit amplitude, the field at the output of the grating plane $U_0(x_0,y_0)$ is simply equal to the transmission $t(x_0,y_0)$. So as to obtain the Fraunhofer diffraction pattern of the grating, we calculate the Fourier transform of $U_0(x_0,y_0)$. Using the convolution theorem, we have:

$$F\{U_0(x_0,y_0)\} = F\left\{\frac{1}{2}[1 + m\cos(2\pi f_0 x_0)]\right\} * F\left\{\text{rect}\left(\frac{x_0}{2w}\right)\text{rect}\left(\frac{y_0}{2w}\right)\right\}$$ [2.79]

as

$$F\left\{\frac{1}{2}[1 + m\cos(2\pi f_0 x_0)]\right\} = \frac{1}{2}\delta(f_x,f_y) + \frac{m}{4}\delta(f_x - f_0,f_y) + \frac{m}{4}\delta(f_x + f_0,f_y)$$ [2.80]

$$F\left\{\text{rect}\left(\frac{x_0}{2w}\right)\text{rect}\left(\frac{y_0}{2w}\right)\right\} = 4w^2\text{sinc}(2wf_x)\text{sinc}(2wf_y)$$ [2.81]

We suppose that the area of the grating is $S = 4w^2$; using the convolution property of the δ function, we obtain:

$$F\{U_0(x_0, y_0)\} = \frac{S}{2} \text{sinc}(2wf_y)$$

$$\times \left\{ \text{sinc}(2wf_x) + \frac{m}{2} \text{sinc}\left[2w(f_x - f_0)\right] + \frac{m}{2} \text{sinc}\left[2w(f_x + f_0)\right] \right\}$$

[2.82]

Following from equation [2.63], the Fraunhofer diffraction from the sinusoidal-amplitude grating can be expressed by:

$$U(x, y) = \frac{S}{j2\lambda d} \exp(jkd) \exp\left[j\frac{k}{2d}(x^2 + y^2) \right] \text{sinc}\left(\frac{2w}{\lambda d} y\right)$$

$$\times \left\{ \text{sinc}\left(\frac{2w}{\lambda d} x\right) + \frac{m}{2} \text{sinc}\left[2w\left(\frac{x}{\lambda d} - f_0\right)\right] + \frac{m}{2} \text{sinc}\left[2w\left(\frac{x}{\lambda d} + f_0\right)\right] \right\}$$

[2.83]

Taking the modulus squared of expression [2.83], we obtain the intensity of the diffracted field. We note that if the observation position is shifted by a number of periods $T = \lambda d/w$ with respect to the center of the sinc function, the value of the sinc function tends to zero. If the frequency f_0 of the grating is markedly greater than $1/w$, the overlap of the three x-dependant sinc functions will be negligible. Under these conditions:

$$I(x, y) \cong \left(\frac{S}{2\lambda d}\right)^2 \text{sinc}^2\left(\frac{2w}{\lambda d} y\right)$$

[2.84]

$$\times \left\{ \text{sinc}^2\left(\frac{2w}{\lambda d} x\right) + \frac{m^2}{4} \text{sinc}^2\left[2w\left(\frac{x}{\lambda d} - f_0\right)\right] + \frac{m^2}{4} \text{sinc}^2\left[2w\left(\frac{x}{\lambda d} + f_0\right)\right] \right\}$$

Considering $m = 1$, $w = 2$ mm, $\lambda = 0.532$ μm, and $d = 200$ mm, Figure 2.5(a) shows the intensity distribution of Fraunhofer diffraction from a sinusoidal-amplitude grating and Figure 2.5(b) shows its profile along the x-axis. The diffraction efficiency of the grating is defined as the ratio between the diffracted intensity in a certain order and the total incident intensity. With this definition, the diffraction intensities of the +1 and −1 orders (i.e. the intensity of the bands on either side of the central spot) are proportional to the coefficients of the δ function in expression [2.80], and from this their diffraction efficiencies are:

$$\eta_{+1} = \eta_{-1} = m^2/4$$

[2.85]

To use such a grating, we need good diffraction efficiency at orders ±1; the preceding result shows that the sinusoidal-amplitude grating must have a high contrast m. Nevertheless, as the maximum value of m is 1, the maximum efficiency at orders ±1 is only 0.25.

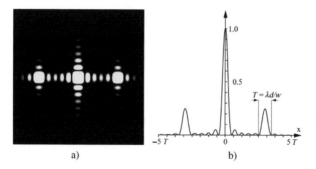

Figure 2.5. *The intensity distribution of the Fraunhofer diffraction pattern from a sinusoidal-amplitude grating for m = 1: a) the intensity distribution (0.532 mm × 0.532 mm); b) normalized intensity curve along the x-axis*

2.4. Some examples and uses of Fresnel diffraction

2.4.1. *Fresnel diffraction from a sinusoidal-amplitude grating*

The study of Fresnel diffraction from a sinusoidal-amplitude grating allows us to give a good explanation of the physical phenomenon called the Talbot effect, from the name of the man who first observed it [TAL 36]. The Talbot effect is a phenomenon of space-periodic self-imaging from the grating. Supposing that the transmission of a diaphragm satisfies:

$$t(x_0, y_0) = \frac{1}{2}[1 + m\cos(2\pi f_0 x_0)]$$

[2.86]

where f_0 is the frequency of the grating whose lines are parallel to the y_0-axis and m is a positive number less than or equal to one. If the grating is illuminated at normal incidence by a monochromatic plane wave of unit amplitude, the distribution of the field after the plane containing the grating $U_0(x_0, y_0)$ is simply equal to the transmission $t(x_0, y_0)$. Using formula [2.50] and the Fresnel transfer function, the field diffracted at a distance d is expressed by:

$$U(x, y) = F^{-1}\{F\{U_0(x_0, y_0)\}H_F(f_x, f_y)\}$$

[2.87]

with

$$H_F(f_x, f_y) = \exp\left[jkd\left(1 - \frac{\lambda^2}{2}(f_x^2 + f_y^2)\right)\right]$$

[2.88]

Substituting expression [2.86] for U_0, the Fourier transform $F\{U_0(x_0,y_0)\}$ in [2.87] is:

$$F\{U_0(x_0,y_0)\}=\frac{1}{2}\delta(f_x,f_y)+\frac{m}{4}\delta(f_x-f_0,f_y)+\frac{m}{4}\delta(f_x+f_0,f_y) \qquad [2.89]$$

Since the value of the transfer function at the origin of the frequency space basis is $\exp(jkd)$, the value at $(f_x,f_y)=(\pm f_0,0)$ will be:

$$H_F(\pm f_0,0)=\exp\left[jkd\left(1-\frac{\lambda^2}{2}f_0^2\right)\right] \qquad [2.90]$$

Thus, [2.87] simplifies to:

$$U(x,y)=\exp(jkd)F^{-1}\left\{\begin{array}{l}\frac{1}{2}\delta(f_x,f_y)+\exp\left(-jkd\frac{\lambda^2}{2}f_0^2\right)\\[2mm]\times\left[\frac{m}{4}\delta(f_x-f_0,f_y)+\frac{m}{4}\delta(f_x+f_0,f_y)\right]\end{array}\right\} \qquad [2.91]$$

Using the characteristics of the Fourier transform of the δ function, we immediately obtain the inverse transformation of this expression:

$$U(x,y)=\exp(jkd)\left\{\frac{1}{2}+\exp\left(-jkdf_0^2\frac{\lambda^2}{2}\right)\times\left[\frac{m}{4}\exp(j2\pi f_0x)+\frac{m}{4}\exp(-j2\pi f_0x)\right]\right\} \qquad [2.92]$$

From Euler's formula, we have:

$$U(x,y)=\frac{\exp(jkd)}{2}\left\{1+m\exp\left(-jkdf_0^2\frac{\lambda^2}{2}\right)\cos(2\pi f_0x)\right\} \qquad [2.93]$$

Taking the modulus squared of expression [2.93], and with $k=2\pi/\lambda$, we obtain the intensity of the diffracted field:

$$I(x,y)=\frac{1}{4}\left\{1+2m\cos\left(-\pi\lambda df_0^2\right)\cos(2\pi f_0x)+m^2\cos^2(2\pi f_0x)\right\} \qquad [2.94]$$

From this expression, three noteworthy conditions are discussed concerning an integer n:

– The diffraction distance d satisfies $\pi \lambda d f_0^2 = 2n\pi$, i.e. $d = 2n / \lambda f_0^2$. In this case, expression [2.94] becomes:

$$I(x,y) = \frac{1}{4}[1 + m\cos(2\pi f_0 x)]^2 \qquad [2.95]$$

Comparing this with [2.86], we note that $I(x,y) = t^2(x,y)$. In other words, the diffracted field is an ideal intensity image of the object field. This phenomenon that forms an image without a lens is called the Talbot effect.

– The diffraction distance d satisfies $\pi \lambda d f_0^2 = (2n+1)\pi$, i.e. $d = (2n+1) / \lambda f_0^2$. In this case, we have:

$$I(x,y) = \frac{1}{4}[1 - m\cos(2\pi f_0 x)]^2 \qquad [2.96]$$

Note that the field is also an intensity image of the object field, but this image is phase-shifted by 180°. This means that there is a solarization of the intensity image distribution (with respect to the previous case, the brightest zone corresponds to the darkest zone). This phenomenon is also called the Talbot effect.

– The diffraction distance d satisfies $\pi \lambda d f_0^2 = (2n-1)\pi$, i.e. $d = (2n-1) / \lambda f_0^2$. In this case, we have:

$$I(x,y) = \frac{1}{4}\left[1 + m^2\cos(2\pi f_0 x)\right] = \frac{1}{4}\left[\left(1 + \frac{m^2}{2}\right) + \frac{m^2}{2}\cos(4\pi f_0 x)\right] \qquad [2.97]$$

Note that the diffracted field is also an image of the grating, but its frequency has doubled compared to the original grating. Moreover, its contrast is relatively low. This type of image is called a Talbot subimage. We note that, if $m \ll 1$, $m^2 \to 0$, the Talbot subimage will no longer be observable.

Figure 2.6 illustrates the positions of the Talbot images in the space after the grating. The Talbot effect can also be observed in cases other than the sinusoidal grating: if the initial field has a periodic structure, we can show that the Talbot effect exists in the diffraction process.

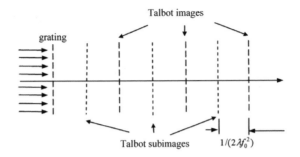

Figure 2.6. *Diagram of the Talbot image positions*

2.4.2. *Fresnel diffraction from a rectangular aperture*

Let us consider a diaphragm with a rectangular aperture centered at the origin of the coordinates, and let $\{w_x, w_y\}$ be the respective half-widths of the aperture in the x_0 and y_0 directions. As in the previous case, if the aperture is illuminated at normal incidence by a monochromatic plane wave of unit amplitude, the distribution of the field is:

$$U_0(x_0, y_0) = \mathrm{rect}\left(\frac{x_0}{2w_x}\right)\mathrm{rect}\left(\frac{y_0}{2w_y}\right) \tag{2.98}$$

After diffraction along a distance d, the field is expressed by the Fresnel diffraction integral:

$$U(x, y) = \frac{\exp(jkd)}{j\lambda d} \int_{-\infty}^{\infty}\int_{-\infty}^{\infty} U_0(x_0, y_0)\exp\left\{\frac{jk}{2d}\left[(x - x_0)^2 + (y - y_0)^2\right]\right\}dx_0 dy_0 \tag{2.99}$$

Considering a separation of variables, this expression can be rewritten as:

$$U(x, y) = -j\exp(jkd)U_x(x)U_y(y) \tag{2.100}$$

with

$$U_x(x) = \frac{1}{\sqrt{\lambda d}}\int_{-w_x}^{w_x} \exp\left[\frac{jk}{2d}(x - x_0)^2\right]dx_0 \tag{2.101}$$

$$U_y(y) = \frac{1}{\sqrt{\lambda d}}\int_{-w_y}^{w_y} \exp\left[\frac{jk}{2d}(y - y_0)^2\right]dy_0 \tag{2.102}$$

Introducing $\alpha = \sqrt{2/\lambda d}\,(x - x_0)$ and $\beta = \sqrt{2/\lambda d}\,(y - y_0)$, we obtain:

$$U_x(x) = \frac{1}{\sqrt{2}} \int_{\alpha_1}^{\alpha_2} \exp\left(j\frac{\pi}{2}\alpha^2 \right) d\alpha \qquad\qquad [2.103]$$

$$U_y(y) = \frac{1}{\sqrt{2}} \int_{\beta_1}^{\beta_2} \exp\left(j\frac{\pi}{2}\beta^2 \right) d\beta \qquad\qquad [2.104]$$

where the limits of integration are:

$$\alpha_1 = \sqrt{\frac{2}{\lambda d}}\,(w_x + x)$$

$$\alpha_2 = \sqrt{\frac{2}{\lambda d}}\,(w_x - x)$$

$$\beta_1 = \sqrt{\frac{2}{\lambda d}}\,(w_y + y)$$

$$\beta_2 = \sqrt{\frac{2}{\lambda d}}\,(w_y - y) \qquad\qquad [2.105]$$

Introducing the two Fresnel functions [GAD 80]:

$$S(z) = \int_0^z \sin(\frac{\pi}{2}t^2)dt \qquad\qquad [2.106]$$

$$C(z) = \int_0^z \cos(\frac{\pi}{2}t^2)dt \qquad\qquad [2.107]$$

The two expressions $U_x(x)$ and $U_y(y)$ can be rewritten as:

$$U_x(x) = \frac{1}{\sqrt{2}}\{[C(\alpha_2) - C(\alpha_1)] + j[S(\alpha_2) - S(\alpha_1)]\} \qquad\qquad [2.108]$$

$$U_y(y) = \frac{1}{\sqrt{2}}\{[C(\beta_2) - C(\beta_1)] + j[S(\beta_2) - S(\beta_1)]\} \qquad\qquad [2.109]$$

After a substitution into [2.100], we finally obtain the field in the observation plane:

$$U(x,y) = \frac{\exp(jkd)}{2j}\{[C(\alpha_2) - C(\alpha_1)] + j[S(\alpha_2) - S(\alpha_1)]\}$$
$$\times \{[C(\beta_2) - C(\beta_1)] + j[S(\beta_2) - S(\beta_1)]\} \qquad [2.110]$$

The intensity distribution of the diffraction pattern in the observation plane is, therefore, given by:

$$I(x,y) = |U(x,y)|^2$$
$$= \frac{1}{4}\{[C(\alpha_2) - C(\alpha_1)]^2 + [S(\alpha_2) - S(\alpha_1)]^2\} \qquad [2.111]$$
$$\times \{[C(\beta_2) - C(\beta_1)]^2 + [S(\beta_2) - S(\beta_1)]^2\}$$

If we managed to solve the two Fresnel functions, the expression of the Fresnel diffraction pattern would be obtained by this relation. Unfortunately, the solution to the Fresnel functions can only be obtained numerically [GAD 80]. Nevertheless, there exist different approximations of these functions [LI 07a, SIE 86]. Here, we introduce the approximation from [SIE 86]. We have:

$$S(z) = \frac{1}{2} - \left[f(z)\cos(\pi z^2/2) + g(z)\sin(\pi z^2/2)\right] \qquad [2.112]$$

$$C(z) = \frac{1}{2} - \left[g(z)\cos(\pi z^2/2) - f(z)\sin(\pi z^2/2)\right] \qquad [2.113]$$

where

$$f(z) \approx \frac{1 + 0.962z}{2 + 1.792z + 3.014z^2} \qquad [2.114]$$

$$g(z) \approx \frac{1}{2 + 4.142z + 3.492z^2 + 6.670z^3} \qquad [2.115]$$

Let $w_x = w_y = 2$ mm and $\lambda = 0.532$ µm. Using the results of [2.111] and the relevant relationships, Figure 2.7 shows the respective intensity patterns corresponding to diffraction distances of $d = 100$, 1,000, and 20,000 mm.

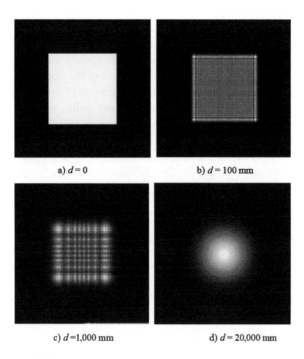

a) $d = 0$ b) $d = 100$ mm

c) $d = 1,000$ mm   d) $d = 20,000$ mm

Figure 2.7. *Fresnel diffraction pattern from a rectangular aperture for different distances*

We note that because of diffraction, the observed patterns are very different to those predicted by geometric optics. They demonstrate an essential law of Fresnel diffraction: if the diffraction distance is small, the diffraction pattern conserves the shape of the aperture with interference fringes at the border and the intensity distribution stays relatively homogeneous; on the other hand, when the diffraction distance increases, the width of the interference fringes increases and their influence stretches toward the center, giving an inhomogeneous intensity distribution. If the distance is very large, the shape of the aperture disappears, and the pattern tends toward that of Fraunhofer diffraction.

2.5. Collins' formula

Practically, the propagation of light is to be considered across an optical system composed of multiple convergent or divergent lenses. If the pieces are positioned symmetrically with respect to the optical axis, the system is said to be a centered system. If the light propagates in the neighborhood of the optical axis (paraxial optics), the Fresnel approximation conditions are often satisfied. Thus, based on the Fresnel diffraction integral or on the other classical formulae of Kirchhoff or

Rayleigh–Sommerfeld, or on the angular spectrum, it is possible to successively calculate the diffracted field between two neighboring elements so as to determine the complex amplitude of the wave traversing the optical system. However, it will be necessary to take into account the filtering effect of the aperture diaphragm of the system and to neglect the filtering due to other elements of the system. Based on this approximation, there are two equivalent coexisting points of view concerning the calculation of diffraction across an optical system [GOO 72, GOO 05]. The first proposition was formulated for the first time by Ernst Abbe in 1873. According to Abbe's theory, only part of the spatial components of an object passes into the entrance pupil, which determines the diffraction of the system. The second proposition was formulated by Lord Rayleigh in 1896, according to which the diffraction effects result from the finite dimension of the exit pupil. These two remarks rest upon an equivalent definition of the pupil: on the one hand it is the conjugate object of the aperture diaphragm and, on the other, it is its conjugate image. It seems that these two points of view are absolutely equivalent and that we obtain coherent results when applying one or the other of the two methods.

Following the matrix approach of geometric optics [KEA 02], the optical properties of a centered system can be described by a matrix of four elements A, B, C, and D. Thus, we can wonder whether it is possible to establish a formula relating the elements $ABCD$ so as to simply calculate diffraction across the system. In 1970, using the Fresnel approximation and eikonal theory, S.A. Collins proposed a formulation [COL 70] called Collins' formula. We are going to show that this formula is an exact mathematical description of the diffraction calculation across an optical system [LI 02a].

2.5.1. Description of an optical system by an ABCD transfer matrix

According to geometric optics, the trajectory of a ray in a plane that includes the optical axis z is sufficient to describe the properties of a system. In the plane containing the optical axis z, the position of any ray can be determined by two parameters: the distance r between the intersection of the ray in the reference plane and the z-axis and the angle of inclination θ between the ray and the optical axis. We can represent it by a two-element column vector $\begin{bmatrix} r & \theta \end{bmatrix}^T$. The transformation of a ray $\begin{bmatrix} r_1 & \theta_1 \end{bmatrix}^T$ from the input plane at $z = z_1$ to the output plane $z = z_2$ is described by its product with a matrix M of four elements A, B, C, D, i.e.

$$\begin{bmatrix} r_2 \\ \theta_2 \end{bmatrix} = M \begin{bmatrix} r_1 \\ \theta_1 \end{bmatrix} = \begin{bmatrix} A & B \\ C & D \end{bmatrix} \begin{bmatrix} r_1 \\ \theta_1 \end{bmatrix}$$

[2.116]

Each optical element and the surrounding medium can be considered as elementary systems, each having a transfer matrix. If the system is structured into N elements, the transformation of the ray can be expressed by the product of the elementary matrices describing the elements that the ray successively traverses, i.e.

$$\begin{bmatrix} r_o \\ \theta_o \end{bmatrix} = \begin{bmatrix} A_N & B_N \\ C_N & D_N \end{bmatrix} \cdots \begin{bmatrix} A_2 & B_2 \\ C_2 & D_2 \end{bmatrix} \begin{bmatrix} A_1 & B_1 \\ C_1 & D_1 \end{bmatrix} \begin{bmatrix} r_i \\ \theta_i \end{bmatrix} = M_N \cdots M_2 M_1 \begin{bmatrix} r_i \\ \theta_i \end{bmatrix} \qquad [2.117]$$

This relation indicates the method that allows us to determine the transfer matrix of the system: we determine the elementary matrices of the elements that the ray passes through $M_1, M_2, ..., M_N$, then following the order in which these elements are traversed, we take the product of the elementary matrices from right to left. The transfer matrix of the system can be expressed as:

$$M = M_N \cdots M_2 M_1 = \begin{bmatrix} A_N & B_N \\ C_N & D_N \end{bmatrix} \cdots \begin{bmatrix} A_2 & B_2 \\ C_2 & D_2 \end{bmatrix} \begin{bmatrix} A_1 & B_1 \\ C_1 & D_1 \end{bmatrix} \qquad [2.118]$$

Note that, for the determination of the transfer matrix of a system, the product of the elementary matrices does not commute and we must strictly conserve the order given by this expression. Otherwise, the result of the product will correspond to another, differently structured, optical system with the same elements.

We can demonstrate an important property of the transfer matrix of a system: if the refractive index of the medium in the input plane is n_1 and that in the output plane is n_2, the value of the determinant of the transfer matrix will be n_1 / n_2, i.e.

$$\det M = AD - BC = n_1 / n_2 \qquad [2.119]$$

Practically, however, the elements of the system are generally in the same medium, and this relation then becomes:

$$\det M = AD - BC = 1 \qquad [2.120]$$

These two relations can be used as proof of the veracity of the calculation of the transfer matrix of a complex system. In the context of the Gaussian approximation [KEA 02], the transfer matrix of an elementary system is constructed in a simple manner. We must establish certain notions and respect some sign rules. The sign convention is as shown in Figure 2.8, which describes an optical system composed of two spherical refracting surfaces of two different homogeneous media [LI 02a].

We represent the curvature center of the spherical surface separating the two media of refractive indices n_1 and n_2 by C. The line SC, the radius of curvature, is written as R, i.e. $R = \overline{SC}$. The z-axis passes through the center C and the apex S of the left refracting surface. The plane comprising the z-axis is the meridian plane. Let us consider the object point A_1 on the optical axis. In the meridian plane, the position of the ray is determined by the distance to the axis and the aperture angle. The object distance is the algebraic distance between the apex S and the object point A_1, i.e. $L_1 = \left| \overline{SA_1} \right|$. The aperture angle is the oriented angle between the incident ray and the axis $\theta_1 = (SA_1E)$. In Figure 2.8, the ray A_1E coming from the point A_1 crosses the spherical surface at the point E. After refraction, the refracted ray EA_2 crosses the axis at the point A_2. The position of the ray EA_2 is determined by the distance SA_2 and the image aperture angle $\theta_2 = (SA_2E)$. For the description of the optical system, we apply certain rules for the location and orientation of distances and angles:

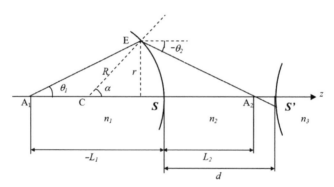

Figure 2.8. *Sign convention*

The figure gives absolute values of the distance and angle parameters:

– The sign convention of distances is from left to right, for example the object distance SA_1 is $\overline{SA_1} = -L_1$.

– For the sizes of objects, the upward direction is positive, or negative if the object is oriented downward.

– For the angle between a ray and the optical axis, the sign is determined by the direction of rotation from the optical axis to the ray. If the rotation is clockwise, it is negative, otherwise it is positive; for example, we have $\theta_2 < 0$ on the diagram.

– For the interval between two refracting surfaces, the sign is determined by the direction of the apex of the first toward the apex of the second; if the direction is the same as that of the propagating light, the sign is positive, otherwise it is negative; in Figure 2.8, the interval between the two surfaces is d ($d>0$).

It must be noted that the sign rules are not strictly obligatory, but by following them we obtain correct and coherent results. Considering Figure 2.8, we can determine the transfer matrix of the refracting surface on the left, which separates the two media of indices n_1 and n_2. Let us consider the plane perpendicular to the optical axis, passing through the apex S, as a reference plane. The incident point E is at height r from the optical axis, and we may consider that the refracted ray is also at this height, i.e. $r_1 = r_2 = r$. Following the sign rules of angles, the absolute values of the angles of incidence and refraction are $\alpha - \theta_1$ and $\alpha - \theta_2$, respectively. As, in Gauss' approximation, the law of refraction is given by $n_1(\alpha - \theta_1) = n_2(\alpha - \theta_2)$, with $\alpha = -\arctan(r/R) \approx -r/R$, we have therefore:

$$\theta_2 = -\frac{(n_2 - n_1)r}{n_2 R} + \frac{n_1 \theta_1}{n_2} \qquad [2.121]$$

Expressing these results in matrix form:

$$\begin{bmatrix} r_2 \\ \theta_2 \end{bmatrix} = \begin{bmatrix} 1 & 0 \\ -\dfrac{n_2 - n_1}{n_2 R} & \dfrac{n_1}{n_2} \end{bmatrix} \begin{bmatrix} r_1 \\ \theta_1 \end{bmatrix} \qquad [2.122]$$

Consequently, the transfer matrix of the spherical refracting surface is:

$$M = \begin{bmatrix} 1 & 0 \\ -\dfrac{n_2 - n_1}{n_2 R} & \dfrac{n_1}{n_2} \end{bmatrix} \qquad [2.123]$$

Making R tends to infinity, we obtain the transfer matrix of a plane refracting surface perpendicular to the optical axis, separating two media of refractive indices n_1 and n_2:

$$M = \begin{pmatrix} 1 & 0 \\ 0 & \dfrac{n_1}{n_2} \end{pmatrix} \qquad [2.124]$$

Table 2.2 gives the matrices of the widely used optical elements [GER 75].

(1) Transmission in a homogeneous medium	$n \quad\quad n \quad\quad n$ $\xrightarrow{\quad\quad l \quad\quad} z$ RP1 $\quad\quad$ RP2	$\begin{bmatrix} 1 & l \\ 0 & 1 \end{bmatrix}$
(2) Plane refracting surface	$n_1 \quad\quad n_2$ $\xrightarrow{\quad\quad\quad} z$ RP1 RP2	$\begin{bmatrix} 1 & 0 \\ 0 & \dfrac{n_1}{n_2} \end{bmatrix}$
(3) Spherical refracting surface separating two media	$n_1 \quad n_2$ R $\xrightarrow{\quad\quad} z$ RP1 RP2	$\begin{bmatrix} 1 & 0 \\ -\dfrac{n_2 - n_1}{n_2 R} & \dfrac{n_1}{n_2} \end{bmatrix}$
(4) Thin lens	f $\xrightarrow{\quad\quad\quad} z$ RP1 RP2	$\begin{bmatrix} 1 & 0 \\ -\dfrac{1}{f} & 1 \end{bmatrix}$
(5) Spherical mirror	R $\xrightarrow{\quad\quad\quad} z$ RP1 RP2	$\begin{bmatrix} 1 & 0 \\ -\dfrac{2}{R} & 1 \end{bmatrix}$
(6) Plane mirror	$\xrightarrow{\quad\quad\quad} z$ RP1 RP2	$\begin{bmatrix} 1 & 0 \\ 0 & 1 \end{bmatrix}$
(7) Totally internally reflecting prism	RP1 RP2 $\xrightarrow{\quad\quad\quad} z$ d	$\begin{bmatrix} -1 & -\dfrac{2d}{n} \\ 0 & -1 \end{bmatrix}$

Table 2.2. *Transfer matrices of optical elements*

2.5.2. *ABCD law and paraxial systems equivalent to a lens*

2.5.2.1. *ABCD law of a spherical wave propagating across an optical system*

We will now analyze the transformation of a spherical wave passing through an optical system. This case constitutes one of the main uses of the transfer matrix. In Figure 2.9, a system is represented by a matrix *ABCD*. The input plane of the system, Rp1, is marked by a dotted line and Rp2 is the output plane. The spherical wave of radius R_1, originating at the point O_1 on the optical axis, can be described by a ray coming from point O_1, intercepting P_1 in the plane Rp1, using the vector $\begin{bmatrix} r_1 & \theta_1 \end{bmatrix}^T$, where r_1 is the height of P_1 and θ_1 is the angle of inclination of the ray. In the same manner, the spherical wave at the output of the system is represented by the ray coming out of the plane Rp2 using the vector $\begin{bmatrix} r_2 & \theta_2 \end{bmatrix}^T$, where r_2 is the height of the intersection P_2 with the plane Rp2 and θ_2 is the angle of inclination of the output ray. From the matrix relation, we have:

$$\begin{cases} r_2 = Ar_1 + B\theta_1 \\ \theta_2 = Cr_1 + D\theta_1 \end{cases}$$
[2.125]

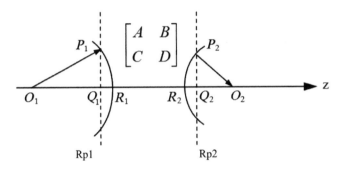

Figure 2.9. *Transformation of a spherical wave by a paraxial system*

In Gauss' approximation, the radii of curvature R_1 and R_2 of the spherical waves at the input and the output, respectively, can be expressed by:

$$\begin{cases} R_1 = \dfrac{r_1}{\theta_1} \\ R_2 = \dfrac{r_2}{\theta_2} \end{cases}$$
[2.126]

From the two preceding relations, we then have:

$$R_2 = \frac{AR_1 + B}{CR_1 + D}$$
[2.127]

This expression constitutes the *ABCD* law of a spherical wave passing through a central system.

Following the sign rules, if the propagation of the rays corresponds to what is shown in Figure 2.9, since $r_1 > 0$ and $\theta_1 > 0$, we have $R_1 = r_1/\theta_1 > 0$. This means that the input spherical wave is divergent. Since $r_2 > 0$ and $\theta_2 < 0$, we have $R_2 = r_2/\theta_2 < 0$, the output spherical wave is convergent. Consequently, if we consider the plane passing through the point O_1 perpendicular to the axis as the object plane, the plane containing O_2 and perpendicular to the axis will be the image plane. Thus, the *ABCD* law of a spherical wave passing through a paraxial system can be considered as another representation of the laws of the formation of images in geometrical optics.

2.5.2.2. *System equivalent to a lens*

A system, represented by the four matrix elements *ABCD*, can be considered as equivalent to a lens allowing the formation of an image. Let us consider ourselves with the relation between the matrix elements and the parameters of a lens. Figure 2.10 shows a system where Rp1 and Rp2 are the input and output planes, respectively, H_1 and H_2 are the respective image and object principal planes, and h_2 is the distance between H_2 and Rp2. If an incoming ray is parallel to the optical axis, from expression [2.125], the relation between the input and output rays is:

$$\begin{cases} r_2 = Ar_1 \\ \theta_2 = Cr_1 \end{cases}$$

[2.128]

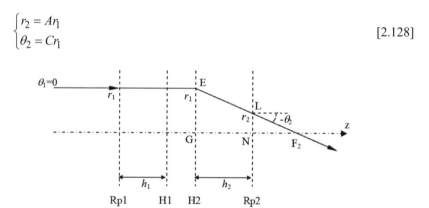

Figure 2.10. *System equivalent to a lens*

Following the definition of the principal planes [KEA 02], the ray, being incident parallel to the axis, intercepts the principal image plane H_2, and will then be deviated toward the focal point F_2. Let the line segment $GF_2 = f_e$ be the focal distance. Following the sign rules, $\theta_2 < 0$, we then have:

$$\begin{cases} -\theta_2 = \dfrac{r_1}{f_e} \\[2mm] \dfrac{r_1}{f_e} = \dfrac{r_2}{f_e - h_2} \end{cases} \qquad [2.129]$$

from which we obtain:

$$f_e = -\frac{1}{C} \qquad [2.130]$$

$$h_2 = \frac{A-1}{C} \qquad [2.131]$$

Let h_1 be the distance between the principal object plane H_1 and Rp1. Considering that the propagation direction is reversed by the return of the light, we obtain a symmetric relation given by:

$$h_1 = \frac{D-1}{C} \qquad [2.132]$$

The previous three expressions [2.130], [2.131], and [2.132] give the relation between the matrix elements and the parameters of the system. These results will be used in the proof of Collins' formula.

2.5.2.3. *Properties of the transfer matrix*

When an element of the transfer matrix of an optical system is zero, the system presents some particular properties. We use relation [2.125] [LI 02a]. Figure 2.11 describes the propagation of a ray in the case where one of the elements of the transfer matrix is zero.

– If $A = 0$, $r_2 = B\theta_1$. In other words, any ray incident at angle θ_1 will be focused on the same point in the plane Rp2. Rp2 is therefore the focal image plane of the system.

– If $B = 0$, $r_2 = Ar_1$. In other words any incident ray passing by the same point in the input plane Rp1 will be focused on the same point in Rp2 regardless of its angle of incidence. This means that Rp1 and Rp2 are conjugated stigmatic planes. In this case, the matrix element corresponds to the transverse magnification $A = r_2 / r_1$.

– If $C = 0$, $\theta_2 = D\theta_1$. We observe that all parallel incident beams passing the input plane Rp1 come out parallel from the plane Rp2. In this case, the matrix element corresponds to the angular magnification $D = \theta_2 / \theta_1$.

– If $D = 0$, $\theta_2 = C r_1$. We observe that all incident beams that converge to the same point in the input plane will come out parallel from the plane Rp2. This means that Rp1 is the focal object plane of the system.

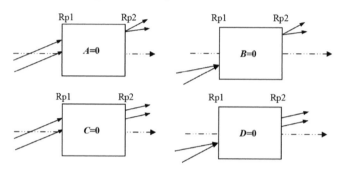

Figure 2.11. *Diagram of the propagation of a ray in the case where one of the elements of the transfer matrix is zero*

2.5.3. *Proof of Collins' formula*

By neglecting the diffraction limit of the optical system and by using Fresnel's approximation for diffraction, Collins [COL 70] established a formula allowing the calculation of the optical field across an optical system. This formula is written as follows:

$$U_2(x_2, y_2) = \frac{\exp(jkL)}{j\lambda B} \int_{-\infty}^{\infty} \int_{-\infty}^{\infty} U_1(x_1, y_1) \times$$

$$\exp\left\{ \frac{jk}{2B} \left[A(x_1^2 + y_1^2) + D(x_2^2 + y_2^2) - 2(x_1 x + y_1 y_2) \right] \right\} dx_1 dy_1$$

[2.133]

where L is the optical path along the optical axis, $U_1(x_1, y_1)$ is the complex amplitude of the light wave in the input plane of the system, $U_2(x_2, y_2)$ is that of the wave at the output plane, and $ABCD$ are the matrix elements of the optical system. From a practical point of view, the Fresnel diffraction integral only permits the calculation of the field in the case of propagation in a homogeneous medium; Collins' formula allows us to calculate the diffracted field across an optical system represented by a transfer matrix $ABCD$. This formulation can, therefore, be very useful for treating certain cases. Relation [2.133] can be obtained theoretically in different ways and here we will give a proof using the Rayleigh approach. Collins' formula can be considered as a mathematical representation of the diffraction effects that result from the finite dimensions or the exit pupil. As the proof uses the transfer properties of a thin lens for the diffracted field and the expression of the field in the ideal image, we will begin with these two points.

2.5.3.1. Transmission from a thin lens

The optical path taken in a thin lens is drawn in Figure 2.12. After the transformation due to the lens, two rays coming from the object point S on the optical axis z will be focused on the image point S_i. The formation of the image can be considered as a transformation of a divergent spherical wave to a convergent spherical wave.

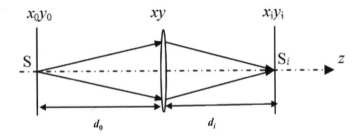

Figure 2.12. *Image formation by a thin lens*

Let d_i be the distance between the origin and the image, d_0 the distance between the origin and the object (following the sign rules, $d_0 < 0$), x and y the coordinates of the lens plane, and $t(x,y)$ the transmission function of the lens. Following from the representation of the complex amplitude of a light wave, the field across the lens can be expressed by the product of $t(x, y)$ with the field incident at the lens, i.e.

$$a\exp\left[-\frac{jk}{2d_i}\left(x^2 + y^2\right)\right] = t(x, y)a\exp\left[-\frac{jk}{2d_0}\left(x^2 + y^2\right)\right] \qquad [2.134]$$

where a is the amplitude of the light wave. From this relation, we can easily obtain:

$$t(x, y) = \exp\left[-\frac{jk}{2}\left(\frac{1}{d_i} - \frac{1}{d_0}\right)\left(x^2 + y^2\right)\right] \qquad [2.135]$$

If f is the focal distance of the lens, using the conjugation relation of thin lenses [KEA 02], $1/f = 1/d_i - 1/d_0$, we can rewrite this expression in the form:

$$t(x,y) = \exp\left[-\frac{jk}{2f}\left(x^2 + y^2\right)\right]$$

[2.136]

We note that the action of transformation of the field by a lens of focal distance f is the product of the field with a quadratic phase factor having a radius of curvature f.

2.5.3.2. Expression of the ideal image

In Figure 2.12, the two planes perpendicular to the z-axis, which pass through S and S$_i$ are the object and image planes, respectively. Let x_0 and y_0 be the coordinates in the object plane and x_i and y_i those in the image plane. According to linear systems theory, if we neglect the aberrations of the system, and on the condition that we are able to obtain the impulse response, the image field of any object is determined by a convolution relation. Next, we will consider the impulse response of an optical system for a point source of unit amplitude $\delta(x_0-\xi, y_0-\eta)$ located in the object plane. The incident field in the plane of the lens and coming from the point source $\delta(x_0-\xi,y_0-\eta)$ is given by the Fresnel diffraction integral:

$$u_\delta\left(x,y;\xi,\eta\right) = -\frac{\exp(-jkd_0)}{j\lambda d_0}$$

$$\times \int\limits_{-\infty}^{\infty}\int\limits_{-\infty}^{\infty} \delta(x_0 - \xi, y_0 - \eta)\exp\left\{-\frac{jk}{2d_0}\left[(x-x_0)^2 + (y-y_0)^2\right]\right\} dx_0 dy_0$$

[2.137]

Owing to the translation property of the δ function, we have:

$$u_\delta(x, y;\xi,\eta) = -\frac{\exp(-jkd_0)}{j\lambda d_0}\exp\left\{-\frac{jk}{2d_0}\left[(x-\xi)^2 + (y-\eta)^2\right]\right\}$$

[2.138]

Using the transmittance of a thin lens, the field coming out of the lens then becomes:

$$u'_\delta(x, y;\xi,\eta) = \exp\left(-jk\frac{x^2 + y^2}{2f}\right)u_\delta(x, y;\xi,\eta)$$

[2.139]

Using the Fresnel diffraction integral once again, we obtain the field incident to the image plane:

$$h(x_i, y_i; \xi, \eta) = \frac{\exp(jkd_i)}{j\lambda d_i} \int_{-\infty}^{\infty} \int_{-\infty}^{\infty} u'_\delta(x, y; \xi, \eta) \exp\left[jk \frac{(x - x_i)^2 + (y - y_i)^2}{2d_i} \right] dxdy$$

[2.140]

This expression represents the field given in the image plane by a point source of coordinates (ξ, η) in the object plane and it constitutes the impulse response of the system [GOO 72, GOO 05]. Substituting the corresponding elements into [2.140], we obtain:

$$h(x_i, y_i; \xi, \eta) = \frac{\exp\left[jk(d_i - d_0) \right]}{\lambda^2 d_i d_0} \exp\left(-jk \frac{\xi^2 + \eta^2}{2d_0} \right) \exp\left(jk \frac{x_i^2 + y_i^2}{2d_i} \right)$$

[2.141]

$$\times \int_{-\infty}^{\infty} \int_{-\infty}^{\infty} \exp\left\{ -jk \left[\left(\frac{x_i}{d_i} - \frac{\xi}{d_0} \right) x + \left(\frac{y_i}{d_i} - \frac{\eta}{d_0} \right) y \right] \right\} dxdy$$

As $L_i = d_i - d_0$ is the optical path from the object plane to the image plane, the transverse magnification is $A = d_i / d_0$, and we have $x_a = A\xi$ and $y_a = A\eta$. Expression [2.141] can be rewritten as:

$$h(x_i, y_i; \xi, \eta) = \frac{A \exp(jkL_i)}{\lambda^2 d_i^2} \exp\left(-jk \frac{x_a^2 + y_a^2}{2Ad_i} \right) \exp\left(jk \frac{x_i^2 + y_i^2}{2d_i} \right)$$

[2.142]

$$\int_{-\infty}^{\infty} \int_{-\infty}^{\infty} \exp\left\{ -j \frac{2\pi}{\lambda d_i} \left[(x_i - x_a) x + (y_i - y_a) y \right] \right\} dxdy$$

We then have:

$$h(x_i, y_i; \xi, \eta) =$$

$$A \exp(jkL_i) \exp\left(-jk \frac{x_a^2 + y_a^2}{2Ad_i} \right) \exp\left(jk \frac{x_i^2 + y_i^2}{2d_i} \right) \delta(x_i - x_a, y_i - y_a) \quad [2.143]$$

We have obtained the impulse response of an ideal system constituted by a thin lens. The impulse response is the optical field in the image plane coming from a point source object of unit amplitude, having coordinates (ξ, η) in the object plane.

Considering $U_0(x_0, y_0)$ as the optical field in the object plane, the field in the image plane can then be expressed by a superposition integral:

$$U(x_i, y_i) = \exp\left(jk\frac{x_i^2 + y_i^2}{2d_i}\right)\exp(jkL_i) \times$$

$$\times \int_{-\infty}^{\infty}\int_{-\infty}^{\infty} U_0(\xi, \eta) A \exp\left(-jk\frac{x_a^2 + y_a^2}{2Ad_i}\right) h(x_i, y_i; \xi, \eta)\,d\xi\,d\eta \quad [2.144]$$

Substituting the coordinates $x_a = A\xi$, $y_a = A\eta$, and expression [2.143] into this relation, we obtain:

$$U(x_i, y_i) = \exp\left(jk\frac{x_i^2 + y_i^2}{2d_i}\right)\exp(jkL_i)$$

$$\times \int_{-\infty}^{\infty}\int_{-\infty}^{\infty} \frac{1}{A}U_0\left(\frac{x_a}{A}, \frac{y_a}{A}\right)\exp\left(-jk\frac{x_a^2 + y_a^2}{2Ad_i}\right)\delta(x_i - x_a, y_i - y_a)\,dx_a\,dy_a \quad [2.145]$$

With the translation property of the δ function, we readily obtain the ideal image field:

$$U(x_i, y_i) = \frac{1}{A}U_0\left(\frac{x_i}{A}, \frac{y_i}{A}\right)\exp(jkL_i)\exp\left[jk\frac{x_i^2 + y_i^2}{2d_i}\left(1 - \frac{1}{A}\right)\right] \quad [2.146]$$

The lens plane can be considered as the principal image plane of the paraxial optical system. The distance d_i is then the distance between the principal image plane and the image plane. Consequently, [2.146] is generally considered as the expression of the optical field of the ideal image formed by a paraxial system.

2.5.3.3. Proof of Collins' formula

Since the *ABCD* system can be considered as an image formation system, we will now tackle this question: if the smallest diaphragm of the system is situated in the object principal plane, considering the diffraction by the *ABCD* system due to the exit pupil in the image space, what will the expression corresponding to the optical field in an observation plane be?

This scenario is illustrated in Figure 2.13. The *ABCD* system is formed from the input plane Rp1 to the output plane Rp2, in which a subsystem *abcd* (the matrix elements of this subsystem are expressed by the four lower case letters *abcd*) forms an image situated between the input plane Rp1 and the output plane Rp2. The field in the plane Rp is the image of the field $U_1(x_1, y_1)$ of the input plane Rp1. Let z_i be the distance between the image plane Rp and the output plane Rp2, after diffraction along the distance z_i. Let us consider the expression of the field $U_2(x_2, y_2)$ in the output plane Rp2.

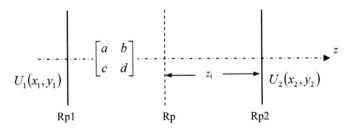

Figure 2.13. *Diffraction due to the exit pupil*

Since the subsystem *abcd* is a system allowing the formation of an image, with $b = 0$, the relation between the elements of the two transfer matrices is then:

$$\begin{bmatrix} A & B \\ C & D \end{bmatrix} = \begin{bmatrix} 1 & z_i \\ 0 & 1 \end{bmatrix} \begin{bmatrix} a & 0 \\ c & d \end{bmatrix} = \begin{bmatrix} a + cz_i & dz_i \\ c & d \end{bmatrix}$$

[2.147]

Using this relation and the property of the determinant ($AD - BC = 1$), we then have:

$$\begin{cases} a = A - CB/D = 1/D \\ \quad z_i = B/D \\ \quad c = C \\ \quad d = D \end{cases}$$

[2.148]

Let x and y be the coordinate of the image plane. Using the previous expression of the ideal image, the image field in the plane Rp can be expressed by:

$$U(x, y) = \frac{1}{a} U_1\left(\frac{x}{a}, \frac{y}{a}\right) \exp(jkL_i) \exp\left[jk\frac{x^2 + y^2}{2d_i}\left(1 - \frac{1}{a}\right)\right]$$

[2.149]

where L_i is the optical path from the input plane Rp1 to the image plane Rp. Given that d_i can be considered as the distance between the image principal plane of the subsystem Rp1–Rp and the image plane Rp, following from [2.131], its value is determined by:

$$d_i = \frac{a-1}{c}$$

[2.150]

Substituting d_i into [2.149], we observe that $L = L_i + z_i$ is the path from the input plane to the observation plane Rp2. The field in the plane Rp2 is expressed by the Fresnel approximation:

$$U_2(x_2,y_2) = \frac{\exp(jkL)}{j\lambda z_i}$$

$$\int_{-\infty}^{\infty}\int_{-\infty}^{\infty} \frac{1}{a}U_1\left(\frac{x}{a},\frac{y}{a}\right)\exp\left(jkc\frac{x^2+y^2}{2a}\right)\exp\left\{\frac{jk}{2z_i}\left[(x_2-x)^2+(y_2-y)^2\right]\right\}dxdy$$

[2.151]

With relation [2.148], we rewrite a, c, z_i as the matrix elements $ABCD$, i.e. $x_1 = Dx$, $y_1 = Dy$, we then obtain:

$$U_2(x_2,y_2) = \frac{\exp(jkL)}{j\lambda B}$$

$$\int_{-\infty}^{\infty}\int_{-\infty}^{\infty} U_1(x_1,y_1)\exp\left\{\frac{jk}{2B}\left[A(x_1^2+y_1^2)+D(x_2^2+y_2^2)-2(x_1x_2+y_1y_2)\right]\right\}dx_1dy_1$$

[2.152]

This expression is identical to Collins' formula [2.133]. In conclusion, Collins' formula is a mathematical representation of the Rayleigh approach with respect to diffraction by a paraxial optical system.

2.5.4. Comparison between Collins' formula and the Fresnel integral

Rewriting Collins' formula:

$$U(x,y) = \frac{\exp(jkL)}{j\lambda B}\int_{-\infty}^{\infty}\int_{-\infty}^{\infty}U_1(x_1,y_1)$$

$$\times\exp\left\{\frac{jk}{2B}\left[A(x_1^2+y_1^2)+D(x^2+y^2)-2(x_1x+y_1y)\right]\right\}dx_1dy_1 \quad [2.153]$$

with $U_1(x_1, y_1)$ the complex amplitude in the input plane and $U(x, y)$ the complex amplitude in the output plane of the optical system. Developing the complex coefficients of the variable x in the exponent of [2.153], we have:

$$Ax_1^2 + Dx^2 - 2x_1 x$$

$$= A(x_1^2 - \frac{2}{A}x_1 x + \frac{x^2}{A^2} - \frac{x^2}{A^2}) + Dx^2 \qquad\qquad [2.154]$$

$$= A(x_1 - \frac{x}{A})^2 - \frac{x^2}{A} + Dx^2$$

$$= \frac{1}{A}(Ax_1 - x)^2 - \left(\frac{1}{A} - D\right)x^2$$

In the same way, we develop the coefficients of the variable y in the exponent. Substituting the results into [2.153] and using the relation $AD - BC = 1$, we obtain:

$$U(x,y) = \frac{\exp(jkL)}{j\lambda B} \exp\left[j\frac{kC}{2A}(x^2 + y^2)\right]$$

$$\int\int_{-\infty}^{\infty} U_1(x_1, y_1) \exp\left\{j\frac{k}{2BA}\left[(Ax_1 - x)^2 + (Ay_1 - y)^2\right]\right\} dx_1 dy_1 \qquad [2.155]$$

Substituting $x_a = Ax_1$ and $y_a = Ay_1$ into this expression, we have:

$$U(x,y) = \frac{\exp(jkL)}{j\lambda BA^2} \exp\left[j\frac{kC}{2A}(x^2 + y^2)\right]$$

$$\int\int_{-\infty}^{\infty} U_1\left(\frac{x_a}{A}, \frac{y_a}{A}\right) \exp\left\{j\frac{k}{2BA}\left[(x_a - x)^2 + (y_a - y)^2\right]\right\} dx_a dy_a \qquad [2.156]$$

We may observe that, except for the phase factor in the double integral, expression [2.156] is analogous to the Fresnel diffraction integral expressed in the form of a convolution [2.55]. From the point of view of numerical analysis, the method for calculating these two expressions is identical. Developing and rearranging [2.156], we now obtain:

$$U(x,y) = \frac{\exp(jkL)}{j\lambda B} \exp\left\{\frac{jk}{2B}D(x^2 + y^2)\right\} \times$$

$$\int\int_{-\infty}^{\infty} \left\{U_0(x_0, y_0) \exp\left[\frac{jk}{2B}A(x_0^2 + y_0^2)\right]\right\} \exp\left[-j2\pi\left(x_0\frac{x}{\lambda B} + y_0\frac{y}{\lambda B}\right)\right] dx_0 dy_0$$

$$[2.157]$$

This is also an analogous expression to that of the Fresnel diffraction integral expressed in the form of Fourier transform [2.56]. The calculation of Collins' formula can also be carried out by a Fourier transform. Since Collins' formula allows us readily to calculate the field across a system *ABCD*, whereas the Fresnel diffraction integral can only be calculated in homogeneous space, we may consider Collins' formula as a generalized expression of the Fresnel diffraction integral.

Let us recall some elements of the proof of Collins' formula: we know that this formula does not take into account the spatial filtering effect from the outline of the optical elements making up the optical system. The use of Collins' formula only applies in the case where this spatial filtering effect from the outline of the optical elements can be neglected. Otherwise, the studied system must be separated into several subsystems in series so that the spatial filtering effect of each subsystem can be neglected. In this case, we may take into account the diffraction effects occurring in the intermediary planes between these subsystems, successively calculating the propagation of light crossing each subsystem to obtain the definitive result. Figure 2.14 shows this principle.

It must be noted that if a system is not centered, we cannot determine the paraxial ray by these two parameters: the distance r between the intersection of the ray with a reference plane and the z-axis and the angle of inclination θ of the ray. In this case, we must use four parameters to determine the trajectory of the ray. Furthermore, the system is represented by a 4×4 matrix. The calculation of the field across the system is based on another more complex formulation, not dealt with in this book, which the reader will be able to find in [LIN 88].

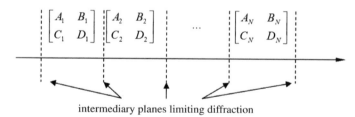

intermediary planes limiting diffraction

Figure 2.14. *Diagram of the principle for the calculation of diffraction across a complex system*

2.6. Conclusion

This chapter has laid out the basics of diffraction phenomena described by a scalar wave. We have exhaustively described the different approaches for the calculation of the field propagating a certain distance from an aperture or a diffracting object. We have addressed matrix optics, which describes optical systems from a geometric point of view, using four parameters. This approach allowed us to discuss Collins' formula, which lets us determine the diffracted field across an optical system.

These fundamentals will be used in Chapter 3 to study how to numerically calculate a diffracted field, in Chapter 4 for the fundamentals of holography, and then in Chapter 5 to study digital Fresnel holography.

Chapter 3

Calculating Diffraction by Fast Fourier Transform

In Chapter 2, we discussed the Kirchhoff, Rayleigh-Sommerfeld, and angular spectrum formulations from the scalar approach to the theory of diffraction. These three formulae rigorously satisfy the scalar wave equation [GOO 05], and their paraxial approximation, the Fresnel diffraction integral, is a formula that is relatively simple to apply. We may consider these four formulations as "classical diffraction formulae" [LI 07a]. Since they can be represented by a Fourier transform, and "the physical possibility is a sufficient condition of validity to justify the existence of a transformation" [GOO 05], we must be able to obtain theoretical diffraction calculations by the application of the Fourier transform. Nevertheless, for a large number of diffraction problems encountered in practice, the Fourier transform almost never gives a simple analytical solution. As a result, we are led to a numerical resolution of the problem, and thus the diffraction is calculated by a discrete Fourier transform (DFT).

At first sight, the numerical calculation to obtain a workable result seems tedious. In the early days of computing, it was very difficult to resolve a practical problem. In 1965, Cooley and Tukey established the fast Fourier transform (FFT) algorithms [COO 65], totally changing the calculation constraints. With a computer and some basic knowledge, the FFT algorithms can be routinely used for a large number of applications [OPP 89, PRO 96, MAR 96, LYO 04], and henceforth these algorithms are widely utilized for calculating the diffraction of a light beam.

In this chapter, we will discuss the relationship between the Fourier transform and its discrete version. Then, by considering Shannon's sampling theorem, the different methods of calculating the classical diffraction formulae by FFT will be studied. Finally, these methods will be generalized for the numerical calculation of Collins' formula.

Most of the calculations presented in this chapter can be carried out by the two programs – LIM1.m and LIM2.m – in the Appendix with the use of the software MATLAB.

3.1. Relation between the discrete and analytical Fourier transforms

3.1.1. Sampling and periodic expansion of a continuous two-dimensional function

If a two-dimensional function can be transformed by a DFT, it has the properties of being discrete and periodic in infinite two-dimensional space, [LI 02b]. In practice, the function to be transformed is generally continuous and defined in an infinite plane. It follows from this that, to carry out a DFT, the original function must first be truncated into a finite rectangular zone, and then sampled by the "two-dimensional Dirac comb" function. To periodize the function both in direct and Fourier space, the sampled rectangular zone must be considered as the two-dimensional period of a function defined in infinite space. Figure 3.1 illustrates this property.

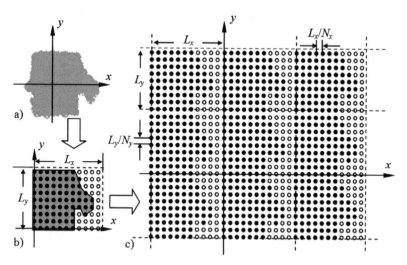

Figure 3.1. *Sampling and periodization of the continuous two-dimensional function*

Figure 3.1(a) illustrates a continuous function located in the gray zone. The sampling process is as follows:

– We move the function into the first quadrant and transform the *xy*-coordinates and then truncate it along the *x*- and *y*-axes in a rectangular zone of sides L_x and L_y.

– Considering the sampling interval along the *x*- and *y*-axes to be $T_x = L_x/N_x$ and $T_y = L_y/N_y$, respectively, the truncated function is sampled in a discrete two-dimensional distribution containing $N_x \times N_y$ points. Figure 3.1(b) shows this operation. The black dots represent the sampled values in the zone of the initial function and the empty dots correspond to the null values.

– Considering the discrete distribution of $N_x \times N_y$ points as a fundamental period, we construct a two-dimensional discrete, periodic distribution. Figure 3.1(c) illustrates nine repetitions of the discrete function in the neighborhood of the origin.

3.1.2. *The relation between the discrete and continuous Fourier transforms*

Having truncated and sampled the original function, its properties have changed. To simplify the study, we will consider only one dimension along the *x*-axis. The result will then be generalized into two dimensions. Fixing a *y*-value, Figure 3.2 outlines the relation between the discrete and continuous functions. The figures in the column on the left are the profiles of the spatial functions, and those on the right are the modules of the Fourier transforms of the figures on the left. For example, Figure 3.2(*a*1) is the spatial function $g(x,y)$ and Figure 3.2(*a*2) represents the modulus of its spectrum $G(f_x, y)$.

The operation of sampling the original continuous function can be described as the product of the Dirac comb (see Chapter 1) with the original function in Figure 3.2(*b*1) [GOO 05], i.e.:

$$g_{T_x}(x,y) = g(x,y)\delta_{T_x}(x) = g(x,y)\sum_{n=-\infty}^{\infty}\delta(x-nT_x) \qquad [3.1]$$

As the Dirac comb $\delta_{T_x}(x)$ is a series of δ functions of period T_x, it can be represented by a Fourier series:

$$\delta_{T_x}(x) = \sum_{n=-\infty}^{\infty}\delta(t-nT_x) = \sum_{k=-\infty}^{\infty}A_k\exp\left(jk\frac{2\pi}{T_x}x\right) \qquad [3.2]$$

where $j = \sqrt{-1}$, and

$$A_k = \frac{1}{T_x} \int_{-T_x/2}^{T_x/2} \delta_{T_x}(x)\exp\left(-jk\frac{2\pi}{T_x}x\right)dx = \frac{1}{T_x} \qquad [3.3]$$

i.e.:

$$g_{T_x}(x,y) = g(x,y)\frac{1}{T_x}\sum_{k=-\infty}^{\infty}\exp\left(jk\frac{2\pi}{T_x}x\right) \qquad [3.4]$$

This means that the sampled signal is no longer identical to the initial function. It has become a signal modulated by the analytic function $g(x, y)$ (see Figure 3.2(c1)). Using the continuous Fourier transform, we now study the relation between the spectra of signals before and after sampling.

Considering the Fourier transform of the earlier expression of $g_{T_x}(x,y)$, we have:

$$\begin{aligned}
G_{T_x}(f_x,y) &= \int_{-\infty}^{\infty} g_{T_x}(x,y)\exp(-j2\pi f_x x)dx \\
&= \int_{-\infty}^{\infty} g(x,y)\frac{1}{T_x}\sum_{k=-\infty}^{\infty}\exp\left(jk\frac{2\pi}{T_x}x\right)\exp(-j2\pi f_x x)dx \\
&= \frac{1}{T_x}\sum_{k=-\infty}^{\infty}\int_{-\infty}^{\infty} g(x,y)\exp\left(-j2\pi(f_x - \frac{k}{T_x})t\right)dx = \frac{1}{T_x}\sum_{k=-\infty}^{\infty} G\left(f_x - \frac{k}{T_x},y\right)
\end{aligned} \qquad [3.5]$$

This expression shows that the spectrum $G_{T_x}(f_x,y)$ of the sampled signal includes the spectrum of the continuous signal, made periodic with period $1/T_x$ (see Figure 3.2(c2)). Notice that if the spectral width of the continuous function is greater than the period $1/T_x$, there is an aliasing of the spectrum with the adjacent motifs. Following the properties of the Fourier transform for a convolution in frequency space, Figure 3.2(c2) can also be obtained by the convolution of the frequency function $G(f_x,y)$ (see Figure 3.2(a2)) with the Dirac comb function $\Delta_{T_x}(f_x)$ (see Figure 3.2(b2)), i.e.:

$$G_{T_x}(f_x,y) = G(f_x,y)*\Delta_{T_x}(f_x) \qquad [3.6]$$

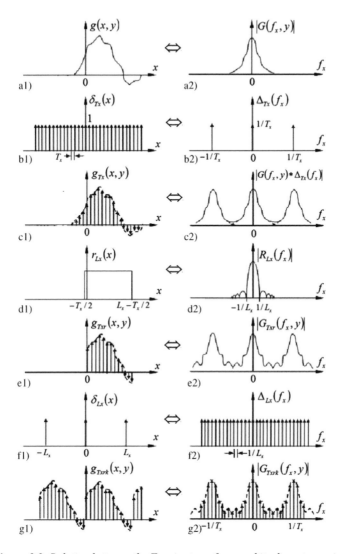

Figure 3.2. *Relation between the Fourier transform and its discrete version*

The result of this is that, after sampling a continuous function by the Dirac comb of period T_x, its spectrum possesses two peculiar properties compared with that of the original:

– The spectrum is periodic with period $1/T_x$; if the bandwidth of the spectrum is greater than $1/2T_x$, a spectral aliasing phenomenon will occur, which results in a modification of the spectrum. Consequently, to obtain a correct result, we must choose a suitable sampling interval for the period $1/T_x$, being at least twice as large as the bandwidth of the continuous function. This property is known as the Shannon sampling theorem [GOO 05] (see Chapter 1).

– The amplitude of the spectrum $G_{T_x}(f_x, y)$ of the discrete function is equal in value to that of the original function multiplied by $1/T_x$.

We note that the earlier results give only theoretical results of a sampling operation by an infinite series of Dirac distributions. In practice, we cannot use an infinite number of samples in the execution of a numerical calculation. The discrete and non-periodic function in Figure 3.2(c1) must therefore be truncated by a rectangle function (see Figure 3.2(d1)), expressed by:

$$\text{rect}_{Lx}(x) = \begin{cases} 1 & \text{if } -T_x/2 < x < L_x - T_x/2 \\ 0 & \text{if not} \end{cases} \qquad [3.7]$$

Thus, we obtain a discrete distribution of N_x points (Fig. 3.2(e1)):

$$g_{Txr}(x, y) = g(x, y)\delta_{Tx}(x)\text{rect}_{Lx}(x) \qquad [3.8]$$

This discrete distribution is then periodized with a period L_x in infinite space (see Figure 3.2(g1)):

$$g_{T_x rk}(x, y) = g_{T_x r}(x + kL_x, y), \ k = 0, \pm 1, \pm 2, \cdots \qquad [3.9]$$

The spectrum of the product of the rectangular function (see Figure 3.2(d1)) with the discrete Dirac series (see Figure 3.2(c1)) is expressed as a convolution of the rectangle function spectrum $R_{L_x}(f_x)$ (see Figure 3.2(d2)) with the spectrum in Figure 3.2(c2), which corresponds to the spectrum of the discrete function (see Figure 3.2(c1)):

$$G_{T_x r}(f_x, y) = \left[G(f_x, y) * \Delta_{T_x}(f_x) \right] * R_{L_x}(f_x) \qquad [3.10]$$

The corresponding curve is drawn in Figure 3.2(e2).

We note that there are secondary maxima of both sides of the central maximum of the spectrum $R_{L_x}(f_x)$, and the spectrum obtained by the convolution is therefore deformed (to underline this problem, the deformation of the spectrum in Figure 3.2($e2$) is a little exaggerated). Comparing Figure 3.2($e2$) with Figure 3.2($a2$), we note that the obtained result is a periodic curve with recurrence $1/T_x$ – the period being the slightly deformed spectrum of the original function. Since the DFT deals with the calculation of the Fourier transform of periodic and discrete functions, the curve in Figure 3.2($e2$) must, again, be sampled by a Dirac comb function of period $1/L_x$ (see Figure 3.2($f2$)). Indeed, the calculator cannot calculate an infinity of spectral values (see Figure 3.2($g2$)).

When we take samples from the frequency domain by a product with the Dirac comb function, this operation corresponds to a convolution of their original functions in the spatial domain. We give the result of the convolution of Figure 3.2($e1$) with Figure 3.2($f1$) in Figure 3.2($g1$), which corresponds to a discrete, periodic function of period L_x in the spatial domain.

The two discrete functions in Figures 3.2($g1$) and ($g2$) are periodic with N_x points per period. The DFT therefore allows to obtain the theoretical values at these N_x points in the fundamental period of the spectrum, from the N_x-sampled points of the continuous function. Naturally, the result will only be true to analytic calculations if Shannon's conditions are respected. In practice, the FFT algorithms quickly calculate the DFT. However, for the algorithm to be "fast", it is necessary that the number of calculation points N_x be a power of two, i.e. {128, 256, 512, 1,024, 2,048, 4,096, 8,192, etc.}. The structure of the FFT algorithms will not be discussed in this book; for all complementary information, the reader is invited to refer to the references [BEL 00], [OPP 89], [PRO 96], [MAR 96], and [LYO 04].

From the results shown in Chapter 2, the diffraction formulae are expressed in the form of either a Fourier transform or a convolution. On the basis of the relation between the Fourier transform and its discrete version, and respecting the conditions of Shannon's theorem, it will now be possible to calculate the diffraction of a light beam using an FFT algorithm.

3.2. Calculating the Fresnel diffraction integral by FFT

In the first instance, we study the Fresnel diffraction integral that can be calculated either by FFT or by fast convolution. Calculating the convolution first requires the execution of a direct FFT, and then an inverse fast Fourier transform (IFFT). To simplify the notation, we write the first method as S-FFT (simple FFT) and the second as D-FFT (double FFT). We will see that to correctly treat a practical diffraction problem we must properly choose one of these two methods [MAS 99, MAS 03, LI 07a].

3.2.1. *Calculating diffraction by the S-FFT method*

Let the complex amplitude be $U_0(x_0,y_0)$ in the object plane, $U(x,y)$ in the observation plane, and d the distance between these two planes. The Fresnel diffraction integral in the form of a Fourier transform (equation [2.56]) is given by:

$$U(x,y) = \frac{\exp(jkd)}{j\lambda d} \exp\left[\frac{jk}{2d}(x^2 + y^2)\right]$$

$$\times \int_{-\infty}^{\infty}\int \left\{ U_0(x_0,y_0)\exp\left[\frac{jk}{2d}(x_0^2 + y_0^2)\right]\right\}\exp\left[-j\frac{2\pi}{\lambda d}(x_0 x + y_0 y)\right]dx_0 dy_0 \qquad [3.11]$$

where $j = \sqrt{-1}$, λ is the wavelength, and $k = 2\pi/\lambda$. The evaluation of this expression consists of the two following calculations:

– Using the FFT, we first calculate the Fourier transform of the function $U_0(x_0,y_0)\exp\left[\dfrac{jk}{2d}(x_0^2 + y_0^2)\right]$.

– The earlier result is multiplied by the phase factor $\dfrac{\exp(jkd)}{j\lambda d}\exp\left[\dfrac{jk}{2d}(x^2 + y^2)\right]$.

Let L_0 be the width of a square zone in the object plane, sampled at $N \times N$ points; the sampling interval is $\Delta x_0 = \Delta y_0 = L_0/N$. Expression [3.11] can be rewritten in discrete form:

$$U(p\Delta x, q\Delta y) = \frac{\exp(jkd)}{j\lambda d}\exp\left[\frac{jk}{2d}\left((p\Delta x)^2 + (q\Delta y)^2\right)\right]$$

$$\text{FFT}\left\{ U_0(m\Delta x_0, n\Delta y_0)\exp\left[\frac{jk}{2d}\left((m\Delta x_0)^2 + (n\Delta y_0)^2\right)\right]\right\}_{\frac{p\Delta x}{\lambda d},\frac{q\Delta y}{\lambda d}} \qquad [3.12]$$

with $\{p,q,m,n\} \in \{-N/2, -N/2 + 1, ..., N/2-1\}$ and where $\Delta x = \Delta y$ is the spatial sampling interval after the FFT. To determine this interval, we must remember the periodicity of the DFT. The result calculated by the earlier expression is a discrete two-dimensional distribution of $N \times N$ points whose interval is $1/\Delta x_0$ (see Figure 3.2) in the frequency domain, i.e.:

$$\frac{L}{\lambda d} = \frac{1}{\Delta x_0} = \frac{N}{L_0} \qquad [3.13]$$

Let $L = \lambda dN/L_0$, from which

$$\Delta x = \Delta y = \frac{L}{N} = \frac{\lambda d}{L_0} \qquad [3.14]$$

We note that if we wish to obtain a correct result, the sampling must obey the Shannon sampling theorem. We now analyze expression [3.11]. The function to be transformed is a product of the object function with a quadratic phase factor. The Fourier transform of this phase factor is an analytic function $j\lambda d \exp\left(-j\lambda d\pi\left(u^2 + v^2\right)\right)$ whose bandwidth is infinite. In other words, it is not a theoretical bandwidth-limited function. According to the properties of convolution, the spectrum of function [3.11] results from the convolution of the spectrum of $U_0(x_0, y_0)$, with this expression. The width of the result of this convolution is an addition of the widths of the two functions [BEL 00]. Thus, the result of the convolution is no longer a bandwidth-limited function, which means that for the discrete calculation of expression [3.12] the Shannon sampling conditions are not realizable in practice. Nevertheless, the number of sample points must be at least two per period. From this principle, we can determine the conditions for which the quadratic function will be correctly sampled [MAS 99, MAS 03, LI 07a]. In the sampled zone, there must be at least two sample points for a phase variation of 2π at the edge of the zone, where the variation is most important for $m = n = \pm N/2$. It is therefore sufficient to solve the following inequality:

$$\left.\frac{\partial}{\partial m}\frac{k}{2d}\left(\left(m\Delta x_0\right)^2 + \left(n\Delta y_0\right)^2\right)\right|_{m,n=N/2} \leq \pi \qquad [3.15]$$

from which we deduce:

$$\Delta x_0^2 \leq \frac{\lambda d}{N} \quad \text{or also } L_0 = L = \sqrt{\lambda dN} \qquad [3.16]$$

Relation [3.16] can be considered as the condition obeying the sampling theorem for the quadratic phase factor. However, the final result of calculating [3.12] by S-FFT is the product of the FFT with another proportionality factor, itself being a quadratic phase factor. Using the method given in [3.16], the sampling interval of the proportionality factor must satisfy:

$$\Delta x^2 \leq \frac{\lambda d}{N} \qquad [3.17]$$

Furthermore, from [3.13], we have $N\Delta x = \lambda dN / N\Delta x_0$ or also $\Delta x = \lambda d / N\Delta x_0$. Substituting this relation into [3.17], we have $\left(\lambda d / N\Delta x_0\right)^2 \leq \lambda d / N$, i.e. $\Delta x_0^2 \geq \lambda d / N$. This condition is contradictory to [3.16] and leads us to impose equality onto these two inequalities:

$$\Delta x_0 = \Delta x = \sqrt{\frac{\lambda d}{N}} \text{ or also } L_0 = L = \sqrt{\lambda d N} \qquad [3.18]$$

Under these conditions, the calculation of [3.12] by S-FFT will obey the sampling theorem. Three conclusions (for a constant wavelength) follow from these results:

– From [3.13], the width of the obtained diffracted field is $L = \lambda d N / L_0$. The result of this is that if the diffraction distance d is very close to 0, L will tend toward 0; this means that if the observation plane is close to the object plane, a large number of sampling points must be used to obtain a zone of usable size. It follows that in practice we cannot use the S-FFT method to calculate the diffraction across small distances d.

– From [3.16], if the sampling interval Δx_0 obeys $\Delta x_0 < \sqrt{\lambda d / N}$ or equally $L_0 < \sqrt{\lambda d N}$, the result of the calculation can be considered as being correctly sampled, as the quadratic phase factor of proportionality does not influence the intensity of the calculated field.

– From [3.18], if we wish to obtain a discrete field approximately verifying the sampling theorem, the widths of the object and observation planes must be equal to $L_0 = L = \sqrt{\lambda d N}$.

The S-FFT method is illustrated in the Appendix by the program "LIM1.m" written in the MATLAB language. The reader will be able to confirm the earlier discussions by running this program.

3.2.2. Numerical calculation and experimental demonstration

As an example, we will consider Figure 3.3 that describes a diffraction setup. We will study the sampling condition for the S-FFT method. We consider an "iris"-type diaphragm whose aperture has 12 edges of equal length, with a diagonal length of 4.8 mm. A collimated laser beam of wavelength 532 nm illuminates this diaphragm at normal incidence. The intensity distribution of the diffracted field is recorded by a Charge-Coupled Device (CCD) detector of area 4.9×6.6 mm^2 consisting of $1{,}536 \times 2{,}048$ pixels. The recorded image will thus be comparable to the result of a numerical calculation. When using the S-FFT method, the respective lengths L_0 and L of the object and observation plane are generally not equal. To facilitate the comparison, using relation [3.18], we consider $L_0 = L = \sqrt{\lambda d N} = 10$ mm. Furthermore, we suppose $N = \{256, 512, 1{,}024\}$ and consequently $d \approx \{734$ mm, 367 mm, 184 mm$\}$, respectively.

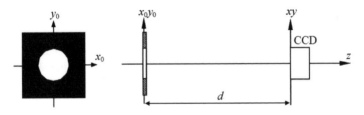

Figure 3.3. *Diffraction scheme*

Substituting these parameters into [3.12], the measured and simulated intensity patterns are given in Figure 3.4. For comparison, the dimensions of the experimental images are 10 mm × 10 mm (3,103 × 3,103 pixels) and are presented with zero padding around the CCD image. The different values of N obey Shannon's conditions corresponding to the different diffraction distances; the smaller the diffraction distance, the greater the number of samples must be.

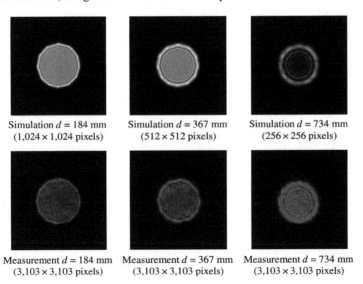

Simulation d = 184 mm (1,024 × 1,024 pixels)	Simulation d = 367 mm (512 × 512 pixels)	Simulation d = 734 mm (256 × 256 pixels)
Measurement d = 184 mm (3,103 × 3,103 pixels)	Measurement d = 367 mm (3,103 × 3,103 pixels)	Measurement d = 734 mm (3,103 × 3,103 pixels)

Figure 3.4. *Comparison of the patterns obtained by numerical simulation with those obtained by measurement (10 mm × 10 mm)*

Figure 3.4 shows a very good agreement between theory and practice. It confirms that if we wish to calculate Fresnel diffraction by S-FFT on a plane very close to the object plane, the number of samples will very quickly become prohibitive.

3.2.3. *The D-FFT method*

Let $U_0(x_0, y_0)$ be again the complex amplitude of the object plane, $U(x, y)$ that of the observation plane, and d the distance between these two planes. The Fresnel diffraction integral in convolution form (see expression [2.55]) is written as:

$$U(x,y) = \frac{\exp(jkd)}{j\lambda d} \int_{-\infty}^{\infty} \int_{-\infty}^{\infty} U_0(x_0, y_0) \exp\left\{ \frac{jk}{2d}\left[(x-x_0)^2 + (y-y_0)^2 \right] \right\} dx_0 dy_0 \qquad [3.19]$$

Using the convolution theorem (see Chapter 1), the Fourier transform of this expression is:

$$F\{U(x,y)\} = F\{U_0(x_0, y_0)\} F\left\{ \frac{\exp(jkd)}{j\lambda d} \exp\left[\frac{jk}{2d}(x^2 + y^2) \right] \right\} \qquad [3.20]$$

With (f_x, f_y) as the frequency coordinates, the Fresnel transfer function is defined as:

$$H_F(f_x, f_y) = F\left\{ \frac{\exp(jkd)}{j\lambda d} \exp\left[\frac{jk}{2d}(x^2 + y^2) \right] \right\} \qquad [3.21]$$

It is straightforward to show that the exact solution is:

$$H_F(f_x, f_y) = \exp\left\{ jkd\left[1 - \frac{\lambda^2}{2}(f_x^2 + f_y^2) \right] \right\} \qquad [3.22]$$

Since the Fourier transform can be evaluated by FFT, the two transfer functions [3.21] and [3.22] are theoretically identical. However, and once again, we must take into account the sampling problem of [3.21]. Relation [3.21] will be examined later during the study of the Kirchhoff and Rayleigh-Sommerfeld formulae. For now, we concentrate on the transfer function [3.22], as it is widely used in practical calculations [YU 05]. By Fourier transform of both sides of [3.20], we obtain the formula for calculating diffraction by convolution:

$$U(x, y) = F^{-1}\{F\{U_0(x_0, y_0)\} H_F(f_x, f_y)\} \qquad [3.23]$$

This result shows that the spectrum in the observation plane is the product of the object spectrum $F\{U_0(x_0, y_0)\}$ with the transfer function $H_F(f_x, f_y)$. The interpretation of this relation was already discussed earlier: the physical process of Fresnel diffraction can be considered as a linear transformation of the object field filtered by a linear shift-invariant system.

Let L_0 be the width of the diffracted field to be calculated and N be the number of samples. The sampling interval is $\Delta x_0 = L_0/N$. In the spectral domain of [3.20], the sampling interval of the transfer functions is $\Delta f_x = \Delta f_y = 1/L_0$. After taking the product and the inverse FFT, the width of the observation plane will be the same as that of the object plane, i.e. $L = 1/\Delta f_x = L_0$. Thus, calculation by D-FFT does not modify the spatial scale of the calculated field. If the discrete distribution of the initial field obeys the sampling theorem, and since the product with the transfer functions does not modify the bandwidth of the initial field, on the condition that the transfer function is continuous (see [3.22]), the obtained result will satisfy the sampling theorem [LI 11a].

In the spectral plane, we write the frequency sampling interval as $(\Delta f_x, \Delta f_y)$. Considering [3.15], an identical reasoning with relation [3.22] leads to the following inequality:

$$\frac{\partial}{\partial p} kd \left[1 - \frac{\lambda^2}{2} \left(p^2 \Delta f_x^2 + q^2 \Delta f_y^2 \right) \right]_{p,q=N/2} \leq \pi \qquad [3.24]$$

from which we deduce:

$$\Delta f_x^2 \leq \frac{1}{\lambda d N} \qquad [3.25]$$

The frequency sampling interval is imposed by the FFT algorithm, and we have $\Delta f_x = 1/N\Delta x_0 = 1/L_0$. Thus, [3.25] is also equivalent to $\sqrt{\lambda d N} \leq L_0$ and we note that the inequality is reversed compared to [3.16]. Function [3.22] will be correctly sampled on the whole numerical spectrum up to a number of points N such that $N \geq \lambda d / \Delta x_0^2$. This means that as the distance increases, the number of points increases, the inverse being equally true. The Fresnel transfer function will be used judiciously in the case of small diffraction distances. In the opposite case, the number of points necessary for a correct sampling will be prohibitive. For example, for $d = 600$ mm, $\lambda = 532$ nm, and $\Delta x_0 = 5$ µm, we must calculate the spectrum with $N \geq 12{,}768$ and if $d = 6$ mm, $N \geq 128$ will suffice.

3.2.4. *Practical sampling conditions due to the energy conservation principle*

Given that the function to be inversely transformed in [3.23] is the product of the spectrum of the object function with the transfer function, the calculation of diffraction by the D-FFT method will satisfy the sampling theorem on the condition that the sampling of $U_0(x_0, y_0)$ itself verifies the theorem. However, from a practical point of view, we must qualitatively evaluate the sampling conditions of $U_0(x_0, y_0)$. Let E be the total energy of the field. Each sample point in frequency space corresponds to an area of size $1/L_0^2$, for which the energy is N^4/L_0^4 times that of the continuous function. The energy of the coordinate point $(p/L_0, q/L_0)$ is $(1/L_0^2) \times |\text{DFT}\{U_0(mL_0/N, nL_0/N)\}(p,q)|^2 (L_0/N)^4$. Using Parseval's theorem (see Chapter 1), the correct sampling of the DFT must satisfy [LI 11a]:

$$E = \frac{L_0^2}{N^4} \sum_{p=-N/2}^{N/2-1} \sum_{q=-N/2}^{N/2-1} \left| \text{DFT}\left\{ U_0\left(m\frac{L_0}{N}, n\frac{L_0}{N} \right) \right\}(p,q) \right|^2 \approx \text{Constant} \qquad [3.26]$$

The increase in the number of sampled points in $U_0(x_0, y_0)$ does not change the total energy E, as long as this number is properly chosen. Thus, to evaluate whether this value is suitable, we can determine the total energy by [3.24], and then by modifying the number N, $N/2$, or $2N$, for example calculate once again the total energy. If there is no difference between the obtained results, the initial number N can be considered suitable. This approach will be confirmed in the following section by comparisons between theoretical calculations and experiment.

3.2.5. *Experimental demonstration of the D-FFT method*

Let us again consider the optical system in Figure 3.3 and the parameters that we used. The object zone is a square of sides $L_0 = 10$ mm containing at the center an aperture of 12 equally sized edges (the diaphragm of the object plane). Using the three values $N = \{128, 256, 512\}$ to sample the diaphragm, we obtain the object field $U_0(x_0, y_0)$. After carrying out DFTs of the object, the normalized spectra are presented in Figure 3.5. These patterns show that the spectral energy is situated in a central neighborhood of the frequency plane. Furthermore, the energies of these three figures are $\{6,469, 6,466, 6,467\}$, respectively. Following from the discussion leading to [3.24], these three values are constant, and we may consider that the sampling satisfies Shannon's theorem.

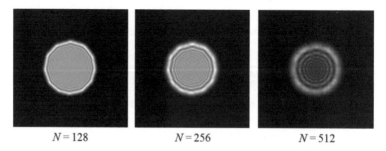

$N = 128$ $\qquad\qquad$ $N = 256$ $\qquad\qquad$ $N = 512$

Figure 3.5. *Spectral distributions for three sampling numbers*

Figure 3.6(a) is the intensity image recorded by the CCD for $d = 184$ mm. Figures 3.6(b), (c), and (d) give the three intensity images simulated for $N = \{128, 256, 512\}$, respectively.

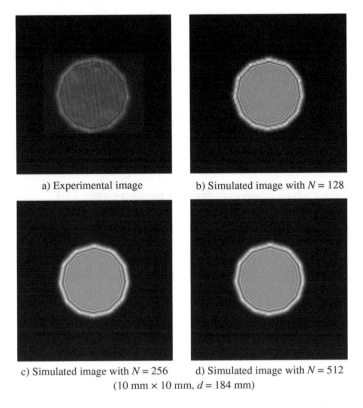

a) Experimental image   b) Simulated image with $N = 128$

c) Simulated image with $N = 256$ d) Simulated image with $N = 512$

(10 mm × 10 mm, $d = 184$ mm)

Figure 3.6. *Comparison between the real image and some simulated images with different numbers of sample points*

Figure 3.6 shows that the numerical simulation of the images coincides well with the image captured by the CCD. However, for $N = 128$, the resolution is relatively weak, which is observed by the lack of sharpness of the diffraction fringes at the edge of the object. The maximum of the frequency bandwidth corresponding to this sampling is $128/(2L_0) = 6.4$ mm^{-1}. If the number of fringes per millimeter exceeds 6.4, the fine structure of the fringes will no longer be distinguishable.

We note that according to the angular spectrum description of diffraction [GOO 05], the field is a superposition of the spectral components of the initial field. As the diffraction distance increases, the diffracted field zone widens linearly. We recall that the D-FFT method conserves the same physical scale for both the object and observation planes: if the diffraction distance is large, this method cannot completely construct the field. It follows that the D-FFT method will be, instead, used in cases where the diffraction distance is relatively small and the angles of the angular spectrum components are likewise relatively small.

In contrast, the characteristic principle of the S-FFT method is that it allows the calculation of diffraction across long distances. In order to obtain useable results, the choice of calculation method must be analyzed as a function of the distance and the size of the field.

The program LIM2.m in the Appendix, written in the MATLAB language, lets us verify the properties of the D-FFT method. After some modifications, this program may be used for the resolution of some practical diffraction problems.

3.3. Calculation of the classical diffraction formulae using FFT

According to the scalar theory of diffraction described in Chapter 2, the angular spectrum, Kirchhoff, and Rayleigh-Sommerfeld formulae are three solutions rigorously satisfying the scalar wave equation [GOO 05]. These three formulations and their paraxial approximation, the Fresnel diffraction integral, are considered to be the classical diffraction formulae. We will show that these classical formulae are expressed in the form of a convolution, and that each formula possesses its own transfer function. Then, we will study the sampling conditions for each formula [LI 07a]. Some theoretical results will then be verified by experimental results.

3.3.1. *Kirchhoff and Rayleigh-Sommerfeld formulae in convolution form*

Figure 3.7 shows the geometry of the diffraction between the object plane $x_0 y_0$ and the observation plane xy. d is the distance between these two planes, and we write r, the vector, from the point (x_0, y_0) of the object plane to the point (x, y) in the observation plane, and n the vector normal to the object plane.

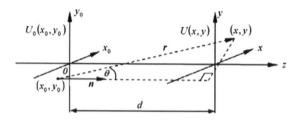

Figure 3.7. *Diagram of the diffraction between the object plane $(x_0 y_0)$ and the observation plane (xy)*

Considering the Kirchhoff relation [2.48] and the obliquity factor $K(\theta) = (\cos(\boldsymbol{n,r}) + 1)/2$ [GOO 05]:

$$U(x,y) = \frac{1}{j\lambda}\iint_{\Sigma_0} U_0(x_0,y_0)\frac{\exp(jkr)}{r} \times \frac{\cos(\boldsymbol{n,r})+1}{2}dx_0dy_0 \qquad [3.27]$$

where $\cos(\boldsymbol{n,r})$ is the cosine of the angle between $\boldsymbol{r}$ and $\boldsymbol{n}$.

Likewise, considering the obliquity factor $K(\theta) = \cos(\boldsymbol{n,r})$ to be equal to 1, the two Rayleigh-Sommerfeld formulae are given by [GOO 05]:

$$U(x,y) = \frac{1}{j\lambda}\iint_{\Sigma_0} U_0(x_0,y_0)\frac{\exp(jkr)}{r} \times \cos(\boldsymbol{n,r})dx_0dy_0 \qquad [3.28]$$

$$U(x,y) = \frac{1}{j\lambda}\iint_{\Sigma_0} U_0(x_0,y_0)\frac{\exp(jkr)}{r}dx_0dy_0 \qquad [3.29]$$

Following the definition of the coordinate system in Figure 3.7, we have:

$$r = \sqrt{d^2 +(x-x_0)^2 +(y-y_0)^2}$$

$$\cos(\boldsymbol{n,r}) = \frac{d}{r} = \frac{d}{\sqrt{d^2 +(x-x_0)^2 +(y-y_0)^2}} \qquad [3.29a]$$

Kirchhoff's formula is rewritten as:

$$U(x,y) = \frac{1}{j\lambda}\iint_{\Sigma_0} U_0(x_0,y_0)\times \qquad [3.30]$$

$$\frac{\exp\left(jk\sqrt{d^2 +(x-x_0)^2 +(y-y_0)^2}\right)}{2\left(d^2 +(x-x_0)^2 +(y-y_0)^2\right)}\left(\sqrt{d^2 +(x-x_0)^2 +(y-y_0)^2} +d\right)dx_0dy_0$$

and the two Rayleigh-Sommerfeld formulae are now:

$$U(x,y) = \frac{d}{j\lambda}\iint_{\Sigma_0} U_0(x_0,y_0)\times\frac{\exp\left(jk\sqrt{d^2 +(x-x_0)^2 +(y-y_0)^2}\right)}{d^2 +(x-x_0)^2 +(y-y_0)^2}dx_0dy_0 \qquad [3.31]$$

$$U(x,y)=\frac{1}{j\lambda}\iint_{\Sigma_0} U_0(x_0,y_0)\times\frac{\exp\left(jk\sqrt{d^2+(x-x_0)^2+(y-y_0)^2}\right)}{\sqrt{d^2+(x-x_0)^2+(y-y_0)^2}}dx_0dy_0 \qquad [3.32]$$

These three formulae [3.30], [3.31], [3.32] exhibit a two-dimensional convolution on the x and y coordinates. According to the convolution theorem (see Chapter 1), they can be rewritten as Fourier transforms, and consequently they can be calculated by FFT.

3.3.2. *Unitary representation of the classical diffraction formulae*

From the above discussions, the classical diffraction formulae can be written in a unitary form:

$$U(x,y)=F^{-1}\left\{F\{U_0(x_0,y_0)\}H(f_x,f_y)\right\} \qquad [3.33]$$

where $F\{\}$ and $F^{-1}\{\}$ are the symbols for the direct and inverse Fourier transforms, f_x,f_y the frequency coordinates, and $H(f_x,f_y)$ the associated transfer function. The corresponding transfer functions are, respectively [MAS 03]:

– The Kirchhoff transfer function:

$$H(f_x,f_y)=F\left\{\frac{\exp\left[jk\sqrt{d^2+x^2+y^2}\right]}{j2\lambda\left(d^2+x^2+y^2\right)}\left(\sqrt{d^2+x^2+y^2}+d\right)\right\} \qquad [3.34]$$

– The Rayleigh-Sommerfeld transfer functions:

$$H(f_x,f_y)=F\left\{d\frac{\exp\left[jk\sqrt{d^2+x^2+y^2}\right]}{j\lambda\left(d^2+x^2+y^2\right)}\right\} \qquad [3.35]$$

$$H(f_x,f_y)=F\left\{\frac{\exp\left[jk\sqrt{d^2+x^2+y^2}\right]}{j\lambda\sqrt{d^2+x^2+y^2}}\right\} \qquad [3.36]$$

– The Fresnel approximation transfer function:

$$H(f_x,f_y)=F\left\{\frac{\exp(jkd)}{j\lambda d}\exp\left[\frac{jk}{2d}(x^2+y^2)\right]\right\} \qquad [3.37]$$

– The Fresnel approximation transfer function (see equation [3.22]):

$$H\left(f_x, f_y\right) = \exp\left\{jkd\left[1 - \frac{\lambda^2}{2}\left(f_x^2 + f_y^2\right)\right]\right\}$$ [3.38]

– The angular spectrum transfer function:

$$H\left(f_x, f_y\right) = \exp\left[jkd\sqrt{1 - \left(\lambda f_x\right)^2 - \left(\lambda f_y\right)^2}\right]$$ [3.39]

The Kirchhoff and Rayleigh-Sommerfeld transfer functions are evaluated by Fourier transform, whereas the Fresnel transfer function can be expressed either as a Fourier transform or as an analytical expression. The angular spectrum transfer function is also an analytic expression. To calculate the Kirchhoff and Rayleigh-Sommerfeld formulae, as well as the Fourier transform of the Fresnel impulse response, we must therefore carry out two direct FFTs and one inverse FFT. When the Fresnel or angular spectrum transfer functions are used in their analytic form, the calculation requires only one direct and one inverse FFT. Accordingly, for reasons of calculation speed, the last two transfer functions are more widely used in practice than the previous transfer functions [PIC 09]. In addition, we also note that the angular spectrum formula rigorously satisfies the scalar wave equation, and its use is widespread in holography [YU 05, LI 09b, LI 00].

3.3.3. Study of the sampling conditions of the classical formulae

We suppose that the distribution of the initial field $U_0(x_0, y_0)$ is limited to a square zone of sides L_0. With the D-FFT method, the result of the calculation of $U(x, y)$ (expression [3.34]) will conserve the same physical scale [LI 02b]. Figure 3.8 shows a diagram of the spatial relationship between the initial plane and the diffracted plane.

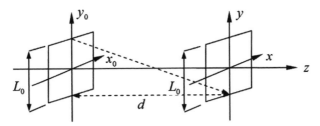

Figure 3.8. *Spatial relationship between the initial and observation planes for the D-FFT method*

We now study the sampling conditions of expression [3.33]. The function between the brackets of the inverse Fourier transform is the product of two terms $F\{U_0(x_0, y_0)\}$ and $H(f_x, f_y)$. The two terms must, simultaneously, satisfy the sampling theorem. We will therefore successively study the different transfer functions $H(f_x, f_y)$ of [3.34], [3.35], and [3.36]. The sampling of the phase function

$$\exp\left[jk\sqrt{d^2 + x^2 + y^2}\right]$$ of these expressions must also satisfy the sampling theorem,

as this oscillating function imposes the conditions. Referring to the principle invoked to get inequality [3.15], the condition is determined by the following inequality [LI 07a]:

$$\left|\frac{\partial}{\partial x}\frac{2\pi}{\lambda}\sqrt{d^2 + x^2 + y^2}\right|_{x,y=L_0/2} \times \frac{L_0}{N} \leq \pi \qquad [3.40]$$

From which we directly elicit:

$$N \geq \frac{L_0^2}{\lambda\sqrt{d^2 + L_0^2/2}} \qquad [3.41]$$

With the same approach as for the sampling of the quadratic phase function from equation [3.11], the sampling condition of the Fresnel transfer function must satisfy:

$$\left|\frac{\partial}{\partial x}\frac{\pi}{\lambda d}(x^2 + y^2)\right|_{x,y=L_0/2} \times \frac{L_0}{N} \leq \pi \qquad [3.42]$$

Leading to an equivalent relation to [3.16]:

$$N \geq \frac{L_0^2}{\lambda d} \qquad [3.43]$$

Comparing [3.43] and [3.41] shows that if $d \gg L_0$, these two conditions are identical.

We will now consider the angular spectrum expression [3.39]. The complex exponential function contains a nonlinear phase term varying with (f_x, f_y), giving it a non-stationary character [OPP 89, PRO 96, MAR 96, LYO 04]. The local spatial period of the angular spectrum on the axis f_x ($f_y = 0$) is given by [GOO 05]:

$$T_{ix} = \frac{1}{2\pi}\frac{\partial}{\partial f_x}kd\sqrt{1 - \lambda^2 f_x^2} = \frac{\lambda d f_x}{\sqrt{1 - \lambda^2 f_x^2}} \qquad [3.44]$$

The maximum spatial period is obtained at the edge of the spectrum, i.e. at $f_x = f_x^{max} = N/2L_0$. The sampling of the angular spectrum in the spectral plane must also fulfill Shannon's theorem, which imposes that the spatial periodization as a consequence of the spectral sampling satisfies $L_0 \geq 2T_{ix}^{max}$, leading to:

$$L_0 \geq \frac{\lambda d N}{\sqrt{L_0^2 - \lambda^2 N^2}} \qquad [3.45]$$

If $L_0 \gg \lambda N$, [3.45] is equivalent to [3.25]. Expression [3.45] also leads to:

$$N \leq \frac{L_0}{\lambda\sqrt{d^2 + L_0^2}} \qquad [3.46]$$

We find an inequality in the opposite direction to [3.41], as mentioned for [3.25] and [3.16]. Given that [3.46] comes from rigorous considerations of the angular spectrum, from the point of view of its physical meaning, it is also the best sampling condition for the angular spectrum and Fresnel diffraction transfer functions.

3.3.4. Example of calculations of the classical diffraction formulae

We take again the test in Figure 3.4, fixing $N = 256$. Given that there is almost no difference between the diffraction patterns simulated by the two Rayleigh-Sommerfeld forms of diffraction, we will consider only the first formulation in what follows. Let us consider the diaphragm illuminated by a plane wave. Let $L_0 = 10$ mm and $\lambda = 532$ nm. We consider $d = 184$ mm, 367 mm, and 734 mm. Figures 3.9–3.11, give the respective comparisons between the diffraction patterns captured by the CCD and the simulations obtained by the different classical formulae. Note that the difference between the measurements and simulations varies with the transfer function and the diffraction distance. These differences are analyzed, taking into consideration the sampling condition.

For the Fresnel transfer function calculated by FFT, the sampling condition [3.43] can be rewritten as:

$$L_0 \leq \sqrt{N\lambda d} \qquad [3.47]$$

Substituting the parameters used in Figures 3.9–3.11 into this relation, we have:

– $d = 184$ mm (see Figure 3.9): $\sqrt{256 \times 0.532 \times 10^{-3} \times 184} \approx 5.01 < L_0$, which does not satisfy the sampling theorem;

– $d = 367$ mm (see Figure 3.10): $\sqrt{256 \times 0.532 \times 10^{-3} \times 367} \approx 7.07 < L_0$, which does not satisfy the sampling theorem;

– $d = 734$ mm (see Figure 3.11): $\sqrt{256 \times 0.532 \times 10^{-3} \times 734} \approx 10.00 = L_0$, which satisfies the sampling theorem.

For the Kirchhoff and Rayleigh-Sommerfeld transfer functions, the sampling condition [3.41] can be rewritten as:

$$L_0^2 \leq N\lambda\sqrt{d^2 + L_0^2 / 2} \qquad\qquad [3.48]$$

By substituting the parameters into this relation, the reader may note that the sampling theorem is satisfied only for the case $d = 734$ mm.

For the angular spectrum with $d \gg L_0$, we saw that inequality [3.47] must be reversed, i.e. $L_0 \geq \sqrt{N\lambda d}$, leading to $L_0 = 10 > 9.9982$ mm for $d = 734$ mm. Shannon's conditions are therefore respected for the calculation by angular spectrum and for the Fresnel transfer function, whatever be the distance.

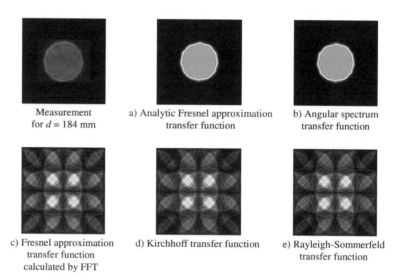

Measurement for $d = 184$ mm	a) Analytic Fresnel approximation transfer function	b) Angular spectrum transfer function
c) Fresnel approximation transfer function calculated by FFT	d) Kirchhoff transfer function	e) Rayleigh-Sommerfeld transfer function

Figure 3.9. *Experimental and simulated diffraction patterns for $d = 184$ mm. The simulations were obtained by discrete convolution calculations using the different transfer functions*

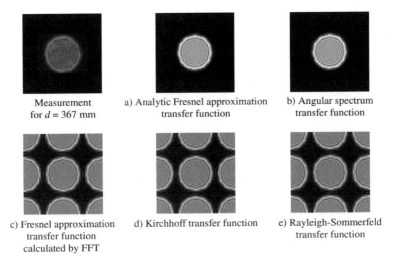

Measurement
for *d* = 367 mm

a) Analytic Fresnel approximation
transfer function

b) Angular spectrum
transfer function

c) Fresnel approximation
transfer function
calculated by FFT

d) Kirchhoff transfer function

e) Rayleigh-Sommerfeld
transfer function

Figure 3.10. *Experimental and simulated diffraction patterns for d = 367 mm. The simulations were obtained by discrete convolution calculations using the different transfer functions*

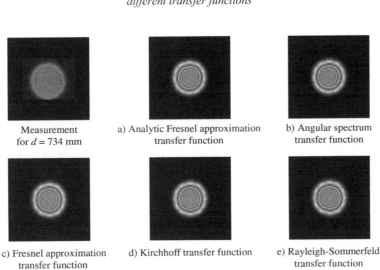

Measurement
for *d* = 734 mm

a) Analytic Fresnel approximation
transfer function

b) Angular spectrum
transfer function

c) Fresnel approximation
transfer function
calculated by FFT

d) Kirchhoff transfer function

e) Rayleigh-Sommerfeld
transfer function

Figure 3.11. *Experimental and simulated diffraction patterns for d = 734 mm. The simulations were obtained by discrete convolution calculations using the different transfer functions*

We observe that Figures 3.9(a,b), 3.10(a,b) and 3.11(a,b) show that the conditions are respected for the calculation by Fresnel transfer function in its analytic form and by the angular spectrum method.

For $d = 734$ mm, the sampling conditions are satisfied for all the classical formulae and Figures 3.11(a–e) confirm this.

For the case where $d = 367$ mm, the central part of Figures 3.10(c–e) appears to correspond to the experimental result. Nevertheless, the sampling does not satisfy the conditions and an "aliasing" phenomenon occurs [OPP 89, PRO 96, MAR 96, LYO 04, BEL 00]. This phenomenon can also be observed in Figures 3.9(c–e). The diffraction pattern is obtained by an inverse DFT. If the frequency sampling is not sufficient to satisfy the sampling theorem, the spatial period determined by the inverse of the frequency sampling interval will be short. Taking into account the fact that the observation window remains constant, this will introduce the appearance of the periods adjacent to the motif in this window, causing the phenomenon of spatial aliasing. In Figures 3.10(c–e), the central part may be approximately considered to be the diffraction pattern: this is a consequence of the fact that the energy of the object field is localized at the center of the spectrum. In this particular case, the aliasing has not yet noticeably impinged upon the useful zone of the image. When the number of sample points is very far from the sampling condition, for example in the case where $d = 184$ mm, the spatial period will be even smaller, and the aliasing phenomenon will be much more important. We then observe in Figures 3.9(c–e) that the result of the calculation is no longer workable. These results show the importance of taking into account the sampling conditions for the execution of a correct diffraction calculation, regardless of the theoretical formulation employed [LI 02c].

3.3.5. *Calculation of diffraction by convolution: summary*

In the scalar theory of diffraction, the angular spectrum, Kirchhoff, and Rayleigh-Sommerfeld formulae rigorously satisfy the scalar wave equation [GOO 05]. They are therefore equivalent presentations of the physical phenomenon of diffraction. Since they can be analyzed in the form of a convolution, the FFT may be used to numerically calculate their transfer functions. However, the major difference between these transfer functions is that the angular spectrum transfer function is mathematically defined, whereas the others must be evaluated by FFT. The sampling theorem must be verified before applying the FFT, and it is necessary to carry out three FFTs to calculate the Kirchhoff and Rayleigh-Sommerfeld formulae. On the other hand, the application of the angular spectrum formula only requires two. This approach, however, may be used only for "small" diffraction distances, satisfying relation [3.45]. Conversely, when the diffraction distance is "small", the number of sample points of the Kirchhoff and Rayleigh-Sommerfeld transfer function increases very quickly toward large values, as relation [3.43] must be satisfied. If the sampling conditions are not satisfied, the result suffers from aliasing and the obtained diffraction differs strongly from the exact result.

The earlier analyses show that, for a given problem, the angular spectrum method is more efficient than the others for "small" diffraction distances. The sampling condition and the calculation time of this formula are equivalent to those coming from the Fresnel approximation, with the use of the Fresnel transfer function. Given that the angular spectrum gives a precise theoretical solution, it will be necessary to favor this approach in practice.

3.4. Numerical calculation of Collins' formula

Within Gauss' approximation, Collins' formula [COL 70] and its inverse calculation [LI 08b] are extremely useful for the study of diffraction across an optical system. For example, in digital holography, if the object wave received by the CCD sensor has crossed an optical system, the inverse Collins' formula simplifies the reconstruction of the object image [LI 07c]. The study of these two formulae shows that they may be calculated either by the S-FFT method or by the D-FFT method. We will discuss which sampling conditions are to be satisfied and will confirm this analysis by an experiment/simulation comparison [LI 08b].

3.4.1. *Collin's direct and inverse formulae*

We suppose that a centered optical system is described in the context of Gauss' approximation, by a matrix *ABCD* [KEA 02]. We recall the equation proved by Collins in 1970, relating the field in the output plane of the system $U(x,y)$, with the field in the input plane $U_0(x_0,y_0)$ [COL 70]:

$$U(x,y) = \frac{\exp(jkz_{\text{axis}})}{j\lambda B} \int_{-\infty}^{\infty}\int_{-\infty}^{\infty} U_0(x_0,y_0) \times$$

$$\exp\left\{\frac{jk}{2B}\left[A(x_0^2+y_0^2)+D(x^2+y^2)-2(xx_0+yy_0)\right]\right\} dx_0 dy_0$$

[3.49]

where z_{axis} is the optical path along the axis of the optical system. Substituting $x_a = Ax_0$ and $y_a = Ay_0$ into [3.49], we have:

$$U(x,y)\exp\left[j\frac{k}{2B}\left(\frac{1}{A}-D\right)(x^2+y^2)\right]=$$

$$\int_{-\infty}^{\infty}\int_{-\infty}^{\infty}U_0\left(\frac{x_a}{A},\frac{y_a}{A}\right)\frac{\exp(jkz_{axis})}{j\lambda BA^2}\exp\left\{j\frac{k}{2BA}\left[(x_a-x)^2+(y_a-y)^2\right]\right\}dx_a dy_a$$

[3.50]

Carrying out a Fourier transform on both sides of [3.50] and using the convolution theorem:

$$F\left\{U(x,y)\exp\left[j\frac{k}{2B}\left(\frac{1}{A}-D\right)(x^2+y^2)\right]\right\}$$

$$=F\left\{U_0\left(\frac{x}{A},\frac{y}{A}\right)\right\}F\left\{\frac{\exp(jkz_{axis})}{j\lambda BA^2}\exp\left\{j\frac{k}{2BA}\left[x^2+y^2\right]\right\}\right\}$$

[3.51]

$$=F\left\{U_0\left(\frac{x}{A},\frac{y}{A}\right)\right\}\frac{\exp(jk(z_{axis}-BA))}{A}\exp\left\{jkBA\left[1-\frac{\lambda^2}{2}\left(f_x^2+f_y^2\right)\right]\right\}$$

We then have:

$$F\left\{U_0\left(\frac{x}{A},\frac{y}{A}\right)\right\}$$

$$=A\exp(-jk(z_{axis}-BA))\exp\left\{-jkBA\left[1-\frac{\lambda^2}{2}\left(f_x^2+f_y^2\right)\right]\right\}\times$$

$$F\left\{U(x,y)\exp\left[j\frac{k}{2B}\left(\frac{1}{A}-D\right)(x^2+y^2)\right]\right\}$$

$$=AF\left\{\frac{\exp(-jkz_{axis})}{-j\lambda BA}\exp\left[-j\frac{k}{2BA}(x^2+y^2)\right]\right\}F\left\{U(x,y)\exp\left[j\frac{k}{2B}\left(\frac{1}{A}-D\right)(x^2+y^2)\right]\right\}$$

[3.52]

Applying an inverse Fourier transform to both sides of this expression, we obtain:

$$U_0\left(\frac{x_a}{A},\frac{y_a}{A}\right)=\frac{\exp(-jkz_{axis})}{-j\lambda B}\int_{-\infty}^{\infty}\int_{-\infty}^{\infty}U(x,y)\exp\left[j\frac{k}{2B}\left(\frac{1}{A}-D\right)(x^2+y^2)\right]\times$$

$$\exp\left\{-j\frac{k}{2BA}\left[(x-x_a)^2+(y-y_a)^2\right]\right\}dxdy$$

[3.53]

Using the two relations $x_a = Ax_0$ and $y_a = Ay_0$, this expression becomes:

$$U_0(x_0, y_0) = \frac{\exp(-jkz_{axis})}{-j\lambda B}$$

[3.54]

$$\int\limits_{-\infty}^{\infty}\int\limits_{-\infty}^{\infty} U(x,y)\exp\left\{-\frac{jk}{2B}\left[D\left(x^2+y^2\right)+A\left(x_0^2+y_0^2\right)-2\left(x_0 x+y_0 y\right)\right]\right\}dxdy$$

Thus, the two expressions [3.49] and [3.54] constitute a pair of direct and inverse relations between the input and output fields.

3.4.2. Calculating Collins' formula by S-FFT

Collins' formula [3.49] can be expressed by the Fourier transform:

$$U(x,y) = \frac{\exp(jkz_{axis})}{j\lambda B}\exp\left[\frac{jk}{2B}D\left(x^2+y^2\right)\right]\times$$

$$F\left\{U_0(x_0,y_0)\exp\left[\frac{jk}{2B}A\left(x_0^2+y_0^2\right)\right]\right\}_{f_x=\frac{x}{\lambda B}, f_y=\frac{y}{\lambda B}}$$

[3.55]

with f_x, f_y the spatial frequency coordinates. This expression means that the Collins' calculation can be carried out by taking the Fourier transform of the function $U_0(x_0,y_0)\exp\left[jkA\left(x_0^2+y_0^2\right)/2B\right]$ and multiplying the result by a quadratic phase factor $\exp(jkz_{axis})\exp\left[jkD\left(x^2+y^2\right)/2B\right]/j\lambda B$.

We write L_0, L as the respective widths of the input and output plane. As indicated earlier, with $N \times N$ samples, the width of the frequency plane will be $N/L_0 \times N/L_0$, and we therefore have:

$$\frac{L}{\lambda|B|} = \frac{N}{L_0} \quad \text{or} \quad L_0 L = \lambda|B|N$$

[3.56]

The sampling interval in the output plane is $L/N = \lambda|B|/L_0$. Using the acronym FFT for the fast Fourier transform, the discrete expression of [3.55] is then:

$$U\left(p\frac{\lambda|B|}{L_0}, q\frac{\lambda|B|}{L_0}\right) = \frac{\exp(jkz_{axis})}{j\lambda B}\exp\left[j\pi\frac{\lambda BD}{L_0^2}\left(p^2+q^2\right)\right]\times$$

$$FFT\left\{U_0\left(m\frac{L_0}{N}, n\frac{L_0}{N}\right)\exp\left[j\pi\frac{AL_0^2}{\lambda BN^2}\left(m^2+n^2\right)\right]\right\}$$

[3.57]

with $\{p,q,m,n\} \in \{-N/2, -N/2+1, \ldots, N/2-1\}$.

Inside the brackets of the FFT, the spatial variation of the object function U_0 is generally weaker than that of the quadratic phase factor. This phase factor therefore determines the sampling conditions [LI 08b]. The maximum spatial variation of the phase factor is found at the edges of the square zone in the input plane whose sampling coordinates are $m,n = \pm N/2$. On the basis of the principles studied for the Fresnel integral (the S-FFT method), the maximum phase variation must be less than π, i.e.:

$$\left| \frac{\partial}{\partial m}\left(\pi \frac{AL_0^2}{\lambda BN^2}\left(m^2 + n^2\right)\right)\right|_{m,n=N/2} \le \pi \qquad [3.58]$$

from which we deduce:

$$|B| \ge \frac{|A|L_0^2}{\lambda N} \qquad [3.59]$$

This relation imposes the sampling condition to get a unaliased diffraction pattern. Likewise, for the complex amplitude of the field calculated by S-FFT to satisfy the sampling theorem, the proportionality term behind the FFT in [3.57] must satisfy the following inequality:

$$\left| \frac{\partial}{\partial p}\, \pi \frac{\lambda BD}{L_0^2}\left(p^2 + q^2\right)\right|_{p,q=N/2} \le \pi \qquad [3.60]$$

from which the solution leads to:

$$|B| \le \frac{L_0^2}{N\lambda|D|} \qquad [3.61]$$

Synthesizing the two expressions [3.59] and [3.61], we have:

$$|A| \le \frac{|B|\lambda N}{L_0^2} \le \frac{1}{|D|} \qquad [3.62]$$

This inequality is the relation that must be satisfied by the matrix coefficients of the optical system to comply with the sampling theorem.

Considering $|A| = |B|\lambda N / L_0^2$, on the left of [3.62], we obtain a particular case:

$$L_0 = \sqrt{|B\lambda N / A|} \qquad [3.63]$$

This means if the width of the input plane is $L_0 = \sqrt{|B\lambda N / A|}$, the field calculated by [3.57] satisfies the sampling theorem. This relation will be used in the experimental demonstration.

3.4.3. Calculating the inverse Collins' formula by S-FFT

Following a similar reasoning, the inverse Collins' formula [3.54] can be rewritten as an inverse Fourier transform:

$$U_0(x_0, y_0) = \frac{\exp(-jkz_{\text{axis}})}{-j\lambda B} \exp\left[-\frac{jk}{2B} A(x_0^2 + y_0^2)\right]$$

$$\int_{-\infty}^{\infty}\int_{-\infty}^{\infty} U(x, y)\exp\left[-\frac{jk}{2B}D(x^2 + y^2)\right]\exp\left[j\frac{2\pi}{\lambda B}(xx_0 + yy_0)\right]dxdy \qquad [3.64]$$

i.e.

$$U_0(x_0, y_0) = \frac{\exp(-jkz_{\text{axis}})}{-j\lambda B} \exp\left[-\frac{jk}{2B} A(x_0^2 + y_0^2)\right] \times$$

$$F^{-1}\left\{U(x, y)\exp\left[-\frac{jk}{2B}D(x^2 + y^2)\right]\right\}_{f_x=\frac{x_0}{\lambda B}, f_y=\frac{y_0}{\lambda B}} \qquad [3.65]$$

The calculation can be carried out by taking the inverse Fourier transform of the function $U(x, y)\exp\left[-jkD(x^2 + y^2)/2B\right]$, and multiplying by the quadratic phase factor $-\exp(-jkz_{\text{axis}})\exp\left[-jkA(x_0^2 + y_0^2)/2D\right]/j\lambda B$.

Supposing once again that L_0 and L are the respective widths of the input and output planes for the inverse calculation, with $N \times N$ samples, we have:

$$L_0 = \frac{\lambda|B|N}{L} \qquad [3.66]$$

The sampling interval of the output plane being $L/N = \lambda|B|/L_0$, the discrete expression of [3.64] is then (IFFT being the acronym for the inverse FFT):

$$U_0\left(m\frac{\lambda|B|}{L}, n\frac{\lambda|B|}{L}\right) = \frac{\exp(-jkz_{\text{axis}})}{-j\lambda B}\exp\left[-j\pi\frac{\lambda BA}{L^2}(m^2 + n^2)\right] \times$$

$$\text{IFFT}\left\{U\left(p\frac{L}{N}, q\frac{L}{N}\right)\exp\left[-j\pi\frac{DL^2}{\lambda BN^2}(p^2 + q^2)\right]\right\} \qquad [3.67]$$

with $\{p,q,m,n\} \in \{-N/2, -N/2 + 1, \ldots, N/2-1\}$.

We note that if we carry out the change of variables $L_0 \to L$, $z_{axis} \to -z_{axis}$, $A \to D$, $D \to A$, $B \to -B$ in Collins' formula [3.49], we obtain the formula for the inverse calculation [3.64]. A very practical consequence follows from this: using these changes, we may determine the sampling conditions for the evaluation of the inverse Collins' formula by S-IFFT. From [3.58], the sample number of the S-IFFT method must satisfy the inequality:

$$|D| \leq \frac{|B| \lambda N}{L^2} \leq \frac{1}{|A|}$$

[3.68]

Considering $1/|A| = |B| \lambda N / L^2$ on the right of [3.68], we obtain the particular case:

$$L = \sqrt{|AB\lambda N|}$$

[3.69]

If the width of the output plane is $L = \sqrt{|AB\lambda N|}$, the reconstituted input field, by [3.67], satisfies the sampling theorem. We recall the physical meaning of relation [3.63]: if $L_0 = \sqrt{|B\lambda N / A|}$, the field in the exit plane calculated by [3.57] satisfies the sampling theorem. It follows from these two conditions that the product $L_0 L$ satisfies $L_0 L = \lambda |B| N$, which constitutes a fundamental relation for calculation by S-FFT and S-IFFT. Consequently, if the two relations [3.63] and [3.69] are both satisfied, the field in the input plane $U_0(x_0, y_0)$ or in the output plane $U(x, y)$ can be mutually calculated, each satisfying the sampling theorem.

The relation $L_0 L = \lambda |B| N$ fixes the limit of the calculations. Given the width of the input plane L_0, the width of the output plane L is proportional to the term $\lambda |B| N$. For a finite number N, if the matrix element B tends to 0 then so too does the width of the output plane. On the other hand, if the width of the output plane L is fixed and $B \to 0$, then the width of the input plane L_0 also tends to 0. The case $B = 0$ corresponds to the case where the output plane is merged with the image plane given by the system (object-image conjugation across the system) [KEA 02]. Thus, if $B \to 0$, the S-FFT and S-IFFT methods are no longer necessary for the evaluation of Collins' formula since the image plane is up to a factor equivalent to the input plane.

3.4.4. Calculating Collins' formula by D-FFT

From expression [3.50], Collins' formula can be rewritten in the form of a convolution:

$$U(x,y) = \frac{\exp(jkz_{\text{axis}})}{jA^2\lambda B}\exp\left[-j\frac{k}{2B}\left(\frac{1}{A}-D\right)(x^2+y^2)\right] \times$$
$$\left[U_0\left(\frac{x}{A},\frac{y}{A}\right)*\exp\left(\frac{jk}{2BA}(x^2+y^2)\right)\right]$$

[3.70]

We have:

$$F\left\{\exp\left(\frac{jk}{2BA}(x^2+y^2)\right)\right\} = j\lambda BA\exp\left(-j\pi\lambda BA\left(f_x^2+f_y^2\right)\right)$$

[3.71]

Using the convolution theorem, expression [3.70] can be rewritten again as:

$$U(x,y) = \exp(jkz_{\text{axis}})\exp\left[-j\frac{k}{2B}\left(\frac{1}{A}-D\right)(x^2+y^2)\right] \times$$
$$F^{-1}\left\{F\left\{\frac{1}{A}U_0\left(\frac{x}{A},\frac{y}{A}\right)\right\}\exp\left(-j\pi\lambda BA\left(f_x^2+f_y^2\right)\right)\right\}$$

[3.72]

This relation shows that Collins' formula is a linear transformation whose transfer function is $\exp\left(-j\pi\lambda BA\left(f_x^2+f_y^2\right)\right)$ and input term is $(1/A)U_0(x/A,y/A)$. In other words, the field U_0 experiences a spatial contraction ($|A| < 1$) or dilation ($|A| > 1$) from element A [LI 10a]. The input plane of width L_0 is sampled at N points and the frequency width of $F\{(1/A)U_0(x/A,y/A)\}$ is N/L_0. Since taking the product with the transfer function does not change the bandwidth of the function, the spatial width of the inverse Fourier transform obtained by IFFT is $L = (1/L_0)^{-1} = L_0$. As a result, expression [3.70] calculated by FFT and IFFT is re-expressed as:

$$U\left(p\frac{L_0}{N},q\frac{L_0}{N}\right) = \exp(jkz_{\text{axis}})\exp\left[-j\frac{k}{2B}\left(\frac{1}{A}-D\right)\left(\frac{L_0}{N}\right)^2(p^2+q^2)\right] \times$$
$$\text{IFFT}\left\{\text{FFT}\left\{\frac{1}{A}U_0\left(r\frac{L_0}{AN},s\frac{L_0}{AN}\right)\right\}\exp\left(-j\pi\lambda BA\frac{m^2+n^2}{L_0^2}\right)\right\}$$

[3.73]

with $\{p,q,r,s,m,n\} \in \{-N/2, -N/2 + 1, \ldots, N/2-1\}$.

Let E be the total energy of the input field. As was explained earlier in the analysis of the classical formulae in convolution form (relation [3.26]), the number of suitable sample points for $(1/A)U_0(rL_0/AN, sL_0/AN)$ must satisfy the relation [LI 11a]:

$$E = \frac{A^2L_0^2}{N^4}\sum_{p=-N/2}^{N/2-1}\sum_{q=-N/2}^{N/2-1}\left|\text{FFT}\left\{\frac{1}{A}U_0\left(r\frac{L_0}{AN},s\frac{L_0}{AN}\right)\right\}(p,q)\right|^2 \approx \text{Constant}$$

[3.74]

Numerically applying the method, discussed earlier in section 3.2.3, we can quickly evaluate if the source term is correctly sampled.

The total calculation again includes taking the product with a phase factor proportional to IFFT. The sampling conditions are:

$$
\left| \frac{\partial}{\partial p} \frac{k}{2B} \left(\frac{1}{A} - D \right) \left(\frac{L_0}{N} \right)^2 \left(p^2 + q^2 \right) \right|_{p,q=N/2} \le \pi \tag{3.75}
$$

Taking into account the fact that the determinant of the optical system is $AC-BD = 1$, and developing condition [3.75], we obtain:

$$
\frac{L_0^2}{\lambda} \left| \frac{C}{A} \right| \le N \tag{3.76}
$$

Relations [3.74] and [3.76] are the necessary conditions for the evaluation of Collins' formula by the D-FFT method.

3.4.5. Calculating the inverse Collins' formula by D-FFT

We may use again the change of variables from section 3.4.3, $z_{axis} \to -z_{axis}$, $A \to D$, $D \to A$, $B \to -B$ in Collins' formula [3.49] and obtain the formula for the inverse calculation [3.54]. These changes readily lead to the sampling conditions for the inverse Collins' formula. On the basis of [3.73], we have:

$$
U_0 \left(r\frac{L}{N}, s\frac{L}{N} \right) = \exp(-jkz_{axis}) \exp\left[j\frac{k}{2B} \left(\frac{1}{D} - A \right) \left(\frac{L}{N} \right)^2 \left(r^2 + s^2 \right) \right] \times
$$
$$
\text{IFFT}\left\{ \text{FFT}\left\{ \frac{1}{D} U\left(p\frac{L}{DN}, q\frac{L}{DN} \right) \right\} \exp\left(j\pi\lambda BD \frac{m^2 + n^2}{L^2} \right) \right\} \tag{3.77}
$$

with $\{r,s,p,q,m,n\} \in \{-N/2, -N/2 + 1, \ldots, N/2-1\}$.

Following from [3.74] and [3.76], the sampling conditions for the calculation of the inverse Collins' formula by D-FFT must satisfy:

$$
E = \frac{D^2 L^2}{N^4} \sum_{r=-N/2}^{N/2-1} \sum_{s=-N/2}^{N/2-1} \left| \text{FFT}\left\{ \frac{1}{D} U\left(p\frac{L}{DN}, q\frac{L}{DN} \right) \right\}(r,s) \right|^2 \approx \text{Constant}
$$
$$
\frac{L^2}{\lambda} \left| \frac{C}{D} \right| \le N \tag{3.78}
$$

The following section offers a numerical and experimental study validating the approaches presented in the earlier sections.

3.4.6. *Numerical calculation and experimental demonstration*

Figure 3.12 shows the optical system and the different planes of interest (λ = 632.8 nm). The incident laser beam propagates along the optical axis z. After crossing a lens L_1, it transforms into a spherical wave coming from the focal point of the lens. This wave then illuminates an aperture in the form of the Chinese letter "dragon". The wave coming from the aperture crosses a second lens L_2 of focal distance f_2 = 698.8 mm, before impacting the CCD detector. The $x_0 y_0$ plane of the aperture is considered as the input plane of the system and the xy plane of the detector as the output plane. We are interested in the diffraction of the laser beam across this simple system. The other parameters of Figure 3.12 are d_0 = 908 mm, d_1 = 147 mm, and d_2 = 1,315 mm.

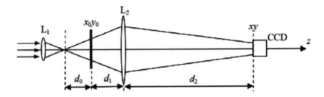

Figure 3.12. *Scheme of the optical system*

We may consider the input plane as a divergent lens of focal distance $-d_0$. The four elements $ABCD$ of the matrix of the optical system are determined by the matrix product:

$$
\begin{bmatrix} A & B \\ C & D \end{bmatrix} = \begin{bmatrix} 1 & d_3 \\ 0 & 1 \end{bmatrix}\begin{bmatrix} 1 & 0 \\ -1/f_2 & 1 \end{bmatrix}\begin{bmatrix} 1 & d_1 \\ 0 & 1 \end{bmatrix}\begin{bmatrix} 1 & 0 \\ 1/d_0 & 1 \end{bmatrix}
$$

$$
= \begin{bmatrix} (d_0 + d_1 + d_3)/d_0 - d_3(d_0 + d_1)/(d_0 f_2) & d_3 - d_1(d_3/f_2 - 1) \\ -(d_0 + d_1 - f_2)/(d_0 f_2) & 1 - d_1/f_2 \end{bmatrix}
$$

[3.79]

Using the numerical values of the experimental parameters, the reader may verify that the matrix elements are $A \approx 0.4388$, $B \approx 1,164$ mm, $C \approx -0.0006$ mm^{-1}, and $D \approx 0.7896$.

3.4.6.1. *Demonstration of the S-FFT and S-IFFT methods*

Let the width of the square input plane $L_0 = \sqrt{|B\lambda N / A|} = 29.32$ mm and $N = 512$. Figure 3.13(a) gives the (intensity) field in the input plane. The surface area of the sensor is 4.64 mm × 6.17 mm and contains 552 × 784 pixels. From relation [3.56], the width of the output plane determined by S-FFT calculation will be $L = \lambda|B|N / L_0 = 12.87$ mm. To simplify the comparison, the intensity distribution detected by the CCD is transformed into a square distribution of sides 12.87 mm with 512 × 512 pixels. After normalization, this intensity distribution is given by Figure 3.13(b). This result serves as experimental proof for the calculation of the field in the output plane.

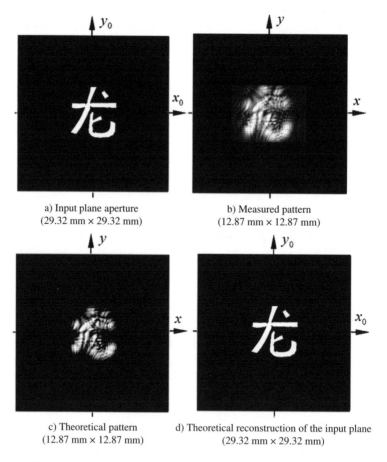

a) Input plane aperture
(29.32 mm × 29.32 mm)

b) Measured pattern
(12.87 mm × 12.87 mm)

c) Theoretical pattern
(12.87 mm × 12.87 mm)

d) Theoretical reconstruction of the input plane
(29.32 mm × 29.32 mm)

Figure 3.13. *Comparison between experiment and calculation using the S-FFT method for the evaluation of Collins' direct and inverse formulae*

Substituting the relevant parameters into [3.57], we obtain the theoretical field $U(x, y)$ in the output plane. The theoretical intensity distribution is given in Figure 3.13(c). Note the strong agreement between theory and experiment.

Relations [3.63] and [3.69] are, respectively, $L_0 = \sqrt{|B\lambda N / A|}$ and $L = \sqrt{|AB\lambda N|}$, which show that the two fields $U_0(x_0, y_0)$ and $U(x, y)$ may be mutually calculated satisfying the sampling theorem. Thus, it is possible to substitute the complex amplitude of the field in Figure 3.13(c) into formula [3.67] of the calculation of the inverse Collins' formula by S-IFFT. The field is reconstructed in the input plane. The obtained result is given in Figure 3.13(d). Note that there is almost no difference between Figures 3.13(d) and 3.13(a). The numerical calculation therefore gives very precise results, and the inverse Collins' formula [3.67] gives a reliable reconstruction in the input plane. We will use this approach in digital holography in Chapter 6.

3.4.6.2. Demonstration of the D-FFT method

We keep $N = 512$ and suppose now that $L_0 = \sqrt{|AB\lambda N|} = 12.87$ mm. The intensity distribution in the input plane is drawn in Figure 3.14(a). The width of the output plane is equal to that of the CCD input (4.64 mm × 6.17 mm). So as to facilitate the comparison of the graphical representations, zeros have been added around the experimental image (Figure 3.14(b)). Having calculated expression [3.73], the result is given in Figure 3.14(c). Comparison of Figure 3.14(c) with Figure 3.14(b) shows that calculation by the D-FFT method very accurately simulates the experimental result.

The sampling condition [3.76] gives $N \geq 357.4$ and condition [3.78] gives $N \geq 198.6$. They are therefore satisfied, since $N = 512$. Substituting the complex amplitude of the output plane into expression [3.77], we obtain the field in the input plane shown in Figure 3.14(d). The reconstructed image corresponds perfectly to Figure 3.14(a).

The reconstructed field may be quantitatively analyzed. Figure 3.15 gives the distributions of the real part U_r and the imaginary part U_i of the recalculated field on the x_0-axis, as well as the modulus of the initial field in the input plane $|U_0|$. We may note that there exists a slight discrepancy between the ideal value and the reconstruction. This discrepancy is essentially due to the phenomenon of truncation in the spatial filtering carried out by the D-FFT method [GOO 05, OPP 89, PRO 96, MAR 96, LYO 04]. These small differences in the results are generally acceptable in many applications.

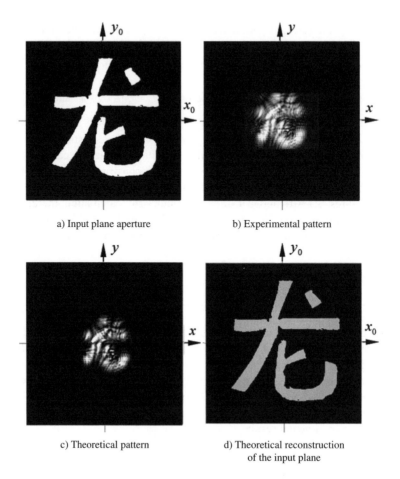

a) Input plane aperture   b) Experimental pattern

c) Theoretical pattern   d) Theoretical reconstruction
                                       of the input plane

Figure 3.14. *Comparison between experiment and calculation using the D-FFT method for the evaluation of Collins' direct and inverse formulae*

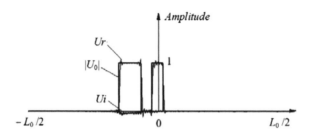

Figure 3.15. *Axial distributions of the real U_r and imaginary U_i parts of the restored field and the modulus of the initial field in the input plane $|U_0|$ along x_0*

3.5. Conclusion

This chapter has presented the methods of the numerical calculation of diffraction. The Single-FFT (S-FFT) and Double-FFT (D-FFT) methods (direct and inverse) have been described in detail. In particular, we have highlighted the optimal sampling conditions for the classical diffraction formulae. The angular spectrum method is very efficient (only two FFTs) but limited to quite small diffraction distances. On the other hand, the direct calculation of the Fresnel transform and the methods requiring three FFTs are better adapted for large diffraction distances. In the Gauss domain, the phenomenon of diffraction across an optical system may also be evaluated with the help of Collins' direct and inverse formulae.

Chapter 4

Fundamentals of Holography

In 1948, to improve the resolution of electronic microscopes, Hungarian scientist Denis Gabor proposed a new process of image formation in two stages, without a lens, that he called the reconstruction of wavefronts [GAB 48]. Gabor made the following remark: if a suitable coherent reference wave is superposed with the light diffracted by an object, then it is possible to record the interference intensity distribution, which he called a hologram. He showed that from such a pattern, it is possible to obtain an image of the original object, containing both the amplitude and the phase of the diffracted waves. The word "holography" comes from the Greek "holos" meaning "whole" and "graphein" meaning "writing". Gabor published two more-detailed articles in 1949 and 1951 considering the applications of the reconstruction of wavefronts to microscopy [GAB 49, GAB 51]. However, this method required a coherent light source. Moreover, the hologram recording system proposed by Gabor being on-axis, the superposition of the twin images diminished the quality of the restored image. Before the advent of the laser, the development of this technique was of interest for a few microscopic techniques [GAR 06a, GAR 06b, KAN 09] and in particle, microholography [ONU 92, ONU 93, COE 02, NIC 06].

In the history of the development of optical holography, American scientists Leith and Upatnieks [LEI 62, YAN 06] made an important contribution. The "off-axis" technique of recording holograms that they proposed allowed the separation of the twin images. We may therefore obtain a holographic image without pollution by the twin image. After the advent of the laser in 1962, even though the electronic microscopy applications that Gabor envisaged did not come to fruition for technical reasons, the development of holographic interferometry in several laboratories was the real beginning of industrial holography [POW 65]. The off-axis method of holographic recording then became widely used in many applications [SMI 94]. Gabor was awarded the Nobel Prize in physics in 1971 for his discovery.

Holograms are classified into different types according to the recording architecture and the characteristics of the recording materials [GOO 05]. However, this book is dedicated to the methods of digital holography and their use in optical metrology; we will not go into detail about the set of methods and materials used in holography, and we invite the reader to refer to [KRE 96]. This chapter presents the fundamentals of Gabor holography and the off-axis method, and discusses the object–image relationship.

4.1. Basics of holography

As a first step, we consider the process of wavefront reconstruction in the original form proposed by Gabor [GAB 48, GOO 05]. Figure 4.1 represents a diagram of the setup for recording a Gabor hologram. The large arrow represents the object situated in the $x_0 y_0$ plane.

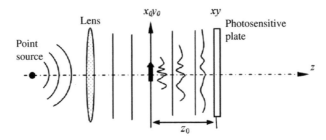

Figure 4.1. *A setup for the recording of a Gabor hologram*

When the object is illuminated with coherent light by the collimator shown in the figure, the transmitted light is formed by two components: a transmitted uniform plane wave and a wave diffused by the object. The hologram is said to be "on-axis", as we see in the figure, the reference wave and the object wave are parallel. Considering R and $O(x,y)$ to be their respective complex amplitudes in the recording plane xy, situated at the distance z_0 from the object plane, the intensity of their interference pattern is expressed by:

$$I(x, y) = |R + O(x, y)|^2$$
$$= |R|^2 + |O(x, y)|^2 + R^* O(x, y) + R O^*(x, y) \qquad [4.1]$$

Here, the recording support is a high-resolution silver-type photosensitive plate [KRE 96]. After chemical treatment, the photographic plate becomes a Gabor hologram. If the exposure is limited to the linear part of the gelatin transmittance, the amplitude transmittance of the hologram is proportional to expression [4.1] [SMI 94]. Introducing the slope of the linear part, written here as β, the transmittance of the recording support after treatment is written as:

$$t_A(x,y) = \beta|R|^2 + \beta\left[|O(x,y)|^2 + R^*O(x,y) + RO^*(x,y)\right]$$ [4.2]

Illuminating the hologram perpendicularly with a plane wave of amplitude A, the wave transmitted by the hologram is decomposed into four terms:

$$At_A(x,y) = A\beta|R|^2 + A\beta|O(x,y)|^2 + A\beta R^*O(x,y) + A\beta RO^*(x,y)$$ [4.3]

The first term is a plane wave that directly crosses the plate, experiencing a uniform attenuation, but without diffusing. If the geometric size of the object is relatively small, i.e. $|O(x,y)| \ll |R|$, the second term is negligible. The third term represents a component proportional to the amplitude of the wave diffused by the object. When we look from the left to the right of the plate (Figure 4.2), we may observe a virtual image of the object at a distance z_0 from the support. As the fourth term is proportional to $O^*(x,y)$, it leads to the formation of a real image situated at the distance z_0 from the plate, but on the other side of that of the virtual image (see Figure 4.2).

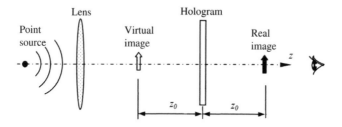

Figure 4.2. *Reconstruction of the Gabor hologram images*

The Gabor hologram therefore simultaneously produces a real and a virtual image of the object, these waves being situated on the axis of the hologram. These images, called twin images, are separated by a distance $2z_0$ and coexist with the coherent front $A\beta|R|^2$. The two terms $\beta|R|^2$ and $A\beta|O(x,y)|^2$ of the transmitted wave will be noise in the useful image. Furthermore, even if the term $A\beta|O(x,y)|^2$ is irrelevant, the focusing of the virtual image is always accompanied by the real unfocused image, due to the presence of the twin image. In the same manner, an observer focusing on the virtual image simultaneously sees an unfocused image coming from the term corresponding to the real image. Thus, with a Gabor hologram, it is possible to form, by wavefront reconstruction, images of an object constituted, for example, by opaque letters on a transparent background, but not by transparent letters on an opaque background [GOO 05]. This seriously limits the use of Gabor holograms. The most satisfactory holographic method was proposed by Leith and Upatnieks, and we will present this in more detail in the next section [LEI 62].

4.1.1. *Leith–Upatnieks holograms*

A Leith–Upatnieks hologram is also called an oblique-reference hologram or an off-axis hologram. The essential difference between this type of hologram and the Gabor type is that during the recording process, the reference wave is introduced at an angle, and is therefore distinct from the wave illuminating the object. Thus, Leith and Upatnieks resolved not only the twin image problem, but also allowed the obtainment of a truly three-dimensional (3D) hologram [YAN 06]. Currently, most holographic methods are based on the oblique reference concept. In this respect, the contribution of Leith and Upatnieks is truly significant in the history of the development of holography.

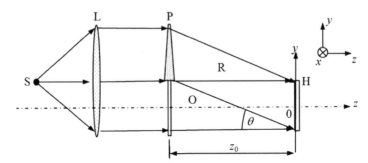

Figure 4.3. *Hologram with an oblique reference*

Figure 4.3 represents a simple setup that may be used to record a Leith–Upatnieks hologram [GOO 05]. Light coming from a point source S is collimated by a lens L. One part of the emergent plane wave meets the object constituted by a transparent object. Another part of the plane wave meets the prism P situated above the object, giving a reference wave. This wave is deviated downward at an angle θ to the axis of the hologram H. Thus, these two coherent waves simultaneously fall on the light-sensitive surface. In this optical system, let us consider a rectangular frame of reference *o-xyz*, where *xy* is the holographic recording plane. The complex amplitude of the reference wave is expressed by:

$$R(x,y) = R_0 \exp[-jk(\sin\theta)y] \qquad [4.4]$$

with R_0, a constant, $k = 2\pi/\lambda$, with λ being the wavelength. Supposing that $O(x,y)$ is the distribution of the object wave in the *xy*-plane:

$$O(x,y) = O_0(x,y)\exp[j\phi_0(x,y)] \qquad [4.5]$$

The distribution of the superposed complex amplitude of these two waves is therefore:

$$u(x,y) = R(x,y) + O(x,y) \qquad [4.6]$$

We thus obtain the intensity distribution in the holographic recording plane:

$$I(x,y) = R_0^2 + |O(x,y)|^2 + $$
$$O(x,y)R_0 \exp[jk(\sin\theta)y] + O^*(x,y)R_0 \exp[-jk(\sin\theta)y] \qquad [4.7]$$

Making a suitable choice of exposure time, the amplitude transmittance of the hologram is proportional to the energy received, i.e.

$$t_A(x,y) = t_0 + \beta R_0^2 + \beta|O(x,y)|^2$$
$$+ \beta R_0 O(x,y)\exp[k(\sin\theta)y] + \beta R_0 O^*(x,y)\exp[-k(\sin\theta)y] \qquad [4.8]$$
$$= t_1 + t_2 + t_3 + t_4$$

with:

$$\begin{cases} t_1 = t_0 + \beta R_0^2 \\ t_2 = \beta|O(x,y)|^2 \\ t_3 = \beta R_0 O(x,y)\exp[k(\sin\theta)y] \\ t_4 = \beta R_0 O^*(x,y)\exp[-k(\sin\theta)y] \end{cases} \qquad [4.9]$$

When the hologram is formed, the image of the object can be reconstructed using different illumination methods for the reconstruction wave. We now analyze two possible illumination methods.

4.1.1.1. *Illumination in the propagation direction of the original reference wave*

We consider $A(x, y) = A_0 \exp[- jk(\sin\theta)y]$ as the complex amplitude of the reconstruction wave (A_0: constant). The field transmitted across the hologram is written as:

$$u(x, y) = A(x, y)t_A(x, y)$$
$$= At_1 + At_2 + At_3 + At_4 \qquad\qquad [4.10]$$

Figure 4.4 represents the four components of the transmitted light. In the following, we successively study their physical meanings.

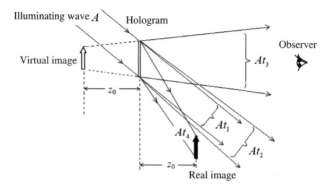

Figure 4.4. *Illumination by a reference wave conforming to the original*

Component At_1 is given by:

$$At_1 = A_0 t_b \exp[- jk(\sin\theta)y] \qquad\qquad [4.11]$$

is none other than an attenuated form of the incident wave, representing a plane wave propagating along the direction of the original reference beam.

Component At_2 given by:

$$At_2 = A_0 \beta |O(x, y)|^2 \exp[- jk(\sin\theta)y] \qquad\qquad [4.12]$$

is also a wave propagating following the direction of the reference beam. It is a wave modulated by the object $|O(x, y)|^2$, whose bandwidth is large, leading to a slightly divergent wave.

These two components constitute what is called zero-order diffraction.

Component At_3 given by:

$$At_3 = A_0 \beta R_0 O(x, y) = A_0 \beta R_0 O_0(x, y) \exp\left[- j\phi_0(x, y)\right] \qquad [4.13]$$

is proportional to the object wave $O(x, y)$ multiplied by the factor $A_0 \beta R_0$. It, therefore, has an identical wavefront to that of the original object wave and propagates along the z-axis. This wave produces a virtual image of the object at a distance z_0 in the holographic plane and is observed along the z-axis (see Figure 4.4).

Component At_4 given by:

$$At_4 = A_0 \beta R_0 O^*(x, y) \exp\left[- jk(2 \sin \theta)y\right] \qquad [4.14]$$

is proportional to the conjugate wave $O^*(x, y)$ multiplied by an exponential factor whose exponent is a linear function of y. Since $O(x, y)$ represents a divergent wave diffused by the object, $O^*(x, y)$ will be a convergent wave producing a real image of the object. The linear phase factor means that this image is tilted with regard to the plate, z. The inclination angle is:

$$\theta' = \arcsin(2 \sin \theta) \approx 2\theta \qquad [4.15]$$

The positions of the real and virtual images are shown in Figure 4.4.

4.1.1.2. *Illumination with a wave propagating along the z-axis*

Let us consider the reconstruction wave to be propagating along the z-axis, i.e. $A(x,y) = A_0$. Figure 4.5 represents the illumination geometry, and the meaning of the four terms At_1, At_2, At_3, and At_4 is explained underneath.

Component At_1 given by:

$$At_1 = A_0\left(t_0 + \beta R_0^2\right) \qquad [4.16]$$

is a plane wave propagating along the z-axis.

Component At_2 given by:

$$At_2 = A_0 \beta |O(x, y)|^2 \qquad [4.17]$$

is a divergent wave, also propagating along the z-axis.

Component At_3 given by:

$$At_3 = A_0 \beta R_0 O(x, y) \exp\left[jk(\sin\theta)y\right]$$ [4.18]

includes the term $O(x,y)$ multiplied by a constant factor $A_0\beta R_0$ and a linear phase factor, which means that it has the same characteristics as the object wave. Its propagation direction makes the angle θ with the z-axis and the virtual image is situated to the left of the plate (see Figure 4.5a).

Component At_4 given by:

$$At_4 = A_0 \beta R_0 O^*(x, y) \exp\left[-jk(\sin\theta)y\right]$$ [4.19]

includes the complex conjugate object wave $O^*(x,y)$ multiplied by a constant factor $A_0\beta R_0$ and an exponential factor $\exp\left[-jk(\sin\theta)y\right]$. This wave forms a real image situated to the right of the plate.

The real and virtual images are symmetric about the plane of the hologram (see Figure 4.5a).

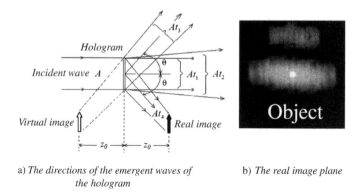

a) *The directions of the emergent waves of the hologram*   b) *The real image plane*

Figure 4.5. *Illumination by a wave propagating along the z-axis*

As an illustration, in Figure 4.5, the object is the string of characters "object". In the plane $z = z_0$, the virtual image and two other patterns formed by the two other diffraction orders may be observed (see Figure 4.5b). The real image has certain properties, which, in general, make it less interesting than the virtual image

[GOO 05]. This pattern is obtained by a numerical calculation from a digital hologram; this method will be studied in Chapter 5.

Other cases where the direction of illumination is tilted with regard to the z-axis or from the direction of the original reference wave may also be studied [GOO 05]. The positions of the real and virtual images are displaced relative to the inclination angle of the reconstruction wave.

4.1.2. Condition for the separation of the twin images and the zero order

The previous studies show that if the inclination angle θ is greater than a minimum value θ_{min}, then the twin images and the zero order will be separated from each other. To evaluate this minimum, it is sufficient to determine the minimum carrier wave frequency for which the spatial frequency spectra of At_3 and At_4 do not overlap with each other, nor with the spectra of At_1 and At_2.

When recording the hologram, the reference light is not necessarily a plane wave. To simplify the study, we consider the reference wave to be plane [GOO 05] and the hologram to be illuminated perpendicularly by a plane wave. We will determine the minimum inclination angle of the reference to the optical axis, θ_{min}, allowing the separation of the twin images and the zero-order diffracted wave. The result will be later generalized for the case of non-plane reference wave [LI 08c].

4.1.2.1. Case where the reference wave is planar

Considering (f_x, f_y) to be the spectral coordinates, the Fourier transforms of the four terms At_1, At_2, At_3, and At_4 are, respectively, given by:

$$G_1(f_x, f_y) = F\{At_1(x,y)\} = A_0 t_b \delta(f_x, f_y) \tag{4.20}$$

$$G_2(f_x, f_y) = F\{At_2(x,y)\} = A_0 \beta \tilde{O}(f_x, f_y) \otimes \tilde{O}(f_x, f_y) \tag{4.21}$$

$$G_3(f_x, f_y) = F\{At_3(x,y)\} = A_0 \beta R_0 \tilde{O}\left(f_x, f_y - \frac{\sin\theta}{\lambda}\right) \tag{4.22}$$

$$G_4(f_x, f_y) = F\{At_4(x,y)\} = A_0 \beta R_0 \tilde{O}^*\left(-f_x, -f_y - \frac{\sin\theta}{\lambda}\right) \tag{4.23}$$

in which the symbol $\otimes$ signifies the autocorrelation product and $\tilde{O}(f_x, f_y)$ represents the spectrum of the object wave.

According to the theory of diffraction by angular spectrum, the spectrum $\tilde{O}(f_x, f_y)$ is the product of the spectrum of the optical field in the object plane with the transfer function $\exp[jkz_0(1-(\lambda f_x)^2-(\lambda f_y)^2)^{1/2}]$ (see Chapter 3). The bandwidth of the function $\tilde{O}(f_x, f_y)$ is therefore identical to that of the spectrum in the object plane, as the product of the spectral functions does not modify the bandwidth.

Supposing that the spectrum of the object does not have any frequency components larger than B. From the characteristics of the autocorrelation product, the spectral bandwidth of the zero-order $G_2(f_x, f_y)$ extends up to the $2B$ frequency. To visually describe the distribution of $G_2(f_x, f_y)$ and of the other relevant spectra, using Figure 4.5b, the spectrum of the hologram is shown in Figure 4.6. The spectrum $G_1(f_x, f_y)$ is reduced to a δ-function at the origin of the spectral plane. The term $G_2(f_x, f_y)$ is simply proportional to $\tilde{O}(f_x, f_y)$, but centered at the coordinate point $(f_x, f_y) = (0, \sin\theta/\lambda)$. The spectrum $G_4(f_x, f_y)$ is proportional to the symmetric of $\tilde{O}(f_x, f_y)$, centered at the coordinate point $(f_x, f_y) = (0, -\sin\theta/\lambda)$.

The study in Figure 4.6 shows that $G_3(f_x, f_y)$ and $G_4(f_x, f_y)$ may be isolated from $G_2(f_x, f_y)$ if $\sin\theta/\lambda > 3B$, i.e. $\sin\theta > 3B\lambda$. In other words, the minimum value of the reference angle for which there is a separation is given by:

$$\theta_{min} = \arcsin(3B\lambda) \tag{4.24}$$

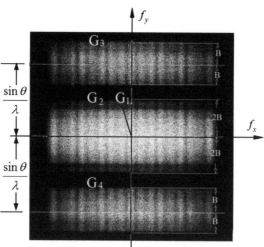

Figure 4.6. *The spectrum of the hologram*

When the reference wave is more intense than the object wave, i.e. $R_0 \gg O_0$, this condition may be somewhat relaxed. The order of magnitude of the amplitude of $G_2(f_x,f_y)$ is less than that of $G_1(f_x,f_y)$, $G_3(f_x,f_y)$, and $G_4(f_x,f_y)$. In this case, $G_2(f_x,f_y)$ may be neglected, and the minimum reference angle is that which separates $G_3(f_x,f_y)$ and $G_4(f_x,f_y)$, i.e.

$$\theta_{min} = \arcsin(B\lambda) \qquad [4.25]$$

4.1.2.2. The case where the reference wave is no longer planar

Let us consider the reference wave:

$$R(x,y) = r(x,y)\exp[jk\varphi_r(x,y)] \qquad [4.26]$$

where $r(x,y)$ is a function that varies slowly with coordinates (x,y) and $\varphi_r(x,y)$ is a non-plane wavefront. The phase may be developed as:

$$\varphi_r(x,y) = a_1 x + b_1 y + \psi_r(x,y) \qquad [4.27a]$$

with:

$$\psi_r(x,y) = a_0 + a_2 x^2 + b_2 y^2 + c_2 xy + \cdots \qquad [4.27b]$$

with a_0, a_1, b_2, c_2, etc., being the real constants.

The intensity distribution in the recording plane of the hologram becomes:

$$
\begin{aligned}
I_H(x,y) &= O_0^2(x,y) + r^2(x,y) \\
&+ O_0(x,y)r(x,y)\exp[jk(\phi_0(x,y) - \psi_r(x,y))]\exp[-jk(a_1 x + b_1 y)] \\
&+ O_0(x,y)r(x,y)\exp[-jk(\phi_0(x,y) - \psi_r(x,y))]\exp[jk(a_1 x + b_1 y)]
\end{aligned}
\qquad [4.28]
$$

We have:

$$[4.29]$$

$$F\{\exp[\mp jk(a_1 x + b_1 y)]\} = \delta\left(f_x \pm \frac{a_1}{\lambda}, f_y \pm \frac{b_1}{\lambda}\right)$$

Taking the Fourier transform of [4.28] and using the convolution property of the δ-function, we then have:

$$F\{I_H(x,y)\} = G_0(f_x,f_y) + G_1\left(f_x + \frac{a_1}{\lambda}, f_y + \frac{b_1}{\lambda}\right) + G_1^*\left(f_x - \frac{a_1}{\lambda}, f_y - \frac{b_1}{\lambda}\right) \qquad [4.30]$$

with

$$G_0(f_x, f_y) = F\{O_0^2(x, y) + r^2(x, y)\}$$
$$= F\{O_0^2(x, y)\} + F\{r^2(x, y)\}$$

[4.31]

and

$$G_1(f_x, f_y) = F\{O_0(x, y)r(x, y)\exp[jk(\phi_0(x, y) - \psi_r(x, y))]\}$$
$$= F\{O_0(x, y)\exp[jk\phi_0(x, y)]\} * F\{r(x, y)\exp[-jk\psi_r(x, y)]\}$$

[4.32]

Let us first examine the term $G_0(f_x, f_y)$. Since $F\{O_0^2(x, y)\} = \tilde{o}(f_x, f_y) \otimes \tilde{o}^*(f_x, f_y)$, the maximum of the spectrum will be less than $2B$, supposing that the spectrum $\tilde{o}^*(f_x, f_y)$ does not have any frequency components greater than B. Furthermore, since $r(x, y)$ is a function that varies slowly with the coordinates (x, y), the distribution of the spectrum of the term $F\{r^2(x, y)\}$ will be localized at the center of the spectrum. Consequently, the maximum of the spectrum of $G_0(f_x, f_y)$ will be less than $2B$.

For the term $G_1(f_x, f_y)$: considering that the spectrum $F\{r(x, y)\exp(-jk\psi_r(x, y))\}$ has no frequency component greater than B_r, according to the correlation property, the maximum frequency of the spectrum of $G_1(f_x, f_y)$ will be $B + B_r$.

Consequently, using a similar analysis, if the reconstruction wave is plane and propagates along the axis of the hologram, then $|a_1/\lambda|$ and $|b_1/\lambda|$ must be greater than $3B + B_r$, i.e.

$$|a_1|, |b_1| > 3B\lambda + B_r\lambda$$

[4.33]

Under this condition, the three diffracted waves emerging from the hologram may be separated from each other.

As an example, let us consider a spherical reference wave coming from the point with coordinates $(\xi, \eta, -z_r)$:

$$R(x, y) = R_0 \exp\left\{ j\frac{k}{2z_r}\left[(x - \xi)^2 + (y - \eta)^2 \right] \right\}$$
$$= R_0 \exp\left\{ j\frac{k}{2z_r}\left[x^2 + y^2 - 2\xi x - 2\eta y + \xi^2 + \eta^2 \right] \right\}$$

[4.34]

Relation [4.33] can then be rewritten as:

$$\left|\frac{\xi}{z_r}\right|, \left|\frac{\eta}{z_r}\right| > 3B\lambda + B_r\lambda \qquad\qquad [4.35]$$

Note that if the reference wave is spherical, the position of the reconstructed images will vary in size and position [GOO 05]. We may equally use a spherical wave of a different wavelength to reconstruct the image with an adjustable magnification [GOO 05].

4.2. Partially coherent light and its use in holography

Let us consider the previous results: an analysis of the intensity distribution of the interference between the object and reference waves contains the key information. Considering the light from a point source to be totally coherent and monochromatic, we have presented the basic principle of optical holography. However, ideal point sources and monochromatic light do not exist in practice. Even laser beams are only quasi-monochromatic sources and partially coherent. The initial hypothesis therefore brings us to an approximate theoretical analysis. To determine the feasibility and limits of this hypothesis, this section studies the interference between partially coherent waves in detail, considering a source of some spatial extent. The results will be useful in practice for the design of a holographic setup.

4.2.1. *Analytic signal describing a non-monochromatic wave*

Using the complex amplitude description of optical waves, we introduce a theoretical approach describing a non-monochromatic wave [CHE 02, GOO 05].

4.2.1.1. *Analytic signal describing a monochromatic wave*

Let us consider a set of reference axis *o-xyz*; an optical vibration $u^r(P,t)$ at the point $P(x,y,z)$ at time t may be described by [GOO 05]:

$$u^r(P,t) = A\cos\big(\phi(P) - 2\pi v_0 t\big) \qquad\qquad [4.36]$$

where A is the amplitude, v_0 the frequency, and $\phi(P)$ the initial phase. The vibration may be described by a complex function given by:

$$u(P,t) = A\exp\big[-j\big(2\pi v_0 t - \phi(P)\big)\big] \qquad\qquad [4.37]$$

This expression constitutes the analytic signal of the monochromatic wave, whose real part $\text{Re}[u(P,t)]$ is the original real signal $u^r(P,t)$ and the complex amplitude is $A\exp[j\phi(P)]$. Using Euler's formula, expression [4.36] can be rewritten as:

$$u^r(P,t) = \frac{1}{2} A\{\exp[j(2\pi v_0 t - \phi(P))] + \exp[-j(2\pi v_0 t - \phi(P))]\} \tag{4.38}$$

Carrying out the Fourier transform of this expression with respect to t, we obtain the spectrum of this signal:

$$\tilde{u}^r(P,v) = \frac{1}{2} A[\exp(-j\phi(P))\delta(v + v_0) + \exp(j\phi(P))\delta(v - v_0)] \tag{4.39}$$

In the same manner, after taking the Fourier transform of [4.37] with respect to t, we then have the spectrum of the analytic signal:

$$\tilde{U}(P,v) = A\exp(j\phi(P))\delta(v - v_0) \tag{4.40}$$

Examination of the previous two relations shows that by suppressing the negative-frequency part of $\tilde{u}^r(P,v)$ and doubling the amplitude of the rest, we will obtain $\tilde{U}(P,v)$. Since the inverse Fourier transform of $\tilde{U}(P,v)$ is the analytic signal of the monochromatic wave, this approach will help in the establishment of the analytic signal of a non-monochromatic wave.

4.2.1.2. Analytic signal describing a non-monochromatic wave

Let $u^r(P,t)$ be a real non-monochromatic signal. Its Fourier transform with respect to t is:

$$\tilde{u}^r(P,v) = \int_{-\infty}^{\infty} u^r(P,t)\exp(-j2\pi vt)dt \tag{4.41}$$

From the reasoning that led to the analytic signal of a monochromatic wave, to obtain the description of the non-monochromatic wave, we must suppress the negative-frequency part of $\tilde{u}^r(P,v)$ and double the rest. Taking into account the fact that the frequency component for $v = 0$ must not be doubled, the analytic signal of a non-monochromatic wave is then expressed by:

$$u(P,t) = \int_{-\infty}^{\infty} [1 + \text{sgn}(v)]\tilde{u}^r(P,v)\exp(j2\pi vt)dv \tag{4.42}$$

with the "sign" function, defined in Chapter 1 as:

$$\text{sgn}(v) = \begin{cases} +1 & v > 0 \\ 0 & v = 0 \\ -1 & v < 0 \end{cases} \qquad [4.43]$$

From this result, we will now study the analytic signal of a laser beam.

4.2.1.3. Analytic signal and spectrum of a laser wave

A laser wave is the sum of electromagnetic radiation coming from various elementary sources constituting the gain medium (atoms and molecules) [TAR 85]. As the radiation from an elementary source may be considered as a monochromatic wave train having a duration τ_c and an initial random phase, the optical vibration $u^r(P,t)$ at the point $P(x,y,z)$ may be represented by:

$$u^r(P,t) = A\cos(\phi(P) - 2\pi v_0 t)\text{rect}\left(\frac{t}{\tau_c}\right) \qquad [4.44]$$

The analytic signal of the monochromatic wave train is therefore given by:

$$u(P,t) = A\exp[-j(2\pi v_0 t - \phi(P))]\text{rect}\left(\frac{t}{\tau_c}\right) \qquad [4.45]$$

whose real part $\text{Re}[u(P,t)]$ is the initial signal $u^r(P,t)$. Using Euler's formula, expression [4.44] may be rewritten as:

$$u^r(P,t) = \frac{1}{2}A\{\exp[j(2\pi v_0 t - \phi(P))] + \exp[-j(2\pi v_0 t - \phi(P))]\}\text{rect}\left(\frac{t}{\tau_c}\right) \qquad [4.46]$$

The Fourier transform (with respect to time t) of this relation gives:

$$\tilde{u}^r(P,v) = \frac{1}{2}A[\exp(-j\phi(P))\delta(v + v_0) + \exp(j\phi(P))\delta(v - v_0)] * \tau_c \text{sinc}(v\tau_c) \qquad [4.47]$$

Suppressing the negative-frequency part and doubling the positive-frequency part, we obtain the spectrum of the wave train:

$$\tilde{U}(P,v) = A\tau_c \exp[j\phi(P)]\text{sinc}[\tau_c(v - v_0)] \qquad [4.48]$$

This shows that the laser beam is not a monochromatic wave. From the characteristics of the "sinc" function, the distribution of the spectrum of a laser of frequency v_0 possesses a maximum at the point v_0 and the first two zeros are found at the coordinates $v_0 - 1/\tau_c$ and $v_0 + 1/\tau_c$ (see Figure 4.7).

Since most of the energy of the spectrum is kept in the zone delimited by $v_0 \pm 1/\tau_c$, the spectral bandwidth of the laser is generally considered to be:

$$\Delta v = 1/\tau_c$$

[4.49]

Evidently, if the duration of the train satisfies $\tau_c \to \infty$, the spectral bandwidth of the laser tends to 0, i.e. $\Delta v \to 0$. It is unique in this case that the laser beam may be considered to be an ideal monochromatic wave. As this perfect property does not exist in practice, the time τ_c is called the "coherence time" [GOO 05].

Let c be the speed of light. The width of the monochromatic wave train is expressed by:

$$L_c = c\tau_c$$

[4.50]

In general, L_c is called the coherence length.

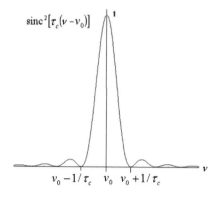

Figure 4.7. *Intensity distribution of the laser spectrum*

Taking into account the fact that the frequency of the wave is $v = c/\lambda$ and that $\Delta v = c\Delta\lambda/\lambda^2$, by substitution into [4.49] we obtain another well-known expression of the coherence length [GOO 05]:

$$L_c = \frac{\lambda^2}{\Delta\lambda}$$

[4.51]

For example, for a ruby laser, $\lambda = 0.6943$ µm, $\Delta\lambda = 0.5 \times 10^{-8}$ mm, we have $L_c \approx 10$ mm.

4.2.2. *Recording a hologram with non-monochromatic light*

As previously discussed, point sources and monochromatic waves do not exist in practice. The use of a non-monochromatic source requires the knowledge of the limiting conditions to be satisfied.

Figure 4.8 shows a classic Young's experiment where the two small circular apertures P_0, P_1 on screen A are illuminated by a non-monochromatic line source S_0–S_1. If the point P_0 is considered as an object point and the wave coming from P_1 is considered as the reference wave, we can record the Leith–Upatnieks hologram on screen H. Since the wave diffused or transmitted by a real object may always be considered as the sum of the waves coming from point sources situated at the surface of the object, we may generalize the result for the study.

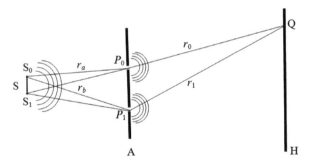

Figure 4.8. *A classic Young's experiment using a non-monochromatic line source*

Let us consider Q to be the observation point and r_0 the distance between P_0 and Q. If the analytic signals at the two points P_0 and P_1 are expressed by $u(P_0,t)$ and $u(P_1,t)$, respectively, according to the linear superposition principle, the analytic signal of the wave at the point Q is then expressed by:

$$U(Q,t) = K_0 u(P_0, t - t_0) + K_1 u(P_1, t - t_1)$$

[4.52]

where $t_0 = r_0/c$ and $t_1 = r_1/c$ (c is the propagation speed), and K_0 and K_1 are propagation coefficients that are inversely proportional to r_0 and r_1, respectively. Since the exposure time of a hologram is much longer than the coherence time, the light intensity at the point Q is an average response for the duration of the recording [GOO 05], i.e.

$$I(Q) = \langle U(Q,t)U^*(Q,t)\rangle \qquad [4.53]$$

Substituting [4.52] into [4.53], we have:

$$I(Q) = K_0^2 \langle u(P_0,t-t_0)u^*(P_0,t-t_0)\rangle + K_1^2 \langle u(P_1,t-t_1)u^*(P_1,t-t_1)\rangle +$$
$$K_0 K_1 \langle u(P_0,t-t_0)u^*(P_1,t-t_1)\rangle + K_0 K_1 \langle u^*(P_0,t-t_0)u(P_1,t-t_1)\rangle \qquad [4.54]$$

In practice, we may consider the wave field to be stationary [LAU 10, GOO 05]. In this case, supposing:

$$\tau = t_1 - t_0 = (r_1 - r_0)/c \qquad [4.55]$$

we may define the coherence function $\Gamma_{01}(\tau)$ as:

$$\Gamma_{01}(\tau) = \langle u(P_0,t-t_0)u^*(P_1,t-t_1)\rangle = \langle u(P_0,t+\tau)u^*(P_1,t)\rangle \qquad [4.56]$$

$$\Gamma_{01}^*(\tau) = \langle u^*(P_0,t-t_0)u(P_1,t-t_1)\rangle = \langle u(P_0,t+\tau)u^*(P_1,t)\rangle^* \qquad [4.57]$$

In the same manner, the complex coherence function at P_0 may be written as:

$$\langle u(P_0,t+\tau)u^*(P_0,t)\rangle = \Gamma_{00}(\tau) \qquad [4.58]$$

The coherence function at P_1 is then given by:

$$\langle u(P_1,t+\tau)u^*(P_1,t)\rangle = \Gamma_{11}(\tau) \qquad [4.59]$$

When $\tau = 0$, the last two expressions become:

$$\langle u(P_0,t-t_0)u^*(P_0,t-t_0)\rangle = \langle u(P_0,t)u^*(P_0,t)\rangle = \Gamma_{00}(0) \qquad [4.60]$$

$$\langle u(P_1,t-t_1)u^*(P_1,t-t_1)\rangle = \langle u(P_1,t)u^*(P_1,t)\rangle = \Gamma_{11}(0) \qquad [4.61]$$

These are the respective intensities of the field at the two points P_0 and P_1. The intensity at the point Q of the waves coming from P_0 and P_1 may be rewritten as:

$$I_0(Q) = K_0^2 \Gamma_{00}(0) \tag{4.62}$$

$$I_0(Q) = K_0^2 \Gamma_{00}(0) \tag{4.63}$$

respectively. Using the previous definitions, [4.54] is finally rewritten as:

$$\begin{aligned} I(Q) &= I_0(Q) + I_1(Q) + K_0 K_1 \left[\Gamma_{01}(\tau) + \Gamma_{01}^*(\tau) \right] \\ &= I_0(Q) + I_1(Q) + 2 K_0 K_1 \, \mathrm{Re}\left[\Gamma_{01}(\tau) \right] \end{aligned} \tag{4.64}$$

If we define the complex degree of coherence by [GOO 05]:

$$\gamma_{01}(\tau) = \frac{\Gamma_{01}(\tau)}{\left[\Gamma_{00}(0) \Gamma_{11}(0) \right]^{1/2}} \tag{4.65}$$

and knowing the following inequality to be proven by [LAU 10]:

$$\left| \Gamma_{01}(\tau) \right| \leq \left[\Gamma_{00}(0) \Gamma_{11}(0) \right]^{1/2} \tag{4.66}$$

we have $|\gamma_{01}(\tau)| \leq 1$. Relation [4.64] may be rewritten again in the form:

$$I(Q) = I_0(Q) + I_1(Q) + 2\sqrt{I_0(Q) I_1(Q)} \, \mathrm{Re}\left[\gamma_{01}(\tau) \right] \tag{4.67}$$

The value of the degree of coherence distinguishes the following different cases:

$-|\gamma_{01}(\tau)| = 1$: total coherence. The two waves coming from P_0 and P_1 are totally coherent at Q.

$-|\gamma_{01}(\tau)| = 0$: total incoherence. The two waves coming from P_0 and P_1 are totally incoherent at Q.

$-0 < |\gamma_{01}(\tau)| < 1$: partial coherence. The two waves coming from P_0 and P_1 are partially coherent at Q.

The contrast of the fringes in the hologram depends on the maximum and minimum intensities I_{max} and I_{min}. We have:

$$C = \frac{I_{max} - I_{min}}{I_{max} + I_{min}} \tag{4.68}$$

from which

$$I_{\max} = I_0(Q) + I_1(Q) + 2\sqrt{I_0(Q)I_1(Q)}|\gamma_{01}(\tau)| \qquad [4.69]$$

$$I_{\min} = I_0(Q) + I_1(Q) - 2\sqrt{I_0(Q)I_1(Q)}|\gamma_{01}(\tau)| \qquad [4.70]$$

The contrast is then expressed by:

$$C = \frac{2\sqrt{I_0(Q)I_1(Q)}}{I_0(Q) + I_1(Q)}|\gamma_{01}(\tau)| = \frac{2K_0K_1}{K_0^2 + K_1^2}|\gamma_{01}(\tau)| \qquad [4.71]$$

The contrast is therefore a function of $|\gamma_{01}(\tau)|$ and when $K_1 = K_0$ (identical intensities at Q), we have maximum contrast $C_{\max} = |\gamma_{01}(\tau)|$.

4.2.3. Total coherence approximation conditions

4.2.3.1. Identical wave train model

According to [TAR 85], a laser beam is the sum of electromagnetic radiation coming from multiple independent elementary sources (excited atoms or molecules). To approximate this phenomenon, we may use a simple model such as that shown in Figure 4.9.

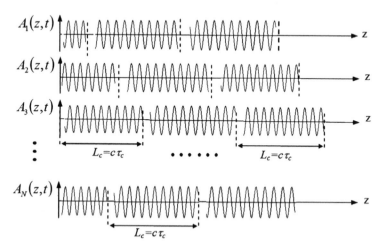

Figure 4.9. *Model of identical wave trains*

In this model, we will consider N elementary sources, with $A_n(z,t)$ the amplitude distribution along the z-axis at time t of the nth elementary source. We again suppose each wave train to have the same width τ_c, frequency, amplitude, and polarization. In reality, there exists a small constant interval between consecutive trains, which is due to the excitation time of the atom or molecule, in which the latter jumps from a lower to a higher energy level. We will assume that this interval is small enough that we may consider each elementary source to consecutively emit wave trains of identical wavelength, whose initial phase is random in $[0,2\pi]$.

4.2.3.2. Temporal coherence of a source emitting identical wave trains

To simplify, we will first consider each source illuminating screen A in Figure 4.8 to be a quasi-point source S_0 situated above source S, and whose emissions are modeled by identical wave trains. The result will be used to generalize in the case of a source of some spatial extent. We consider r_a to be the distance between S_0 and P_0 and r_b to be the distance between S_0 and P_1. The analytic signal of the point Q formed by the sum of N wave trains passing through the hole P_0 can be expressed by:

$$\sum_{m=1}^{N} K_0 U_m(t) = K_0 \sum_{m=1}^{N} u_m \exp(-j2\pi vt)\exp[j\phi_m(t)] = K_0 U(t) \qquad [4.72]$$

where the coefficient K_0 is inversely proportional to $(r_a + r_0)$.

Similarly, the analytic signal of the point Q formed by the sum of N wave trains passing through the hole P_1 can be expressed by:

$$\sum_{n=1}^{N} K_1 U_n(t + \tau) \qquad [4.73]$$

$$= K_1 \sum_{n=1}^{N} u_n \exp[-j2\pi v(t + \tau)]\exp[j\phi_n(t + \tau)] = K_1 U(t + \tau)$$

with coefficient K_0 inversely proportional to $(r_b + r_1)$ and

$$\tau = \frac{(r_b + r_1) - (r_a + r_0)}{c} \qquad [4.74]$$

The analytic signal at the point Q is the sum of these two signals, i.e.

$$U_Q = K_1 U(t + \tau) + K_0 U(t) \qquad [4.75]$$

Note that the amplitudes of the trains are identical. The complex coherence function of source S_0 is therefore:

$$\Gamma_{01}(\tau) = \langle U(t+\tau)U^*(t)\rangle$$
$$= \exp(-j2\pi\nu\tau)\left\langle \sum_{n=1}^{N}\sum_{m=1}^{N} u_n u_m^* \exp\{j[\phi_n(t+\tau)-\phi_m(t)]\}\right\rangle \qquad [4.76]$$

Splitting this expression into two parts corresponding to the cases $m = n$ and $m \neq n$, we have:

$$\Gamma_{01}(\tau) = \exp(-j2\pi\nu\tau)\left\langle \sum_{n=1}^{N}|u_n|^2 \exp\{j[\phi_n(t+\tau)-\phi_n(t)]\} + (\text{cross terms})\right\rangle \qquad [4.77]$$

with

$$(\text{cross terms}) = \sum_{\substack{n=1 \\ }}^{N}\sum_{\substack{m=1 \\ (m\neq n)}}^{N} u_n u_m^* \exp\{j[\phi_n(t+\tau)-\phi_m(t)]\} \qquad [4.78]$$

The "cross terms" correspond to the case $m \neq n$. Since the initial phase of each wave train has a random value between 0 and 2π, the phase offset between different wave trains $\phi_n(t+\tau)-\phi_m(t)$ will be a random value. Consequently, we have:

$$\langle\text{cross terms}\rangle = \left\langle \sum_{\substack{n=1 \\ }}^{N}\sum_{\substack{m=1 \\ (m\neq n)}}^{N}|u_m|^2 \exp\{j[\phi_n(t+\tau)-\phi_m(t)]\}\right\rangle = 0 \qquad [4.79]$$

Let us now examine the first term of expression [4.77] corresponding to the case $m = n$. Within the sum symbol, each term is a product of two analytic signals of the nth wave train: the analytic signal and its conjugate with a time shift τ. These two signals are two components of the same electromagnetic radiation from an elementary source. Therefore, if the measurement time t satisfies $0 \leq t \leq \tau$, when the wave train of the nth source taking the path S_0-P_0-Q has arrived at Q, the other wave train taking the path S_0-P_1-Q is retarded. The retarded wave train is that emitted previously by the same elementary source. In this case, there is a phase difference of $[\phi_n(t+\tau)-\phi_n(t)]=\Delta\phi_n$. However, if $\tau \leq t \leq \tau_c$, then the two wave trains are two components of the same electromagnetic radiation from the same elementary source. In this case, their initial phases are identical, i.e. $\phi_n(t+\tau)-\phi_n(t)=0$.

Consequently, when the measurement time satisfies $0 \le t \le \tau_c$, then the phase difference is expressed by:

$$\phi_n(t+\tau)-\phi_n(t) = \begin{cases} \Delta\phi_n & 0 \le t < \tau \\ 0 & \tau \le t < \tau_c \end{cases} \qquad [4.80]$$

The average of the complex exponential in [4.77] over the interval $0 \le t \le \tau_c$ can therefore be calculated as:

$$\frac{1}{\tau_c}\int_0^{\tau_c}\exp\{j[\phi_n(t+\tau)-\phi_n(t)]\}dt = \frac{1}{\tau_c}\left[\int_0^{\tau}\exp(j\Delta\phi_n)dt + \int_{\tau}^{\tau_c}dt\right]$$

$$= \frac{\tau}{\tau_c}\exp(j\Delta\phi_n)+1-\frac{\tau}{\tau_c} \qquad [4.81]$$

The initial phases of two neighboring wave trains emitted by the same elementary source are random. If the average is calculated over a sufficiently long time, then we will have $\langle\exp(j\Delta\phi_n)\rangle = 0$. We therefore obtain:

$$\langle\exp\{j[\phi_n(t+\tau)-\phi_n(t)]\}\rangle = 1-(\tau/\tau_c) \qquad [4.82]$$

Thus, we have:

$$\left\langle\sum_{n=1}^{N}|u_n|^2\exp\{j[\phi_n(t+\tau)-\phi_n(t)]\}\right\rangle = \sum_{n=1}^{N}|u_n|^2\left(1-\frac{\tau}{\tau_c}\right) = I_0\left(1-\frac{\tau}{\tau_c}\right) \qquad [4.83]$$

In this relation, I_0 is the total intensity of the source S_0, i.e.

$$I_0 = \sum_{n=1}^{N}|u_n|^2 = N|u_0|^2 \qquad [4.84]$$

The complex coherence function of source S_0 (relation [4.77]) may be simplified as:

$$\Gamma_{01}(\tau) = I_0\exp(-j2\pi\nu\tau)[1-(\tau/\tau_c)] \qquad [4.85]$$

We note that if $\tau < 0$, we must consider the value $-\tau$. Relation [4.85] is finally written as:

$$\Gamma_{01}(\tau) = I_0\exp(-j2\pi\nu\tau)[1-(|\tau|/\tau_c)]$$

$$= I_0\exp(-j2\pi\nu\tau)\Lambda(|\tau|/\tau_c) \qquad [4.86]$$

where $\Lambda(x)$ is the triangle function defined as (see Chapter 1):

$$\Lambda\left(|\tau|/\tau_c\right)=\begin{cases}1-|\tau|/\tau_c & |\tau|<\tau_c \\ 0 & |\tau|\geq\tau_c\end{cases} \qquad [4.87]$$

Following the same procedure, it may be shown that $\Gamma_{00}(\tau)=\Gamma_{11}(\tau)=\Gamma_{01}(\tau)$. The complex degree of coherence is then given by:

$$\gamma_{01}(\tau)=\frac{\Gamma_{01}(\tau)}{\left[\Gamma_{00}(0)\Gamma_{01}(0)\right]^{1/2}}=\exp(-j2\pi v\tau)\Lambda\left(\frac{|\tau|}{\tau_c}\right) \qquad [4.88]$$

Let us consider relation [4.67], which expresses the intensity at the point Q. We must again find the two terms $I_0(Q)$ and $I_1(Q)$. Since $\Gamma_{00}(\tau)=\Gamma_{11}(\tau)=\Gamma_{01}(\tau)$, we are led to:

$$I_0(Q)=K_0^2\Gamma_{00}(0)=K_0^2 N|u_0|^2$$

$$I_1(Q)=K_1^2\Gamma_{11}(0)=K_1^2 N|u_0|^2 \qquad [4.89]$$

Substituting [4.88] and these two relations into [4.67], we have:

$$I(Q)=K_0^2 N|u_0|^2+K_1^2 N|u_0|^2+2K_0 K_1 N|u_0|^2\cos(2\pi v\tau)\Lambda\left(\frac{\tau}{\tau_c}\right) \qquad [4.90]$$

From [4.68], the contrast of the interference fringes is therefore:

$$C=\frac{2|K_0 K_1|}{K_0^2+K_1^2}\Lambda\left(\frac{\tau}{\tau_c}\right) \qquad [4.91]$$

As an example, Figure 4.10 shows the evolution of $I(Q)$ for two values of the ratio between K_0 and K_1. The curves show that the contrast is diminished with the increase in time τ. Moreover, τ is proportional to the optical path length difference between the two optical routes $|(r_b+r_1)-(r_a+r_0)|$. Thus, to ensure the best contrast in the interference pattern encoding the hologram, the difference of the two optical paths must be as small as possible. We also note that the greater the time τ_c of an optical wave train, the better the coherence.

The previous studies are based on the model of identical wave trains. Experimental results have shown the adequacy of the model [XIO 09]. To record a hologram, we must limit the difference in optical path length between the object and reference waves, such that they are less than the coherence length $L_c = c\tau_c$. Taking into account the fact that the coherence length of the different laser sources available on the market is generally not infinitely large (from centimeters for a laser diode to several meters for a single longitudinal mode diode-pumped solid-state laser), good regulation of the holographic setup is preferable for the obtainment of nearly identical optical paths for the object and reference waves.

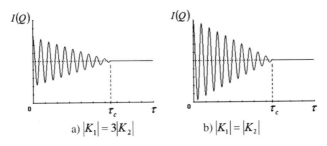

Figure 4.10. *Curves of I(Q) for the identical wave train model*

We recall the previous results: considering the light coming from a quasi-point source, we have determined the limiting conditions allowing the recording of a high-contrast hologram. Nevertheless, the cross section of a laser always has a certain extent (the size of the beam waist, for example). To analyze the influence of the width of the source, we may consider that a source with some spatial extent is the sum of point sources situated in different points on the surface of the source. In this case, supposing the intensity at the point Q to be the sum of all the intensities of the elementary sources, it can be shown that this factor will also diminish the contrast of the interference fringes [GOO 05]. The direct consequence of this is that we must use a source that is as point-like as possible [SMI 94]. In practice, we use a "spatial filter" consisting of a microscope lens focusing the laser beam onto a microscopic diaphragm situated in the focal plane. Since the intensity distribution in the focal plane is related to the Fourier transform of the beam, the small aperture consisting of the hole, filters the smallest spatial frequency component. Thus, having filtered the laser beam, we will obtain a spherical wave coming from the focal point whose amplitude distribution will be relatively homogeneous.

4.2.4. *Recording a Fresnel hologram*

From the studies in the previous section, and according to the Leith–Upatnieks concept, Figure 4.11 shows a setup for recording a Fresnel hologram.

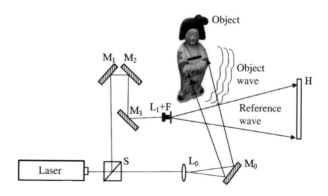

Figure 4.11. *Recording setup for a Fresnel hologram*

The object is a figurine and the laser is separated into two parts by the beam splitter S. One part of the emergent wave, having crossed the lens L_0, is reflected by the mirror M_0, and illuminates the figurine. The wave diffused by the figuring constitutes the object wave. The part of the beam reflected by the splitter S will be reflected successively by mirrors M_1, M_2, and M_3, and focused by the microscope lens L_1. After filtering with the spatial filter F, we obtain a spherical reference wave. In this setup, M_1 and M_2 constitute an optical path compensator. To ensure good coherence between the object and reference waves, the optical path can be adjusted by vertically displacing the position of the compensator.

To reconstruct the images, the hologram can be illuminated by different reconstruction waves, as discussed earlier. For example, if a replica of the original reference wave illuminates the hologram as indicated in Figure 4.12, the two reconstructed images are symmetric relative to the hologram plane.

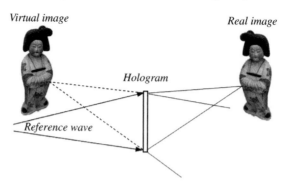

Figure 4.12. *Reconstruction of the images by diffraction of the reference wave*

The transformation of the object amplitude to the reconstructed wave amplitude is still a linear operation. The wave diffused by the surface of the object can still be represented by the sum of point sources situated at its surface. Fundamentally, the properties of the object image may be obtained by studying the image given by a point source. Thus, considering a spherical reference wave, in the following section, we will study the properties of images of a point source reconstructed by illuminating the hologram according to different possibilities [GOO 05].

4.3. Study of the Fresnel hologram of point source

Let us consider a set of reference axis o-xyz and the recording setup shown in Figure 4.13. The plane $z = 0$ represents the plane of the photosensitive material H. A point source P_0 with coordinates $(x_0, y_0, -z_0)$ emits an object wave and a spherical reference wave is coming from the point $P_r(x_r, y_r, -z_r)$. The point P_B with coordinates $(x_B, y_B, -z_B)$ is the location of the source used for the reconstruction. Using a parabolic approximation of the spherical wave, the object and reference waves in the plane H are, respectively, expressed by:

$$u_0(x, y) = A_0' \exp\left\{ j \frac{k}{2z_0} \left[(x - x_0)^2 + (y - y_0)^2 \right] \right\}$$

[4.92]

and

$$u_r(x, y) = A_r' \exp\left\{ j \frac{k}{2z_r} \left[(x - x_r)^2 + (y - y_r)^2 \right] \right\}$$

[4.93]

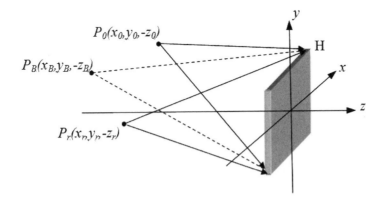

Figure 4.13. *Schematic diagram for recording the hologram of a point source*

Let us consider the following complex coefficients:

$$A_0 = A'_0 \exp\left[\frac{jk}{2z_0}(x_0^2 + y_0^2)\right]$$

$$A_r = A'_r \exp\left[\frac{jk}{2z_r}(x_r^2 + y_r^2)\right] \tag{4.94}$$

Equations [4.92] and [4.93] may be rewritten as:

$$u_0(x,y) = A_0 \exp\left[\frac{jk}{2z_0}(x^2 + y^2)\right]\exp\left[-jk\left(\frac{x_0}{z_0}x + \frac{y_0}{z_0}y\right)\right]$$

$$u_r(x,y) = A_r \exp\left[\frac{jk}{2z_r}(x^2 + y^2)\right]\exp\left[-jk\left(\frac{x_r}{z_r}x + \frac{y_r}{z_r}y\right)\right] \tag{4.95}$$

The transmittance of the hologram is given by:

$$t_A = t_0 + \beta I = t_b + \beta|u_0|^2 + \beta u_0 u_r^* + \beta u_0^* u_r \tag{4.96}$$

Using these relations, the reconstruction of images using different types of hologram illumination is studied in the following section.

4.3.1. Reconstructing the hologram of a point source

4.3.1.1. Hologram illuminated by a spherical wave with the same wavelength

We consider a spherical reconstruction wave coming from the point P_B. Taking into account the previous discussion, its complex amplitude at the hologram is written as:

$$u_B(x,y) = A_B \exp\left[\frac{jk}{2z_B}(x^2 + y^2)\right]\exp\left[-jk\left(\frac{x_B}{z_B}x + \frac{y_B}{z_B}y\right)\right] \tag{4.97}$$

where A_B is a constant. Illuminating the hologram with this wave, the wave diffracted by transmission is then expressed by:

$$u_B t_A = u_B t_b + u_B \beta|u_0|^2 + u_B \beta u_0 u_r^* + u_B \beta u_0^* u_r$$
$$= u_1 + u_2 + u_3 + u_4 \tag{4.98}$$

Henceforth, we will only be interested in the two transmitted waves u_3 and u_4, which encode the amplitude of the object. The wave u_3 can be developed as:

$$u_3 = u_B \beta u_0 u_r^*$$

$$= A_3 \exp\left[\frac{jk}{2}\left(\frac{1}{z_B} + \frac{1}{z_0} - \frac{1}{z_r}\right)(x^2 + y^2)\right] \times \exp\left\{-jk\left[\left(\frac{x_B}{z_B} + \frac{x_0}{z_0} - \frac{x_r}{z_r}\right)x + \left(\frac{y_B}{z_B} + \frac{y_0}{z_0} - \frac{y_r}{z_r}\right)y\right]\right\}$$

$$= A_3 \exp\left[\frac{jk}{2z_p}(x^2 + y^2)\right] \times \exp\left[-jk\left(\frac{x_p}{z_p}x + \frac{y_p}{z_p}y\right)\right]$$

[4.99]

with

$$A_3 = \beta A_B A_0 A_r^*$$ [4.100]

$$\frac{1}{z_p} = \frac{1}{z_B} + \frac{1}{z_0} - \frac{1}{z_r}$$ [4.101]

$$\frac{x_p}{z_p} = \frac{x_B}{z_B} + \frac{x_0}{z_0} - \frac{x_r}{z_r}$$ [4.102]

$$\frac{y_p}{z_p} = \frac{y_B}{z_B} + \frac{y_0}{z_0} - \frac{y_r}{z_r}$$ [4.103]

Relations [4.101]–[4.103] constitute the conjugation relations of holography. These expressions show that u_3 represents a spherical wave originating at the point P_P with coordinates $(x_p, y_p, -z_p)$. If the reconstruction point source is situated at the same point as the original reference source, i.e. $x_B = x_r$, $y_B = y_r$, and $z_B = z_r$, we then have $x_p = x_0$, $y_p = y_0$, and $z_p = z_0$. That is $P_P(x_p, y_p, -z_p)$ coincides with $P_0(x_0, y_0, -z_0)$. In this case, u_3 reconstructs the wave u_0 coming from the original object point. When $z_p = z_0 > 0$, u_3 is a divergent spherical wave and an observer to the right of the hologram may observe the virtual image situated to the left of the hologram plane. Since this wave is similar to that coming from the original object point, it reconstitutes the initial object wave. Conversely, when $z_p < 0$, u_3 is a convergent wave that forms the real image of the original object point at the point $(x_p, y_p, |z_p|)$.

Following an identical reasoning, the term u_4 can be developed as:

$$u_4 = u_B \beta u_0^* u_r$$

$$= A_4 \exp\left[\frac{jk}{2}\left(\frac{1}{z_B} - \frac{1}{z_0} + \frac{1}{z_r}\right)\left(x^2 + y^2\right)\right] \times \exp\left\{-jk\left[\left(\frac{x_B}{z_B} - \frac{x_0}{z_0} + \frac{x_r}{z_r}\right)x + \left(\frac{y_B}{z_B} - \frac{y_0}{z_0} + \frac{y_r}{z_r}\right)y\right]\right\}$$

$$= A_4 \exp\left[\frac{jk}{2z_c}\left(x^2 + y^2\right)\right] \times \exp\left[jk\left(\frac{x_c}{z_c}x + \frac{y_c}{z_c}y\right)\right]$$

[4.104]

with

$$A_4 = \beta A_B A_0^* A_r$$

[4.105]

Comparing the corresponding factors, we have:

$$\frac{1}{z_c} = \frac{1}{z_B} - \frac{1}{z_0} + \frac{1}{z_r}$$

[4.106]

$$\frac{x_c}{z_c} = \frac{x_B}{z_B} - \frac{x_0}{z_0} + \frac{x_r}{z_r}$$

[4.107]

$$\frac{y_c}{z_c} = \frac{y_B}{z_B} - \frac{y_0}{z_0} + \frac{y_r}{z_r}$$

[4.108]

These results show that the diffracted wave u_4 represents a spherical wave originating in a similar manner from the point $P_C(x_c, y_c, -z_c)$.

If the reconstruction point source is situated at the same point as the original reference source, i.e. $x_B = x_r$, $y_B = y_r$, and $z_B = z_r$, then we have:

$$\frac{1}{z_c} = \frac{2}{z_r} - \frac{1}{z_0} \quad \text{or identically} \quad z_c = \frac{z_0 z_r}{2z_0 - z_r}$$

[4.109]

The wave u_4 is called the conjugate object wave and the image formed is called the conjugate image. Relation [4.109] indicates that if $z_0 > z_r/2$, i.e. $z_c > 0$, u_4 is a divergent wave, and the image is virtual. On the other hand, if $z_0 < z_r/2$, i.e. $z_c < 0$, u_4 is a convergent wave, and the image formed is real.

4.3.1.2. *Hologram illuminated by a spherical wave with a different wavelength*

Let us consider λ_1 to be the wavelength used to record the hologram and λ_2 to be the wavelength of the reconstruction wave. Carrying out similar calculations to those conducted in the previous section, we may establish the conjugation relations describing the coordinates of the image formed by u_3 by diffraction from the hologram [GOO 05]:

$$\frac{1}{z_p} = \frac{1}{z_B} + \mu\left(\frac{1}{z_0} - \frac{1}{z_r}\right) \hspace{3cm} [4.110]$$

$$\frac{x_p}{z_p} = \frac{x_B}{z_B} + \mu\left(\frac{x_0}{z_0} - \frac{x_r}{z_r}\right) \hspace{3cm} [4.111]$$

$$\frac{y_p}{z_p} = \frac{y_B}{z_B} + \mu\left(\frac{y_0}{z_0} - \frac{y_r}{z_r}\right) \hspace{3cm} [4.112]$$

with $\mu = \lambda_2/\lambda_1$.

We can also establish the relations concerning the coordinates of the conjugate image formed by the wave u_4:

$$\frac{1}{z_c} = \frac{1}{z_B} - \mu\left(\frac{1}{z_0} - \frac{1}{z_r}\right) \hspace{3cm} [4.113]$$

$$\frac{x_c}{z_c} = \frac{x_B}{z_B} - \mu\left(\frac{x_0}{z_0} - \frac{x_r}{z_r}\right) \hspace{3cm} [4.114]$$

$$\frac{y_c}{z_c} = \frac{y_B}{z_B} - \mu\left(\frac{y_0}{z_0} - \frac{y_r}{z_r}\right) \hspace{3cm} [4.115]$$

4.3.1.3. *Case where the reference and reconstruction waves are plane waves*

When the reference and reconstruction waves are plane, the discussion may be carried out by considering $z_r \to \infty$ and $z_B \to \infty$ in the relations established previously. If the reconstruction wave has the same wavelength, then [4.101], [4.102] and [4.103] become:

$$\frac{1}{z_p} = \frac{1}{z_0}$$

$$\frac{x_p}{z_p} = \frac{x_0}{z_0}$$

$$\frac{y_p}{z_p} = \frac{y_0}{z_0} \qquad [4.116]$$

Otherwise, if the reconstruction wave no longer has the same wavelength as during the recording of the hologram, [4.113], [4.114] and [4.115] become:

$$\frac{1}{z_p} = \mu \frac{1}{z_0}$$

$$\frac{x_p}{z_p} = \mu \frac{x_0}{z_0}$$

$$\frac{y_p}{z_p} = \mu \frac{y_0}{z_0} \qquad [4.117]$$

4.3.2. Magnifications

4.3.2.1. Transverse magnification of the reconstructed image

The transverse magnification of the reconstructed image may be studied in a similar manner for the x and y directions of the set of reference coordinates. To simplify, we will only consider the x direction. When the x_0 coordinate of the object point changes slightly and the other parameters do not vary, the transverse magnification G_{yp} of the reconstructed image is defined as the ratio of the variation in the image coordinates, x_p, to the variation in the object coordinates, x_0. From the conjugation relation [4.114], the transverse magnification G_{yp} at the point P is given by:

$$G_{yp} = \frac{\partial x_p}{\partial x_0} = \mu \frac{z_p}{z_0} \qquad [4.118]$$

From [4.116], the transverse magnification G_{yc} of the conjugate image is defined by:

$$G_{yc} = \frac{\partial x_c}{\partial x_0} = -\mu \frac{z_c}{z_0} \qquad [4.119]$$

4.3.2.2. *Longitudinal magnification*

When the z_0 coordinate of the object point changes slightly and the other parameters do not vary, the longitudinal magnification G_{zp} of the reconstructed image is defined as the ratio of the variation in the image coordinate z_p, to the variation in the object coordinate, z_0. Carrying out the partial differentiation of [4.110], we obtain:

$$\frac{\Delta z_p}{z_p^2} = \mu \frac{\Delta z_0}{z_0^2} \qquad [4.120]$$

from which we extract the expression for the longitudinal (or axial) magnification:

$$G_{zp} = \frac{\Delta z_p}{\Delta z_0} = \mu \frac{z_p^2}{z_0^2} \qquad [4.121]$$

In a similar way, with [4.110], the longitudinal magnification G_{zc} of the conjugate image is obtained by:

$$G_{zc} = \frac{\Delta z_c}{\Delta z_0} = -\mu \frac{z_c^2}{z_0^2} \qquad [4.122]$$

4.3.3. *Resolution of the reconstructed image*

The resolution of the image reconstructed by diffraction depends on parameters such as the size of reference source used during the recording of the hologram, the size of the reconstruction source, the spectral extent of the light used, and any aberrations in the wavefronts (deviations from a spherical wavefront). This section offers a study of the image resolution, considering there to be no aberrations.

4.3.3.1. *Influence of the size of the illuminating source*

Let us consider a variable x_B. After partial differentiation of [4.102] with respect to x_p, we obtain:

$$\Delta x_p = \frac{z_p}{z_B} \Delta x_B \qquad [4.123]$$

In the same way, from relations [4.103], [4.107] and [4.108] we have:

$$\Delta y_p = \frac{z_p}{z_B} \Delta y_B \qquad [4.124]$$

$$\Delta x_c = \frac{z_c}{z_B} \Delta x_B \qquad\qquad [4.125]$$

$$\Delta y_c = \frac{z_c}{z_B} \Delta y_B \qquad\qquad [4.126]$$

These results indicate that if the hologram of the object point is illuminated by a wave coming from a line source of width $\overline{BB'}$, the image obtained will be of extent $\overline{PP'}$. For the real and virtual images, respectively, we can establish two relations expressing this influence:

$$\overline{PP'} = \frac{z_p}{z_B} \overline{BB'} \qquad\qquad [4.127]$$

$$\overline{PP'} = \frac{z_c}{z_B} \overline{BB'} \qquad\qquad [4.128]$$

We suppose that the wave diffused by an object may still be considered as the sum of multiple point sources. The magnification of the image brings about a superposition of neighboring images, one on top of the other, and therefore diminishes the clarity of the image. To assure the quality of the restored image, the value of $\overline{PP'}$ must be less than a certain minimum value. However, according to [4.127] and [4.128], for a given $\overline{PP'}$, if z_p tends to zero, $\overline{BB'}$ must be large. Consequently, so as to guarantee the clarity of the reconstructed image, when recording the hologram, the object must be placed at the smallest possible distance from the photosensitive support. Under this condition, we may use a source of some spatial extent to reconstruct clear images. In practice, to decrease the distance z_p, we can make the image of the object on the photosensitive support with a lens, or with a reconstruction of the real image of the hologram.

4.3.3.2. Influence of the spectral width of the light source

If the source is not monochromatic, the image of each point source constituting the surface of the object will be slightly spread out and the object image will become blurred. This phenomenon is known by the name of chromatic aberration or chromatic distortion. Chromatic aberration can be classified by considering the transverse and the longitudinal aberrations.

Let us consider λ_2 and $\Delta\lambda$ to be the reconstruction wavelength and spectral width of the source, respectively. Relation [4.114] can also be written in the form:

$$x_p = \frac{x_B}{z_B} z_p + \frac{\lambda_2}{\lambda_1}\left(\frac{x_0}{z_0} - \frac{x_r}{z_r}\right)z_p \qquad\qquad [4.129]$$

Note that z_p is also a function of the wavelength. Calculating the differential Δx_p, we obtain the transverse chromatic aberration in the x dimension:

$$\Delta x_p = \frac{x_B}{z_B}\Delta z_p + \frac{\Delta\lambda}{\lambda_1}\left(\frac{x_0}{z_0} - \frac{x_r}{z_r}\right)z_p + \frac{\lambda_2}{\lambda_1}\left(\frac{x_0}{z_0} - \frac{x_r}{z_r}\right)\Delta z_p \qquad [4.130]$$

In the same manner, we find the differential Δy_p of relation [4.115]. The transverse chromatic aberration in the y dimension is:

$$\Delta y_p = \frac{y_B}{z_B}\Delta z_p + \frac{\Delta\lambda}{\lambda_1}\left(\frac{y_0}{z_0} - \frac{y_r}{z_r}\right)z_p + \frac{\lambda_2}{\lambda_1}\left(\frac{y_0}{z_0} - \frac{y_r}{z_r}\right)\Delta z_p \qquad [4.131]$$

To calculate the two previous expressions, it is necessary to know the longitudinal chromatic aberration Δz_p. From [4.116], we perform the differential Δz_p and obtain:

$$\Delta z_p = -\frac{\Delta\lambda}{\lambda_1}\left(\frac{1}{z_0} - \frac{1}{z_r}\right)z_p^2 \qquad [4.132]$$

We have established the relations giving the transverse and longitudinal chromatic aberrations. Analysis of these results shows that if $z_0 \rightarrow 0$, then we have $z_p \rightarrow 0$ for the coordinate of the reconstructed image. Having examined relations [4.129], [4.130] and [4.131], we have $\Delta x_p \rightarrow 0$, $\Delta y_p \rightarrow 0$, and $\Delta z_p \rightarrow 0$. This means that the transverse and longitudinal chromatic aberrations will be very small, and we may use natural "white" light to reconstruct a clear image of the object. A practical example will be discussed at the end of the following section (see Figure 4.20).

4.4. Different types of hologram

In general practice, a hologram is recorded using the Fresnel configuration. Nevertheless, there exist other recording configurations, each having a different name. The following sections will give details of these different configurations.

4.4.1. *The Fraunhofer hologram*

Using the Fresnel diffraction integral and the previous notation, the object wave in the plane of the photosensitive support is expressed by [GOO 05]:

$$O(x,y) = \frac{\exp(jkz_0)}{j\lambda z_0} \exp\left[\frac{jk}{2z_0}(x^2 + y^2)\right] \times$$

$$\int_{-\infty}^{\infty}\int_{-\infty}^{\infty} O_0(x_0,y_0)\exp\left[\frac{jk}{2z_0}(x_0^2 + y_0^2)\right]\exp\left\{-j2\pi\left(\frac{x}{\lambda z_0}x_0 + \frac{y}{\lambda z_0}y_0\right)\right\}dx_0 dy_0$$

[4.133]

If the size of the object is much smaller than the distance z_0, i.e. $(k/2z_0)(x_0^2 + y_0^2) \ll \pi$, then we may neglect the quadratic phase factor in the double integral. In this case, $O(x,y)$ can be approximated by Fraunhofer diffraction:

$$O(x,y) = \frac{\exp(jkz_0)}{j\lambda z_0} \exp\left[\frac{jk}{2z_0}(x^2 + y^2)\right] \times$$

$$\int_{-\infty}^{\infty}\int_{-\infty}^{\infty} O_0(x_0,y_0)\exp\left\{-j2\pi\left(\frac{x}{\lambda z_0}x_0 + \frac{y}{\lambda z_0}y_0\right)\right\}dx_0 dy_0$$

[4.134]

and the hologram thus recorded is called a "Fraunhofer hologram".

The condition satisfying the Fraunhofer approximation can be rewritten as:

$$z_0 \gg \frac{1}{\lambda}(x_0^2 + y_0^2)$$

[4.135]

In order to illustrate this condition, we will consider the following example: an object is of circular form with radius a. We have $x^2 + y^2 = a^2$, and therefore $z_0 \gg a^2/\lambda$. If we use a HeNe laser of wavelength $\lambda = 0.6328$ µm and $a = 10$ mm, to record a Fraunhofer hologram, the distance z_0 must be greater than 15 km.

Evidently, it is not possible to obtain a Fraunhofer hologram under such conditions. However, even though we cannot record a Fraunhofer hologram of the object in a laboratory, according to [4.135], if the recording distance z_0 is of the order of a meter, the size of the object must be less than $\sqrt{\lambda z_0}$. This condition is adapted from the case where the object is a field of particles. In addition, we will see later that using a lens, the recording distance of a Fraunhofer hologram will become of the same order as that of the focal distance, thereby making the recording possible.

4.4.2. The Fourier hologram

The recording setup for a Fourier hologram is shown in Figure 4.14. We insert a convergent lens of focal image length f between the object and the photosensitive support. The surface of the object is in the neighborhood of the focal object plane $z = -2f$ (to the left of the lens). The recording plane is situated in the plane $z = 0$, which is the focal image plane (on the right side of the lens).

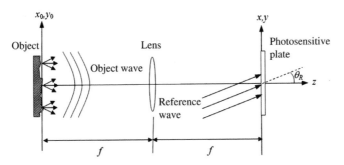

Figure 4.14. *Setup for recording a Fourier hologram*

From the studies in Chapter 2 concerning the propagation of light through an optical system, the object field is described by Collins' formula [COL 70]:

$$O(x,y) = \frac{\exp(jkL)}{j\lambda B}\exp\left\{\frac{jk}{2B}D(x^2+y^2)\right\} \times$$

$$\int_{-\infty}^{\infty}\int_{-\infty}^{\infty}\left\{O_0(x_0,y_0)\exp\left[\frac{jk}{2B}A(x_0^2+y_0^2)\right]\right\}\exp\left[-j2\pi\left(x_0\frac{x}{\lambda B}+y_0\frac{y}{\lambda B}\right)\right]dx_0dy_0 \qquad [4.136]$$

with

$$\begin{bmatrix} A & B \\ C & D \end{bmatrix} = \begin{bmatrix} 1 & f \\ 0 & 1 \end{bmatrix}\begin{bmatrix} 1 & 0 \\ -1/f & 1 \end{bmatrix}\begin{bmatrix} 1 & f \\ 0 & 1 \end{bmatrix} = \begin{bmatrix} 0 & f \\ -1/f & 0 \end{bmatrix} \qquad [4.137]$$

Substituting the optical elements of the *ABCD* system into [4.136], we then have:

$$O(x,y) = \frac{\exp(j2kf)}{j\lambda f}\int_{-\infty}^{\infty}\int_{-\infty}^{\infty}O_0(x_0,y_0)\exp\left[-j2\pi\left(x_0\frac{x}{\lambda f}+y_0\frac{y}{\lambda f}\right)\right]dx_0dy_0 \qquad [4.138]$$

This means that the object field in the recording plane is the Fourier transform of $O_0(x,y)$ multiplied by a constant factor without interest. Considering that the reference wave in the recording plane is given by:

$$R(x,y) = R_0\exp(jk\sin\theta_R x) \qquad [4.139]$$

The result of the interference between the object and reference waves is given by:

$$I_H(x,y) = R_0^2 + O(x,y)O^*(x,y) +$$
$$R_0 \exp(-jk\sin\theta_R x)O(x,y) + R_0 \exp(jk\sin\theta_R x)O^*(x,y)$$

[4.140]

The transmittance of the hologram is given by:

$$t_A(x,y) = t_0 + \beta I_H(x,y) = t_1 + t_2 + t_3 + t_4$$

[4.141]

with

$$t_1 = t_0 + \beta R_0^2$$

[4.142]

$$t_2(x,y) = \beta O(x,y)O^*(x,y)$$

[4.143]

$$t_3(x,y) = \beta R_0 \exp(-jk\sin\theta_R x)\frac{\exp(j2kf)}{j\lambda f} \times$$
$$\int_{-\infty}^{\infty}\int_{-\infty}^{\infty} O_0(x_0,y_0)\exp\left\{-j2\pi\left(\frac{x}{\lambda f}x_0 + \frac{y}{\lambda f}y_0\right)\right\}dx_0 dy_0$$

[4.144]

$$t_4(x,y) = \beta R_0 \exp(jk\sin\theta_R x)\frac{\exp(-j2kf)}{-j\lambda f} \times$$
$$\int_{-\infty}^{\infty}\int_{-\infty}^{\infty} O_0^*(x_0,y_0)\exp\left\{j2\pi\left(\frac{x}{\lambda f}x_0 + \frac{y}{\lambda f}y_0\right)\right\}dx_0 dy_0$$

[4.145]

We now study the case where a reconstruction plane wave of amplitude A illuminates the hologram situated in the plane $z = 0$ along the z-axis. The plane of the hologram is now the focal plane to the left of the lens, whose focal distance is f (see Figure 4.15). The observation plane is placed in the focal plane on the right of the lens. The complex field diffracted by the hologram is given by:

$$u(x,y) = At_A(x,y) = At_1 + At_2 + At_3 + At_4$$
$$= u_1(x,y) + u_2(x,y) + u_3(x,y) + u_4(x,y)$$

[4.146]

Let us consider the (x_i,y_i) coordinate in the observation plane. The complex amplitude of the wave in the observation plane is given by a Fourier transform:

$$\tilde{u}(x_i,y_i) = \frac{\exp(j2kf')}{j\lambda f'}F\{u(x_i,y_i)\}\left(\frac{x_i}{\lambda f'},\frac{y_i}{\lambda f'}\right)$$

[4.147]

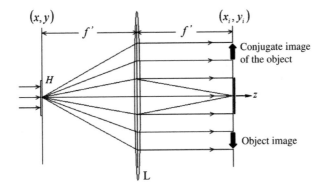

Figure 4.15. *Image reconstruction from a Fourier hologram*

Using [4.146], we can rewrite [4.145] as:

$$\tilde{u}(x_i, y_i) = \frac{\exp(j2kf')}{j\lambda f'} \left[\tilde{u}_1(x_i, y_i) + \tilde{u}_2(x_i, y_i) + \tilde{u}_3(x_i, y_i) + \tilde{u}_4(x_i, y_i) \right] \qquad [4.148]$$

The four terms in parentheses, respectively, correspond to the Fourier transforms of the terms u_1, u_2, u_3, and u_4 of [4.146]. To simplify, we write C as the constant complex factor before the brackets. We will now successively study the four emergent waves corresponding to the four components of [4.148].

4.4.2.1. *Component* $C\tilde{u}_1(x_i, y_i)$

We have:

$$C\tilde{u}_1(x_i, y_i) = C \times F\{At_1\} = C \times A \times \delta(x_i, y_i) \qquad [4.149]$$

This is a very bright spot in the center of the observation plane.

4.4.2.2. *Component* $C\tilde{u}_2(x_i, y_i)$

We have:

$$C\tilde{u}_2(x, y) = C \times F\{At_2\} = C \times A \times F\left\{O(x,y)O^*(x,y)\right\}\left(\frac{x_i}{\lambda f'}, \frac{y_i}{\lambda f'}\right) \qquad [4.150]$$

This expression is the autocorrelation of the wave $F\{O(x,y)\}$. In the observation plane, we may observe a halo whose width is two times $F\{O(x,y)\}$.

4.4.2.3. Component $C\widetilde{u}_3(x_i, y_i)$

We have:

$$C\widetilde{u}_3(x,y) = C\beta AR_0 \frac{\exp(j2kf)}{j\lambda f}$$

$$\int_{-\infty}^{\infty}\int_{-\infty}^{\infty} O_0(x_0,y_0)dx_0dy_0 \int_{-\infty}^{\infty}\int_{-\infty}^{\infty}\exp\left\{-j2\pi\left[\left(\frac{x_0}{\lambda f}+\frac{x_i}{\lambda f'}+\frac{\sin\theta_R}{\lambda}\right)x+\left(\frac{y_0}{\lambda f}+\frac{y_i}{\lambda f'}\right)y\right]\right\}dxdy$$

$$= C\beta AR_0 \frac{\exp(j2kf)}{j\lambda f}\int_{-\infty}^{\infty}\int_{-\infty}^{\infty} O_0(x_0,y_0)\delta\left(\frac{x_0}{\lambda f}+\frac{x_i}{\lambda f'}+\frac{\sin\theta_R}{\lambda},\frac{y_0}{\lambda f}+\frac{y_i}{\lambda f'}\right)dx_0dy_0$$

$$[4.151]$$

giving

$$C\widetilde{u}_3(x,y) = C\beta AR_0(\lambda f)^2 \frac{\exp(j2kf)}{j\lambda f}\int_{-\infty}^{\infty}\int_{-\infty}^{\infty} O_0(\lambda fX,\lambda fY)\delta\left(X+\frac{x_i}{\lambda f'}+\frac{\sin\theta_R}{\lambda},Y+\frac{y_i}{\lambda f'}\right)dXdY$$

$$= C\beta AR_0(\lambda f)^2 \frac{\exp(j2kf)}{j\lambda f}O_0\left(-\frac{x_i}{f'/f}-f\sin\theta_R,-\frac{y_i}{f'/f}\right)$$

$$[4.152]$$

Posing $G'_y = f'/f$, and substituting C into this relation, we have:

$$C\widetilde{u}_3(x,y) = \beta AR_0 \frac{\exp(j2k(f+f'))}{-G_y'}O_0\left(-\frac{x_i+f'\sin\theta_R}{G_y'},-\frac{y_i}{G_y'}\right) \qquad [4.153]$$

Note that this is an inverted image of the object with magnification of G'_y, whose center is situated at the coordinates $x_i = -f\sin\theta_R$ and $y_i = 0$, as shown in Figure 4.15.

4.4.2.4. Component $C\widetilde{u}_4(x_i, y_i)$

We have:

$$C\widetilde{u}_4(x,y) = C\beta AR_0 \frac{\exp(-j2kf)}{-j\lambda f}$$

$$\int_{-\infty}^{\infty}\int_{-\infty}^{\infty} O_0^*(x_0,y_0)dx_0dy_0 \int_{-\infty}^{\infty}\int_{-\infty}^{\infty}\exp\left\{-j2\pi\left[\left(-\frac{x_0}{\lambda f}+\frac{x_i}{\lambda f'}-\frac{\sin\theta_R}{\lambda}\right)x+\left(-\frac{y_0}{\lambda f}+\frac{y_i}{\lambda f'}\right)y\right]\right\}dxdy$$

$$= C\beta AR_0 \frac{\exp(-j2kf)}{-j\lambda f}\int_{-\infty}^{\infty}\int_{-\infty}^{\infty} O_0^*(x_0,y_0)\delta\left(-\frac{x_0}{\lambda f}+\frac{x_i}{\lambda f'}-\frac{\sin\theta_R}{\lambda},-\frac{y_0}{\lambda f}+\frac{y_i}{\lambda f'}\right)dx_0dy_0$$

$$[4.154]$$

giving

$$C\tilde{u}_4(x,y) = C\beta AR_0(\lambda f)^2 \frac{\exp(-j2kf)}{-j\lambda f} \times$$

$$\int_{-\infty}^{\infty}\int_{-\infty}^{\infty} O_0^*(\lambda f X, \lambda f Y)\delta\left(-X + \frac{x_i}{\lambda f'} - \frac{\sin\theta_R}{\lambda}, -Y + \frac{y_i}{\lambda f'}\right)dXdY$$ [4.155]

$$= C\beta AR_0(\lambda f)^2 \frac{\exp(-j2kf)}{-j\lambda f} O_0^*\left(\frac{x_i}{f'/f} - f\sin\theta_R, \frac{y_i}{f'/f}\right)$$

and we obtain:

$$C\tilde{u}_4(x,y) = \beta AR_0 \frac{\exp[j2k(f'-f)]}{G_y'} O_0^*\left(\frac{x_i - f'\sin\theta_R}{G_y'}, \frac{y_i}{G_y'}\right)$$ [4.156]

This expression shows that the fourth term is the conjugate image of the object with a magnification of G_y', whose center is situated at the coordinates $x_i = f'\sin\theta_R$ and $y_i = 0$ (see Figure 4.15).

Proceeding in a similar manner, we may also demonstrate that, when the illumination direction of the plane wave is identical to that of the original reference wave, the center of the object image will be at the center of the observation plane and will be inverted with a magnification of G_y'.

4.4.3. The lensless Fourier hologram

It is possible to record a lensless Fourier transform hologram when the reference wave is spherical and divergent from a point situated in the object plane. The recording setup is shown in Figure 4.16.

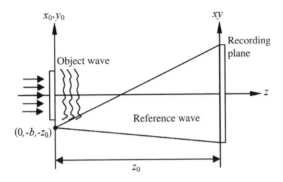

Figure 4.16. *Lensless Fourier hologram recording setup*

The object field in the recording plane is given by relation [4.133]. Supposing that the reference wave is spherical, coming from the point with coordinates $(0,-b,-z_0)$. The reference wave in the recording plane is:

$$R(x,y) = r_0 \exp\left\{\frac{jk}{2z_0}\left[x^2 + (y+b)^2\right]\right\}$$

$$= r_0 \exp\left(\frac{jk}{2z_0}b^2\right)\exp\left(\frac{jk}{z_0}by\right)\exp\left[\frac{jk}{2z_0}(x^2+y^2)\right] \qquad [4.157]$$

The important terms of the hologram are $O(x,y)R^*(x,y)$ and $O^*(x,y)R(x,y)$. Having examined [4.133] and [4.157], we note that the phase factor $\exp[jk/2z_0(x^2 + y^2)]$ disappears from the two orders of diffraction +1 and −1.

We neglect the constant coefficient $\exp[jk/2z_0b^2]$ in [4.157]. Posing:

$$O_g(x,y) = \frac{\exp(jkz_0)}{j\lambda z_0} \times$$

$$\int_{-\infty}^{\infty}\int_{-\infty}^{\infty}\left\{O_0(x_0,y_0)\exp\left[\frac{jk}{2z_0}(x_0^2+y_0^2)\right]\right\}\exp\left\{-j2\pi\left(\frac{x}{\lambda z_0}x_0 + \frac{y}{\lambda z_0}y_0\right)\right\}dx_0 dy_0 \qquad [4.158]$$

Relation [4.1] can be rewritten as:

$$I_H(x,y) = |O(x,y)|^2 + r_0^2 + r_0 O_g^*(x,y)\exp\left(\frac{jk}{z_0}by\right) + r_0 O_g(x,y)\exp\left(-\frac{jk}{z_0}by\right) \qquad [4.159]$$

We will demonstrate that the reconstruction of a Fourier hologram can be carried out in two different ways, as described in Figures 4.17(a) and (b). The hologram is placed in the plane $z = 0$. Illuminating it with a convergent spherical wave of radius of curvature z_c (see Figure 4.17a), we observe in the plane $z = z_c$ two real images of the object, one inverted relative to the other. If we illuminate the hologram using a divergent spherical wave of radius of curvature z_c, in the plane $z = -z_c$ (see Figure 4.17b) we will observe two virtual images of the object, one inverted relative to the other.

As an example, we carry out a demonstration of the method shown in Figure 4.17(a). The diffracted wave in the observation plane is described by the Fresnel diffraction integral:

$$U(x_i, y_i) = \frac{\exp(jkz_c)}{j\lambda z_c} \times$$

$$\int_{-\infty}^{\infty}\int_{-\infty}^{\infty} I_H(x,y)\exp\left[-\frac{jk}{2z_c}\left(x^2+y^2\right)\right]\exp\left\{\frac{jk}{2z_c}\left[\left(x-x_i\right)^2+\left(y-y_i\right)^2\right]\right\}dxdy$$

[4.160]

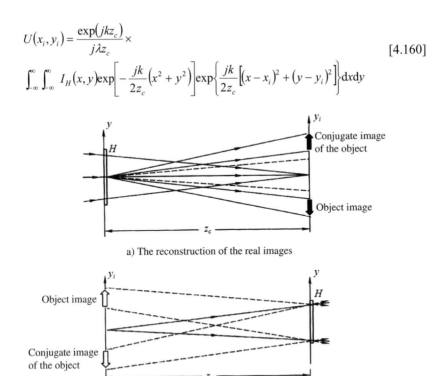

a) The reconstruction of the real images

b) The reconstruction of the virtual images

Figure 4.17. *Two different ways of reconstructing a lensless Fourier hologram*

Substituting $I_H(x,y)$ into this integral, we obtain an expression composed of three terms:

$$U(x_i, y_i) = U_{12}(x_i, y_i) + U_3(x_i, y_i) + U_4(x_i, y_i)$$

[4.161]

The term $U_{12}(x_i, y_i)$ represents the Fourier transform of $|O(x, y)|^2 + R_0^2$, which is generally localized around the center of the z-axis.

The term $U_3(x_i, y_i)$ is:

$$U_3(x_i, y_i) = \frac{\exp(jkz_c)}{j\lambda z_c} \times$$

$$\int_{-\infty}^{\infty}\int_{-\infty}^{\infty} r_0 O_g^*(x,y)\exp\left(\frac{jk}{z_0}by\right)\exp\left[-\frac{jk}{2z_c}\left(x^2+y^2\right)\right]\exp\left\{\frac{jk}{2z_c}\left[\left(x-x_i\right)^2+\left(y-y_i\right)^2\right]\right\}dxdy$$

[4.162]

After substituting $O_g^*(x,y)$ into this relation, we obtain:

$$U_3(x_i, y_i) = r_0 \frac{\exp(jk(z_c - z_0))}{z_c / z_0} \exp\left[\frac{jk}{2z_c}(x_i^2 + y_i^2)\right] \times$$

$$\int_{-\infty}^{\infty} \int_{-\infty}^{\infty} Q(x, y; x_0', y_0') \exp\left(-j2\pi\left[\frac{x_i}{\lambda z_c}x + \frac{1}{\lambda z_c}\left(y_i - \frac{z_c}{z_0}b\right)y\right]\right) dx dy \qquad [4.163]$$

with

$$Q(x, y; x_0', y_0')$$

$$= \int_{-\infty}^{\infty} \int_{-\infty}^{\infty} \left\{ \begin{matrix} O_0^*(\lambda z_0 x_0', \lambda z_0 y_0') \times \\ \exp\left[-\frac{jk}{2z_0}(\lambda z_0)^2(x_0'^2 + y_0'^2)\right] \end{matrix} \right\} \exp[j2\pi(x_0' x + y_0' y)] dx_0' dy_0' \qquad [4.164]$$

and $x_0' = x_0/\lambda z_0$, $y_0' = y_0/\lambda z_0$. Analysis of [4.163] shows that $U_3(x_i, y_i)$ is the Fourier transform of the function $Q(x, y; x_0', y_0')$, which itself is the inverse Fourier transform of the function $O_0^*(\lambda z_0 x_0', \lambda z_0 y_0')\exp\left[-(jk/2z_0)\times(\lambda z_0)^2(x_0'^2 + y_0'^2)\right]$. In fact, this is the conjugate object wave enlarged by a factor of $1/(\lambda z_0)$ and multiplied by a phase factor. Since the coordinates of the Fourier transform are $(x_i/\lambda z_c, (y_i - z_c/z_0)/\lambda z_c)$, this means that the transformed field is enlarged by a factor of λz_c. Synthesizing these two operations, we may observe the real image of the object with a magnification of z_c/z_0, centered at the point with coordinates $(0, z_c/z_0)$, as the phase factor $\exp\left[-jk/2z_0(x_0^2 + y_0^2)\right]$ does not play a role in the distribution of the reconstructed image (see the conjugate image in Figure 4.17a).

In the same way, we can show that $U_3(x_i, y_i)$ forms the inverted real image of the object with a magnification of z_c/z_0, whose center is situated at the point with coordinates $(0, -z_c/z_0)$ (see Figure 4.17b).

4.4.4. *The image hologram*

We will obtain an image hologram if, during the recording, the object (or its image) is close to the photosensitive support. In practice, two methods are often used.

Figure 4.18 illustrates one method using a lens to form the real image of the object on the photosensitive material.

Another method uses the reconstructed real image of a hologram. This is shown in Figure 4.19. If we already have a Fresnel hologram of an object (written H_1) at our disposal, by illuminating it with a reconstruction wave R_1, we may form a real image on the photosensitive support H. In this case, by introducing another reference wave R, we can record the image hologram of the original object.

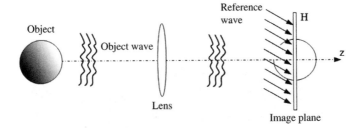

Figure 4.18. *The use of a lens to record an image hologram*

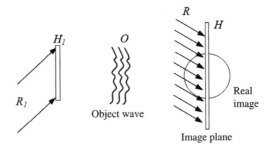

Figure 4.19. *Recording an image hologram using the reconstructed real image from another hologram*

In these two setups, the object and reconstruction distances tend to zero, and as we saw in section 4.3.3.1, the clarity of the reconstructed image is better. As mentioned in the previous section, we may even use natural light to reconstruct the 3D image. As an example, Figure 4.20 shows a reconstruction of an image hologram of a model of the planet Saturn. The hologram is illuminated by an incandescent lamp, and the three photographs are taken from three different heights. When the hologram was recorded, the plane of the photographic plate was exposed to the 3D image of the object. The reconstructed image gives the appearance of a real object crossing the plane of the support.

4.4.5. *The phase hologram*

Throughout the previous studies, we have always considered the transmittance of the hologram to be proportional to the intensity of the interference pattern of the object wave with the reference wave. In fact, using certain special techniques [XIO 09], the transmittance of the hologram may also be expressed by a phase function according to:

$$t_H(x, y) = t_A(x, y)\exp[j\phi_H(x, y)] \qquad [4.165]$$

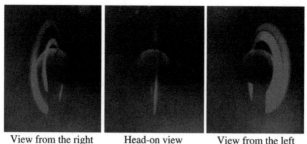

View from the right   Head-on view   View from the left
(Photographs taken at the Kunming university of science and technology)

Figure 4.20. *Images reconstructed from an image hologram. (Photographs taken at the Kunming University of Science and Technology - for a color version of this figure, see www.iste.co.uk/picart/digiholog.zip)*

When the function $\phi_H(x,y)$ is constant, the hologram is an amplitude hologram, and if $t_A(x,y)$ is constant, the hologram is a pure phase hologram. Supposing that the object and reference waves in the photosensitive plane are:

$$O(x, y) = O_0(x, y)\exp[j\varphi_0(x, y)] \qquad [4.166]$$

and

$$R(x, y) = R_0(x, y)\exp[j\varphi_r(x, y)] \qquad [4.167]$$

respectively. The intensity resulting from the interference of these two waves is given by:

$$I_H(x, y) = O_0^2(x, y) + R_0^2(x, y) + 2O_0(x, y)R_0(x, y)\cos[\varphi_0(x, y) - \varphi_r(x, y)] \qquad [4.168]$$

By using an appropriate treatment for certain photosensitive materials [KRE 96], we may obtain a phase hologram whose transmittance is expressed by the function:

$$t_H(x, y) = t_a \exp[jgI_H(x, y)] \qquad [4.169]$$

where t_a and g are two real constants.

We pose

$$K(x,y) = \exp\left[jg\left(O_0^2(x,y) + R_0^2(x,y)\right)\right]$$ [4.170]

$$\alpha(x,y) = 2gO_0(x,y)R_0(x,y)$$ [4.171]

$$\psi(x,y) = \varphi_0(x,y) - \varphi_r(x,y)$$ [4.172]

Relation [4.169] may be rewritten as:

$$t_H(x,y) = K(x,y)\exp\left[j\alpha(x,y)\cos\psi(x,y)\right]$$ [4.173]

Expression [4.173] can be developed as Bessel functions of the first kind $J_n(\alpha)$ [XIO 09]:

$$t_H(x,y) = K(x,y)\sum_{n=-\infty}^{\infty} J_n(\alpha(x,y))\exp\left[jn\psi(x,y)\right]$$ [4.174]

We note that when a phase hologram is illuminated by a plane wave of unit amplitude, the emergent wave contains multiple components: one diffraction wave of the order zero, corresponding to $n = 0$, and other diffraction wave propagating symmetrically on both sides of the axis, corresponding to $n = \pm1, \pm2, \ldots$

In practice, only three orders of diffraction corresponding to the three terms $n = 0$ and $n = \pm1$ are observed. For example, when the hologram is recorded, if the object wave propagates along the z-axis, and if the reference wave is plane and has a direction described by the angle θ_x (to the z-axis), we have $\varphi_r(x,y) = 2\pi/\lambda \times x\sin\theta_x$. Since we have:

$$n\psi(x,y) = \frac{n\pi}{2} - n\varphi_0(x,y) + \frac{2\pi}{\lambda}nx\sin\theta_x$$ [4.175]

the wave corresponding to $|n\sin\theta_x|\geq1$ does not exist. Therefore, if $\theta_x \geq 30°$, we may only observe three diffracted waves corresponding to the three terms $n = 0$ and $n = \pm1$.

From [4.174], we have:

$$|J_n(\alpha(x,y))| \propto O_0(x,y)R_0(x,y)$$ [4.176]

Generally, $R_0(x,y)$ varies slowly with the spatial coordinates (x,y) and $K(x,y)$ is a phase factor that has no influence on the modulus squared of the wave. Consequently, the wave diffracted by a phase hologram consists of three waves:

$$n = 0 \quad K(x,y)J_0(\alpha(x,y))$$

$$n = 1 \quad K(x,y)J_1(\alpha(x,y))\exp\left[-j\varphi_0(x,y) + j\frac{2\pi}{\lambda}x\sin\theta_x\right]\exp\left[j\frac{\pi}{2}\right]$$

$$n = -1 \quad -K(x,y)J_1(\alpha(x,y))\exp\left[j\varphi_0(x,y) - j\frac{2\pi}{\lambda}x\sin\theta_x\right]\exp\left[-j\frac{\pi}{2}\right]$$

[4.177]

To determine the relations given in [4.177], we have used the equality:

$$J_n(\alpha(x,y)) = (-1)^n J_{-n}(\alpha(x,y))$$

[4.178]

Considering the recording distance z_0, the analysis of these three terms show that:

– The wave of order 0 ($n = 0$) propagates along the z-axis.

– The wave of order +1 ($n = 1$) propagates at an angle θ_x to the z-axis and will form a real image in the plane $z = z_0$, and whose center has the coordinates $(z_0\tan\theta_x, 0, z_0)$.

– The wave of order −1 ($n = -1$) propagates at an angle $-\theta_x$ to the z-axis and will form a virtual image in the plane $z = -z_0$, and whose center is at $(-z_0\tan\theta_x, 0, z_0)$.

These results indicate that the wave diffracted by the phase hologram illuminated by a plane wave presents the same properties as that obtained with an amplitude hologram. However, considering that the diffraction efficiency of the hologram is the ratio of the light flux forming the image to the incident light flux, then the diffraction capacity of a phase hologram is better than that of an amplitude hologram [XIO 09]. The greater the diffraction capacity, the greater the energy of the reconstructed object wave, and so the better the visibility of the image is. Phase holograms are thus widely used for holographic art [GEN 00, HUB 91, BJE 96].

We note that there exist other types of hologram and other types of material and support for the recording of holograms [KRE 96, XIO 09]. Nevertheless, this chapter has presented the basic knowledge necessary for the comprehension of holography in general, and of digital holography in particular, which can be transcribed to every type of method or holographic material.

4.5. Conclusion

This chapter has described in detail the theoretical fundamentals of optical holography. The principle of recording interference fringes was presented; then we studied the aspects relating to the reconstruction of the object wave by diffraction on the hologram. We have explicitly described the different types of hologram and the resulting formation of images. These fundamental principles will be used in digital holography where the physical diffraction of a laser beam will be replaced by a numerical calculation.

Chapter 5

Digital Off-Axis Fresnel Holography

Recording a hologram on a photosensitive support consisting of a photographic plate or film generally requires a chemical process. This type of process is often limiting for most applications, for which it is often required to record multiple holograms. This makes any industrial use difficult, for quality control in production lines, for example. The idea of digitally reconstructing the optical wavefront was born in the 1960s. The oldest study on the subject dates back to 1967 with the article published by J.W. Goodman in *Applied Physics Letters* [GOO 67]. The idea was to replace the "analog" recording/decoding of the object by a "digital" recording/decoding simulating diffraction from a digital grating consisting of the recorded image. Holography thus became "digital", replacing the photographic plate with a matrix of the discrete values of the hologram. Then, in 1971, Huang discussed the computer analysis of optical wavefronts and introduced for the first time the concept of "digital holography" [HUA 71]. The works presented in 1972 by Kronrod [KRO 72] historically constitute the first attempts at reconstruction by the calculation of an object coded in a hologram. At the time, 6 hours of calculation was required for the reconstruction of a field of 512×512 pixels with the Minsk-22 computer, the discrete values being obtained from a holographic plate of 64-bit digitization with a scanner. However, it took until the 1990s for array detector-based digital holography to materialize [SCH 94]. In effect, there have been important developments in two sectors of technology:

– Since this period, microtechnological processes have resulted in charge-coupled device (CCD) arrays with sufficiently small pixels to fulfill the Shannon condition for the spatial sampling of a hologram.

– The computational treatment of images has become accessible, thanks in large part to the significant improvement in microprocessor performance, in particular their processing units as well as their storage capacities.

The physical principle of digital holography is similar to that of traditional holography. The term "digital off-axis Fresnel holography" means that the recording system is generally based on the oblique reference method and that the object field is obtained by diffraction in a free field across a certain distance. This type of architecture was described by Leith–Upatnieks [LEI 62]. However, the size of the pixels in an image detector (CCD or complementary metal-oxide semiconductor -CMOS) is clearly greater than that of the grains of a traditional photographic plate (typically 2–3 µm, compared with some 25 nm). These constraints require that we take into account certain parameters (pixel area, number of pixels, and pixel pitch), which were more or less clear in analog holography.

This chapter aims to describe the different reconstruction methods in digital Fresnel holography and introduce digital color holography. Image quality is discussed through a theoretical analysis and methods for removing the zero-order are presented.

5.1. Digital off-axis holography and wavefront reconstruction by S-FFT

The Fresnel diffraction integral is the most commonly used mathematical expression for the reconstruction of a digital wavefront [GOO 72, KRE 97a, KRE 04, SCH 94]. There exist different calculation algorithms [MAS 99, LI 07b, LI 09a, LI 09b]. The most direct form is the Fresnel diffraction integral written in the form of a Fourier transform, as it can be calculated by only one Fast Fourier Transform (FFT) (see Chapter 3). Thus, the method restoring the wavefront by the Fresnel integral calculated by only one FFT will be described as reconstruction by Single Fast Fourier Transform (S-FFT) or reconstruction by discrete Fresnel transform. In the first part of this chapter, we will study the design of the optical system recording a digital off-axis hologram, the method of wavefront reconstruction by S-FFT, and the quality of restored images. The program LIM4.m in the Appendix reconstructs a hologram by S-FFT.

5.1.1. *Characteristics of the diffraction from a digital hologram impacted by a spherical wave*

In holography, digital or analog, the reference wave may be a plane or spherical. During the reconstruction of the image, the fictitious light simulating the illumination of the hologram is manufactured by computer and it may also be either a plane or a spherical wave. A plane wave may be considered as a spherical wave that has a radius of curvature tending to infinity. Generally, assuming that the reference and reconstruction waves are spherical, we will study in detail the distribution of the diffracted waves that form the real image, the virtual image, and the zero order in the image plane reconstructed by S-FFT [PIC 08a, PAV 10, LI 10b].

Figure 5.1 shows a simplified digital holographic system. The x_0y_0-plane represents the object plane and the x_iy_i-plane represents the image plane reconstructed with a spherical wave. The distances between the two planes and the plane of the CCD (xy) are represented by z_0 and z_i, respectively. To simplify matters, the coherent (laser) beam illuminating the object is not represented in the diagram.

In accordance with the properties of diffusion from rough surfaces [GOO 07, GOO 85], the light coming from a source object having an optically rough surface is the result of the sum of all its elementary wavelets. We may represent an elementary wavelet at a diffusing element with coordinates (ξ, η) in the object plane with the following equation:

$$u_0\left(x_0,y_0;\xi,\eta\right)= o(\xi,\eta)\delta(x_0 - \xi, y_0 - \eta)\exp\left[j\phi_o(\xi,\eta)\right] \qquad [5.1]$$

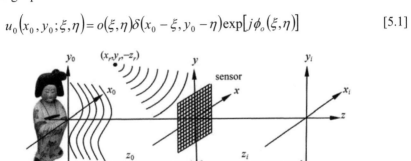

Figure 5.1. *Simplified scheme for the recording of a digital hologram*

The phase $\phi_o(\xi, \eta)$ is random, belonging to the interval $[-\pi, +\pi]$. Using the Fresnel diffraction formula across the distance z_0, the field reaching the plane of the detector is presented in the following form:

$$u_\delta\left(x, y;\xi,\eta\right)= \frac{\exp\left[jkz_0 + j\phi_o(\xi,\eta)\right]}{j\lambda z_0}o(\xi,\eta)\exp\left\{\frac{jk}{2z_0}\left[(x - \xi)^2 + (y - \eta)^2\right]\right\} \qquad [5.2]$$

with $k = 2\pi/\lambda$ and λ being the wavelength. The wave coming from the full object and impacting the recording plane is represented by the sum:

$$U(x,y)= \sum_{\xi}\sum_{\eta} u_\delta\left(x,y;\xi,\eta\right) \qquad [5.3]$$

We assume that the reference beam of (almost) uniform amplitude A_r, coming from the point $(x_r, y_r, -z_r)$ is a spherical wave:

$$R(x,y) = A_r \exp\left\{\frac{jk}{2z_r}\left[(x-x_r)^2 + (y-y_r)^2\right]\right\} \qquad [5.4]$$

The intensity resulting from the interference between the object and reference waves is:

$$I_H(x,y) = |U(x,y)|^2 + A_r^2 + R(x,y)U^*(x,y) + R^*(x,y)U(x,y) \qquad [5.5]$$

We consider the spherical wave, $R_c(x, y) = \exp[jk/2z_c(x^2 + y^2)]$, as being the reconstruction wave. From [5.5], simulating the illumination of the hologram by this wave, the waves diffracted by the hologram will be composed of the following terms:

$$U_{0U}(x,y) = w(x,y)R_c(x,y)|U(x,y)|^2$$

$$U_{0R}(x,y) = w(x,y)R_c(x,y)A_r^2$$

$$U_+(x,y) = w(x,y)R_c(x,y)R(x,y)U^*(x,y)$$

$$U_-(x,y) = w(x,y)R_c(x,y)R^*(x,y)U(x,y) \qquad [5.6]$$

where $w(x, y)$ is the window function of the detector, U_{0U} and U_{0R} are the zero order diffracted waves, U_+ is the conjugate wave of the object, and U_- is the wave directly related to the object.

We will first of all study the wave that forms the virtual image and the relation between the geometric position of the reconstructed image in the image plane and the experimental variables. We will then study the conjugate object wave and the zero order.

5.1.1.1. Virtual object

According to the theory of diffraction, the complex amplitude of the virtual wave after having traveled the distance z_i may be expressed by the following equation (see Chapters 2 and 4):

$$U_{i-}(x_i,y_i) = \frac{\exp(jkz_i)}{j\lambda z_i}\int\limits_{-\infty}^{\infty}\int U_{i-}(x,y)\exp\left\{\frac{jk}{2z_i}\left[(x-x_i)^2 + (y-y_i)^2\right]\right\}dxdy \quad [5.7]$$

Considering the different variables, the equation can be transformed into:

$$U_{i-}(x_i,y_i) = \frac{\exp(jkz_i)}{j\lambda z_i}\exp\left[\frac{jk}{2z_i}(x_i^2+y_i^2)\right]\exp\left\{-\frac{jk}{2z_r}[x_r^2+y_r^2]\right\}\times$$

$$\sum_\xi\sum_\eta\frac{\exp[jkz_0+j\phi_o(\xi,\eta)]}{j\lambda z_0}o(\xi,\eta)A_r\exp\left[\frac{jk}{2z_0}(\xi^2+\eta^2)\right]\times \qquad [5.8]$$

$$\int\int_{-\infty}^{\infty\,\infty}w(x,y)\exp\left[\frac{jk}{2}\left(\frac{1}{z_c}-\frac{1}{z_r}+\frac{1}{z_i}+\frac{1}{z_0}\right)(x^2+y^2)\right]\times$$

$$\exp\left\{-j2\pi\left[\left(x_i-\frac{z_i}{z_r}x_r+\frac{z_i}{z_0}\xi\right)\frac{x}{\lambda z_i}+\left(y_i-\frac{z_i}{z_r}y_r+\frac{z_i}{z_0}\eta\right)\frac{y}{\lambda z_i}\right]\right\}dxdy$$

Considering the condition $1/z_c-1/z_r+1/z_i+1/z_0=0$ to be satisfied, the diffraction distance leading to a focused image coinciding to the object corresponds to:

$$z_i=-\left(\frac{1}{z_0}+\frac{1}{z_c}-\frac{1}{z_r}\right)^{-1} \qquad [5.9]$$

The integration in equation [5.8] corresponds to the diffraction from the aperture of the image detector, $w(x,y)$. Letting $G_y=-z_i/z_0$, the center of the diffracted image is at the point $(z_ix_r/z_r+G_y\xi,z_iy_r/z_r+G_y\eta)$. Even though the phase of each diffracted image is random, the energy of the diffraction is concentrated at the center of the image. Moreover, the amplitude of the center of the image is proportional to $o(\xi,\eta)$.

In other words, the intensity of the field at the position $(z_ix_r/z_r+G_y\xi,z_iy_r/z_r+G_y\eta)$ is proportional to $|o(\xi,\eta)|^2$. Having calculated all the added values of (ξ,η), the image in the plane $z=z_i$ will be G_y times the object wave whose center is situated at $(z_ix_r/z_r,z_iy_r/z_r)$. The larger the $w(x,y)$ is, the more the intensity is concentrated at the center of the image of each element, and the better the quality of the image will be.

5.1.1.2. Conjugate object

Introducing the term U_+ from [5.6] into the Fresnel integral for diffraction across the distance z_i that satisfies equation [5.9], we obtain the following equation:

$$U_{i+}(x_i,y_i)=\sum_\xi\sum_\eta\Theta_+(\xi,\eta;x_i,y_i)\int\int_{-\infty}^{\infty\,\infty}w(x/G_y',y/G_y')$$

$$\exp\left\{\frac{jk}{2G_y'z_i}\left[\left(x-\left(x_i+\frac{z_i}{z_r}x_r-G_y\xi\right)\right)^2+\left(y-\left(y_i+\frac{z_i}{z_r}y_r-G_y\eta\right)\right)^2\right]\right\}dxdy \qquad [5.10]$$

where $\Theta_+(x_i,y_i)$ is a random function and $G_y'=1-z_i/z_0+z_i/z_r+z_i/z_c$. The integration represents the Fresnel diffraction from the square window across a distance z_i.

The conjugate image is not in focus. The center of the image is located at $(-z_i x_r/z_r + G_y \xi, -z_i y_r/z_r + G_y \eta)$. It is necessary to take into account the interference between the different wavelet sources $o(\xi, \eta)$. An interference field will be formed in the plane $z = z_i$, and the center will be located at $(-z_i x_r/z_r, -z_i y_r/z_r)$, the magnification being G_y. Knowing that the energy of each elementary reconstructed point in this Fresnel diffraction is concentrated in a zone with sides $|G_y'|L$, letting D_0 be the width of the object, the width of the interference field will be approximately equal to $G_y D_0 + |G_y'|L$ (L: width of the sensor, assumed to be square).

5.1.1.3. Zero order

The complex amplitude of the diffracted field U_{0U} is:

$$U_{i0U}(x_i, y_i) = \frac{\exp(jkz_i)}{j\lambda z_i} \int_{-\infty}^{\infty}\int_{-\infty}^{\infty} w(x,y)|U(x,y)|^2 \exp\left[j\frac{k}{2z_c}(x^2 + y^2)\right]\exp\left\{j\frac{k}{2z_i}\left[(x-x_i)^2 + (y-y_i)^2\right]\right\}dxdy$$

[5.11]

where $|U(x,y)|^2 = U(x,y)U^*(x,y)$. The tapering function $w(x,y)$ of the detector has the property $w(x,y) = w^3(x,y)$. Therefore, using the Fourier transform symbol $F\{\}$, the equation [5.11] is rewritten in the following form:

$$U_{i0U}(x_i, y_i) = \frac{\exp(jkz_i)}{j\lambda z_i}\exp\left[j\frac{k}{2z_i}(x_i^2 + y_i^2)\right] \times$$

$$F\{w(x,y)U(x,y)\} * F\{w(x,y)U^*(x,y)\} * F\left\{w(x,y)\exp\left[j\frac{k}{2}\left(\frac{1}{z_c} + \frac{1}{z_i}\right)(x^2 + y^2)\right]\right\}$$

[5.12]

The output coordinates of the Fourier transform are $(x_i/\lambda z_i, y_i/\lambda z_i)$. The distribution of $U_{i0U}(x_i, y_i)$ is determined by two convolutions between three terms coming from Fourier transforms that we will study respectively.

According to [5.2] and [5.3], $F\{w(x,y)U(x,y)\}$ is transformed as:

$$F\{w(x,y)U(x,y)\} = \sum_{\xi}\sum_{\eta} \frac{\exp[jkz_0 + j\phi_o(\xi,\eta)]}{j\lambda G_y z_i} o(\xi,\eta) \times$$

$$\exp\left\{-\frac{jk}{2G_y z_i}\left[(G_y\xi + x_i)^2 + (G_y\eta + y_i)^2\right] + \frac{jk(\xi^2 + \eta^2)}{2z_0}\right\} \times$$

$$\int_{-\infty}^{\infty}\int_{-\infty}^{\infty} w\left(\frac{x'}{G_y}, \frac{y'}{G_y}\right)\exp\left\{\frac{jk}{2G_y z_i}\left[(x' - (G_y\xi + x_i))^2 + (y' - (G_y\eta + y_i))^2\right]\right\}dx'dy'$$

[5.13]

where the integration represents the Fresnel diffraction of the pupil magnified G_y times, whose center is at the point with coordinates $(-G_y\xi, -G_y\eta)$. So as to better explain the physical meaning of the terms in the equation, we introduce the random term $o'(\xi,\eta;x_i,y_i)$ letting its argument be $\arg\{o'(\xi,\eta;x_i,y_i)\}$. The equation becomes:

$$F\{w(x,y)U(x,y)\} = \sum_\xi \sum_\eta \left|o'(\xi,\eta;x_i,y_i)\right| \times$$

$$\exp\left\{-j\frac{k}{2G_y z_i}\left[(G_y\xi + x_i)^2 + (G_y\eta + y_i)^2\right] + j\arg(o'(\xi,\eta;x_i,y_i))\right\} \qquad [5.14]$$

We note that this corresponds to the sum of spherical waves of random phases, which converge toward the point $(-G_y\xi, -G_y\eta, G_y z_i)$. Having calculated this sum for the values of (ξ,η), $F\{w(x,y)U(x,y)\}$ becomes a *speckle* field [DAI 84].

We also have:

$$F\{w(x,y)U^*(x,y)\} = \sum_\xi \sum_\eta \left|o''(\xi,\eta;x_i,y_i)\right| \times$$

$$\exp\left\{j\frac{k}{2G_y z_i}\left[(G_y\xi - x_i)^2 + (G_y\eta - y_i)^2\right] + j\arg(o''(\xi,\eta;x_i,y_i))\right\} \qquad [5.15]$$

where $o''(\xi,\eta;x_i,y_i)$ is another random function. [5.15] is also the sum of spherical waves of random phases, which converge toward $(G_y\xi, G_y\eta, -G_y z_i)$. Thus $F\{w(x,y)U^*(x,y)\}$ is also a *speckle* field.

We can easily prove that:

$$F\left\{w(x,y)\exp\left[j\frac{k}{2}\left(\frac{1}{z_c} + \frac{1}{z_i}\right)(x^2 + y^2)\right]\right\}$$

$$= \Psi(x_i,y_i)\int_{-\infty}^{\infty}\int_{-\infty}^{\infty} w\left(\frac{x}{G_{yc}}, \frac{y}{G_{yc}}\right)\exp\left[j\frac{k}{2G_{yc}z_i}\left[(x-x_i)^2 + (y-y_i)^2\right]\right]dxdy \qquad [5.16]$$

where $\Psi(x_i,y_i)$ is a complex function and $G_{yc} = 1 + z_i/z_c$. Equation [5.16] is the diffraction spot given by the detector window which is a square of width L. Thus, the width of the diffracted field is approximately $|G_{yc}|L$.

From the previous discussions and the properties of convolution, we may transform the result of equation [5.12] into a field of spots whose width is

$|G_{yc}|L + 2G_yD_0$. When $z_i = -z_c$, the expression corresponds to a lens-less Fourier hologram. We may apply the Fourier transform calculation to [5.16], where the distribution area is less than those in the case where $z_i \neq -z_c$. Thus, for the lens-less Fourier hologram, $U_{i0U}(x_i,y_i)$ corresponds to the case where the distribution area is the narrowest.

We may express the diffraction of U_{0R} across a distance z_i as:

$$U_{i0R}(x_i, y_i) = \frac{\exp(jkz_i)}{j\lambda \, z_i G_{yc}^2} A_r^2 \exp\left[-\frac{jk}{2G_{yc}z_i}(x_i^2 + y_i^2)\right] \times$$

$$\int\int_{-\infty}^{\infty\,\infty} w\left(\frac{x}{G_{yc}}, \frac{y}{G_{yc}}\right) \exp\left[j\frac{k}{2G_{yc}z_i}\left[(x_i - x)^2 + (y_i - y)^2\right]\right] dxdy \qquad [5.17]$$

This is a diffracted image whose center is at the origin and whose width is $|G_{yc}|L$.

The fields $U_{i0U}(x_i,y_i)$ and $U_{i0R}(x_i,y_i)$ correspond to the respective perturbations of the zero-order diffraction. Nevertheless, the area of the first is relatively spread out and that of the second is relatively narrow. This is the reason why we often observe the superposition of a large zone of low amplitude with a small square (or rectangular) zone of quite large amplitude in the reconstruction plane. The width of the total diffraction zone of the zero-order diffraction is $|G_{yc}|L+2G_yD_0$, i.e. two times the object size.

5.1.2. Optimization of the experimental parameters

According to the previous analysis, to better isolate the different waves emerging from the hologram, the width of the reconstructed plane must be greater than the sum of the zero-order width and those of the direct and conjugate wave, i.e.:

$$L_i > |G_{yc}L| + 4G_yD_0 + |G_y'|L \qquad [5.18]$$

This expression allows the optimization of the digital hologram [PIC 08a, PAV 09]. Let us now study the optimization of the variables of the experimental apparatus using the characteristics of the discrete Fourier transform.

We suppose the plane of the detector to be composed of $N \times N$ pixels. After a discrete Fourier transform to calculate the Fresnel diffraction, the physical width becomes $L_i = \lambda z_i N/L = \lambda G_y z_0 N/L$. Since this value is proportional to the magnification G_y, the relation between the dimensions of the reconstructed object image and the dimensions of the reconstructed plane does not vary as a function of

G_y. In other words, for any value of G_y for reconstruction by S-FFT, the reconstructed image keeps the same proportion to the reconstruction plane.

Since the width of the zero order is $|G_{yc}|L+2G_yD_0$, in general its value is greater than $2G_yD_0$. Moreover, the sum of the widths of the reconstructed image and the initial object field is slightly greater than $2G_yD_0$. By inserting a variable $\rho \geq 1$, we may define the recording distance of the hologram as:

$$L_i = \lambda G_y z_0 N / L = \rho \times 4G_y D_0 \qquad [5.19]$$

hence,

$$z_0 = \frac{\rho \times 4D_0 L}{\lambda N} \qquad [5.20]$$

Since the amplitude at the edge of the zero order described by [5.12] is relatively small, in practice, experiments show that with $\rho = 1$, we may obtain a reconstructed image of satisfactory quality.

In expression [5.18], we have not taken into account the superposition of different fields. To better isolate the perturbations, we fix the absolute value of the coordinates of the center of the reconstructed image at $3L_i/8$ [PIC 08a, PAV 10], i.e.:

$$\left|\frac{z_i}{z_r} x_r\right| = \frac{3L_i}{8} \quad \text{or} \quad \left|\frac{x_r}{z_r}\right| = \frac{3\lambda N}{8L} \qquad [5.21]$$

Here, x_r/z_r also represents the incidence angle of the reference beam and is related to the spatial frequencies of the microfringes constituting the digital hologram (i.e. $u_r = x_r/\lambda z_r$). On the basis of [5.20] and [5.21], we may define an optical system adapted to the recording of a digital color hologram. In effect, if we manage to isolate the zero order for a particular wavelength from perturbations, we may obtain the same thing for beams of different colors. Some practical examples will be presented during this chapter.

5.1.3. *Experimental reconstruction by S-FFT*

As an illustration, we will consider an experiment. Figure 5.2 represents the experimental system. The beam coming from the laser is separated by a polarizing beam splitter (PBS) cube. The reflected beam is made parallel by the afocal system, and then it illuminates the object at an angle via a mirror. The beam transmitted by the cube is spatially expanded with the spatial filter, then collimated, and constitutes the reference wave. The 50% beam splitter allows the recombination of the object and reference beams in the sensor plane. The object and reference beams are copolarized using half-wave plates (HWP), which allow the rotation of the polarizations. The incidence angles of the reference beams are adjusted by laterally displacing lens L_1. The object is a sports medal with a diameter of 50 mm. The pixels have a size of 4.65 µm. The number of pixels is $N = 1,024$, which means that the sensor width is $L = 4.76$ mm. We use, alternately, a red laser ($\lambda = 632.8$ nm) and a green laser ($\lambda = 532$ nm).

Letting $\rho = 1$ and substituting $\lambda = 632.8$ nm and $\lambda = 532$ nm into [5.20], we have respectively $z_0 = 1,469.2$ mm and $z_0 = 1,745.5$ mm. This result means that if we choose z_0 greater than 1,745.5 mm, we may avoid the perturbation of the zero order in the two reconstructed images at each wavelength. If 1,469.7 mm $< z_0 <$ 1,745.8 mm, we may isolate only the image coming from the red laser, the green image being polluted by the zero order. When $z_0 < 1,469.7$ mm, both reconstructed images will be perturbed by the zero order. So as to verify this theoretical analysis, two experimental proofs were carried out by placing the object at the distances $z_0 = 1,250$ mm and $z_0 = 1,500$ mm relative to the plane of the sensor.

The reference beam is a plane wave coming from the collimator. We adjust the angles of the red and green beams so that the reconstructed images are respectively formed on the first and the second quadrant of the reconstruction plane.

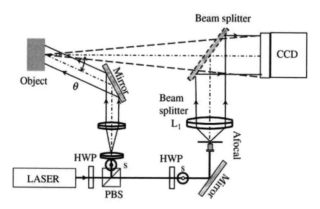

Figure 5.2. *Digital off-axis interferometer*

Letting $G_y = 0.2$, Figures 5.3(a) and (b) correspond to the respective images reconstructed by S-FFT with the two lasers and $z_0 = 1,250$ mm. We note that the physical width of the S-FFT reconstructed plane is proportional to the wavelength: the image reconstructed with the red beam is smaller than the green beam. We also note that the zero-order diffraction is partially superposed with the two reconstructed images. Figures 5.3(c) and (d) correspond to the reconstructed images for $z_0 = 1,500$ mm. Since the width of the reconstructed image plane for red light is four times greater than the real size of the object, the obtained image is separated from the perturbation of the zero order.

We may readily observe that a clear spot is present in the middle of each image. This is an effect of the image $U_{i0R}(x_i,y_i)$. Since the reference beam that we use in our experiment is a plane wave, we may calculate the width of the diffraction spot, which is $|G_{yc}|L = |G_y - 1|L \approx 3.8$mm (by applying $z_r \rightarrow \infty$). The result of the calculation corresponds well to the experimentally measured result.

Thus, the size of the reconstructed images varies with the wavelength of the light, but does not vary with the magnification of the reconstruction. This result will later be applied to the case where the reconstruction wave is spherical, thus generating an adjustable transverse magnification.

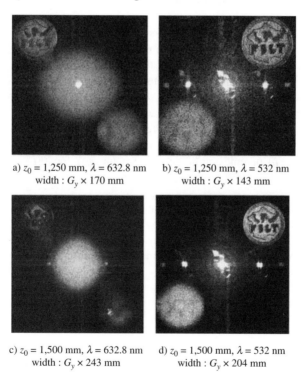

a) $z_0 = 1,250$ mm, $\lambda = 632.8$ nm
width : $G_y \times 170$ mm

b) $z_0 = 1,250$ mm, $\lambda = 532$ nm
width : $G_y \times 143$ mm

c) $z_0 = 1,500$ mm, $\lambda = 632.8$ nm
width : $G_y \times 243$ mm

d) $z_0 = 1,500$ mm, $\lambda = 532$ nm
width : $G_y \times 204$ mm

Figure 5.3. *Comparison of the images reconstructed by S-FFT with different recording distances and wavelengths*

The previous results have been obtained without using a specific method of eliminating the zero order and the conjugate image. It turns out that by using special techniques to eliminate perturbations, we may optimize the recording distances. Zhang [ZHA 04a] proposes the use of a second phase-shifted hologram by an amount less than 2π. The reconstruction of the image obtained by the difference of the two phase-shifted holograms may efficiently eliminate the zero order. Moreover, when the reference wave is more intense than the object wave, the perturbation due to the term $U_{i0U}(x_i, y_i)$ related to the object wave will be very weak, and we may therefore neglect its influence. Under these conditions, the width of the reconstruction plane does not need to be greater than four times the width of the reconstructed image. The detector may therefore be closer to the object so as to record the angular spectra of an object at higher frequencies, and thus we obtain a reconstructed image of better resolution. This point will be tackled in detail later.

5.1.4. *Quality of the reconstructed image*

We may consider the holographic system providing the digital image to be a coherent optical system that forms, in the $x_i y_i$-plane, the image of the object situated in the $x_0 y_0$-plane. Nevertheless, a part of the system exists only in virtual world of the computer. According to linear systems theory and studies on the formation of images in coherent optics [GOO 72], if we can obtain the impulse response of the system, we may then determine the influence of the parameters of the system on the quality of the image. We are, therefore, now interested in the impulse response of the holographic system. The response will be determined by the image of a point source $\delta(x_0-\xi, y_0-\eta)$ of unit amplitude in the plane $x_0 y_0$ ($o\exp(j\phi_o) = 1$) [GOO 72, KRE 02a, KRE 02b].

The optical field in the xy-plane, coming from the point source $\delta(x_0-\xi, y_0-\eta)$, is expressed by the Fresnel approximation by equation [5.2]. After the interference of the object and reference waves, the digital hologram is spatially integrated with the pupil function of the pixel (which is considered to be even) and limited by the pupil function of the detector:

$$
\begin{aligned}
I_{w\delta}(x,y;\xi,\eta) &= \left\{ \int_{x-\alpha\Delta x/2}^{x+\alpha\Delta x/2} \int_{y-\beta\Delta y/2}^{y+\beta\Delta y/2} I_\delta(u,v;\xi,\eta)\,du\,dv \right\} w(x,y) \\
&= \left\{ \int_{-\infty}^{+\infty}\int_{-\infty}^{+\infty} I_\delta(u,v;\xi,\eta)\mathrm{rect}\!\left(\frac{x-u}{\alpha\Delta x},\frac{y-v}{\beta\Delta y}\right) du\,dv \right\} w(x,y) \\
&= \left\{ I_\delta(x,y;\xi,\eta) * \mathrm{rect}\!\left(\frac{x}{\alpha\Delta x},\frac{y}{\beta\Delta y}\right) \right\} w(x,y)
\end{aligned}
\qquad [5.22]
$$

where

$$I_\delta(x,y;\xi,\eta) = |U(x,y;\xi,\eta) + R(x,y)|^2$$
$$= \frac{1}{\lambda^2 z_0^2} + A_r^2 + U^*(x,y;\xi,\eta)R(x,y) + U(x,y;\xi,\eta)R^*(x,y)$$

[5.23]

and

$$U(x,y;\xi,\eta) = \frac{\exp(jkz_0)}{j\lambda z_0}\exp\left[\frac{jk}{2z_0}(x^2+y^2)\right]F\{\tilde{f}(x,y)\}\left[\frac{x}{\lambda z_0},\frac{y}{\lambda z_0}\right]$$

[5.24]

with

$$\tilde{f}(x,y) = \exp\left[\frac{jk}{2z_0}(x^2+y^2)\right]u_0(x_0,y_0;\xi,\eta)$$

[5.25]

and

$$f\left(\frac{x}{\lambda z_0},\frac{y}{\lambda z_0}\right) = F\{\tilde{f}(x,y)\}\left[\frac{x}{\lambda z_0},\frac{y}{\lambda z_0}\right]$$

[5.26]

In these relations, $\alpha\Delta x \times \beta\Delta y$ is the area of a pixel, and Δx and Δy are the pixel pitches along the x- and y-axes, respectively. The filling factors $\alpha,\beta\in[0,1]$ signify that there is a dead zone between the pixels. The area of the pixel matrix is given by the function $w(x,y)$ and is determined by $N\Delta x \times M\Delta y$, where N and M are the number of pixels along the x- and y-axes [PIC 08a]. The structural model of the detector window is represented in Figure 5.4.

In order to simplify the analytical calculation, we will consider the case in which the reference wave is plane and is described by its spatial frequencies. This means that $R(x,y) = A_r \exp[-2j\pi(u_r x + v_r y)]$, where $\{u_r,v_r\} = \lim_{z_r \to \infty}\{x_r/z_r, y_r/z_r\}$. Furthermore, we consider the case of perfect focusing in the virtual image plane, that is $z_i = -z_0$, by considering a digital plane wave in the reconstruction ($z_c = \infty$). The field in the image plane is expressed by the Fresnel diffraction integral at distance $z_i = -z_0$:

$$h_\delta(x_i,y_i;\xi,\eta) = -\frac{\exp(-jkz_0)}{j\lambda z_0}\int_{-\infty}^{\infty}\int I_{w\delta}(x,y;\xi,\eta)\exp\left\{-\frac{jk}{2z_0}\left[(x-x_i)^2+(y-y_i)^2\right]\right\}\mathrm{d}x\mathrm{d}y$$

[5.27]

Since $I_{w\delta}$ is composed of three diffraction orders, expression [5.27] can be decomposed into three contributions:

$$h_\delta(x_i, y_i; \xi, \eta) = h_0(x_i, y_i; \xi, \eta) + h_+(x_i, y_i; \xi, \eta) + h_-(x_i, y_i; \xi, \eta) \qquad [5.28]$$

Here, we are interested in studying the impulse response for the virtual image, i.e. $h_-(x, y; \xi, \eta)$. For the sake of simplicity, let us consider a one-dimensional (1D) expression. Thus, we have:

$$h_-(x_i; \xi) = -\frac{\exp(-jkz_0)}{j\lambda z_0} \exp\left[-\frac{jk}{2z_0} x_i^2\right]$$

$$\times \int_{-\infty}^{+\infty}\left[\left\{R^*(x)U(x;\xi)\right\} * \mathrm{rect}\left(\frac{x}{\alpha\Delta x}\right)\right] \times \exp\left[-\frac{jk}{2z_0} x^2\right] w(x) \exp\left[+2j\pi\left(\frac{xx_i}{\lambda z_0}\right)\right] dx$$

$$= -\frac{\exp(-jkz_0)}{j\lambda z_0} \exp\left[-\frac{jk}{2z_0} x_i^2\right] \times F\left\{\exp\left[-\frac{jk}{2z_0} x^2\right]\right\} * F\left\{\left\{R^*(x)U(x;\xi)\right\} * \mathrm{rect}\left(\frac{x}{\alpha\Delta x}\right)\right\} * F\{w(x)\}$$

$$[5.29]$$

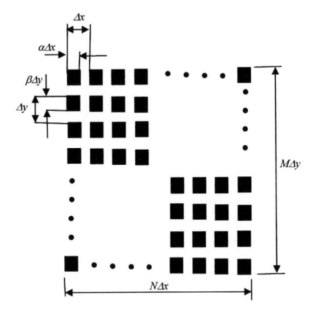

Figure 5.4. *Structure of the detector window*

The Fourier transforms are evaluated at spatial frequencies $\{-x_i/\lambda z_0, -y_i/\lambda z_0\}$. Considering the properties of the Fourier transform, along with the previous expressions, we have:

$$F\left\{\left\{R^*(x)U(x;\xi)\right\} * \text{rect}\left(\frac{x}{\alpha\Delta x}\right)\right\} = \frac{\exp(jkz_0)}{j\lambda z_0}\left[F\left\{\exp\left[\frac{jk}{2z_0}(x^2)\right]\right\} * F\left\{R^*(x)\right\} * F\left\{f\left(\frac{x}{\lambda z_0}\right)\right\}\right] \times F\left\{\text{rect}\left(\frac{x}{\alpha\Delta x}\right)\right\}$$

$$= A_r\sqrt{\lambda z_0}\exp(jkz_0)\left[\exp\left[-\frac{jk}{2z_0}x^2\right] * \tilde{f}(-x+\lambda u_r z_0)\right] \times F\left\{\text{rect}\left(\frac{x}{\alpha\Delta x}\right)\right\}$$

[5.30]

With the properties of convolution with the chirp function, this leads to:

$$F\left\{\left\{R^*(x)U(x;\xi)\right\} * \text{rect}\left(\frac{x}{\alpha\Delta x}\right)\right\}\left(-\frac{x_i}{\lambda z_0}\right) = A_r(\lambda z_0)^{1/2}\exp(jkz_0)\exp\left[-\frac{jk}{2z_0}x_i^2\right]$$

$$\times F\left\{\exp\left[-\frac{jk}{2z_0}x^2\right]\tilde{f}(-x+\lambda u_r z_0)\right\}\left(-\frac{x_i}{\lambda z_0}\right) \times F\left\{\text{rect}\left(\frac{x}{\alpha\Delta x}\right)\right\}\left(-\frac{x_i}{\lambda z_0}\right)$$

[5.31]

Thus, the impulse response is now:

$$h_-(x_i;\xi) = j\frac{(\lambda z_0)^{1/2}}{\lambda z_0}\exp\left[-\frac{jk}{2z_0}x_i^2\right]$$

$$\times\left[\exp\left[-\frac{jk}{2z_0}x_i^2\right]F\left\{\tilde{f}(-x+\lambda u_r z_0)\exp\left[-\frac{jk}{2z_0}x^2\right]\right\}\left(-\frac{x_i}{\lambda z_0}\right) \times \alpha\Delta x\,\text{sinc}\left(\frac{\alpha\Delta x x_i}{\lambda z_0}\right)\right]$$

$$* \exp\left[\frac{jk}{2z_0}x_i^2\right] * F\{w(x)\}$$

[5.32]

By applying once again the convolution with the chirp function, we get:

$$h_-(x_i;\xi) = -\sqrt{\lambda z_0}$$

$$\times F\left\{F\left\{\tilde{f}(-x+\lambda u_r z_0)\exp\left[-\frac{jk}{2z_0}x^2\right]\right\}\left(-\frac{x_i}{\lambda z_0}\right) \times \alpha\Delta x\,\text{sinc}\left(\frac{\pi\alpha\Delta x x_i}{\lambda z_0}\right)\right\}\left[\frac{x_i}{\lambda z_0}\right] * F\{w(x)\}$$

[5.33]

leading to:

$$h_-(x_i;\xi) = -\sqrt{\lambda z_0}\,\tilde{f}(x_i - \lambda u_r z_0)\exp\left[-\frac{jk}{2z_0}x_i^2\right] * \mathrm{rect}\left(\frac{x_i}{\alpha\Delta x}\right) * N\Delta x\,\mathrm{sinc}\left(\frac{N\Delta x x_i}{\lambda z_0}\right)\quad [5.34]$$

Furthermore, we have:

$$\tilde{f}(x - \lambda u_r z_0)\exp\left(-\frac{j\pi}{2z_0}x^2\right) = \exp\left[\frac{jk}{2z_0}(x - \lambda u_r z_0)^2\right]\exp\left(-\frac{j\pi}{2z_0}x^2\right)\delta(x - \lambda u_r z_0 - \xi)$$

$$= \exp\left[\frac{jk}{2}(\lambda u_r)^2 z_0\right]\exp(-j\pi\lambda u_r x)\delta(x - \lambda u_r z_0 - \xi)$$

$$[5.35]$$

In the 1D case, the impulse response is then given by:

$$h_-(x_i;\xi) = -\sqrt{\lambda z_0}\,\exp\left[\frac{jk}{2}z_0\lambda^2 u_r^2\right]\exp(-j\pi\lambda u_r x_i)$$

$$\times \delta(x - \lambda u_r z_0 - \xi) * \mathrm{rect}\left(\frac{x_i}{\alpha\Delta x}\right) * N\Delta x\,\mathrm{sinc}\left(\frac{N\Delta x}{\lambda z_0}x_i\right)\quad [5.36]$$

Consequently, the 2D impulse response of the point source in the focused virtual image plane may be written as:

$$h_-(x_i, y_i; \xi, \eta) = C(x_i, y_i)$$

$$\times \delta(x_i - \lambda u_r z_0 - \xi, y_i - \lambda v_r z_0 - \eta) * \mathrm{rect}\left(\frac{x_i}{\alpha\Delta x}, \frac{y_i}{\beta\Delta y}\right) * \mathrm{sinc}\left(\frac{N\Delta x}{\lambda z_0}x_i, \frac{M\Delta y}{\lambda z_0}y_i\right)$$

$$[5.37]$$

where $C(x_i, y_i)$ represents the terms independent of the coordinates (ξ, η).

Considering the complex amplitude in the object plane as the sum of point sources, the optical field is given by the superposition integral:

$$O_i(x_i, y_i) = \int_{-\infty}^{\infty}\int_{-\infty}^{\infty} O_0(\xi, \eta)h_-(x_i, y_i; \xi, \eta)\mathrm{d}\xi\mathrm{d}\eta \quad [5.38]$$

This result shows that, if we consider $O_0(x_0, y_0)$ as the input signal, the digital holographic system forming the image is a linear system, its impulse response being described by [5.37]. Equation [5.37] also gives the key to understanding resolution in digital holography. It indicates that the reconstructed object is related to the real object by a convolution relation with different contributions. The first contribution is a localization function in the reconstructed field, the second is the pixel function, and the last is the effect of the finite size of the recording. The convolution with the sinc function in equation [5.37] is a result quite coherent with that presented by Kreis [KRE 02a, KRE 02b]. Note that providently, due to the discrete sampling of the hologram, the mathematical expression is the periodic $\sin(Nx)/\sin(x)$ type function rather than the $N\text{sinc}(x)$ type. However, the basic period of $\sin(Nx)/\sin(x)$ has a quite similar profile to $N\text{sinc}(x)$ [PIC 08a]. The paraxial position of the reconstructed object is given by coordinates $(X_0, Y_0) = (u_r \lambda z_0 + \xi, v_r \lambda z_0 + \eta)$, or also $(X_0, Y_0) = (x_r z_0/z_r + \xi, y_r z_0/z_r + \eta)$. So this means that a lateral shift of the object contributes to the localization of the reconstructed image. Equation [5.37] states that the reconstructed object is the real object convoluted with the pixel function. This result is quite compatible with optical imaging properties [PIC 08a]. Indeed, in classical imaging where the object is projected on to the sensor by means of an optical lens, the image is the real image convoluted with the point spread function of the lens and then convoluted with the pixel function. In classical imaging, the filtering of the real object is due to the lens and the pixel surface. Digital holography is a non-conventional imaging method. The filtering is not performed by a lens since there is no lens in the Fresnel configuration. It is instead performed by the double free-space propagation due first to the physical diffraction from object to sensor, and second to the digital diffraction from sensor plane to the reconstructed plane. So, equation [5.37] indicates that the object is convoluted with the point spread function of the filtering, which is given by the sinc function and the pixel function. Note that the sinc function is the diffraction pattern from a digital rectangular aperture and constitutes the main contribution to the resolution function. In classical imaging, one of the terms in the convolution is the diffraction pattern from the pupil of the lens. Finally, the fundamental result given in equation [5.37] is common sense and can be intuitively understood. From this it follows that the influence of the pixel function is a convoluting argument and not a multiplicative sinc function.

The 2D sinc function is related to the width of the detector window $N\Delta x \times M\Delta y$. The larger the window, the more the impulse response will tend toward a δ function, and thus the better will be the quality of the image. The width of the impulse response is given by $\rho_x = \lambda z_0/N\Delta x$ and $\rho_y = \lambda z_0/M\Delta y$ following the x- and y-axes, respectively (Rayleigh criterion). These two parameters fix the spatial resolution limit of the digital holographic apparatus. The spatial resolution is proportional to the wavelength and the distance, and inversely proportional to the width of the detector.

The pixel function is convoluted with the sinc function. If we consider the pixel size to be "large", then there is a low-pass filtering of the resolution function. It follows that active surface of pixels may have a significant effect on the spatial resolution of reconstructed images. Figure 5.5 illustrates this effect and shows the

modulus of the sinc function compared to that of the effective function in the
x-direction. The numerical values are $N = M = 1,024$, $\Delta x = \Delta y = 10$ μm, $\alpha = \beta = 0.95$,
$\lambda = 632.8$ nm, and $z_0 = 150$ mm. Figure 5.5(a) shows that the resulting curve has a
significant decrease in its maximum value and an attenuation of its undulations; thus
the contrast between the peaks and troughs of the function decreases. This decrease
induces a blurring in the image. Figure 5.5(b) shows the normalized degradation of
the resolution function versus pixels size, along the x profile. The numerical values
used are $\lambda = 632.8$ nm and $z_0 = 500$ mm, it is imposed that the observation horizon
be equal to $N\Delta x = L = 6.75$ mm, corresponding to usual size of a commercially
available CCD sensor and the pixel width $\alpha\Delta x$ varies from 3 to 10 μm.

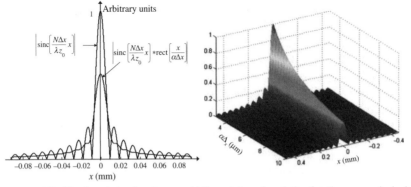

a) Profile of resolution function   b) Degradation of resolution function versus pixels size

Figure 5.5. *Effective profiles of the resolution function versus the pixel area*

We now try to appreciate the influence of the size of the pixel matrix and the
number of reconstructed data points on the quality of the reconstructed image. We
pointed out in Chapter 3 that the spatial sampling in the discrete Fresnel transform is
related to the number of data points used in the FFT algorithms. Consider the
numbers $\{K,J\}$. They can be freely adjusted: we can choose to reduce the number of
calculated data points with $\{K,J\}<\{N,M\}$ or we can choose to increase with
$\{K,J\}\geq\{N,M\}$. This last case is called "zero-padding" and consists of adding
$(K-N,J-M)$ zeros around the hologram matrix. Fundamentally, these zeros do not
add pertinent information; however, they modify the samplings of the diffracted
field that become $\lambda z_0/K\Delta x$ and $\lambda z_0/J\Delta y$. This means that the spatial resolution is not
modified because it is imposed by the number of useful pixels (M,N) of the detector
area and not by the number of data points of the reconstructed field. However, there
is a decrease in the sampling interval leading to an increase of the "definition" of the
image plane. This means that we will see more texture in the image: the resolution
function will be finely sampled and the granular structure of the object will appear to
the observer. Zero-padding of hologram has, as a consequence, the appearance of the

fine speckles of the image but without decreasing their size. Indeed, the presence of speckles in the image is intuitive because the initial rough object is convoluted with enlarging functions from equation [5.37]. This aspect is illustrated in Figure 5.6 in the case of the digital hologram of a 2 euro coin (25 mm in diameter, illuminated with a HeNe laser, placed at $z_0 = 660$ mm, sensor with surface 4.76 mm × 4.76 mm). The number of reconstructed data points is chosen to be (512, 1,024, 2,048, 4,096). When $K = J = 512$ there is a strong reduction of the observation horizon of the hologram since the number of data points used for the computation is smaller than the initial matrix. In this case, the resolution decreases and the reconstructed image appears very poor. When $K = J = 1,024$, the number of data points is equal to that given by the sensor. The image sampling also corresponds to the resolutions ρ_x, ρ_y. Thus the image appears "pixelated". For $K = J = 2,048$, zero-padding is effective and the image sampling is two times smaller than resolution. So, the resolution function is sampled with a better definition and this allows the observation of the fine texture of the image, particularly its speckle. For $K = J = 4,096$, the image sampling is four times smaller than the resolution. The definition in the image plane is again increased, but the speckle does not change its size since it is imposed by the resolution.

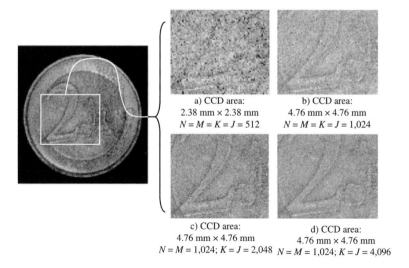

a) CCD area:
2.38 mm × 2.38 mm
$N = M = K = J = 512$

b) CCD area:
4.76 mm × 4.76 mm
$N = M = K = J = 1,024$

c) CCD area:
4.76 mm × 4.76 mm
$N = M = 1,024; K = J = 2,048$

d) CCD area:
4.76 mm × 4.76 mm
$N = M = 1,024; K = J = 4,096$

Figure 5.6. *Comparison of images reconstructed by holograms of different sizes and zero-padding*

5.2. Elimination of parasitic orders with the S-FFT method

We recall the previous discussion: the zero order is a perturbation of the reconstructed field. In order to eliminate this perturbation and to assure the good quality of the reconstructed image, it is necessary to increase the signal-to-noise ratio. In this section, we will study the diffraction efficiency of a digital hologram, and then we will present some widely used techniques for the elimination of the parasitic orders.

5.2.1. *Diffraction efficiency of a digital hologram*

The reconstruction of a digital wavefront does not consume real light energy, as is the case in the process of physical diffraction from a laser by a photographic plate. Nevertheless, the ratio of the waves digitally diffracted may be expressed. The diffraction efficiency is generally defined as the ratio between the intensity of the reconstruction wave and those of the diffracted orders. We will now examine which intensity ratio p between the object and the reference must be imposed to obtain the greatest amplitude of the reconstructed object wave [LI 09a].

Let $O = \sqrt{p} \exp(jk\varphi)$ be the complex amplitude of the object wave, $R = \exp(jk\varphi_r)$ the reference wave, and $R_c = a_c \exp(jk\varphi_c)$ the reconstruction wave. The complex amplitude of the light transmitted by the hologram is:

$$
\begin{aligned}
R_c \times I_H &= R_c \left(|O|^2 + |R|^2 \right) + R_c O^* R + R_c O R^* \\
&= a_c (p+1) \exp(jk\varphi_c) \\
&\quad + a_c \sqrt{p} \exp(-jk\varphi + jk\varphi_r + jk\varphi_c) \\
&\quad + a_c \sqrt{p} \exp(jk\varphi - jk\varphi_r + jk\varphi_c)
\end{aligned}
\tag{5.39}
$$

The mean intensity is the sum of three terms:

$$
I_t = a_c^2 (p+1)^2 + 2a_c^2 p
\tag{5.40}
$$

Whatever the choice of the reconstruction wave (object or conjugate wave), the ratio between the intensity of the reconstructed wave and the mean intensity is always given by:

$$
\eta = \frac{a_c^2 p}{I_t} = \frac{1}{p + 4 + 1/p}
\tag{5.41}
$$

If $p = 1$, the intensity of the reference wave is equal to that of the object wave, this expression is maximal. This condition corresponds to the case where we have the best contrast between interference fringes, and means that there is the best grayscale in the hologram; this result therefore seems logical.

Substituting $p = 1$ into [5.41], we obtain $\eta = 1/6$. In other words, for an amplitude hologram, the proportion of useful energy is only 1/6 when the object–reference ratio attains its optimum value. In this case, the proportion of energy at the zero order is 4/6, constituting the largest perturbation of the object wavefront.

We therefore note that the elimination of the zero order allows us to increase the signal-to-noise ratio in the image. We present some practical methods in the following subsection.

5.2.2. Methods of direct elimination

It is possible to eliminate the parasitic orders by using holograms recorded under different conditions.

5.2.2.1. Method directly eliminating the object and reference waves

If we have recorded a hologram I_H, and we have independently recorded the object and reference waves $|R|^2$ and $|O|^2$, respectively, we may obtain a hologram that only consists of both twin images, i.e.:

$$I'_H = I_H - |O|^2 - |R|^2 = O^* R + OR^*$$ [5.42]

Since the perturbation coming from the zero order has disappeared, and on the condition that there is no superposition between the useful and conjugate images, we may reconstruct the image without perturbation. In this case, we may still decrease the object–detector distance and increase the spatial resolution of the image [KRE 97b, LIU 02, DEM 03b, ZHA 04a, RAM 07, CHE 07]. From relation [5.20], the recording distance is determined by the following relation:

$$z_0 = \rho \times \frac{2D_0 L}{\lambda N}$$ [5.43]

This relation may be intuited, by considering Figure 5.7, which shows, in a system of rectangular coordinates, the relationship between the detector ($z = 0$) and the reconstruction ($z = z_0$) planes. The center of the reconstructed image is situated at the center of the first quadrant [PAV 09].

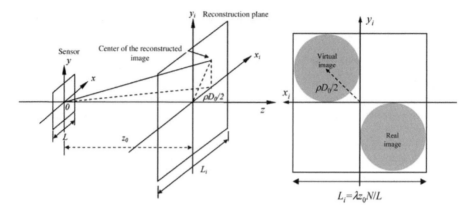

Figure 5.7. *Relation between the sensor plane, the image plane, and the propagation direction of the reference wave*

As an illustration, a simulation may aid the comprehension of this result. The parameters of this simulation are as follows:

– the object has the dimension $D_0 = 25$ mm, its transmittance is proportional to the brightness distribution of the famous "Mona Lisa" painting;

– wavelength $\lambda = 532$ nm;

– detector with $L = 4.76$ mm and $N = 1,024$.

From [5.41] we have $z_0 \geq 2D_0L/(N\lambda) = 436.88$ mm. We suppose the object-sensor distance to be $z_0 = 450$ mm, which corresponds to the case where $\rho \approx 1.03$ for [5.43]. For the reconstructed image to be located in the first quadrant, from Figure 5.7, we consider the reference wave to be plane and propagating in a direction given by the direction cosines:

$$\cos\alpha = \cos\beta = \frac{\rho D_0 / 2}{\sqrt{\rho^2 D_0^2 / 4 + z_0^2}} \approx \frac{\rho D_0}{2z_0}$$

$$\cos\gamma = \frac{z_0}{\sqrt{D_0^2 / 4 + z_0^2}} \approx 1 \qquad\qquad [5.44]$$

Adding zeros around the image of the "Mona Lisa", we obtain an object plane of sides $2D_0 = 50$ mm distributed over $1,024 \times 1,024$ pixels. Furthermore, we suppose the phase of each pixel to be random. Figure 5.8(a) shows the image in the object plane.

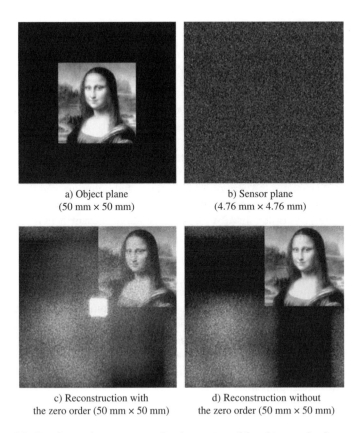

a) Object plane
(50 mm × 50 mm)

b) Sensor plane
(4.76 mm × 4.76 mm)

c) Reconstruction with
the zero order (50 mm × 50 mm)

d) Reconstruction without
the zero order (50 mm × 50 mm)

Figure 5.8. *Simulation demonstrating the elimination of the object and reference waves*
(number of pixels: 512 × 512)

The steps of the simulation process are as follows:

– We calculate the complex amplitude of the object in the detector plane by S-FFT. The intensity pattern calculated is shown in Figure 5.8(b); we note that it is a speckle pattern.

– We take the mean value of the object wave amplitude as the amplitude of the reference wave and the direction cosines are evaluated with [5.44].

– We calculate the digital hologram $|R + O|^2$, then reconstruct the object by calculating by S-FFT the field diffracted across the distance z_0.

Figure 5.8(c) is the image in the reconstruction plane: it is greatly perturbed by the zero order.

– We then calculate $|R + O|^2 - |R|^2 - |O|^2$ and reconstruct it in the same manner, and we obtain a decontaminated image, as demonstrated in Figure 5.8(d).

In practice, the recording of a hologram, the reference, and then object waves is carried out sequentially, which generates a noise fluctuation in what is obtained. Thus, the decontamination is not total and there may remain a slight trace of the zero order.

Note that other methods based on the use of a single off-axis digital hologram exist in the literature [PAV 09, PAV 10]. In the reference [PAV 10], the method is iterative, and it estimates the zero order from the initial hologram and the filtering of the +1 order, then by iteration converges to the +1 order decontaminated from the presence of the zero order. In [PAV 09], the authors present a nonlinear method based on filtering in the Fourier plane of the logarithm of the hologram. These two methods also give very good results.

5.2.2.2. Method with an arbitrary phase shift of the reference wave

The method presented in the previous section requires three images to be recorded sequentially, and presents some limitations. Here, we present another method that requires only two phase-shifted images [ZHA 04a].

If we add a phase shift δ whose value is not a multiple of 2π, the intensity of the hologram now corresponds to:

$$I'_H(x,y) = |O|^2 + |R|^2 + RO^* \exp(j\delta) + R^* O \exp(-j\delta) \qquad [5.45]$$

The difference between the initial and phase-shifted hologram is:

$$I_H(x,y) - I'_H(x,y) = RO^*[1 - \exp(j\delta)] + R^* O[1 - \exp(-j\delta)] \qquad [5.46]$$

It is therefore possible to reconstruct the object field without the zero order by taking the difference $I_H - I'_H$. The exponential factor inside the brackets in [5.46] does not influence the spatial distribution of the reconstructed image. Of course, the phase shift may take any value except $\delta = \pi$.

With this method, the distance may be decreased so as to improve the spatial resolution (relation [5.43], Figure 5.7). Simulations show the quality of the reconstructed image to be identical to those of the previous method.

5.2.3. *Method of extracting the complex amplitude of the object wave*

It is possible to directly extract the complex amplitude of the object wave by using phase-shifting methods [CRE 88, DOR 99]. This approach was described by Yamaguchi [YAM 97] in 1997 and allows the reconstruction of an image free from the zero order and the twin image.

We write the complex amplitude of the object and reference waves as $O = o_0\exp(j\varphi_0)$ and $R = r_0\exp(j\varphi_r)$, respectively. The hologram is:

$$I_H(x,y) = o^2(x,y) + r^2(x,y) + 2o(x,y)r(x,y)\cos[\varphi(x,y) - \varphi_r(x,y)] \quad [5.47]$$

We consider a phase-shifted hologram with a phase shift that is an integer division of 2π, i.e. $2\pi/P$, with integer P. We have:

$$I_{Hp}(x,y) = o^2(x,y) + r^2(x,y) + 2o(x,y)r(x,y)\cos[\varphi(x,y) - \varphi_r(x,y) + 2n\pi/P] \quad [5.48]$$

with $p = 1, 2, ..., P$. For $P \geq 3$, the phase of the object wave in the detector plane may be calculated by [GRE 84]:

$$\varphi_0 = \varphi_r + \arctan\left\{\frac{\sum_{n=1}^{P} I_{Hp}\sin(2\pi p/P)}{\sum_{n=1}^{P} I_{Hp}\cos(2\pi p/P)}\right\} \quad [5.49]$$

and the amplitude is calculated by:

$$o_0 = \frac{1}{2r_0}\sqrt{\left(\sum_{p=1}^{P} I_{Hp}\sin(2\pi p/P)\right)^2 + \left(\sum_{p=1}^{P} I_{Hp}\cos(2\pi p/P)\right)^2} \quad [5.50]$$

If the reference wave is plane or spherical, that is, free from aberrations, the phase $\varphi_r(x,y)$ may be determined without ambiguity and compensated in [5.49]. The complex wave may be evaluated and the object may be directly reconstructed by S-FFT. Using the conjugate complex wave, we may calculate the twin image.

Letting $P = 4$, we obtain the most widely used method that was proposed by [YAM 97], using four $\pi/2$ phase-shifted holograms [CRE 88, WYA 75]. In this case, relations [5.49] and [5.50] become:

$$\varphi_0 = \varphi_r + \arctan\left\{\frac{I_{H4} - I_{H2}}{I_{H1} - I_{H3}}\right\}$$

$$o_0 = \frac{1}{4r_0}\sqrt{[I_{H1} - I_{H3}]^2 + [I_{H4} - I_{H2}]^2} \qquad\qquad [5.51]$$

As an illustration, Figure 5.9 shows the result obtained with the "Mona Lisa" and four phase shifts 0, $\pi/2$, π, and $3\pi/2$. The parameters are $L_0 = 75$ mm, $N = 1,024$, and the pixel matrix width is $L = 4.76$ mm. The recording distance is given by $z_0 = LL_0/(\lambda N) \approx 551$ mm. Figure 5.9(a) shows the reconstructed image, similar to the initial image, and Figure 5.9(b) shows one of the four phase-shifted holograms.

a) Reconstructed image	b) One of the four holograms
(75 mm × 75 mm,	(4.76 mm × 4.76 mm,
1,024 × 1,024 pixels)	1,024 × 1,024 pixels)

Figure 5.9. *Simulation of reconstruction by phase shift*

Phase-shifting methods reproduce all the information, on the condition that the amplitude and phase of the reference beam are well known. In practice, these conditions are difficult to satisfy [LI 10b]. Moreover, a number of studies have considered the influence of errors on the reconstructed image following different algorithms [RAS 94]. Note that the phase shift cannot be an exact integer division of 2π and that the increment between each phase-shifted hologram may be different. Some methods of phase demodulation were recently proposed and integrate the possibility of a random phase shift. The reader will be able to find the algorithms corresponding to these methods in the references [CRE 88], [QIA 01], [CAI 03], [CAI 04] and [XU 06].

5.3. Wavefront reconstruction with an adjustable magnification

The method of reconstruction by S-FFT is relatively simple. Nonetheless, the physical width of the reconstructed plane depends on the wavelength, the diffraction distance, and the number of samples. Most of the reconstructed field is occupied by parasitic orders while the image of interest occupies a limited zone. Furthermore, when we make a digital holographic recording using waves of different wavelengths, or when we use digital color holography to measure displacement fields (see Chapter 7), the physical size of the reconstructed images must be identical regardless of the wavelength. The normalization of the physical scale of the reconstructed images corresponding to different wavelengths has stimulated researchers during recent years.

In 2004, F. Zhang [ZHA 04b] proposed an algorithm called double Fresnel-transform algorithm (DBFT) based on a double discrete Fourier transform and the Fresnel approximations. The author claimed an adjustable magnification. The proposed method was based on phase-shifting to obtain the object wave then takes advantage of the fact that the size of the field by S-FFT depends on the reconstruction distance. We will show that even though this method does not rigorously satisfy the sampling theorem, it allows us to obtain suitable results. Another algorithm that rigorously obeys the scalar wave equation and satisfies the sampling theorem also enables the reconstruction of the image with a variable magnification [LI 09b, LI 10c, LI 11b, PIC 09]. We will begin by studying this algorithm and then we will discuss the DBFT algorithm.

The fundamentals of holography show that, considering a spherical reconstruction wave, we may observe the image reconstructed with a magnification that depends on the curvature of this wave. If the reconstruction wave is spherical, the previous study of the S-FFT method showed that the physical width of the reconstructed plane is proportional to the magnification of the image. This means that it is not possible to obtain an image of a different size to that of the plane reconstructed using S-FFT (see the discussion of [5.19] in section 5.1). It is therefore necessary to consider another approach and, in particular, the methods of calculation by convolution. The theoretical aspects of the numerical calculation of diffraction using the transfer function of the angular spectrum presented in Chapter 3 show that, in this case, the width of the reconstructed plane is identical to that of the detector. Consequently, from the relation between the size of the object and that of the pixel matrix, we may determine a spherical reconstruction wave suitable for reconstructing an image that occupies the entire surface of the calculated plane.

The different transfer functions of Chapter 3 correspond to different mathematical formulae. So as to increase the calculation speed, it is necessary to estimate the number of FFTs to be calculated.

From equation [3.33] in Chapter 3, when we know the object field $U(x,y)$ in the detector plane, the reconstructed image is expressed by:

$$U_i(x,y) = F^{-1}\{F\{U(x,y)\}H(f_x,f_y)\}$$

[5.52]

According to relations [3.30], [3.31], and [3.32] in Chapter 3, the Kirchhoff and Rayleigh–Sommerfeld transfer functions are given by a Fourier transform. The numerical result of $H(f_x, f_y)$ must therefore be obtained by an FFT. With [5.52], we must first calculate the spectrum of the object field, and then calculate its product with the transfer function, and finally, for the reconstruction, we require one inverse Fourier transform. This means it is necessary to carry out three FFTs to obtain a result.

However, if we use the two other transfer functions, either the angular spectrum or the Fresnel, that we presented in Chapter 3, we will have two analytical expressions directly defined in frequency space. Having multiplied this transfer function by the spectrum and calculating the reconstruction by inverse FFT, we will have only carried out two fast transforms. As we need to take two FFTs with this method, it may then be called "convolution with an adjustable magnification". Taking into account the calculation time, we generally use the D-FFT with angular spectrum method. The program LIM5.m in the Appendix reconstructs a hologram by D-FFT.

5.3.1. *Convolution with adjustable magnification*

Using the same notation as in section 5.1, the hologram recorded by the detector is (the pixels are considered to have no spatial extent):

$$I_H(x,y) = w(x,y)\left[|U(x,y)|^2 + A_r^2 + R(x,y)U^*(x,y) + R^*(x,y)U(x,y)\right]$$ [5.53]

Illuminating the hologram with a spherical wave, the spectrum of the diffracted wave is given by:

$$F\{R_c(x,y)I_H(x,y)\} = G_0(f_x,f_y) + G_+(f_x,f_y) + G_-(f_x,f_y)$$ [5.54]

The terms on the right of this expression are the spectra of the zero order, the conjugate wave, and the object wave, respectively. These spectra are given by the following relations:

$$G_0(f_x,f_y) = F\left\{\left[|U(x,y)|^2 + A_r^2\right]w(x,y)R_c(x,y)\right\}$$ [5.55a]

$$G_+\left(f_x, f_y\right) = F\{R(x,y)U^*(x,y)w(x,y)R_c(x,y)\} \qquad [5.55b]$$

$$G_-\left(f_x, f_y\right) = F\{R^*(x,y)U(x,y)w(x,y)R_c(x,y)\} \qquad [5.55c]$$

Here again we take up Goodman's notation [GOO 72, GOO 05]: $G_+(f_x,f_y)$ corresponds to the spectrum of the conjugate beam forming a real image in the direction of illumination, and $G_-(f_x,f_y)$ is the spectrum of the beam that leads to the formation of a virtual image in the opposite to the propagation direction. Since either of these two terms can be used for the reconstruction of the object wavefront, we will study only $G_-(f_x,f_y)$ in the following.

Substituting $R(x,y)$ into $G_-(f_x,f_y)$:

$$G_-\left(f_x, f_y\right) = F\left\{A_r \exp\left\{-\frac{jk}{2z_r}\left[(x-x_r)^2 + (y-y_r)^2\right]\right\}U(x,y)w(x,y)R_c(x,y)\right\}$$

$$= A_r \exp\left[-\frac{jk}{2z_r}\left(x_r^2 + y_r^2\right)\right]F\left\{\exp\left[-\frac{jk}{2z_r}\left(x^2+y^2\right)\right]\exp\left[+j2\pi\left(\frac{x_r}{\lambda z_r}x + \frac{y_r}{\lambda z_r}y\right)\right] \times U(x,y)w(x,y)R_c(x,y)\right\}$$

$$[5.56]$$

and supposing

$$G'_-\left(f_x, f_y\right) = F\left\{\exp\left[-\frac{jk}{2z_r}\left(x^2 + y^2\right)\right]U(x,y)R_c(x,y)\right\} \qquad [5.57]$$

Equation [5.56] may be rewritten as:

$$G_-\left(f_x, f_y\right)$$

$$= A_r \exp\left[-\frac{jk}{2z_r}\left(x_r^2 + y_r^2\right)\right]G'_-\left(f_x, f_y\right) * F\{w(x,y)\} * \delta\left(f_x - \frac{x_r}{\lambda z_r}, f_y - \frac{y_r}{\lambda z_r}\right) \quad [5.58]$$

$$\approx A_r \exp\left[-\frac{jk}{2z_r}\left(x_r^2 + y_r^2\right)\right]G'_-\left(f_x - \frac{x_r}{\lambda z_r}, f_y - \frac{y_r}{\lambda z_r}\right)$$

This expression shows that, in the spectral plane, the spectrum $G'_-(f_x,f_y)$ is centered at the spatial frequencies $(x_r/\lambda z_r, y_r/\lambda z_r)$. The study of reconstruction by illumination with a spherical wave (section 5.1) showed that when the diffraction distance satisfies [5.9], i.e.

$$z_i = -\left(\frac{1}{z_0} + \frac{1}{z_c} - \frac{1}{z_r}\right)^{-1} \qquad [5.59]$$

we obtain an image of the object field whose center is displaced from the origin. The magnification is:

$$G_y = -z_i / z_0$$ [5.60]

In order to form an image centered on the origin, it is necessary to extract the spectrum $G'_-(f_x, f_y)$ described by [5.57]. To do this, we use a window filter $W(f_x, f_y)$ in the Fourier plane and we consider the product by the spectrum of the hologram. Then, shifting of spectral coordinates $(x_r/\lambda_r, y_r/\lambda z_r)$ and calculating the inverse Fourier transform, we obtain the object field [LI 09b, PIC 09]:

$$U_i(x, y) = F^{-1}\left\{ W\left(f_x + \frac{x_r}{\lambda z_r}, f_y + \frac{y_r}{\lambda z_r} \right) G_-\left(f_x + \frac{x_r}{\lambda z_r}, f_y + \frac{y_r}{\lambda z_r} \right) H(f_x, f_y, z_i) \right\}$$ [5.61]

where $H(f_x, f_y, z_i)$ is the transfer function of the diffraction across the distance z_i. From equations [3.34]–[3.39] in Chapter 3, the transfer functions correspond to the different classical diffraction formulae, and, respecting the sampling theorem, we can always reconstruct the object wavefront with a variable magnification. Taking into account the efficiency of calculation, we will use only the two following analytical functions:

– The angular spectrum transfer function:

$$H(f_x, f_y, z_i) = \exp\left[jkz_i \sqrt{1 - (\lambda f_x)^2 - (\lambda f_y)^2} \right]$$ [5.62]

– The Fresnel approximation transfer function:

$$H(f_x, f_y, z_i) = \exp\left\{ jkz_i\left[1 - \frac{\lambda^2}{2}(f_x^2 + f_y^2) \right] \right\}$$ [5.63]

From [5.9], the radius of curvature of the spherical wave is given by:

$$z_c = \left(\frac{1}{z_0} + \frac{1}{z_i} - \frac{1}{z_r} \right)^{-1}$$ [5.64]

Generally, the distance z_0 between the object and the detector as well as the radius of curvature z_r of the reference wave are known. The magnification G_y necessary for the reconstruction of the object in the window of the detector, is given by the ratio of the detector and object sizes. Once the magnification is determined, using [5.60] and [5.64], we may determine the new reconstruction distance z_i (which is different to z_0) and the radius of curvature z_c of the reconstruction wave.

Following the procedure presented in this section, the reconstruction of the wavefront will be achieved by [5.61].

Considering that G_- and G_+ contain the same information about the object, we may find similar expressions which allow the image of the term G_+ to be reconstructed.

5.3.2. *Experiment with adjustable magnification*

The experimental apparatus is presented in Figure 5.2 in which we consider the green laser wave ($\lambda = 532$ nm). The reference wave is plane ($z_r = \infty$) and given by the spatial filter. The pixel matrix contains $1,024 \times 1,360$ pixels of size 4.65 µm. The object is the bronze medal of the "2000 Paris 20 km" whose diameter is 60 mm and the object–detector distance is $z_0 = 1,500$ mm. In practice, we will use a hologram of $1,024 \times 1,024$ pixels for the reconstruction of the wavefront, which corresponds to a pixel matrix of width $L = 4.76$ mm. The ratio between the width of the pixel matrix and the diameter of the medal is $L/D_0 \approx 0.079$. So the reconstructed image completely occupies the reconstruction field, we will consider $G_y = 0.075$. From [5.60], we have $z_i = -112.5$ mm. Substituting $z_r = \infty$ into [5.64], we obtain $z_c = -121.6$ mm. Figure 5.10(a) shows the spectrum of the hologram illuminated by the spherical wave. The amplitude of the zero order being greater than the other two, its maximum is clipped in order to see the whole spectrum. The spectral repartition of the zero order is similar to the Fresnel pattern from a rectangular pupil. This image shows that, if we use the spectrum of the object (or conjugate) wave for the reconstruction, the determination of its center is an important point not to be neglected. The center of the spectrum of the conjugate object wave is marked by a cross and the filter window is marked by a rectangular line.

Having chosen the useful part of the spectrum, we consider this zone as the center of a new spectral plane, and, by adding zeros all around it, we obtain the spectrum of the conjugate object wave across $1,024 \times 1,024$ pixels. With [5.61] and the angular spectrum transfer function, the reconstructed image of the object is given in Figure 5.10(b).

We note that the image obtained by the calculation covers the reconstruction plane. Since the choice of magnification is independent of the wavelength, we may reconstruct identically sized images of different wavelengths. However, since the window filter includes a part of the zero order, there exists a strong perturbation in the image of Figure 5.10(b). The perturbation has the form of the Fraunhofer diffraction pattern from a rectangular pupil. It may be shown that this perturbation corresponds to the intensity distribution of the reference wave $w(x, y)A_r^2$ of [5.53]. When the magnification of the reconstruction varies, the position of the perturbation moves in the plane, but keeps the same appearance. For example, Figures 5.11 and 5.12 correspond to the images obtained with the magnifications $G_y = 0.055$ and $G_y = 0.035$.

These figures show that when the magnification decreases the spectrum of the zero order expands. The elimination of the perturbation due to the zero order is therefore essential if the quality of the reconstruction is to be increased. This point is discussed in the following section.

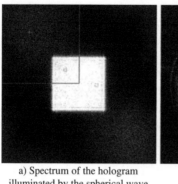 

a) Spectrum of the hologram illuminated by the spherical wave and window filtering function	b) Reconstructed image $z_i = -112.5$ mm $z_c = -121.6$ mm

Figure 5.10. *Spectrum of the hologram and reconstructed image with a magnification of $G_y = 0.075$*

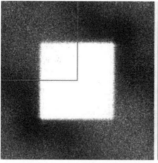 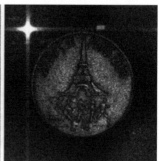

a) Spectrum of the hologram illuminated by the spherical wave and window filtering function	b) Reconstructed image $z_i = -82.5$ mm $z_c = -87.3$ mm

Figure 5.11. *Spectrum of the hologram and the image reconstructed with a magnification of $G_y = 0.055$*

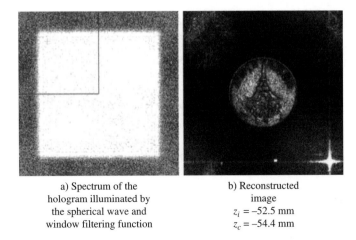

<table>
<tr><td>a) Spectrum of the hologram illuminated by the spherical wave and window filtering function</td><td>b) Reconstructed image
$z_i = -52.5$ mm
$z_c = -54.4$ mm</td></tr>
</table>

Figure 5.12. *Spectrum of the hologram and the image reconstructed with a magnification of $G_y = 0.035$*

5.3.3. *Elimination of the perturbation due to the zero order*

As pointed out previously, the form of the perturbation due to the zero order is very different from that of the image reconstructed by the S-FFT method. Naturally, it is possible to apply phase-shifting methods, as previously discussed, to obtain the useful wave and eliminate all perturbations. However, it is often favorable to only work with a single off-axis hologram (or one fast time sequence) so as to limit the acquisition time of the hologram, and conserve the real-time character of holography. Thus, we now look into the elimination of perturbations in an off-axis hologram reconstructed by convolution with an adjustable magnification.

5.3.3.1. *Spectral distribution and determination of the center of the object wave*

The previous study of wavefront reconstruction showed that the spectral distribution of the object wave (or the conjugate wave) given by a digital hologram illuminated by a spherical wave is a wide distribution of diffuse nature. Its center is shifted relative to the center of the spectral plane. Its coordinates depend on the spatial frequencies of the reference wave. The correct positioning of the center is necessary so that the window filter may correctly reconstruct the image. On the basis of previous studies, we present two methods permitting the reduction of the perturbation due to the zero order, and one method that allows the determination of the spectral center of the object wave.

Taking equations [5.56] anew, the expression of $G_-(f_x, f_y)$ is given by:

$$G_-(f_x, f_y) = A_r \exp\left[-\frac{jk}{2z_r}(x_r^2 + y_r^2)\right]$$

$$* F\left\{\exp\left[\frac{jk}{2}\left(\frac{1}{z_c} - \frac{1}{z_r}\right)(x^2 + y^2)\right]w(x,y)\right\} * F\{U(x,y)\} \qquad [5.65]$$

$$* F\left\{\exp\left[+j\frac{k}{z_r}(x_r x + y_r y)\right]\right\}$$

We have:

$$F\left\{\exp\left[+j\frac{k}{z_r}(x_r x + y_r y)\right]\right\} = \delta\left(u - \frac{x_r}{\lambda z_r}, v - \frac{y_r}{\lambda z_r}\right) \qquad [5.66]$$

Supposing

$$\frac{1}{z_-} = \frac{1}{z_c} - \frac{1}{z_r} \qquad [5.67]$$

Equation [5.65] may be simplified to:

$$G_-(f_x, f_y) \approx C \times F\left\{\exp\left[\frac{jk}{2z_-}(x^2 + y^2)\right]w(x,y)\right\}$$

$$* F\{U(x,y)\} * \delta\left(u - \frac{x_r}{\lambda z_r}, v + \frac{y_r}{\lambda z_r}\right) \qquad [5.68]$$

Given that the convolution between the last term on the right of [5.68] and $F\{U(x, y)\}$ simply displaces the function $F\{U(x, y)\}$ and does not play any role in its spatial distribution, the distribution of $G_-(f_x, f_y)$ depends only on the convolution between $F\left\{\exp\left[jk/2z_-(x^2 + y^2)\right]w(x,y)\right\}$ and $F\{U(x, y)\}$. It may be shown that:

$$F\left\{\exp\left[\frac{jk}{2z_-}(x^2 + y^2)\right]w(x,y)\right\} = (\lambda z_-)^2 \exp\left[-j\pi\lambda z_-(f_x^2 + f_y^2)\right] \times$$

$$\int\limits_{-\infty}^{\infty}\int\limits_{-\infty}^{\infty} w(\lambda z_- f_{xc}, \lambda z_- f_{yc})\exp\left\{j\pi\lambda z_-\left[(f_{xc} - f_x)^2 + (f_{yc} - f_y)^2\right]\right\}df_{xc}df_{yc}$$

$$[5.69]$$

In frequency space, this is the diffraction pattern from a rectangular pupil. Considering that the pixel matrix is square:

$$w\left(\lambda z_- f_x, \lambda z_- f_y\right) = \mathrm{rect}\left(\frac{\lambda z_- f_x}{L}, \frac{\lambda z_- f_y}{L}\right) \qquad [5.70]$$

The convolution between $F\left\{\exp\left[jk/2z_-\left(x^2 + y^2\right)\right]w(x, y)\right\}$ and $F\{U(x, y)\}$ will enlarge the latter. The enlargement is determined by [5.70] and is approximately equal to $|L/\lambda z_-|$.

In the same way, for $G_+(f_x, f_y)$, and with [5.55b], supposing

$$\frac{1}{z_+} = \frac{1}{z_c} + \frac{1}{z_r} \qquad [5.71]$$

The spectrum of the object wave $G_-(f_x, f_y)$ will be stretched by the extension width $|L/\lambda z_+|$. Since, in general, $|L/\lambda z_+|$ and $|L/\lambda z_-|$ are not equal, the enlargements of the spectra of the object and conjugate waves are not identical. Nevertheless, from [5.67] and [5.71], the smaller the radius of curvature of the spherical reconstruction wave, the greater $|L/\lambda z_+|$ and $|L/\lambda z_-|$ will be. This means that the spectral widths of the object and conjugate waves increase when z_c decreases.

We now study the spectrum of the zero order. From [5.55a], $G_0(f_x, f_y)$ is rewritten as:

$$G_0\left(f_x, f_y\right) = G_{01}\left(f_x, f_y\right) + G_{02}\left(f_x, f_y\right) \qquad [5.72]$$

with:

$$G_{01}\left(f_x, f_y\right) = F\left\{|U(x, y)|^2\right\} * F\{R_c(x, y)w(x, y)\} \qquad [5.73a]$$

$$G_{02}\left(f_x, f_y\right) = A_r^2\, F\{R_c(x, y)w(x, y)\} \qquad [5.73b]$$

First, we study the distribution of $F\{R_c(x, y)w(x, y)\}$. Developing it, we obtain:

$$F\{R_c(x, y)w(x, y)\} = \left(\lambda z_c\right)^2 \exp\left[-j\pi\lambda z_c\left(f_x^2 + f_y^2\right)\right]\times$$

$$\int_{-\infty}^{\infty}\int_{-\infty}^{\infty} w\left(\lambda z_c f_x', \lambda z_c f_y'\right)\exp\left\{j\pi\lambda z_c\left[\left(f_x' - f_x\right)^2 + \left(f_y' - f_y\right)^2\right]\right\}df_x' df_y'$$

$$[5.74]$$

In frequency space, this expression corresponds to the diffraction pattern from a square pupil whose width is $|L/\lambda z_c|$.

In [5.73a], the width of $F\left\{|U(x,y)|^2\right\} = F\{U(x,y)\} * F\{U^*(x,y)\}$ is twice that of $F\{U(x,y)\}$. Since the surface of the object is generally rough, $F\left\{|U(x,y)|^2\right\}$ is a speckle pattern in frequency space. Thus, the width of $G_{01}(f_x,f_y)$ is approximately the sum of $|L/\lambda z_c|$ and twice the width of $F\{U(x,y)\}$.

In summary, the spectral width of the zero order is the sum of the widths of $F\{|U(x,y)|^2\}$ and $|L/\lambda z_c|$, and there is a square pattern of width $|L/\lambda z_c|$ situated at the center of the spectrum. The width of each spectral zone increases when the radius of curvature z_c decreases, that is when the magnification G_y decreases, and the spectra are superposed. This is what is seen in Figures 5.10(a), 5.11(a), and 5.12(a). The spectral appearance of the zero order is essentially manifested as a high amplitude Fresnel diffraction pattern from a square pupil. The smaller the absolute value of the radius $|z_c|$, the greater the extent of the spectrum. These experimental results coincide well with the theoretical analysis. The spectra mix strongly when the magnification G_y is small.

The following section discusses the problem of the spectral localization of the useful wave.

5.3.3.2. Spectral position of the object wave

We will now demonstrate that the spectral center of the object wave may be determined by taking the position of the image reconstructed by S-FFT as a reference. We take up equation [5.68] again: this expression shows that $G_-(f_x,f_y)$ is located at the frequency coordinates $(x_r/\lambda z_r, y_r/\lambda z_r)$.

The calculation of the spectrum is carried out by FFT. The $N \times N$ pixel matrix has sides L and the spectral plane has a width equal to N/L. The center of the useful wave will be located at the pixel coordinates $(x_r L/\lambda z_r, y_r L/\lambda z_r)$ in the spectral plane.

Consider the discussion about wavefront reconstruction by S-FFT developed in the first section; when the diffraction distance satisfies [5.09], an image of magnification G_y, centered at the spatial coordinates $(x_r z_i/z_r, y_r z_i/z_r)$, is formed in the reconstructed plane at $z = z_i$. The sensor matrix being composed of $N \times N$ pixels, the physical width of the plane reconstructed by S-FFT is $L_i = \lambda z_i N/L = \lambda G_y z_0 N/L$ [LI 09a]. In this case, considering the pixel as a measurement cell of the image plane, the coordinates of the center of the object image are $(x_r L/\lambda z_r, y_r L/\lambda z_r)$. Thus, the image reconstructed by S-FFT and the spectral zone are located at the same pixel coordinates. Considering an image calculated by S-FFT as a reference, we may therefore determine the center of the spectrum of the object wave without ambiguity.

As an example, Figure 5.13(a) shows the image reconstructed by S-FFT. The spectral image of a hologram illuminated by a spherical wave is given in Figure 5.13(b). Considering the center of the reconstructed image marked by the white cross (see Figure 5.13a) as a reference, the position of the spectral center is determined in Figure 5.13(b) by the same cross.

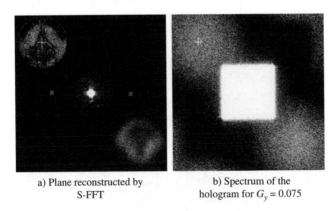

a) Plane reconstructed by	b) Spectrum of the
S-FFT	hologram for $G_y = 0.075$

Figure 5.13. *Relation between the center of the image given by S-FFT and that of the spectrum of the object wave*

5.3.4. *Method eliminating the perturbation due to the zero order*

Figure 5.13(b) shows that, even though we are able to correctly determine the center of the spectrum of the object wave, the superposition between the spectra must be treated. We may potentially use a small window to limit the perturbation, but, on the other hand, we will lose some components of the object wave spectrum, which translates into a degradation of the edges of the object. We present a simple method allowing the elimination of the perturbation without degrading the quality of the reconstructed image [LI 10d, LIU 02].

Let us consider again the expression of the hologram recorded by the detector:

$$I_H(x,y) = w(x,y)\left[|U(x,y)|^2 + A_r^2 + R(x,y)U^*(x,y) + R^*(x,y)U(x,y)\right] \quad [5.75]$$

From a statistical point of view, the mean of the last two terms in a neighborhood $\Delta \in (x \pm k\Delta x, y \pm k\Delta y)$, k being a non-zero integer, around the observation point (x,y), tends toward zero. We may therefore make the following approximation:

$$\bar{I}_{H \in \Delta}(x,y) \approx w(x,y)\left[|U(x,y)|^2 + A_r^2\right] \quad [5.76]$$

We consider the difference

$$I_H(x,y) - \bar{I}_{H \in \Delta}(x,y) \approx w(x,y)\big[R(x,y)U^*(x,y) + R^*(x,y)U(x,y)\big]$$ [5.77]

By suitably choosing the neighborhood Δ and using the "difference hologram" expressed by [5.77], we may reconstruct the image, eliminating the perturbations due to the zero order.

In order to show the validity of this approach, we use a zone Δ formed by eight pixels neighboring each pixel ($k = 1$). Figure 5.14(a) shows the spectrum of the "difference hologram" $I_H(x,y) - \bar{I}_{H \in \Delta}(x,y)$ illuminated by a spherical wave. The spectral center of the object wave and the window filter are noted. Figure 5.17(b) shows the reconstructed image.

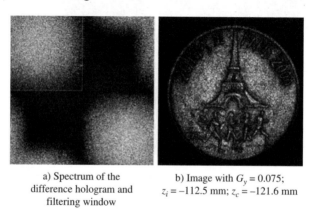

a) Spectrum of the
difference hologram and
filtering window

b) Image with $G_y = 0.075$;
$z_i = -112.5$ mm; $z_c = -121.6$ mm

Figure 5.14. *Spectrum of the hologram and the image reconstructed by the mean-value suppression method*

A comparison between Figures 5.10(b) and 5.14(b) shows that the pollution by the zero order is eliminated.

5.4. Filtering in the image and reconstruction planes by the FIMG4FFT method

The S-FFT method has shown that the information of the object is entirely contained in the reconstructed image, even though we may not in reality vary the relative size of the image by the variation of the radius of curvature of the spherical reconstruction wave. If we apply a window filter in the reconstructed plane, which allows the direct extraction of the complex amplitude of the image, then, by calculating the inverse Fresnel transformation, we may obtain the object field at detector plane. In this case the use of the Fourier transform gives its spectrum, then, by multiplying it by a transfer function, it will be possible to reconstruct the object with an adjustable magnification [LI 11b].

This method requires four FFTs: the first forms the image by the S-FFT method; the second, after filtering, calculates the inverse diffraction; the third leads to the spectrum; and the fourth allows the reconstruction with the desired size. So as to simplify the notation, this method is called reconstruction by "FIMG4FFT", an acronym for "Filtering the IMaGe and reconstruction by 4 FFTs".

The reconstructions show that the FIMG4FFT method leads to good-quality images. We will study this in detail in the following.

5.4.1. *Adjustable magnification reconstruction by the FIMG4FFT method*

5.4.1.1. *Filtering the image plane*

We again make use of the notation used previously. The complex amplitude of the virtual image may be expressed by the Fresnel diffraction integral:

$$U_i(x_i, y_i) = \frac{\exp(jkz_i)}{j\lambda z_i} \exp\left[\frac{jk}{2z_i}\left(x_i^2 + y_i^2\right)\right] \times$$

$$\int\int_{-\infty-\infty}^{\infty\ \infty} R_c(x,y)R^*(x,y)w(x,y)U(x,y)\exp\left[\frac{jk}{2z_i}\left(x^2 + y^2\right)\right] \times$$

$$\exp\left[-j2\pi\left(x\frac{x_i}{\lambda z_i} + y\frac{y_i}{\lambda z_i}\right)\right]dxdy \qquad [5.78]$$

After reduction, we have

$$U_i(x_i, y_i) = \frac{\exp(jkz_i)}{j\lambda z_i} \exp\left[\frac{jk}{2z_i}\left(x_i^2 + y_i^2\right)\right] \exp\left\{-\frac{jk}{2z_r}\left[x_r^2 + y_r^2\right]\right\} u_i(x_i, y_i) \qquad [5.79]$$

with

$$u_i(x_i, y_i) = A_r \int\int_{-\infty-\infty}^{\infty\ \infty} w(x,y)U(x,y)\exp\left[\frac{jk}{2}\left(\frac{1}{z_c} - \frac{1}{z_r} + \frac{1}{z_i}\right)\left(x^2 + y^2\right)\right]$$

$$\exp\left[-j2\pi\left(x\frac{x_i - x_r}{\lambda z_i} + y\frac{y_i - y_r}{\lambda z_i}\right)\right]dxdy \qquad [5.80]$$

The previous analysis showed that we obtain an image of the object field centered at the point $(x_r z_i/z_r, y_r z_i/z_r)$ in the image plane. Extracting the image and applying a window filter, we displace the origin to the point $(x_r z_i/z_r, y_r z_i/z_r)$. We then obtain:

$$u'_i(x_i, y_i) = A_r \int_{-\infty}^{\infty} \int_{-\infty}^{\infty} w(x,y) U(x,y) \exp\left[\frac{jk}{2}\left(\frac{1}{z_c} - \frac{1}{z_r} + \frac{1}{z_i}\right)(x^2 + y^2)\right]$$

$$\exp\left[-j2\pi\left(x\frac{x_i}{\lambda z_i} + y\frac{y_i}{\lambda z_i}\right)\right] dxdy \qquad [5.81]$$

Carrying out an inverse transform on both sides and multiplying by $\exp\left[-jk/2z_i(x^2 + y^2)\right]$, we then have:

$$F^{-1}\{u'_i(x_i, y_i)\}\left(\frac{x_i}{\lambda z_i}, \frac{y_i}{\lambda z_i}\right) \times \exp\left[-\frac{jk}{2z_i}(x^2 + y^2)\right]$$

$$= A_r w(x,y) U(x,y) \exp\left[\frac{jk}{2}\left(\frac{1}{z_c} - \frac{1}{z_r}\right)(x^2 + y^2)\right] \qquad [5.82]$$

$$= R_c(x,y) R^*(x,y) w(x,y) U(x,y)$$

We note that the right side of [5.82] is exactly the complex amplitude that propagates along the optical axis, and that contributes to the formation of the virtual image.

From this, the field of the real image in the plane $z = z_i$ may be described by the angular spectrum diffraction formula:

$$U_i(x,y) =$$

$$F^{-1}\left\{F\left\{F^{-1}\{u'_i(x_i, y_i)\}\left(\frac{x_i}{\lambda z_i}, \frac{y_i}{\lambda z_i}\right) \times \exp\left[-\frac{jk}{2z_i}(x^2 + y^2)\right]\right\} \exp\left[jkz_i\sqrt{1 - \lambda^2(f_x^2 + f_y^2)}\right]\right\}$$

$$[5.83]$$

If this expression is calculated by FFT and Inverse Fast Fourier Transform (IFFT), the result will keep the same physical size as that of the pixel matrix [MAS 99, LI 09a, LI 07b, PIC 09]. Choosing a suitable magnification taking into account the size of the object relative to the detector, the method leads to the reconstruction of a very good quality image of the object.

The reconstruction process is summarized in the following steps:

Step 1: Choose a magnification G_y, determine the reconstruction distance z_i by $G_y = -z_i/z_0$, then determine the radius of curvature of the spherical reconstruction wave; next calculate an FFT of the expression $F\left\{I_H(x,y)R_c(x,y)\exp\left[\dfrac{jk}{2z_i}\left(x^2+y^2\right)\right]\right\}$

Step 2: Select the image of the object by a window filter, then displace the image to the center of the plane and add zeros around the image; we obtain a discrete function $u_i'(x_i, y_i)$

Step 3: Determine the complex amplitude in the plane $z = 0$ using an inverse FFT.

Step 4: Reconstruct the object with the desired magnification by applying [5.83].

5.4.1.2. Experimental results

The experimental setup is, as shown in Figure 5.2, with $\lambda = 532$ nm. The parameters are similar to those mentioned in section 5.3.2. With $G_y = 0.075$ we have $z_i = -112.5$ mm and $z_c = -121.6$ mm. Figure 5.15(a) shows the image reconstructed after the first step. Next, the image is extracted by a window of 200×200 pixels, then we apply the second step. The image is displaced to the center of the plane and we add zeros around it. The result is given in Figure 5.15(b). Having obtained the object field in the detector plane by step 3, the spectrum of the conjugate object field is calculated by FFT and represented in Figure 5.15(c). Figure 5.15(d) shows the image reconstructed by the method. A comparison between Figures 5.15(d) and 5.13(b) shows that, even though it is longer, the FIMG4FFT method allows us to efficiently get rid of the perturbations due to the zero order.

We may show numerically that for any magnification, the *space-bandwidth product* of the reconstructed image is constant. Thus, there is no loss of information in the image which is reconstructed at a very high quality [LI 11b].

5.4.1.3. Local reconstruction by the FIMG4FFT method

In the previous demonstration, the image of the entire object is extracted by a window of 200×200 pixels from the image plane given by S-FFT. Choosing a local area in the image plane, we may reconstruct the local area of the object and display it completely in the reconstructed plane.

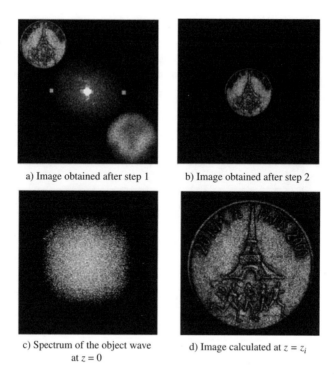

a) Image obtained after step 1   b) Image obtained after step 2

c) Spectrum of the object wave   d) Image calculated at $z = z_i$
at $z = 0$

Figure 5.15. *Reconstruction with magnification $G_y = 0.075$ by the FIMG4FFT method*
($z_i = -112.5$ mm, $z_c = -121.6$ mm)

Let L_0 be the physical width of the reconstruction plane obtained by S-FFT with N sample points and L be the width of the detector window. If a local area to the image situated in a square frame with sides composed of N_s points is reconstructed in the reconstruction plane, the transverse magnification G_y must satisfy the relation $L = N_s L_0 G_y / N$. Since $L_0 = \lambda z_0 N / L$ (see Chapter 3), we have:

$$G_y = \frac{L^2}{\lambda z_0 N_s} \qquad [5.84]$$

As an example, using the hologram of the medal presented previously, and considering $N_s = \{100,200\}$, Figure 5.16 shows two images reconstructed with magnifications $G_y = 0.0711$ and $G_y = 0.1421$. These results show that the method allows the reconstruction of any area of the object with any magnification.

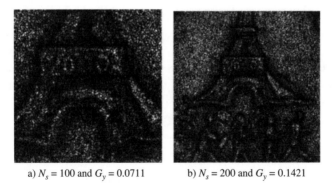

a) $N_s = 100$ and $G_y = 0.0711$ b) $N_s = 200$ and $G_y = 0.1421$

Figure 5.16. *Local images calculated by the FIMG4FFT method*

5.5. DBFT method and the use of filtering in the image plane

As previously mentioned, in 2004, F. Zhang proposed the algorithm called DBFT, enabling the reconstruction of the wavefront of the object field with an adjustable magnification [ZHA 04b]. The author based his method on the use of four phase-shifted holograms recorded at different times with phase differences of 0, $\pi/2$, π, and $3\pi/2$ relative to the reference wave (see section 5.2.3). The DBFT method may be applied to the case of non-demodulated off-axis holograms, given certain arrangements that are discussed forthwith.

We will show that some improvements allow the obtainment of satisfactory results even though the DBFT algorithm does not rigorously satisfy the sampling theorem and is based on Fresnel's approximations.

5.5.1. *DBFT method*

The notation is similar to that used previously. Knowing $U(x,y)$, the field in the observation plane after diffraction across a distance z_1 is calculated by the discrete Fresnel transform:

$$
\begin{aligned}
U_1(x_1, y_1) = & \frac{\exp(jkz_1)}{j\lambda z_1} \exp\left[\frac{jk}{2z_1}\left(x_1^2 + y_1^2\right)\right] \\
& \times \int\int_{-\infty}^{\infty}\left\{U(x,y)\exp\left[\frac{jk}{2z_1}\left(x^2 + y^2\right)\right]\right\}\exp\left[-j2\pi\left(\frac{x_1}{\lambda z_1}x + \frac{y_1}{\lambda z_1}y\right)\right]dxdy
\end{aligned}
$$

[5.85]

When the calculation is carried out by S-FFT, the physical width of the numerical result is $L_1 = \lambda z_1 N/L$. Let z_0 be the distance between the object and the detector, and let $z_0 = z_1 + z_2$. We wish to obtain the diffracted field having a physical width L_v. We will consider the calculation of the diffraction across the distance z_0 to be carried out by two "relay diffractions" with the two distances z_1 and z_2. In this case, the physical width of the diffracted field obtained by the second calculation is given by:

$$L_v = \lambda z_2 N / L_1 \qquad [5.86]$$

Substituting the relation giving L_1 into [5.86], we obtain:

$$z_1 = \frac{z_0 L}{L_v + L} \qquad [5.87]$$

By making a suitable choice of the two distances z_1 and z_2, we may reconstruct the object image with an adjustable magnification.

5.5.2. Sampling of the DBFT algorithm

The DBFT algorithm is based on two successive S-FFT diffraction calculations. It is therefore necessary that the two calculations satisfy the sampling theorem. We recall the discussion of the S-FFT diffraction calculation in section 3.2.1 of Chapter 3. From relation [3.15], for the first calculation by S-FFT, if we want to obtain the diffracted field verifying the sampling theorem, then the widths of the object and observation plane must be equal and satisfy $L_1 = L = \sqrt{\lambda z_1 N}$.

The feasibility of the second diffraction calculation by S-FFT depends on the good sampling of the intermediary field in the plane $z = z_1$. If the sampling of the intermediary field is not correct, the phenomenon of spectral aliasing occurs, as mentioned in Chapter 3, which diminishes the quality of the reconstructed image. Consequently, the DBFT algorithm may give an image containing some perturbations due to spectral aliasing.

We illustrate this discussion with an experimental example. We use the same system and the same object as presented in Figure 5.13. The hologram is recorded with a red laser ($\lambda = 632.8$ nm). The image reconstructed by S-FFT is shown in Figure 5.17(a). Figure 5.17(b) shows the green image obtained for $\lambda = 532$ nm. The width of the plane of the red image is $L_R = 204$ mm, and that of the green image is $L_G = 171$ mm. The sizes of the images are therefore not identical.

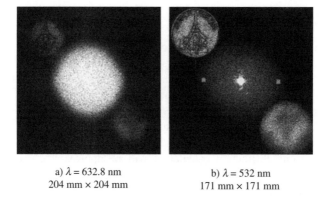

a) $\lambda = 632.8$ nm
204 mm × 204 mm

b) $\lambda = 532$ nm
171 mm × 171 mm

Figure 5.17. *Reconstruction of the images by S-FFT*

The concept of the DBFT algorithm allows the reconstruction of the green image such that its size is equal to that of the red image. We now consider $L_v = L_R = L_G = 204$ mm to be the width of the reconstruction plane. We determine $z_1 = 34.2$ mm using [5.87] ($z_0 = 1,500$ mm).

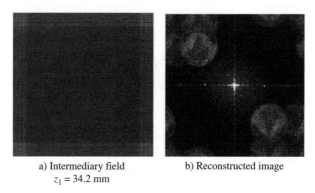

a) Intermediary field
$z_1 = 34.2$ mm

b) Reconstructed image

Figure 5.18. *Problem in the reconstruction of the green image by DBFT*

Figure 5.18(a) shows the distribution of the diffracted field in the intermediary plane. We may observe, at the edge of the plane, the influence of spectral aliasing. This aliasing is due to the breach of the sampling theorem in the calculation of the quadratic phase factor of the integral in [5.85]. Having carried out the second diffraction calculation, the distribution in the reconstruction plane is given in Figure 5.18(b). We obtain a green image of the same size as the red image, but the perturbation due to spectral aliasing notably decreases the quality of the image.

5.5.3. *Improvement of the DBFT method*

If we use the Fresnel diffraction integral for the reconstruction of the object wavefront, the optical system recording the hologram must satisfy the paraxial approximation. In this case, the calculation concerns only the case where the components of the angular spectrum of the object propagate in the neighborhood of the optical axis and may impact the detector. Normally, most of the energy of the diffracted field converges to the neighborhood of the center of the intermediary plane. This means that if a central area of the intermediary plane satisfies the sampling theorem, the second diffraction calculation will be approximately correct. Let us consider N_c to be the number of pixels in the width of this area, and Δx_1, Δy_1 the sampling interval along the x_1 and y_1 axes of the intermediary plane. Referring to the discussions of the sampling of the quadratic phase (see Chapter 3), N_c must satisfy:

$$N_c = \frac{\lambda z_1}{\Delta x_1^2} \tag{5.88}$$

This result gives an interesting indication: in order to theoretically obtain a result without spectral aliasing, we may use a diaphragm, placed in the intermediary plane, open at the center and having sides of width N_c pixels. In this case, the sampling of the intermediary field will satisfy Shannon's theorem for the second calculation.

The method of filtering the image plane allows the reconstruction of the object field in the recording plane by the calculation of the inverse diffraction. Using a single digital hologram, and based on the concept of the DBFT algorithm, we may also get the correct reconstruction of the image with a variable magnification by following this process:

Step 1: Use the S-FFT method to calculate the image of the object.

Step 2: Take a sample of the object image with a window filter placed in the reconstruction plane.

Step 3: From the relation between the geometric position of the center of the image in the reconstruction plane, the diffraction distance, and the inclination angle of the reference beam, determine both inclination angles θ_x and θ_y of the reference beam relative to the optical axis.

Step 4: Use the inverse diffraction calculation across distance z_0 to get the field in the recording plane, that is $U(x,y)\exp\left[jk\left(\theta_x x + \theta_y y\right)\right]$; the object field is multiplied by the linear phase shift from the reference wave.

Step 5: Multiplying the previously obtained result with the linear phase $\exp\left[-jk\left(\theta_x x + \theta_y y\right)\right]$, we obtain the object field $U(x,y)$.

Step 6: From the object field $U(x, y)$, introducing a diaphragm into the intermediary plane, we may apply the DBFT algorithm to reconstruct the image of the object.

Reconstruction by this process requires four discrete Fresnel transforms, which is twice that of the initial DBFT algorithm. This version of the DBFT algorithm will be called double-DBFT algorithm (DDBFT) in the following sections.

5.5.4. *Experimental demonstration of the DDBFT method*

Using again the two holograms in Figure 5.3, we now carry out an experimental demonstration of the DDBFT method. After steps 1 and 2, Figures 5.19(a) and (b) show the red and green images, limited to a rectangular aperture of 168 × 168 pixels and 200 × 200 pixels, respectively, in the two planes reconstructed by S-FFT. We consider the center of each image to determine the components of the inclination angle of each reference wave using the simple relations:

$$\theta_x = \left| N/2 - N_{CX} \right| / N \times L_0 / z_0$$
$$\theta_y = \left| N/2 - N_{CY} \right| / N \times L_0 / z_0$$
$$L_0 = \lambda z_0 N / L, \qquad\qquad [5.89]$$

with N_{CX} and N_{CY} the pixel coordinates of the geometric position of the image center.

The width of the two image planes is imposed as L_v = 70 mm and, following steps 4–6, both reconstructed images are shown in Figures 5.22(c) and (d), respectively. We note that the modification of the DBFT algorithm now makes it possible to reconstruct the image with a single hologram, and without the perturbation of the spectral aliasing.

In practice, we may be interested in the study of only a particular area of the object. We saw in the previous section that, using a local window filter, it is straightforward to reconstruct the local field of the object by the FIMG4FFT method. Applying the same principle of filtering in the image plane, we may also obtain a similar result with the DDBFT method.

If a local area in the image situated in a square frame sides N_s points is reconstructed in the reconstruction plane, the width of this plane must satisfy the relation $L_v = N_s L_0 / N$. Since $L_0 = \lambda z_0 N / L$, we have:

$$L_v = \lambda z_0 N_s / L \qquad\qquad [5.90]$$

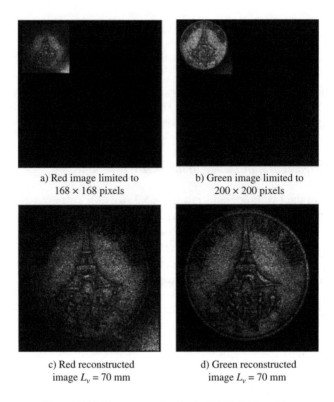

a) Red image limited to
168 × 168 pixels

b) Green image limited to
200 × 200 pixels

c) Red reconstructed
image L_v = 70 mm

d) Green reconstructed
image L_v = 70 mm

Figure 5.19. *Reconstruction by the DDBFT algorithm*

In practice, the experimental system for recording the hologram often satisfies the Fresnel approximation. In this case, the DDBFT algorithm is equivalent to the FIMG4FFT method. Using relation [5.90], it is easy to confirm that the results of reconstructions of a local object image obtained by the DDBFT and the FIMG4FFT methods are perfectly identical. Comparing the calculation time for these two methods, there is almost no difference, since the reconstructions require to carry out four FFT calculations.

5.6. Digital color holography

We saw in previous sections that it is possible to calculate a monochromatic image coded in a monochromatic hologram. In this section, we are interested in the reconstruction and display of color holograms coded in color or monochromatic digital holograms. Using three holograms recorded successively or at the same time by a monochromatic or color detector, we may reconstruct the object field of each chromatic component (*R*: red, *G*: green, and *B*: blue) of the object, and we may also display a color image of the object, by considering the intensity of each reconstruction as a component of the color image [YAM 02, DEM 03, ZHA 08, PIC 09].

The first digital color holograms appeared in the 2000s with the advent of color detectors. Yamaguchi showed the applicability of digital color holography for the color reconstruction of objects [YAM 02]. Since then, numerous applications have been developed, particularly in the domain of contactless metrology (see Chapter 7): flow analysis in fluid mechanics [DEM 06, DES 06a, DES 06b, DES 08, DES 11], surface profilometry by two-color microscopy [KUM 09, KUH 07, MAN 08], and multidimensional metrology of deformed objects [KHM 08a, TAN 10a, TAN 10b, TAN 11].

For the display of a color image, the three components correspond to three different wavelengths. If the reconstructions are carried out by the S-FFT method, the physical scale of the reconstructed objects will depend on the wavelength: it will be impossible to obtain a color image. This section proposes tackling the treatment of digital holograms containing information of three wavelengths so that the reconstructed color image is a correct superposition of the three RGB components.

5.6.1. *Recording a digital color hologram*

There exist different approaches for recording digital color holograms, in particular for *simultaneously* recording the three colors. The simplest method consists of using a monochromatic detector and recording the colors *sequentially*. This method was proposed by Demoli in 2003 [DEM 03] and is only adapted to the case of objects that vary slowly in time.

Figure 5.20 illustrates the different recording strategies. The first possibility consists of using a chromatic filter organized in a Bayer mosaic (Figure 5.20a). However, in such a detector, half of the pixels detect green, and only a quarter detect red or blue [DES 11b]. The spatial color filter creates holes in the mesh and therefore a loss of information, which translates into a loss of resolution. For example, Yamaguchi used a detector with $1,636 \times 1,238$ pixels of size 3.9×3.9 μm^2 [YAM 02], and his results had a relatively weak spatial resolution. The number of effect pixels for each color was 818×619, and the pixel pitch was 7.8 μm.

The second possibility consists of using three detectors organized as a "tri-CCD", the spectral selection being carried out by a prism with dichroic treatments (Figure 5.20b). Such a detector guarantees a high spatial resolution and a spectral selectivity compatible with the constraints of digital color holography for non-contact metrology. Of course, the relative adjustment of the three sensors must be carried out with high precision. For example, Desse [DES 11b] developed a type of holographic color interferometry for use in fluid mechanics, with three detectors of 1,344 × 1,024 pixels of size 6.45 μm × 6.45 μm.

The third possibility consists of using a color detector based on a stack of photodiodes [TAN 10a, TAN 10b, DES 08, DES 11b] (http://www.foveon.com, Figure 5.20c). The spectral selectivity is relative to the mean penetration depth of the photons in the silicon: blue photons at 425 nm penetrate to around 0.2 μm, green photons at 532 nm to around 2 μm, and red photons at 630 nm to around 3 μm. Thus the construction of junctions at depths at around 0.2 μm, 0.8 μm, and 3.0 μm gives the correct spectral selectivity for color imaging. However, the spectral selectivity is not perfect, as green photons may be detected in the blue and the red bands, but the architecture guarantees a maximum spectral resolution since the number of effective pixels for each wavelength is that of the entire matrix. For example, the reference [TAN 10b] uses a stack of photodiodes with 1,060 × 1,414 pixels of size 5 μm ×5 μm.

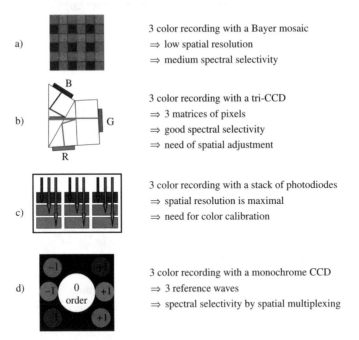

a)   3 color recording with a Bayer mosaic
      ⇒ low spatial resolution
      ⇒ medium spectral selectivity

b)   3 color recording with a tri-CCD
      ⇒ 3 matrices of pixels
      ⇒ good spectral selectivity
      ⇒ need of spatial adjustment

c)   3 color recording with a stack of photodiodes
      ⇒ spatial resolution is maximal
      ⇒ need for color calibration

d)   3 color recording with a monochrome CCD
      ⇒ 3 reference waves
      ⇒ spectral selectivity by spatial multiplexing

Figure 5.20. *Recording a digital color hologram (for a color version of this figure, see www.iste.co.uk/picart/digiholog.zip)*

Finally, the fourth possibility consists of using a monochromatic detector combined with spatial chromatic multiplexing (Figure 5.20d). Each reference wave must have different separately adjusted spatial frequencies according to their wavelengths. The complexity of the experimental apparatus increases with the number of colors. For two-color digital holography, it is acceptable, for three colors, it becomes prohibitive. A demonstration of this approach is given in the references [PIC 09], [MAN 08], [KUH 07], and [TAN 11].

5.6.2. *Standardization of the physical scale of reconstructed monochromatic images*

The reconstruction of the object image in true color is a combination of three reconstructed fields with each wavelength. It is therefore necessary to assure the conservation of the image size for each wavelength. From the studies conducted in previous sections, the calculation of diffraction may also be carried out by the adjustable-magnification D-FFT method, one of the advantages of which is that the width of the observation plane conserves the same scale as that of the detector plane. This approach brings certain advantages for digital color holography and is widely applied in Chapter 7. Moreover, the hologram recording system often satisfies the Fresnel approximation, and, in this case, the DDBFT algorithm is as useful as the FIMG4FFT method. We are now interested in an approach based on the S-FFT reconstruction.

We recall the discussions of diffraction calculation by the S-FFT method. The width of the field diffracted across a distance z_0 is $L_0 = \lambda z_0 N / L$. The pixel pitch of the detector is $\Delta x = L/N$ and that of the plane diffracted by S-FFT is $\Delta x_0 = L_0/N$. We have:

$$\Delta x_0 = \frac{\lambda z_0}{N \Delta x} \qquad\qquad [5.91]$$

The sampling interval varies with the wavelength, but also with the number of points in the reconstruction. Of course, we have already indicated, this characteristic constitutes a major inconvenience for the use of this approach in the reconstruction of color holograms or in multidimensional metrology. From this fact, the reconstructed images must therefore have the same size for a superposition perfect to the nearest pixel. This condition will only be satisfied if we make sure we have a sampling interval which is constant and independent of the wavelength. Relation [5.95] gives a path: adjusting N as a function of the wavelength λ, it is possible to keep Δx_0 constant. This approach was presented in 2004 by Ferraro and called "Fresnel transform with wavelength dependant zero-padding" [FER 04]. In this section, we will present a method that may be considered as an adaptation of the method proposed by Ferraro [TAN 11].

Having presented the Fresnel transform with zero-padding method, we will give an example of color image reconstruction by digital color holography using the three reconstruction methods.

5.6.3. *Fresnel transform with wavelength-dependant zero-padding*

We note that if the wavelength changes, the sampling pitch changes. For the sake of simplicity, we will carry out the study with two wavelengths, knowing that the results can be easily adapted to the case of n wavelengths ($n > 2$). We also note that by modifying the recording distance z_0, we also modify the interval Δx_0 [FER 04, ALF 06, JAV 05a]. This imposes the sequential recording of colors with modification of the distance for each color. This approach is not well adapted to the study of dynamic objects since it is necessary to record the color hologram in real time. Our study is therefore limited to the case where the physical recording distance is fixed.

We will consider the case of two wavelengths given by a HeNe laser ($\lambda_R = 632.8$ nm) and a frequency-doubled NdYAG laser ($\lambda_G = 532$ nm) and we will consider a detector with $N = 1{,}024$ and $\Delta x = 4.65$ µm. We wish to reconstruct using Fresnel transform the color holograms with Δx_R and Δx_G, the sampling intervals of the two reconstructed images and K_R and K_G, the numbers of calculation points along the x-direction. The reconstruction process must respect the following condition:

$$\Delta x_R = \frac{\lambda_R z_0}{K_R \Delta x} = \frac{\lambda_G z_0}{K_G \Delta x} = \Delta x_G \qquad [5.92]$$

i.e.

$$\frac{\lambda_R}{K_R} = \frac{\lambda_G}{K_G} \qquad [5.93]$$

For the two wavelengths mentioned previously, we have:

$$\frac{K_R}{K_G} = \frac{\lambda_R}{\lambda_G} = 1.189473 \qquad [5.94]$$

To carry out the calculation by FFT, K_R and K_G must be even integers. Rounding this fraction to the third decimal place, we may write:

$$1000\frac{K_R}{K_G} = integer \qquad [5.95]$$

with *integer* = 1,189 (rounded by default) or *integer* = 1,190 (rounded by excess).

Table 5.1 presents the different possible options for the parameters K_R and K_G, as well as the corresponding values of Δx_R and Δx_G, for an object placed at $z_0 = 1{,}320$ mm from the detector.

K_G	Δx_G (mm)	*Integer* = 1,189		*Integer* = 1,190	
		$K_R = 1.189 K_G$	Δx_R (mm)	$K_R = 1.190 K_G$	Δx_R (mm)
1,000	0.1510	1,189	0.1511	**1,190**	0.1510
1,200	0.1258	1,426.8	0.1259	**1,428**	0.1258
1,400	0.1079	1,664.6	0.1079	**1,666**	0.1078
1,600	0.0944	1,902.4	0.0944	**1,904**	0.0943
1,800	0.0839	2,140.2	0.0839	**2,142**	0.0839
2,000	0.0755	**2,378**	0.0755	**2,380**	0.0755
2,200	0.0686	2,615.8	0.0687	**2,618**	0.0686
2,400	0.0629	2,853.6	0.0629	**2,856**	0.0629
2,600	0.0581	3,091.4	0.0581	**3,094**	0.0581
2,800	0.0539	3,329.2	0.0540	**3,332**	0.0539
3,000	0.0503	**3,567**	0.0504	**3,570**	0.0503

Table 5.1. *The values of the reconstruction parameters for a fixed reconstruction distance*

The pairs that satisfy the condition of "even integers" are indicated in bold. Taking into account the rounding of the ratio of wavelengths to the third decimal place, we may make a slight modification on the order of some tenths of a millimeter to the reconstruction distance, without degrading the focalization of the image. A study showed that the modification of the reconstruction distance contributed around 2% to the enlargement of the impulse response of the reconstruction [TAN 11], which is relatively acceptable.

Assuming a different reconstruction distance for each wavelength, the equality $\Delta x_R = \Delta x_G$ will be obtained, if

$$\frac{\lambda_R z_R}{K_R} = \frac{\lambda_G z_G}{K_G} \qquad [5.96]$$

For an optimal simultaneous focalization of the two images, we may choose z_R and z_G on both sides of z_0. This amounts to posing $z_R + z_G = 2z_0$, i.e.

$$z_G = 2z_0 - z_R \qquad [5.97]$$

It is sufficient to choose a distance z_R proportional to z_G, i.e. [TAN 11]:

$$z_R = \frac{K_R \lambda_G}{K_G \lambda_R} z_G = \frac{integer \times \lambda_G}{1000 \lambda_R} z_G \qquad [5.98]$$

The combination of equations [5.97] and [5.98] leads to the determination of z_R and z_G defined as follows:

$$\begin{cases} z_R = \dfrac{2z_0 \lambda_G \times integer}{1000 \lambda_R + \lambda_G \times integer} \\ z_G = 2z_0 - z_R \end{cases} \qquad [5.99]$$

The values of Δx_R and Δx_G will now be strictly identical to the desired precision, that is 10^{-3} in this example. These results will be used in the following sections.

5.6.4. Experimental study of the different methods of reconstructing color images

So as to illustrate the feasibility of the different methods standardizing the physical scale of color images, we will consider the setup shown in Figure 5.21. The object studied is a Chinese ceramic head whose height is 40 mm. It is placed at a distance $z_0 = 1,320$ mm from the recording plane and illuminated by light of $\lambda_R = 632.8$ nm and $\lambda_G = 532$ nm. The two holograms are simultaneously recorded on a monochromatic detector with the spatial multiplexing technique (Figure 5.20d) [PIC 03a, PIC 09]. Two beams coming from two laser sources are separated into two by a pair of polarization beam splitter (PBS) cubes. The two reflected beams are made parallel by two afocal systems, and they then illuminate the object at two different incidences via two mirrors (M1 and M2). The two other beams transmitted by the cubes are spatially expanded with two spatial filters (SF1 and SF2), then collimated, and constitute the reference waves. 50% beam splitters (BS1 and BS2) enable the recombination of the object and reference beams in the detector plane. The object and reference beams are copolarized using half-wave plates which allows the rotation of the polarizations. The incidence angles of the two reference beams are adjusted by laterally displacing lenses L_1 and L_3 [PIC 03a]. Thus, we can independently adjust the spatial frequencies of the reference waves. The pixels have a size of 4.65 μm. The number of pixels is $N = 1,024$, which means that the width of the sensor is $L = 4.76$ mm.

We adjust the angles of the red and green reference beams so that the respective reconstructed images are formed on the first and the second quadrants of the reconstruction plane. This principle is called the *spatial multiplexing of two-color holograms*. The detector is, in effect, unable to distinguish the colors since it is a monochromatic detector. On the other hand, the adjustment of the reference beams lets them occupy effectively the reconstructed field, and therefore the spatial bandwidth, so that the color images may be recorded.

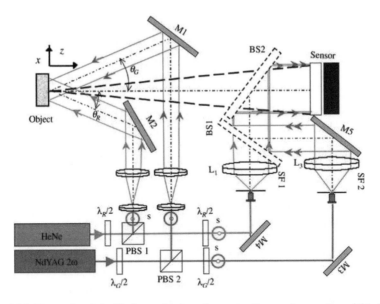

Figure 5.21. *Two-color digital holographic interferometer (for a color version of this figure, see www.iste.co.uk/picart/digiholog.zip)*

Figure 5.22 represents the reconstructed planes, with the focus on the red (left) and green (right) holograms, respectively. We clearly see that the sizes of the two reconstructed images are not identical, since the widths of the two planes are:

$$- L_{0R} = \lambda_R z_0 N/L = 0.6328 \times 10^{-3} \times 1{,}320 \times 1{,}024/4.76 = 179.6 \text{ mm on the left;}$$

$$- L_{0G} = \lambda_G z_0 N/L = 0.532 \times 10^{-3} \times 1{,}320 \times 1{,}024/4.76 = 151.0 \text{ mm on the right.}$$

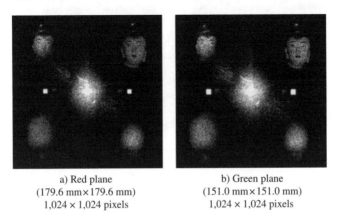

a) Red plane
(179.6 mm × 179.6 mm)
1,024 × 1,024 pixels

b) Green plane
(151.0 mm × 151.0 mm)
1,024 × 1,024 pixels

Figure 5.22. *Reconstructions with S-FFT*

By successively using the methods with zero-padding, FIMG4FFT and DDBFT, we will standardize the physical scale of both images and reconstruct the two-color image of the object.

5.6.4.1. *Two-color image calculated by the zero-padding method*

Using the algorithm with zero-padding and relation [5.95], we chose the parameters from Table 5.1 with *integer* = 1,190, K_G = 3,000, K_R = 3,570, z_R = 1,320.3 mm, and z_G = 1,319.7 mm. Figure 5.23 shows the reconstructed red, green, and two-color images. The red and green holograms have exactly the same size, thus giving a color image with the superposition of the intensity of each component in a 1:1 ratio (900 × 900 pixels for each image). The calculated two-color image is compared to a color photograph obtained with a digital camera at full aperture, under the same lighting conditions. The images show a good agreement. We may also observe the speckle pattern at the surface of the two reconstructed images, which is due to the coherent illumination [GOO 07].

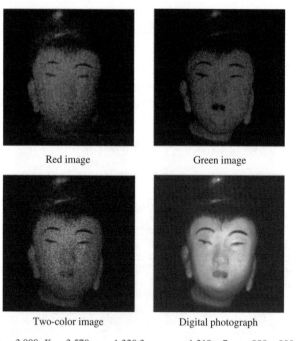

Red image   Green image

Two-color image   Digital photograph

(K_G = 3,000, K_R = 3,570, z_R = 1,320.3 mm, z_G = 1,319 × 7 mm, 900 × 900 pixels)

Figure 5.23. *Holograms reconstructed by Fresnel transform with zero padding (for a color version of this figure, see www.iste.co.uk/picart/digiholog.zip)*

5.6.4.2. *Reconstruction by the FIMG4FFT and the DDBFT with adjustable magnification*

So as to conserve the size of the color image that we saw previously, we take the red image from the red plane in Figure 5.24(a) using a square window whose sides consist of 260 pixels. This window allows the reconstruction of a zone of height 260/1,024 × 151 mm = 38.34 mm, which corresponds to a magnification of G_y = 1,024 × 4.65 μm/38.34 mm = 0.124. From this, we deduce that $z_i = -163.88$ mm and $z_c = -188.67$ mm.

Figure 5.24 shows the image obtained after the displacement of the filtered image in the plane calculated by S-FFT for the red color. The image reconstructed after the application of the complete process is given in Figure 5.24(b). For the green image, we have a window filter of 260 × 632.8/532≈310 pixels. Following the same procedure, the two images for the green part are shown in Figures 5.24(c) and (d).

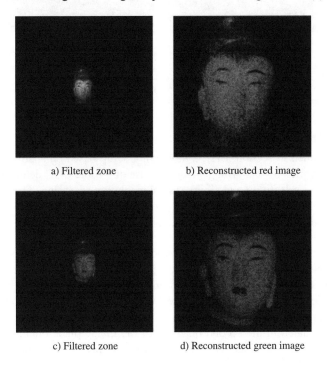

a) Filtered zone   b) Reconstructed red image

c) Filtered zone   d) Reconstructed green image

Figure 5.24. *Images reconstituted by FIMG4FFT for both colors (for a color version of this figure, see www.iste.co.uk/picart/digiholog.zip)*

Combining Figures 5.24(b) and (d), the two-color image is given in Figure 5.25(a). The DDBFT method has also been applied with the same parameters.

The two-color image obtained is given in Figure 5.25(b). We may observe that the results are almost identical. We note that, in this example, the recording of the hologram satisfies the paraxial approximation, and both results are therefore acceptable. The FIMG4FFT method is based on the angular spectrum method, which rigorously respects the scalar wave equation, *a priori* giving a better result than DDBFT.

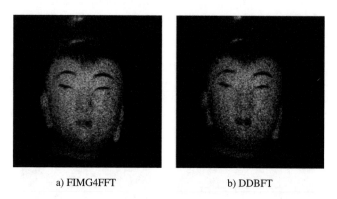

a) FIMG4FFT   b) DDBFT

Figure 5.25. *Comparison of images reconstructed by FIMG4FFT and DDBFT (for a color version of this figure, see www.iste.co.uk/picart/digiholog.zip)*

5.6.4.3. *Three-color digital holography*

As mentioned in section 5.7.1, a three-color setup based on spatial multiplexing requires a complex optical arrangement. The use of a triple CCD detector guarantees a good spectral selectivity and a high spatial resolution recording. The detector used consists of $1,344 \times 1,024$ pixels with a pixel pitch of $\Delta x = \Delta y = 6.45$ µm. We will give one example here of three-color image reconstruction.

The experimental apparatus includes three reference beams oriented in the same direction, as described in Figure 5.26 [TAN 10b]. Dichroic plates allow the combination of the three laser beams into one single beam, which is then separated into one object beam and one reference beam. These beams are copolarized. The incidence angle of the reference beams is adjusted so that the three reconstructed images are situated in the second quadrant of the image plane obtained by discrete Fresnel transform. The object is a Chinese theatrical mask 40 mm high placed at the distance $z_0 = 2,000$ mm from the sensor.

Even though the reconstruction may be carried out by the different methods presented previously, we will only use an adjustable magnification with a spherical reconstruction wave. Removing the mean value of each hologram (see section 5.3.2.1), the reconstruction of the red, green, and blue planes by discrete Fresneltransform is given in Figure 5.27. We note that the width of the blue image is approximately a quarter of that in the reconstruction plane. Its position allows the isolation of the perturbation due to the zero order. Furthermore, because of the very good spectral selectivity of the triple CCD detector, we note that there is no diffusion between the colors.

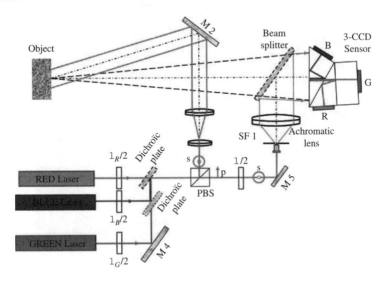

Figure 5.26. *Optical set-up with a single reference beam (for a color version of this figure, see www.iste.co.uk/picart/digiholog.zip)*

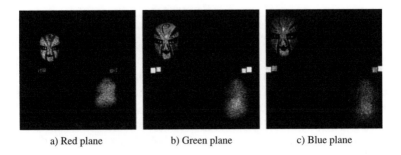

a) Red plane   b) Green plane   c) Blue plane

Figure 5.27. *Reconstruction by discrete Fresnel transform*

The magnification is equal to 0.1, so that the reconstructed image covers the reconstruction plane. Figure 5.28 shows the three holograms reconstructed in each color, as well as the color hologram obtained by their superposition and a weighting of 1:1:1.

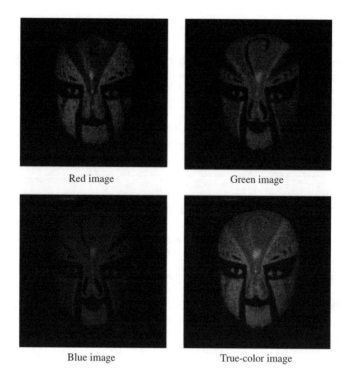

Red image   Green image

Blue image   True-color image

Figure 5.28. *Images reconstructed with adjustable magnification (for a color version of this figure, see www.iste.co.uk/picart/digiholog.zip)*

5.7. Digital phase hologram

In traditional holography with a non-optoelectronic photosensitive medium, there exist two types of hologram: amplitude holograms and phase holograms. Chapter 4 shows that the diffraction efficiency of phase holograms is greater than that of amplitude holograms [MEI 96]. Currently, digital holography is based on calculations from an amplitude hologram. It may be asked if a digital phase hologram is accessible from the recording of interference patterns by a detector, and if its digital diffraction efficiency is as good as that of a digital amplitude hologram. This question is tackled in this section.

In fact, using the interference between the object and reference waves, we may also form a digital phase hologram, but for this, it is necessary to determine a factor called the "shape factor". We carry out an experimental demonstration of object wavefront reconstruction using a digital phase hologram.

5.7.1. *Formation of a digital phase hologram and reconstruction by S-FFT*

We discussed phase holograms in section 4.4.5 of Chapter 4. We recall here some notions. The transmittance of a phase hologram is generally described by:

$$t_H(x, y) = t_0(x, y) \exp\left[j \phi_H(x, y)\right] \qquad [5.100]$$

Let us consider $t_0(x,y) = 1$, $\phi_H(x,y) = g I_H(x,y)$ with g the "shape factor" of the digital phase hologram. The transmittance of the digital phase hologram is then expressed as:

$$t_H(x, y) = \exp\left[j g I_H(x, y)\right] \qquad [5.101]$$

Since we have:

$$I_H = o_0^2 + r_0^2 + 2o_0 r_0 \cos(\varphi_0 - \varphi_r) \qquad [5.102]$$

posing $\alpha = 2 g o_0 r_0$ and $\psi = \pi/2 - \varphi_0 + \varphi_r$, [5.101] is rewritten as:

$$t_H = \beta \exp\left[j \alpha \sin(\psi)\right] \qquad [5.103]$$

Evidently, given that the value of $\sin(\psi)$ varies between -1 and $+1$, for the transmittance to be uniform, the choice of g must satisfy:

$$\alpha = 2 g o_0 r_0 \leq \pi \qquad [5.104]$$

The transmittance is developed as Bessel functions $J_n(\alpha)$ and [5.103] is developed as:

$$t_H(x, y) = \beta(x, y) \sum_{n=-\infty}^{\infty} J_n(\alpha(x, y)) \exp\left[j n \psi(x, y)\right] \qquad [5.105]$$

The $n = 0$ term represents the zero order of diffraction, the $n = -1$ term represents a wave proportional to the object wave in the plane $z = -z_0$, and the $n = +1$ term leads to the formation of a real image of the object situated in the plane $z = z_0$. Figure 5.29 shows two curves of the Bessel function $J_n(\alpha)$ for $n = 0$ and $n = 1$.

From the previous result, if a phase hologram is formed by a digital hologram, then the reconstruction of the object wavefront is also possible. The diffraction amplitude of the zero order is proportional to $J_n(\alpha)$ and $\alpha = 2 g o_0 r_0 \leq \pi$. If we make a choice of g and $o_0 r_0$ so that $J_0(\alpha)$ tends to zero, the perturbation due to the zero order will be automatically eliminated. Moreover, we may also take the maximum value of $J_1(\alpha)$, so that the two diffractions $n = \pm 1$ including the information of the object field reach a maximum.

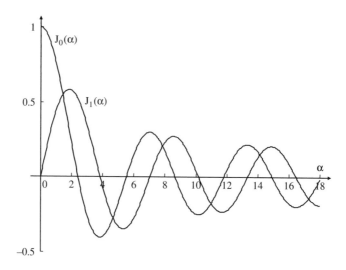

Figure 5.29. *Two curves of the Bessel functions* $J_n(\alpha)$

In the following sections, we will present a method that allows the determination of the "shape factor" g.

Let I_{max} and I_{min} be the respective maximum and minimum of the hologram recorded by the detector. If the variation in the amplitudes of the object and reference waves are weak in the pixel space, we may consider $o_0 r_0$ as a constant: C_{or}. From [5.102], we may demonstrate that $C_{or} = (I_{max} - I_{min})/4$ and we have approximately:

$$g = \frac{2\alpha}{I_{max} - I_{min}} \qquad [5.106]$$

However, this expression only gives an approximate relation between α and g. We must determine a method to fix one of these two factors. For this, we examine the curve of $J_n(\alpha)$. $\alpha \approx 1.9$ corresponds to the first maximum of $J_1(\alpha)$ and $\alpha \approx 2.5$ corresponds to the first zero of $J_0(\alpha)$. Furthermore, when α varies from 1.9 to 2.4, $J_0(\alpha) < J_1(\alpha)$ is satisfied. Consequently, if the variation of α is limited to 1.9~2.5, we are able to recuperate the object wavefront from a phase hologram.

The complex amplitude in the plane of the virtual image at $z = -z_0$ may be calculated by the Fresnel diffraction integral:

$$U(x_i, y_i) = -\frac{\exp(-jkz_0)}{j\lambda z_0} \exp\left[-\frac{jk}{2z_0}\left(x_i^2 + y_i^2\right)\right]$$

$$\times \int\int_{-\infty}^{\infty}\left\{t_H(x,y)\exp\left[-\frac{jk}{2z_0}\left(x^2 + y^2\right)\right]\right\}\exp\left[j\frac{2\pi}{\lambda z_0}\left(x_i x + y_i y\right)\right]dxdy \qquad [5.107]$$

and numerically evaluated by S-FFT.

5.7.2. *Experimental demonstration*

To confirm the previous discussions, we now carry out a study of wavefront reconstruction from a phase hologram using the test from Figure 5.15.

We first consider $\alpha = 2$ and, using the interference pattern recorded by the detector, we determine g by [5.106]. Then, from [5.101], we form a phase hologram. Having calculated [5.107], Figure 5.30(a) gives the result of the reconstruction. Figure 5.30(b) shows the reconstruction corresponding to an amplitude hologram, i.e. directly reconstructed with the hologram recorded in the detector plane. Note that, with the present choice of "shape factor" g, there is almost no difference between these two images.

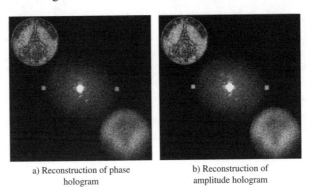

a) Reconstruction of phase hologram

b) Reconstruction of amplitude hologram

Figure 5.30. *Comparison of two types of hologram reconstructed by S-FFT with 1,024 × 1,024 pixels*

We now study the influence of the "shape factor" g or the factor α on the reconstructed image. Let us examine [5.105] and the two curves of the Bessel functions. Between the first maximum of $J_1(\alpha)$ and the first zero of $J_0(\alpha)$, the relation $J_1(\alpha) > J_0(\alpha)$

is always satisfied and this allows us to decrease the perturbation due to the zero order. From [5.100], if α is greater than π, the transmittance is no longer a uniform function. The quality of the object wavefront will be degraded if we increase α. In order to confirm this analysis, we let $\alpha = \{0.5;1;2;4\}$ and using [5.106] to determine the corresponding value of g, Figure 5.31 shows the results of the reconstructions.

We note that the intensity of the reconstructed image increases with α. However, for $\alpha = 4$, a strong perturbation appears in the image. This means that an optimal choice of α is to be made if we wish to obtain a maximum for the signal-to-noise ratio.

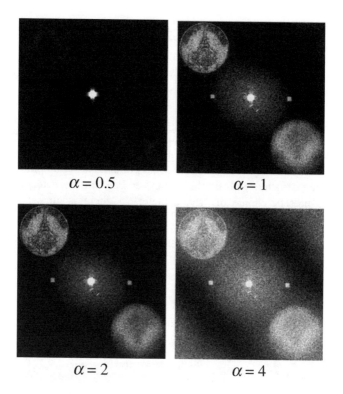

Figure 5.31. *Influence of α on the reconstructed field*

From a theoretical point of view, the information about the object wave included in amplitude and phase holograms is identical. The other reconstruction methods (FIMG4FFT, for example) may also be used to reconstruct an image with an adjustable magnification. However, the physical mechanisms forming the two types of hologram are different, and each method has its own capacity to eliminate the perturbation of the zero order. From a practical point of view, the amplitude hologram is more widely used for a very large number of applications in imaging or in metrology.

5.8. Depth of focus of the reconstructed image

In the previous section, we considered the reconstructed image to always be in perfect focus. However, the parameters of the holographic system (distances and curvature radii, for example) are determined experimentally. Thus small errors can occur and the reconstructed image may not be exactly in focus. This section deals with the depth of focus of the reconstructed image.

5.8.1. *Theoretical analysis*

Here we consider the case where the reconstructed image does not perfectly lie in the ideal focal plane. Writing z_m as the reconstruction distance, $z_m \neq z_i$, the reconstructed field is then given in the Fresnel approximation by:

$$U_m(x_m,y_m) = \frac{\exp(jkz_m)}{j\lambda z_m} \int\int_{-\infty}^{\infty} U_-(x,y)\exp\left\{\frac{jk}{2z_m}\left[(x-x_m)^2+(y-y_m)^2\right]\right\}dxdy$$

[5.108]

Substituting expression $U_-(x,y)$ from [5.6] into [5.108] leads to:

$$U_m(x_m,y_m) = \sum_\xi \sum_\eta \Theta(\xi,\eta;x_m,y_m,z_m) \times$$

$$\int\int_{-\infty}^{\infty} w(x,y)\exp\left[\frac{jk}{2}\left(\frac{1}{z_c}-\frac{1}{z_r}+\frac{1}{z_m}+\frac{1}{z_0}\right)(x^2+y^2)\right] \times$$

[5.109]

$$\exp\left\{-j2\pi\left[\left(x_m-\frac{z_m}{z_r}x_r+\frac{z_m}{z_0}\xi\right)\frac{x}{\lambda z_m}+\left(y_m-\frac{z_m}{z_r}y_r+\frac{z_m}{z_0}\eta\right)\frac{y}{\lambda z_m}\right]\right\}dxdy$$

Considering

$$\frac{1}{z_c}+\frac{1}{z_r}+\frac{1}{z_m}-\frac{1}{z_0}=\frac{1}{z_g}$$

[5.110]

with [5.9], we have:

$$\frac{1}{z_m}-\frac{1}{z_i}=\frac{1}{z_g}$$

[5.111]

The integral in equation [5.109] is the Fourier transform of a quadratic phase factor multiplied by the detector window. We have:

$$\tilde{W}_z\left(x_m, y_m\right) = \int\limits_{-L/2}^{+L/2} \int\limits_{-L/2}^{+L/2} \exp\left[\frac{jk}{2}\left(\frac{1}{z_m} - \frac{1}{z_i}\right)\left(x^2 + y^2\right)\right] \times$$

$$\exp\left\{-j2\pi\left[\left(x_m - \frac{z_m}{z_r}x_r + \frac{z_m}{z_0}\xi\right)\frac{x}{\lambda z_m} + \left(y_m - \frac{z_m}{z_r}y_r + \frac{z_m}{z_0}\eta\right)\frac{y}{\lambda z_m}\right]\right\}dxdy$$

[5.112]

This function is convoluted with the resolution function in equation [5.37], in the case where $z_m \neq z_i$. It disappears if $z_m = z_i$ since Fourier transform of 1 is the Dirac distribution $\delta(x,y)$. Because this function is related to the focus of the digital reconstruction, its spectral extent is limited by the size of the image sensor; this means that limiting its observation horizon imposes a limitation on its energy as well as its spatial bandwidth. Let us consider the x-direction (similar relations hold for the y direction). The quadratic phase factor from [5.112] has local spatial frequencies given by:

$$f_{ix} = \frac{x}{\lambda}\left(\frac{1}{z_m} - \frac{1}{z_i}\right)$$

[5.113]

Then, the maximal spatial frequencies considered at the detector are:

$$f_{ix}^{max} = \frac{L}{2\lambda}\left(\frac{1}{z_m} - \frac{1}{z_i}\right)$$

[5.114]

Such a spatial frequency bandwidth generates a spatial width ΔX in the reconstructed plane via the relation $\Delta X = 2\lambda z_m f_{ix}^{max}$. So, considering the Rayleigh criterion and the profile of $\tilde{W}_z$, the resolution in the presence of a digital defocus in the reconstructed plane can be considered to be the width of a defocusing function, given by:

$$\rho_x^z = L\left|1 - \frac{z_m}{z_i}\right|$$

[5.115]

A similar relation holds for the y-direction. This expression gives the contribution of the focusing error to the blurring of the image. It depends only on the observation horizon in the considered direction and on the ratio z_m/z_i. It vanishes in the case of perfect image focusing, since $z_m = z_i$. In this case, the resolution in the object plane is given by (see section 5.1.4.):

$$\rho_x = \frac{\lambda z_i}{L} = \frac{\lambda z_i}{N \Delta x} \qquad [5.116]$$

A criterion to determine the focal depth of the reconstructed image can be obtained by preposing that the width of the defocusing function must be at most equal to ρ_x. Noting $\Delta z = |z_m - z_i|$, we get:

$$2\Delta z \cong \frac{2\lambda z_i^2}{L^2} = \frac{2\lambda z_i^2}{N^2 \Delta x^2} \qquad [5.117]$$

Thus the focal depth is proportional to the square of the angular aperture of the sensor as seen from the object [YAM 01a].

5.8.2. *Comparison with a digital holographic simulation*

Figure 5.32 shows $\left| \tilde{W}_z(x,0) \right|$ (equation [5.112]) for $\lambda = 632.8$ nm, $\Delta x = 4.65$ μm, $N = 1{,}024$, $z_i = 250$ mm and with z_m varying from -350 mm to -152 mm.

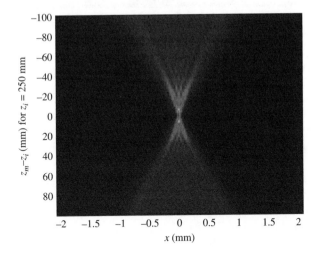

Figure 5.32. *Evolution of the focusing function versus reconstruction distances (for a color version of this figure, see www.iste.co.uk/picart/digiholog.zip)*

Some profiles along the x-direction are represented in Figure 5.33. When $z_m - z_0 \neq 0$, an enlargement is visible, which induces a blur in the reconstructed image due to the enlargement of each point constituting the image. Applying equation

[5.115] with $z_i = 250$ mm and $z_m-z_0 = -100$ mm gives $\rho_x^z = 1.9$ mm, which corresponds to the width of the relevant curve in Figure 5.33; in this example, the spatial resolution is not better than 1.9 mm [PIC 08a].

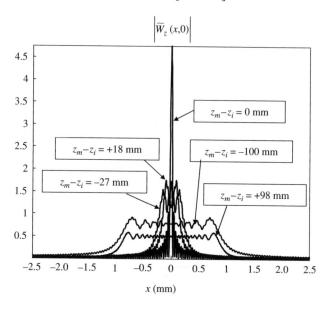

Figure 5.33. *Profiles of the resolution function for different reconstruction distances*

A simulation of the full digital holographic process (recording and reconstruction) can be performed using a digital pinhole as an object [PIC 08a]. Reconstruction is computed with the D-FFT method such that sampling remains invariant. The parameters are $\lambda = 632.8$ nm, $\Delta x = 4.65$ μm, $N = 1,024$, $z_i = 250$ mm, and z_m varying from -350 mm to -152 mm. Figure 5.34 shows the comparison between resolution functions obtained with the full process simulation and the computation of equation [5.112]. The two pictures are quite similar: they have the same width around the axis of perfect focus ($z_m = z_i$). However, their amplitudes are slightly different, which can be seen in the slight variation of the color map representation. The resemblance of the curves in Figures 5.35 and 5.36 can be appreciated, showing the x profile for perfect focusing and the z profile along z-axis. It can be seen that x profiles overlap whereas z profiles are slightly different, although they have equivalent widths according to Rayleigh criterion. Overall, the model presented in this section is a good approximation of spatial resolution in digital Fresnel holography in the presence of focusing errors.

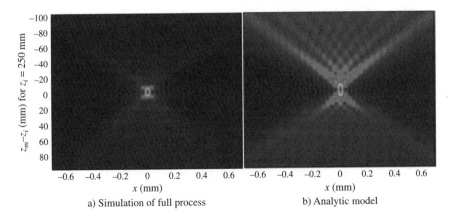

a) Simulation of full process

b) Analytic model

Figure 5.34. *Comparison between the analytical formulation and a numerical simulation versus reconstruction distance (for a color version of this figure, see www.iste.co.uk/picart/digiholog.zip)*

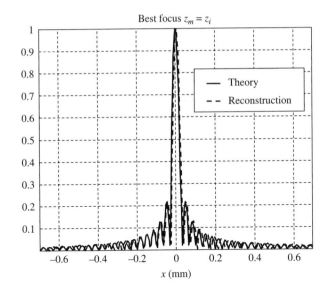

Figure 5.35. *Profiles along the x-direction for the analytical formulation and a numerical simulation at the best focus*

5.8.3. *Experiments*

The object is a 2 euro coin, 25 mm in diameter, illuminated at $\lambda = 0.6328$ nm and placed at $z_0 = 660$ mm from the sensor ($N = 1,024$, $\Delta x = 4.65$ μm). The reference wave is plane, thus $z_r = \infty$. The reconstruction is performed using the D-FFT method with an adjustable magnification of $G_y = 0.35$ and the reconstruction parameters are $z_i = -231$ mm and $z_c = -355.38$ mm. The theoretical ideal focused image will then be obtained with $z_m = -231$ mm, the spatial resolution being $\rho_x = 30.7$ µm in the reconstructed image plane. From [5.117], the depth of focus is $\Delta z \approx 7$ mm.

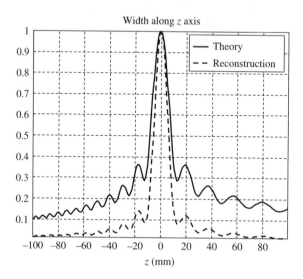

Figure 5.36. *Profiles along the z-axis for the analytical formulation and a full numerical simulation for x = y = 0*

Figure 5.37 shows the reconstructed images. Figure 5.37(a) corresponds to the best focused image. Figure 5.37(b) corresponds to an out of focus image with $z_m = z_i - 50$ mm. The image is highly blurred due to the enlarging function of equation [5.112]. In this case, we have $\rho_x^z = 1.03$mm. Figures 5.27(c) and 5.37(d) correspond to reconstructions included symmetrically within the depth of focus, for which we have $\rho_x^z = 103$ µm, which is about three times the spatial resolution. As can be seen, the images are focused even if there is a slight difference between them. Figures 5.27(e) and 5.37(f) correspond to reconstructions slightly outside the depth of focus, for which we have $\rho_x^z = 206$ µm. The images are blurred by the enlarging function of equation [5.112], whose width increases by $|z_m - z_i|$.

Figure 5.37 shows that if the reconstruction distance differs slightly from the ideal, there is no significant difference between reconstructed images. This result justifies the zero-padding algorithm in section 5.7.3, since a small change in the reconstruction distance does not dramatically degrade the spatial resolution of the image.

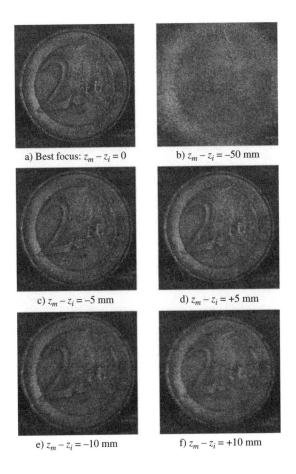

a) Best focus: $z_m - z_i = 0$ b) $z_m - z_i = -50$ mm

c) $z_m - z_i = -5$ mm   d) $z_m - z_i = +5$ mm

e) $z_m - z_i = -10$ mm   f) $z_m - z_i = +10$ mm

Figure 5.37. *Reconstructed images inside and outside of the depth of focus*

5.9. Conclusion

In this chapter, we have presented the principles of digital Fresnel holography (i.e. with diffraction across free space), as well as the associated reconstruction methods. The discrete Fresnel transform is the simplest and most direct calculation method, on the condition that the sampling theorem is respected in the plane of the hologram. This method is certainly the most widely used, even though it does not guarantee the invariance of the reconstructed horizon with the wavelength. Some simple techniques of eliminating the zero order and increasing the spatial resolution of reconstructed images have been discussed. We have presented the methods based on adjustable magnification, which allows the size of the reconstructed image to be adapted to the size of the image sensor. These methods are based on the use of a spherical reconstruction wave, which generates a modification of the reconstruction distance and therefore of the size of the image. These methods give a horizon which is identical to that of the recording detector, and consequently invariant with the wavelength.

We presented some methods of digital color holography. An algorithm based on the Fresnel transform and wavelength-dependant zero-padding was discussed. True color RGB images may thus be reconstructed from the recording of a single three-color hologram.

Finally, we discussed the depth of focus of the reconstruction process. Some useful relations were given for the estimation of the width of the enlarging function that degrades the resolution of the image, as well as the estimation of the depth of focus around the ideal focus.

This chapter has dealt with the case of "off-axis holography". The reconstruction methods are mainly based on Fresnel diffraction. Note that other reconstruction methods based on wavelets are also discussed in the literature. For examples, the reader may refer to the references [ONU 93], [LIE 03], [LIE 04a], and [LIE 04b]. The case of "in-line holography" has been voluntarily omitted. The reason is that it suffers from the overlapping of the twin image and zero order, so that practical applications are limited to particular cases, such as the investigation of particle field extraction [ONU 92, HIN 02] or the microscopy of phase objects [GAR 06a, GAR 06b].

Chapter 6

Reconstructing Wavefronts Propagated through an Optical System

We saw in Chapter 5 how to reconstruct an object field from a digital hologram recorded in a free space, i.e. in a configuration where the object is placed facing the detector. In a large number of experimental problems, it is tempting to adjust the optical system so as to reduce the size of the digital holographic apparatus, the recording distance respecting Shannon's conditions being directly proportional to the size of the object. If the exposed surface of the object is very different (larger or smaller) than that of the pixel matrix of the detector, it is necessary to conceive of an optical system that adapts the object field to the sampling conditions set by the detector. In general, the surface area of the detector is in the order of mm², whereas the object may occupy several cm². In this case, we are interested in reconstructing the wavefront propagated by an optical system. There exist three methods enabling the adaptation of the object wave: the first method consists of synthesizing an aperture, which aims to increase the effective surface area of the detector's pixel matrix by recording different zones by successive displacements of the detector in its plane [BIN 02, MAS 02]; this method is usually called "synthetic aperture holography"; the second method combines the points of view given by several mirrors, so as to increase the spectral width of the recording [YIN 05]; the last method uses an optical system that transforms the wave to display the object at a smaller angle, or to make an image of the object directly in the detector plane [LI 08a, MAN 05]. The techniques used in the last method are similar to those used in speckle interferometry [SLA 11]. The first method may be applied only in the case where the object is immobile or moving very slowly. The second method requires the development of a very complex optical system. The last approach is the most reasonable in terms of the complexity and ease of its implementation.

In particular, this method is implemented in digital holographic microscopes [CUC 99a, CUC 99b].

In this context, we must develop an algorithm for reconstructing the wavefront after the hologram has recorded the object wave propagated through an optical system.

This chapter treats the transformation of the object wave by an optical system and, using Collins' formula and the classical diffraction formulae, we will present some reconstruction algorithms that will be verified by simulations and experimental results [GOO 72, GOO 05, COL 70, LI 08b].

6.1. Theoretical basis

We recall the discussion of relation [5.37] from Chapter 5 concerning the impulse response of the process of image formation in digital Fresnel holography. In the case of diffraction toward the detector in free space (Fresnel holography), there is no optical system transforming the object wave. To study the quality of the reconstructed image, we consider the process of recording the hologram and reconstructing the object image as an image formation process. On the basis of linear systems theory and considering a plane reference wave, the impulse response [5.37] was established [KRE 02a, KRE 02b, KRE 04, PIC 08a], and it is reiterated as equation [6.1] in summary form (the pixels are considered to have no spatial extent):

$$h(x,y) = C \times \text{sinc}\left(\frac{N\Delta x}{\lambda z_0}x\right)\text{sinc}\left(\frac{M\Delta y}{\lambda z_0}y\right) \qquad [6.1]$$

where C is a complex constant, z_0 is the recording distance, λ is the wavelength, Δx and Δy are the pixel pitches, and N and M are the number of pixels in the detector matrix along the x- and y-axes, respectively. The width of the impulse response fixes the spatial resolution of the reconstruction, which is then given by:

$$\rho_x = \frac{\lambda z_0}{N\Delta x}$$
$$\rho_y = \frac{\lambda z_0}{M\Delta y} \qquad [6.2]$$

If the impulse response is close to the δ function, the quality of the image is much better, as the spatial resolution tends to that of the pixels of the detector [PIC 08a]. Since $N\Delta x \times M\Delta y$ is the surface area of the detector, [6.2] shows that the greater the detector surface area and the shorter the recording distance, the better the resolution of the image. In reality, the resolution cannot be indefinitely increased but is instead limited by the exit pupil of the imaging system [SLA 11]. The attainable spatial resolution is ultimately very similar whether recording with free-space propagation or through an imaging system. However, the width of a commercially available detector is typically in the order of millimeters. Compared to photographic holographic plates that have surface areas of 10 cm × 12 cm, digital detectors have a tenth of the resolving power, and it seems that it will be difficult to considerably increase their size in the future. Furthermore, to produce the reference wave, we must add a beam splitter (a 50/50 plate, a cube splitter, or a polarization splitter) between the object and the detector, which hinders the reduction of the recording distance. The transformation of the object wave by an optical system placed between the detector and the object gives the possibility of adjusting the size of the object and the recording distance. In this chapter, we will therefore study images reconstructed with this configuration, where the object wave is propagated through an optical system.

6.1.1. *Case of a convergent lens*

Figure 6.1 illustrates the case where the light from the object crosses a convergent lens [LI 09b]. A hologram may be recorded if we add a reference wave, which is not represented in Figure 6.1. In effect, this holographic recording architecture may be considered as a system forming an image which is unfocussed at the position of the detector. From the Rayleigh or Abbe theory of image formation, the lens mount may be considered as the entrance or exit pupil of the system [GOO 72, LI 08b]. If we consider this system for recording a hologram, the detector is placed anywhere between the planes PC0 and PC1 in Figure 6.1 and the system allows the recording of the components of the angular spectrum crossing the lens. If we use this setup, we may record many more high-frequency components from the object compared to a lens-less system by increasing the geometric extent of the laser beam. The lens then acts as a larger collector than the image sensor.

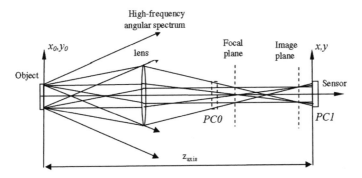

Figure 6.1. *Angular spectrum in an image-forming system*

Practically, the imaging system is generally structured with several optical elements, and Collins' formula, which is presented in Chapter 2, is useful for this study.

6.1.2. Impulse response of the process

6.1.2.1. Matrix description of the digital holographic system

We recall the study of Collins' formula from Chapter 2. If a system may be represented by a transfer matrix of four elements A, B, C, D, letting (x_0,y_0) be the coordinates of the input plane, $U_0(x_0,y_0)$ be the distribution of the complex amplitude of the input field, and (x,y) be the coordinates of the output plane, the output plane $U(x,y)$ is expressed by Collins' formula [COL 70]:

$$U(x, y) = \frac{\exp(jkz_{axis})}{j\lambda B} \int_{-\infty}^{\infty}\int_{-\infty}^{\infty} U_0(x_0, y_0)\exp\left\{\frac{jk}{2B}\left[A(x_0^2 + y_0^2)+ D(x^2 + y^2)- 2(xx_0 + yy_0)\right]\right\}dx_0 dy_0$$

[6.3]

where z_{axis} is the optical path length along the optical axis and $k = 2\pi/\lambda$.

If we consider x_i, y_i to be the coordinates in the image plane, Figure 6.2 shows the digital holographic system containing the physical recording process and the digital reconstruction process of the hologram.

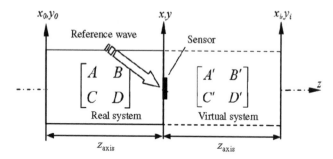

Figure 6.2. *Digital holographic system*

Figure 6.2 shows that the physical processes of the system may be separated into two parts. The first part concerns the light from the object propagating along the z-axis and impacting the detector, then, after interfering with the reference beam, the hologram is recorded. This is a real, physical, optical process. The second part concerns the virtual illumination of the hologram by a digital wave and the calculation of the diffraction by the hologram, giving a reconstruction of an image of the object. This is a purely virtual optical process, since the diffraction does not truly exist. Since the surface area of the detector matrix is generally smaller than the diameters of the other optical elements of the system, using the Abbe and Rayleigh theory [GOO 05], it is sufficient to study the problem of the diffraction of the object wave constrained by the pupil of the detector matrix.

From the previous hypotheses, we will consider the real optical system to be situated between the two planes $x_0 y_0$ and xy and described by the transfer matrix $ABCD$, and the virtual optical system is situated between the two planes xy and $x_i y_i$ and described by the transfer matrix $A'B'C'D'$. If the object wave propagating toward the xy-plane can form an image of the object with a unit magnification in the $x_i y_i$-plane, the two matrices must satisfy the following relation [GER 75]:

$$\begin{bmatrix} A' & B' \\ C' & D' \end{bmatrix} \begin{bmatrix} A & B \\ C & D \end{bmatrix} = \begin{bmatrix} 1 & 0 \\ 0 & 1 \end{bmatrix} \qquad [6.4]$$

We therefore have:

$$A' = D, \quad B' = -B, \quad C' = -C, \quad D' = A \qquad [6.5]$$

Consequently, once the object field in the xy-plane is obtained, we can reconstruct the image field by applying Collins' formula from the coefficients of the transfer matrix of the virtual optical system.

6.1.2.2. *Impulse response from the digital holographic system*

The quality of the reconstructed image is linked to the impulse response of the system forming the image. Let us consider, in the object plane $x_0 y_0$ of Figure 6.2, a point source of unit amplitude with coordinates (ξ, η) as a point object. We may study the structure of its image in the $x_i y_i$-plane. In this case, in a similar way to that which was presented in previous chapters, the object field is described by the function $\delta(x_0 - \xi, y_0 - \eta)$ (see section 5.1.4). Using Collins' formula, neglecting the constant phase factor concerning the optical path length along the axis, the object field in the detector plane is expressed by:

$$O_\delta(x, y; \xi, \eta) = \frac{1}{j\lambda B} \int_{-\infty}^{\infty} \int_{-\infty}^{\infty} \delta(x_0 - \xi, y_0 - \eta) \exp\left\{ \frac{jk}{2B} \left[A(x_0^2 + y_0^2) + D(x^2 + y^2) - 2(xx_0 + yy_0) \right] \right\} dx_0 dy_0$$

$$= \frac{1}{j\lambda B} \exp\left\{ \frac{jk}{2B} \left[A(\xi^2 + \eta^2) + D(x^2 + y^2) - 2(x\xi + y\eta) \right] \right\}$$

$$[6.6]$$

In the previous chapter, we described several methods for recovering the object field. To simplify our study, we suppose that the field $O_\delta(x, y; \xi, \eta)$ has been obtained. We consider the wave at the aperture diaphragm to be the input signal of the virtual system. Let us study the output signal. For simplicity, the pixels are considered to have no spatial extent.

The aperture diaphragm may be represented by:

$$w(x, y) = \text{rect}\left(\frac{x}{N\Delta x}\right)\text{rect}\left(\frac{y}{M\Delta y}\right) \tag{6.7}$$

where N and M are the number of pixels along the x- and y-axes, respectively.

From [6.5] and Collins' formula, we neglect the constant phase factor introduced by the optical path length along the optical axis and the reconstructed field in the $x_i y_i$-plane is given by

$$O_{i\delta}(x_i, y_i; \xi, \eta) = \frac{1}{-j\lambda B} \int\limits_{-\infty}^{\infty}\int\limits_{-\infty}^{\infty} O_\delta(x, y)w(x, y) \times$$
$$\exp\left\{-\frac{jk}{2B}\left[D(x^2 + y^2) + A(x_i^2 + y_i^2) - 2(x_i x + y_i y)\right]\right\}dxdy \tag{6.8}$$

Substituting [6.7] into [6.8], we may rewrite this expression in the form of an inverse Fourier transform:

$$O_{i\delta}(x_i, y_i; \xi, \eta) = \exp\left\{-j\frac{k}{2B}A\left[(x_i^2 + y_i^2) - (\xi^2 + \eta^2)\right]\right\}F^{-1}\{w(x, y)\}\left(\frac{x_i - \xi}{\lambda B}, \frac{y_i - \eta}{\lambda B}\right) \tag{6.9}$$

Substituting $w(x,y)$ into this relation, we may again rewrite it as:

$$O_{i\delta}(x_i, y_i; \xi, \eta) = N\Delta x^2 M\Delta y^2 \exp\left\{-j\frac{k}{2B}A\left[(x_i^2 + y_i^2) - (\xi^2 + \eta^2)\right]\right\}$$
$$\times \text{sinc}\left[N\Delta x\left(\frac{x_i - \xi}{\lambda B}\right)\right]\text{sinc}\left[M\Delta y\left(\frac{y_i - \eta}{\lambda B}\right)\right] \tag{6.10}$$

This expression constitutes the response at the output of the digital holographic system. Letting $O_0(x_0, y_0)$ be the object field, the reconstructed field in the image plane is given by the following superposition integral:

$$O_r(x_i, y_i) = N\Delta x^2 M\Delta y^2 \exp\left[-j\frac{k}{2B}A(x_i^2 + y_i^2)\right] \times$$
$$\int\limits_{-\infty}^{\infty}\int\limits_{-\infty}^{\infty} O_0(x_0, y_0)\exp\left[j\frac{k}{2B}A(x_0^2 + y_0^2)\right]\text{sinc}\left[N\Delta x\left(\frac{x_i - x_0}{\lambda B}\right)\right]\text{sinc}\left[M\Delta y\left(\frac{y_i - y_0}{\lambda B}\right)\right]dx_0 dy_0 \tag{6.11}$$

The digital holographic system in Figure 6.2 therefore has an impulse response given by:

$$h_-(x_i, y_i; x_0, y_0) = N\Delta x^2 M\Delta y^2 \exp\left[-j\frac{k}{2B}A(x_i^2 + y_i^2)\right] \text{sinc}\left[N\Delta x\left(\frac{x_0}{\lambda B}\right)\right] \text{sinc}\left[M\Delta y\left(\frac{y_0}{\lambda B}\right)\right] \quad [6.12]$$

The ideal image corresponds to an impulse response tending toward the δ function. Under these conditions, if B tends to zero, expression [6.12] becomes the product of the two-dimensional δ function with a constant complex factor. Given that the case where $B = 0$ corresponds to the coincidence of the detector and image plane, this means that if the detector is placed in the neighborhood of the object image plane, we should reconstruct the best image of the object. Note that equation [6.12] does not take into account of the limiting aperture of the optical system. Practically, this means that the real impulse response must be convoluted to that of the optical system. So the image plane has a resolution that is at most diffraction-limited by the optical system. However, the diffraction limit depends on the method used to reconstruct the object from the digital hologram. In case of off-axis holography, the digital hologram of the aperture must fulfill Shannon's theorem, so that resolution limits are equivalent in both cases: free space or imaging in the sensor plane [SLA 11].

We know that diffraction across the distance z_0 is equivalent to diffraction across a simple optical system whose transfer matrix has the elements $A = 1$, $B = z_0$, $C = 0$, and $D = 1$. In this case, comparison of [6.12] with [6.1] shows that the impulse response [6.1] may be considered as a particular case of expression [6.12].

6.1.2.3. *Experimental reconstruction with an afocal system*

The optical system in Figure 6.3 is composed of two convergent lenses whose focal distances are $f_1 = 710$ mm for L_1 and $f_2 = 127$ mm for L_2. The setup is an afocal system and is used to record a hologram [LI 09b]. A square diaphragm whose sides are $D_x = D_y = D_0 = 12$ mm with the Chinese letter "dragon" (in reverse) at the center serves as an object. The diaphragm is illuminated by a plane wave of wavelength $\lambda = 632.8$ nm. The light emerging from the diaphragm, having crossed the two lenses L_1 and L_2 and the splitter S, constitutes the object wave incident to the detector plane. The reference wave is that reflected by the splitter S. Let d_1 be the distance between the object plane and the lens L_1 and d_2 the distance from L_2 to the detector. The monochromatic detector consists of 768 × 576 pixels with a pixel pitch of 8.4 μm. We chose as reconstruction parameters a horizon of $N \times N = 512 \times 512$ points that correspond to a detector surface area of 4.3 mm × 4.3 mm.

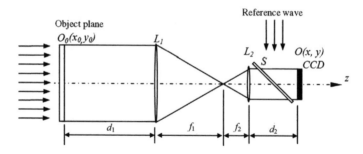

Figure 6.3. *Experimental two-lens system*

The four elements of the matrix are determined by the following relation:

$$\begin{bmatrix} A & B \\ C & D \end{bmatrix} = \begin{bmatrix} 1 & d_2 \\ 0 & 1 \end{bmatrix} \begin{bmatrix} 1 & 0 \\ -1/f_2 & 1 \end{bmatrix} \begin{bmatrix} 1 & f_1 + f_2 \\ 0 & 1 \end{bmatrix} \begin{bmatrix} 1 & 0 \\ -1/f_1 & 1 \end{bmatrix} \begin{bmatrix} 1 & d_1 \\ 0 & 1 \end{bmatrix}$$

$$= \begin{bmatrix} -f_2/f_1 & \left(-d_1 f_2^2 + f_2 f_1^2 + f_1 f_2^2 - d_2 f_1^2\right)/(f_2 f_1) \\ 0 & -f_1/f_2 \end{bmatrix}$$ [6.13]

It is easy to confirm that when $d_1 = f_1$ and $d_2 = f_2$, we have $B = 0$, i.e. the system becomes a "$4f$ system" [KEA 02, GOO 72, GOO 05]. In this case, the exit plane is the image of the input plane. However, by modifying the two distances d_1 and d_2 we may obtain results corresponding to the condition $B \neq 0$.

For the case where $d_1 = f_1$, we record three holograms corresponding to three positions $d_2 = \{80 \text{ mm}, 128 \text{ mm}, 232 \text{ mm}\}$. The results are given in Figure 6.4(a). These three figures show that in the case where $d_2 = 128$ mm we obtain an almost clear image on the detector, as this position is very close to the image plane. In the two other cases, the detector planes are distant from the image plane and the images are blurred.

The complex amplitude of the diffracted field in the detector plane may be calculated by Collins' formula from the image of the letter. Figure 6.4(b) shows the results obtained by the three simulations. The comparison shows a good correlation between experimental and theoretical results. We reconstruct the image from relation [6.8], i.e. with the object field $O(x,y)$:

$$O_i(x_i, y_i) = \frac{1}{-j\lambda B} \int\limits_{-\infty}^{\infty}\int\limits_{-\infty}^{\infty} O(x, y) w(x, y) \times$$

$$\exp\left\{-\frac{jk}{2B}\left[D(x^2 + y^2) + A(x_i^2 + y_i^2) - 2(x_i x + y_i y)\right]\right\} dx dy$$ [6.14]

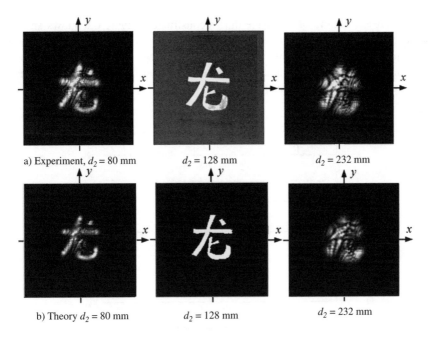

Number of samples: 512 × 512 ; surface: 4.3 mm × 4.3 mm

d_2 = 80 mm: A = –0.1789, B = 262.7559 mm, C = 0, D = –5.5906 mm^{-1}
d_2 = 128 mm: A = –0.1789, B = –5.5906 mm, C = 0, D = –5.5906 mm^{-1}
d_2 = 232 mm: A = –0.1789, B = –587.0079 mm, C = 0, D = 5.5906 mm^{-1}

Figure 6.4. *Comparison between the simulated and experimentally diffracted images*

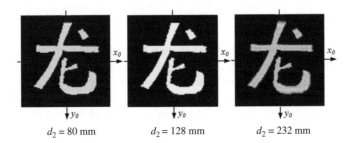

Figure 6.5. *Comparison of the images reconstructed in three cases where the d_2*
values are different (area of each image: 12 mm × 12 mm)

Figure 6.5 shows the three images reconstructed in the object plane using the fields in Figure 6.4(a). We note that the object field may be reconstructed by the field recorded in a plane which is not the image plane given by the optical system.

To estimate the quality of an image thus reconstructed, Figure 6.6 shows an image line along $y_0 = -2$ mm. A comparison is given between the ideal amplitude and the real and virtual parts of the complex reconstructed image. We note that, as theoretically predicted, the smaller the value of the matrix element B, the better the quality of the reconstructed image.

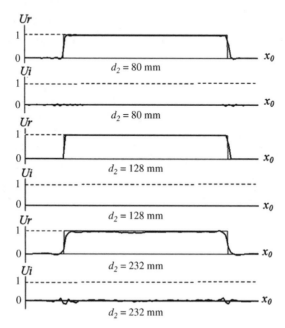

Figure 6.6. *Comparison between the amplitude of the ideal image (thin line) and the real parts Ur (thick line) of the reconstructed image along $y_0 = -2$ mm*

The optical system used previously is only an attempt to confirm the possibility of reconstructing the object wavefront using the field propagated through an optical system. We will see in the following section that if we add a divergent lens between the two convergent lenses, we may obtain a zoom, which is very useful for adapting the size of the object when it is much larger or smaller than the detector [LI 08a].

6.2. Digital holography with a zoom

In numerous practical instances, we often meet the case where the size of the object is much larger or much smaller than the size of the detector. Even though the 4*f* system allows us to transform the object wave so that it can be adapted to the detector size, it is difficult to adapt it to certain practical cases. For example, when the size of the object is much larger than that of the detector, the focal distance of the second lens of the 4*f* system will be very small. In general, the reference wave is introduced behind this lens by a beam splitter cube whose size does not always allow its placement. Consequently, it is of interest to design an optical system that allows us to adapt to the size of the object, giving a correct recording of the hologram.

A zoom is obtained by adding a divergent lens between the two convergent lenses of the 4*f* system. By suitably setting the position of the divergent lens, this system allows the easy adaptation to the variation in the size of the object. If the decrease in object size is properly calculated, there will be the possibility of including a cube into the beam's trajectory so that the reference beam may be introduced before the detector plane

6.2.1. *Principle of the zoom*

This holographic system is similar to a Mach-Zehnder interferometer, into one arm of which we insert the three-lens optical system. Figure 6.7 shows such a holographic interferometer that works in a similar manner as that of a transmitting holographic microscope [CUC 99].

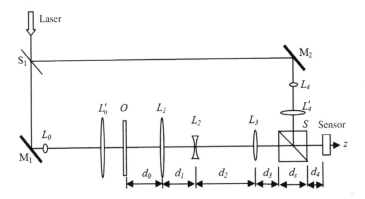

Figure 6.7. *Recording a hologram with a zoom*

In this figure, the incident laser beam is first separated into two by the splitter S_1. The object beam is reflected by the mirror M_1 and propagates across the collimator composed of two lenses L_0 and L'_0, which transform it into a plane wave. The zoom is determined by the three lenses L_1, L_2, and L_3. Here, L_2 is a divergent lens, the other two are convergent, and the convergence point of the light crossing L_1 and L_2 coincides with the focus of L_3. Having crossed the splitter S, the beam is transformed into a quasi-plane wave impacting the detector. The reference beam is reflected by S_1, then by M_2, and crosses the collimator composed of lenses L_4 and L_4'. The cube mixes the two waves at the detector. The focal distances of the three lenses L_1, L_2, and L_3 are noted as f_1, f_2, and f_3. We will show that if $f_1 > f_3$, we may obtain an image of the object plane in the detector plane with a magnification less than f_3/f_1.

6.2.2. Study of the zoom

Figure 6.8 shows a zoom system composed of three lenses L_1, L_2, and L_3, in which the hollow dot represents the focal point F_1' of the lens L_1. For the sake of simplicity, we may consider the lenses to be thin. Lens L_2 is placed between L_1 and F_1', and so the ray incident parallel to the optical axis will be focalized at the output of L_1L_2, at the point P shown by the black dot. The effective lens is determined by extending the ray convergent to P (see Figure 6.8). The virtually extended ray intercepts the ray incident to the principal object plane $[H_0]$ of the effective system. Letting d_h be the distance between H_0 and L_1, and d_f the distance between F_1' and P, the focal distance of the effective system is $d_h + f_1 + d_f$. If the point P coincides with the focal point of lens L_3, then the three lenses are equivalent to the $4f$ system, in which the first lens is situated in the plane $[H_0]$ and whose transverse magnification is given by:

$$G_y = -\frac{f_3}{d_h + f_1 + d_f} \qquad [6.15]$$

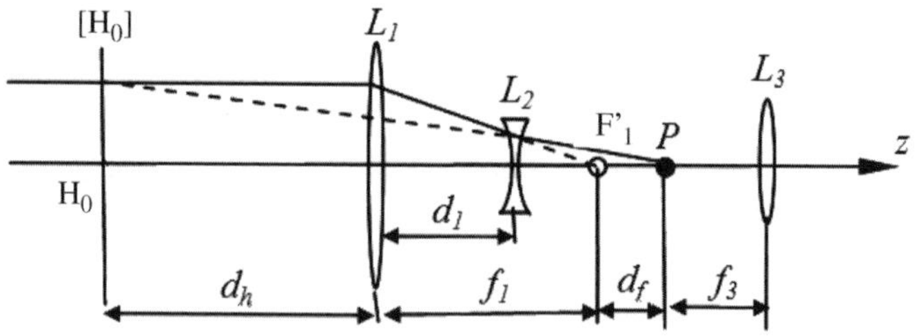

Figure 6.8. *Three lens zoom*

Gauss' approximation and the geometric relations of Figure 6.8 allow us to determine the two parameters d_f and d_h (P being the image of F_1') [KEO 02]. The relations between the parameters are:

$$\frac{1}{-f_2} = \frac{1}{-(f_1 - d_1)} + \frac{1}{(f_1 - d_1) + d_f}$$ [6.16]

$$\frac{f_1 - d_1}{f_1} = \frac{(f_1 - d_1) + d_f}{d_h + f_1 + d_f}$$ [6.17]

6.2.3. Design of the zoom

From a practical point of view, we often know the width L of the detector, the three focal distances of the three lenses, and the width D_0 of the object. The problem is then to design the zoom. From relation [6.15], we also have

$$|G_y| = \frac{L}{D_0} = \frac{f_3}{d_h + f_1 + d_f}$$ [6.18]

Substituting f_1, f_2, and f_3 into [6.16], [6.17], and [6.18], we will be able to determine d_1, d_f, and d_h. In Figure 6.7, we write the refractive index of the beam splitter cube S as n. Considering the system formed from the object plane O to the detector as the system $ABCD$, the transfer matrix will be:

$$\begin{bmatrix} A & B \\ C & D \end{bmatrix} = \begin{bmatrix} 1 & d_4 \\ 0 & 1 \end{bmatrix} \begin{bmatrix} 1 & d_s/n \\ 0 & 1 \end{bmatrix} \begin{bmatrix} 1 & d_3 \\ 0 & 1 \end{bmatrix} \times$$

$$\begin{bmatrix} 1 & 0 \\ -1/f_3 & 1 \end{bmatrix} \begin{bmatrix} 1 & d_2 \\ 0 & 1 \end{bmatrix} \begin{bmatrix} 1 & 0 \\ 1/f_2 & 1 \end{bmatrix} \begin{bmatrix} 1 & d_1 \\ 0 & 1 \end{bmatrix} \begin{bmatrix} 1 & 0 \\ -1/f_1 & 1 \end{bmatrix} \begin{bmatrix} 1 & d_0 \\ 0 & 1 \end{bmatrix}$$ [6.19]

Developing this expression, we obtain:

$$A = (1 - d/f_3)(1 - d_1/f_1) + [d_2 + d(1 - d_2/f_3)][1/f_2 - (1 + d_1/f_2)/f_1]$$

$$B = (1 - d/f_3)[d_0 + d_1(1 - d_0/f_1)] + [d_2 + d(1 - d_2/f_3)] \times$$
$$[d_0/f_2 + (1 + d_1/f_2)(1 - d_0/f_1)]$$

$$C = -(1 - d_1/f_1)/f_3 + (1 - d_2/f_3)[1/f_2 - (1 + d_1/f_2)/f_1]$$

$$D = -[d_0 + d_1(1 - d_0/f_1)]/f_3 + (1 - d_2/f_3) \times$$
$$[d_0/f_2 + (1 + d_1/f_2)(1 - d_0/f_1)]$$ [6.20]

with

$$z_0 = d_4 + d_s/n + d_3$$ [6.21]

Since the case $B = 0$ corresponds to the case where the output plane is the image plane of the input plane, the image–sensor distance is given by:

$$z_0 = \frac{[d_0 + d_1(1 - d_0/f_1)] + [d_0/f_2 + (1 + d_1/f_2)(1 - d_0/f_1)]d_2}{[d_0 + d_1(1 - d_0/f_1)]/f_3 - (1 - d_2/f_3)[d_0/f_2 + (1 + d_1/f_2)(1 - d_0/f_1)]} \quad [6.22]$$

We note that $d_2 = f_1 + d_f + f_3 - d_1$, and so if one of d_0 or z_0 is given, we may determine the other one.

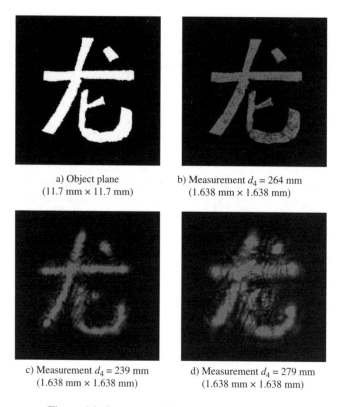

a) Object plane
(11.7 mm × 11.7 mm)

b) Measurement $d_4 = 264$ mm
(1.638 mm × 1.638 mm)

c) Measurement $d_4 = 239$ mm
(1.638 mm × 1.638 mm)

d) Measurement $d_4 = 279$ mm
(1.638 mm × 1.638 mm)

Figure 6.9. *Experimental demonstration of the zoom*

As an example, we will consider three lenses L_1, L_2, and L_3 having the respective focal distances $f_1 = 697$ mm, $f_2 = 60$ mm, and $f_3 = 127$ mm, and a beam splitter cube of width $d_s = 80$ mm and refractive index $n \approx 1.6$. If we use only the two lenses L_1 and L_3 to construct a $4f$ system, the transverse magnification will be $G_y = -f_3/f_1 \approx -0.19$. Since the beam splitter cube must be placed behind lens L_3, the space between L_3 and the image plane is only 47 mm. Taking into account the size of the supports and optical components, the apparatus is therefore difficult to set up.

Furthermore, since the object plane is situated at the distance $f_1 = 697$ mm behind L_1, the space is poorly used. To confirm the validity of these studies, considering $d_0 = 390$ mm and $G_y = -0.14$, the design of the zoom is as follows: from [6.22], we obtain $z_0 = 334$ mm, $d_1 = 665$ mm, and $d_2 = 147$ mm. This means that the space behind the last lens L_3 is sufficient for the placement of the beam splitter cube. We also have $d_3 = 20$ mm, and from [6.21], we find the position of the image with $d_4 = 264$ mm.

6.2.4. *Experimental validation*

We consider the same object as in the previous section (see Figure 6.9(a), the inverted Chinese letter "dragon"). The laser has a wavelength of $\lambda = 532$ nm. Figures 6.9(b)–(d) show the three intensity distributions of the diffracted field recorded by the detector (512×512 pixels with a pixel pitch of 3.2 μm). Each square image has a width of 1.638 mm. A comparison of Figure 6.9(a) with Figure 6.9(b) shows that the imaging system functions perfectly.

Analysis of Figures 6.9(c) and (d) shows that the greater the d_4 is, the more the diffracted field is blurred compared to the initial object. However, since the system is equivalent to a $4f$ system and the incident wave is plane, the light propagated by the ensemble is quasi-parallel to the optical axis, which means that all the information of the object may be received by the detector. The detector records the diffracted field with a lack of focus which will be compensated for during the digital reconstruction of the image [LI 08a].

Considering the transverse magnification to be greater than 1, this zoom design may be generalized for the case where the size of the object is very small compared to the detector, as will be the case for holographic microscopy.

6.3. Reconstructing an image by Collins' formula

In this section we will use Collins' formula to reconstruct the image from a recording after propagation across the optical system interposed between the object and the detector.

6.3.1. *Reconstruction algorithm*

6.3.1.1. *Experimental setup*

Figure 6.10 presents a schema of the holographic system [LI 09a]. The object is the letter "dragon" illuminated by a spherical wave coming from point O. The light from the object crosses the convergent lens L, then the beam splitter cube S_1, and then arrives at the detector. The reference wave comes from the second beam splitter cube S_2. A piezoelectric transducer (PZT) lets us record the phase-shifted holograms, and thus get rid of the parasitic orders (see section 5.2.2.2). A mirror M is attached to the ceramic PZT [YAM 97]. The horizontal displacement of the mirror from the PZT allows the addition of a controlled phase shift between each recorded hologram. In this experiment, we record two arbitrarily phase-shifted holograms so as to eliminate the zero order.

In this system, the focal distance of the lens L is $f = 699$ mm, the detector matrix has 576×768 pixels with a pixel pitch of 8.4 µm and the other parameters are $d_0 = 147$ mm, $d_1 = 135$ mm, $d_2 = 80$ mm, $d_3 = 1,100$ mm, and $R_0 = 1,055$ mm. If the object is of a small size, we may displace it toward the source O to fit the detector size.

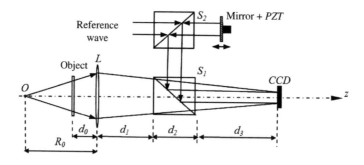

Figure 6.10. *Experimental setup*

The illumination of the object by a spherical wave is equivalent to illuminating it with a plane wave and adding a divergent lens of focal distance R_0-d_0 into the object plane. The *ABCD* matrix of the system will be determined by [LI 07c]:

$$\begin{bmatrix} A & B \\ C & D \end{bmatrix} = \begin{bmatrix} 1 & d_3 \\ 0 & 1 \end{bmatrix} \begin{bmatrix} 1 & d_2/n \\ 0 & 1 \end{bmatrix} \begin{bmatrix} 1 & d_1 \\ 0 & 1 \end{bmatrix} \begin{bmatrix} 1 & 0 \\ -1/f & 1 \end{bmatrix} \begin{bmatrix} 1 & d_0 \\ 0 & 1 \end{bmatrix} \begin{bmatrix} 1 & 0 \\ 1/(R_0-d_0) & 1 \end{bmatrix} \qquad [6.23]$$

With the parameters involved in this expression, we obtain: $A = 0.4387$, $B = 1164.3$ mm, $C = -0.0005613$ mm^{-1}, and $D = 0.7896$.

6.3.1.2. *Reconstruction by calculating the inverse Collins formula*

The aperture of the letter "dragon" has a width of around 10 mm and the area of the pixel matrix is 6.4512 mm × 4.8412 mm, containing 768 × 576 pixels. Since there is not a large difference between these areas, we may directly use the method of double FFT (D-FFT) convolution to carry out the calculation. Using formula [3.77] from Chapter 3:

$$U_0\left(r\frac{L}{N}, s\frac{L}{N}\right) = \exp(-jkz_{axis})\exp\left[j\frac{k}{2B}\left(\frac{1}{D} - A\right)\left(\frac{L}{N}\right)^2(r^2 + s^2)\right]$$

$$\times IFFT\left\{FFT\left\{\frac{1}{D}U\left(p\frac{L}{DN}, q\frac{L}{DN}\right)\right\}\exp\left(j\pi\lambda BD\frac{m^2 + n^2}{L^2}\right)\right\}$$

[6.24]

with $\{r,s,p,q,m,n\} \in \{-N/2, -N/2 + 1, ..., N/2 - 1\}$.

Prior to the calculation of this expression, we must determine the spectral term:

$$FFT\left\{\frac{1}{D}U\left(p\frac{L}{DN}, q\frac{L}{DN}\right)\right\}$$

[6.25]

To obtain the numerical function $(1/D) \times U(pL/DN,qL/DN)$, we may follow these steps:

– *Step 1*: form the hologram with sides of 12.8 mm and $N \times N = 1,024 \times 1,024$ pixels by adding zeros around the recorded digital hologram.

– *Step 2*: form the *difference* hologram coming from the two phase-shifted holograms (see section 5.2.2).

– *Step 3*: carry out a Fourier transform of the *difference* hologram to obtain its spectrum.

– *Step 4*: obtain the spectrum of the object by a window filter.

– *Step 5*: consider the center of the filtered spectrum as the origin of the spectral plane and reform the spectrum across $1,024 \times 1,024$ pixels by adding zeroes around the filtered zone.

– *Step 6*: carry out an inverse Fourier transform to find the object wave $U(pL/N,qL/N)$ in the detector plane, whose sampling interval is L/N.

– *Step 7*: the physical interval of $U(pL/DN,qL/DN)$ being L/DN, we interpolate $U(pL/N,qL/N)$ to obtain $(1/D) \times U(pL/DN,qL/DN)$.

Applying this approach, the reconstruction of the object image is presented in Figure 6.12(a). Figure 6.12(b) shows the object represented on the same physical scale.

A comparison of these two images shows the good correspondence of the obtained result with the original. However, the edges of the reconstructed image are not as sharp as those of the object. This phenomenon is due to diffraction by the mounts of the elements of the optical system, which results in a loss of components of the angular spectrum of the object. The result shown in Figure 6.11 is therefore coherent.

6.3.2. *Adjustable-magnification reconstruction after propagation across an optical system*

In the previous section, we used the D-FFT image reconstruction algorithm based on the inverse Collins formula. If the size of the object is very different than that of the detector, the D-FFT method does not work directly, and we must use the simple fast Fourier transform (S-FFT) method (see Chapter 3). In this case, the size of the calculated image depends on the value of B, the illumination wavelength λ, and the number of pixels N. Calculation by S-FFT presents certain inconveniences for digital color holography. From the study of adjustable magnification reconstruction (see Chapter 5) and of Collins' formula, we notice that there also exists the possibility of reconstructing the object field with an adjustable magnification. We will see in this section that by using the coefficients of the system's transfer matrix, we may determine the radius of curvature of the spherical reconstruction wave and the new digital diffraction distance. Using these two parameters and the classical formulation of diffraction, we may then reconstruct the enlarged field of the object in the detector space.

a) Reconstructed image   b) Object
(12.8 mm × 12.8 mm, 1,024 × 1,024 pixels)

Figure 6.11. *Comparison between the reconstructed image and the real object*

6.3.2.1. *Reconstruction with an adjustable magnification in the detector space*

Consider Figure 6.2 that shows the holographic system for recording and reconstruction. The object wave has been propagated through the optical system whose transfer matrix is *ABCD*. The reference wave is spherical, coming from the point with coordinates $(x_r, y_r, -z_r)$. Moreover, we let $z = 0$ be the plane of the CCD, $z = -z_0$ the object plane, and $z = z_i$ the plane of the reconstructed image (see Figures 5.1 and 6.2). The notation and image formation conform to the equations mentioned in Chapter 5 and at the beginning of this chapter. We are again interested in the image of a point source located at (ξ, η) in the object plane.

We are interested in the third term of equation [5.6], given by:

$$U_-(x,y) = w(x,y)R_c(x,y)R^*(x,y)U(x,y) \tag{6.26}$$

The image field expressed by the Fresnel diffraction integral is then given by:

$$U_{i-}(x_i,y_i;\xi,\eta) = \frac{\exp(jkz_i)}{j\lambda z_i} \int_{-\infty}^{\infty}\int_{-\infty}^{\infty} U_-(x,y;\xi,\eta)\exp\left\{\frac{jk}{2z_i}\left[(x-x_i)^2 + (y-y_i)^2\right]\right\}dxdy \tag{6.27}$$

After substituting the parameters into this integral, we have:

$$U_{i-}(x_i,y_i;\xi,\eta) = A_r\frac{\exp(jkz_i)}{\lambda^2 B z_i}\int_{-\infty}^{\infty}\int_{-\infty}^{\infty} w(x,y)\exp\left\{\frac{jk}{2B}\left[A(\xi^2+\eta^2)+D(x^2+y^2)-2(x\xi+y\eta)\right]\right\}$$

$$\times \exp\left\{-\frac{jk}{2z_r}\left[(x-x_r)^2+(y-y_r)^2\right]\right\}\exp\left[\frac{jk}{2z_c}(x^2+y^2)\right]$$

$$\times \exp\left\{\frac{jk}{2z_i}\left[(x-x_i)^2+(y-y_i)^2\right]\right\}dxdy \tag{6.28}$$

To get a focused image, we must impose the following relation:

$$\frac{D}{B}-\frac{1}{z_r}+\frac{1}{z_c}+\frac{1}{z_i}=0 \tag{6.29}$$

Using this condition, integral [6.28] may be simply rewritten as:

$$U_{i-}(x_i,y_i;\xi,\eta) = \Theta(x_i,y_i;\xi,\eta)$$

$$\times \int_{-\infty}^{\infty}\int_{-\infty}^{\infty} w(\lambda z_i u, \lambda z_i v)\exp\left\{-j2\pi\left[u\left(x_i-\frac{z_i x_r}{z_r}+G_y\xi\right)+v\left(y_i-\frac{z_i y_r}{z_r}+G_y\eta\right)\right]\right\}dudv \tag{6.30}$$

where $G_y = -z_i/B$, $u = x/\lambda z_i$, $v = y/\lambda z_i$, and

$$\Theta(x_i, y_i; \xi, \eta) = A_r G_y \exp(jkz_i)\exp\left\{\frac{jk}{2B}\left[A(\xi^2 + \eta^2)\right]\right\}\exp\left\{-\frac{jk}{2z_r}\left[x_r^2 + y_r^2\right]\right\}\exp\left\{\frac{jk}{2z_i}\left[x_i^2 + y_i^2\right]\right\}$$

[6.31]

Relation [6.30] shows that we obtain an image of the object field with a magnification of G_y centered at the point with coordinates $(z_i x_r/z_r, z_i y_r/z_r)$. Consequently, when the magnification G_y is fixed, the reconstruction distance z_i may be determined by $z_i = -G_y \times B$. The radius of the spherical reconstruction wavefront z_c is then expressed by:

$$z_c = \left(\frac{1}{z_r} - \frac{D}{B} - \frac{1}{z_i}\right)^{-1}$$

[6.32]

Combining the results: once the magnification G_y is fixed, we calculate the reconstruction distance z_i, and then, after substituting the values of z_i and z_r into [6.32], we determine the radius of curvature z_c of the spherical reconstruction wave.

The filtering in the S-FFT image plane presented in Chapter 5 is also useful for this study, but for the image to completely occupy the reconstruction plane, we must know the relationship between the magnification G_y and the filtering width N_s (in pixel units). Since L is the width of the detector, following the same principle giving relation [5.84] from Chapter 5, we find $G_y = L^2/\lambda B N_s$.

Using this technique, and considering the hologram to possess $N \times N$ pixels, the reconstruction of the image may be carried out in the following steps:

– *Step 1*: reconstruct the image using the S-FFT algorithm.

– *Step 2*: select the useful zone in the image plane using a suitable filter window.

– *Step 3*: reform the image plane with a size of $N \times N$ pixels by adding zeroes around the filtered image.

– *Step 4*: find the conjugate object field in the plane of the hologram by carrying out the inverse diffraction calculation.

– *Step 5*: illuminate the hologram with a spherical wave and calculate the resulting spectrum.

– *Step 6*: reconstruct the image using the angular spectrum method to calculate the diffraction across the distance z_i.

We give an experimental demonstration in the following section.

6.3.2.2. *Experimental demonstration for the reconstruction of color images*

As mentioned in Chapter 5, the interest of the adjustable-magnification reconstruction method is to allow the reconstruction of color holograms recorded with several different wavelengths. This feasibility experiment uses three lasers of wavelengths $\lambda = 632.8$, 532, and 473 nm. Figure 6.12 shows a simple scheme for recording a hologram with a monochromatic detector. Here, the recording of each wavelength is sequential.

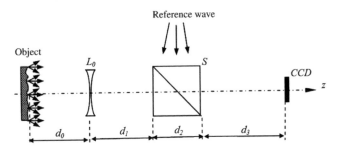

Figure 6.12. *Simple setup recording through a diverging lens*

The reference wave is reflected by the beam splitter cube S, and then it propagates toward the detector with an angle of inclination such that the image reconstructed by S-FFT is situated in the second quadrant of the reconstruction plane. The object is a mask of "the Monkey King", 65 mm in height. Since the size of the object is much larger than the detector (1,024 × 1,024 pixels, $L = 4.76$ mm), we have added a divergent lens between the object and the detector.

For laser illumination at $\lambda = 532$ nm, the parameters of the setup are as follows: $z_r = \infty$ (plane reference wave), the focal distance of the divergent lens is $f_0 = -110$ mm, the refractive index of the cube is $n = 1.5$, $d_0 = 220$ mm, $d_1 = 406$ mm, $d_2 = 25$ mm, and $d_3 = 100$ mm. From the previous parameters, the transfer matrix of the optical system between the object and detector planes is then given by:

$$\begin{bmatrix} A & B \\ C & D \end{bmatrix} = \begin{bmatrix} 1 & d_3 \\ 0 & 1 \end{bmatrix} \begin{bmatrix} 1 & d_2/n \\ 0 & 1 \end{bmatrix} \begin{bmatrix} 1 & d_1 \\ 0 & 1 \end{bmatrix} \begin{bmatrix} 1 & 0 \\ -1/f_0 & 1 \end{bmatrix} \begin{bmatrix} 1 & d_0 \\ 0 & 1 \end{bmatrix} \qquad [6.33]$$

With these parameters, we obtain: $A = 5.9788$, $B = 1713.5$ mm, $C = 0.091$ mm^{-1}, and $D = 2.7727$. From the size of the image in the S-FFT plane, and for reconstruction of an image covering the entire field, a window of $N_s \times N_s = 356 \times 356$ pixels filtering the zone to be reconstructed is used (see Figure 6.14). With the two relations, $G_y = L^2/\lambda B N_s$ and $G_y = z_i/B$, we obtain $G_y = 0.0697$ and $z_i = -119.43$ mm. Next, we calculate $z_c = 148.42$ mm with [6.32]. The image reconstructed by the S-FFT algorithm is given in Figure 6.13(a). Figure 6.13(b) shows the reconstructed image.

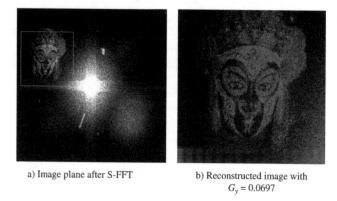

a) Image plane after S-FFT   b) Reconstructed image with
                                                $G_y = 0.0697$

Figure 6.13. *Green images reconstructed by the two methods (for a color version of this figure, see www.iste.co.uk/picart/digiholog.zip)*

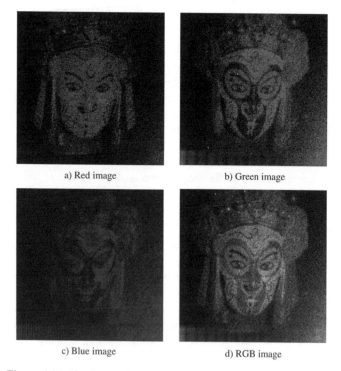

a) Red image   b) Green image

c) Blue image   d) RGB image

Figure 6.14. *The three color components and the RGB image obtained (4.76 mm × 4.76 mm, 1,024 × 1,024 pixels, $G_y = 0.0697$) (for a color version of this figure, see www.iste.co.uk/picart/digiholog.zip)*

For illumination with the other lasers, the elements of the transfer matrix of the system vary with the wavelength and the magnification of the reconstructed image depends on the values of the two matrix elements B and C. Taking this effect into account, we determine the focal length f_i for the wavelength λ_i with the relation $f_i = f_0(n_0 - 1)/(n_i - 1)$, in which n_0 is the refractive index of the lens for the wavelength λ_0, f_0 is the corresponding focal distance, and n_i the refractive index of the lens for another wavelength λ_i [LOU 10].

For the reconstructed image to have the same magnification and the same number of pixels, the window filtering the image given by S-FFT consists of $356 \times 532/632.8 \approx 300$ pixels for the red image and $356 \times 532/473 \approx 400$ pixels for the blue image. With the same procedure as for the green component, we reconstruct the two other color components of the image with magnification $G_y = 0.0697$. Figure 6.14 illustrates the three color components of the image and the color image obtained after recombination.

6.4. Using the classical diffraction formulae to reconstruct the wavefront after propagation across an optical system

In the previous sections, the reconstruction of the wavefronts after propagation across an optical system was conducted using Collins formula. This formula is established using the Fresnel approximation. The Fresnel approximations are a paraxial approximation of the rigorous formulae coming from the scalar theory of diffraction (see Chapter 2). Collins' formula is therefore valid only for paraxial systems. This section treats the possibility of reconstructing wavefronts using the rigorous formulae from the scalar theory of diffraction.

6.4.1. Use of the rigorous diffraction formulae

Every system is composed of different optical systems aligned along the optical axis. The process of the propagation of light across the system is constituted by successive propagations between the elements encountered. If the object field in the output plane of the system is determined with precision, the object wavefront may be determined by successive inverse diffraction calculations between the optical elements. Remember the different methods that were presented in Chapter 3 for the numerical calculation of diffraction along the propagation direction and for inverse diffraction using the classical formulae. Thus, all the classical formulae may be used for reconstruction. However, taking into account the sampling conditions and calculation time, the angular spectrum method has the most interest. As an example, we use this formula to experimentally confirm the theoretical approach.

6.4.1.1. *Simulation of the overall process*

We consider again the imaging part of Figure 6.10. The simulation follows five steps [LI 09a]:

– *Step 1*: obtain the object field in the detector plane by the successive calculation of diffraction between the elements encountered.

– *Step 2*: form two holograms with reference waves of different phases and calculate the difference hologram (see section 5.2.2).

– *Step 3*: calculate the spectrum of the difference hologram and obtain the spectrum of the object wave in the detector plane by spectral filtering.

– *Step 4*: obtain the object wave in the detector plane by an inverse Fourier transform.

– *Step 5*: reconstruct the object field by successively calculating the inverse diffraction between the elements encountered.

The simulation process is explained in detail in the following section.

6.4.1.1.1. Calculating the object field in the detector plane by successively calculating the diffraction between the optical elements encountered

Let x_0, y_0 be the coordinates in the object plane and $o_0(x_0, y_0)$ be the transmittance of the object. The object being illuminated by a spherical wave, the wavefront in the object plane may be expressed by:

$$O_0(x_0, y_0) = o_0(x_0, y_0) \exp\left(jk \frac{x_0^2 + y_0^2}{2(R_0 - d_0)} \right)$$ [6.34]

We consider that the diffracted field has a width of $D_0 = 12.8$ mm sampled at $N = 1{,}024$ points. Figure 6.15(a) shows the intensity distributions of the object in the different planes.

Letting $x_1 y_1$ be the coordinates in the plane of the lens L, the optical field in this plane is expressed by:

$$O_1(x_1, y_1) = F^{-1}\left\{ F\{O_0(x_0, y_0)\} \exp\left[j \frac{2\pi}{\lambda} d_0 \sqrt{1 - (\lambda f_x)^2 - (\lambda f_y)^2} \right] \right\}$$ [6.35]

Figure 6.15(b) shows the results of the field calculated in the plane of the lens.

Let x_2y_2 be the coordinates of the leftmost plane of the cube S. The field in this plane is then given by:

$$O_2(x_2,y_2)=F^{-1}\left\{F\{O_1(x_1,y_1)T_1(x_1,y_1)\}\exp\left[j\frac{2\pi}{\lambda}d_1\sqrt{1-(\lambda f_x)^2-(\lambda f_y)^2}\right]\right\} \qquad [6.36]$$

The function $T_1(x_1,y_1)=\exp(-jk(x_1^2+x_1^2)/2f)$ represents the transmittance of the lens L.

The coordinates of the rightmost plane of the cube S are x_3y_3. The wave crossing the cube is then given by:

$$O_3(x_3,y_3)=F^{-1}\left\{F\{O_2(x_2,y_2)\}\exp\left[j\frac{2\pi}{\lambda_s}d_2\sqrt{1-(\lambda_s f_x)^2-(\lambda_s f_y)^2}\right]\right\} \qquad [6.37]$$

where $\lambda_s=\lambda/n$, with n the refractive index of the cube S ($n=1.5$). Finally, the field in the detector plane is obtained by:

$$O(x,y)=F^{-1}\left\{F\{O_3(x_3,y_3)\}\exp\left[j\frac{2\pi}{\lambda}d_3\sqrt{1-(\lambda f_x)^2-(\lambda f_y)^2}\right]\right\} \qquad [6.38]$$

Figure 6.15(c) shows the intensity distribution in the detector plane. We may observe the effect of the convergent lens L, which reduces the size of the object image in this plane. As the wave emerging from the lens L is convergent, the size of the diffraction pattern has become smaller.

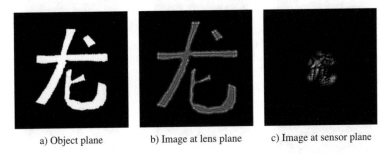

a) Object plane   b) Image at lens plane   c) Image at sensor plane

Figure 6.15. *Simulations of the propagation of the object wave*

6.4.1.1.2. Calculating two phase-shifted holograms and their difference

A plane wave is described by

$$R(x,y)=A_r\exp\left[jk(\theta_x x+\theta_y y)\right] \qquad [6.39]$$

In order to form a hologram with a higher contrast, the amplitude A_r is three times the mean of $|O(x,y)|$. The inclination angle of the reference beam is determined so that the center of the spectrum is localized in the first quadrant of the spectral plane of the hologram. The hologram is calculated by:

$$I_H(x,y) = |R(x,y) + O(x,y)|^2 \qquad\qquad [6.40]$$

The width of the diffracted field calculated by the angular spectrum method is still the same value of 12.8 mm. To simulate the effect of a detector of size 6.4512 mm × 4.8412 mm, the intensity distribution I_H must be limited by the detector window. The simulated hologram is shown in Figure 6.16(a). After adding a phase shift of π/3 into [6.39], we may obtain a phase-shifted hologram and the difference hologram formed by the subtraction of one hologram from another is shown in Figure 6.16(b).

6.4.1.1.3. Calculating the spectrum of the difference hologram and extracting the spectrum of the object wave

Figure 6.16(c) shows the spectrum of the difference hologram. The spectrum of the zero order has disappeared, the spectrum of the object wave is situated in the first quadrant, and that of the conjugate wave is situated in the third quadrant.

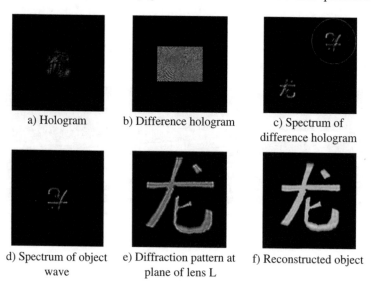

a) Hologram   b) Difference hologram   c) Spectrum of
                                                        difference hologram

d) Spectrum of object   e) Diffraction pattern at   f) Reconstructed object
       wave   plane of lens L

Figure 6.16. *Simulation of the process of reconstructing the object field*

A circular window of radius 240 pixels lets us select the spectrum of the object (see Figure 6.16(c)). Considering the center of the filtered spectrum as the origin, zeros are added around it. The spectrum of the object wave across $1,024 \times 1,024$ pixels is shown in Figure 6.16(d).

6.4.1.1.4. Reconstructing the object field by successively calculating the inverse diffraction between the optical elements

For the inverse diffraction calculations, it is sufficient to change the sign in the complex exponentials of the angular spectrum. For example, the field repropagated from the detector plane toward the rightmost plane of the cube S is calculated by the following relation:

$$O_3(x_3,y_3) = F^{-1}\left\{ F\{O(x,y)\} \exp\left[-j\frac{2\pi}{\lambda} d_3 \sqrt{1 - (\lambda f_x)^2 - (\lambda f_y)^2} \right] \right\} \qquad [6.41]$$

The field in the leftmost plane of the cube S is given by:

$$O_2(x_2,y_2) = F^{-1}\left\{ F\{O_3(x_3,y_3)\} \exp\left[-j\frac{2\pi}{\lambda_s} d_2 \sqrt{1 - (\lambda_s f_x)^2 - (\lambda_s f_y)^2} \right] \right\} \qquad [6.42]$$

The field in the plane to the right of the lens L is:

$$O_1(x_1,y_1) = F^{-1}\left\{ F\{O_2(x_2,y_2) T_0(x_1,y_1)\} \exp\left[-j\frac{2\pi}{\lambda} d_1 \sqrt{1 - (\lambda f_x)^2 - (\lambda f_y)^2} \right] \right\} \qquad [6.43]$$

The intensity distribution $O_1(x,y)$ is shown in Figure 6.16(e). We note the good correspondence with Figure 6.15(b).

To retrieve the object field, we must take into account the effect of the inverse transformation of the lens L by taking the complex conjugate of its transmittance. We therefore have:

$$O_0(x_0,y_0) = F^{-1}\left\{ F\{O_1(x_1,y_1) T_1^*(x_1,y_1)\} \exp\left[-j\frac{2\pi}{\lambda} d_0 \sqrt{1 - (\lambda f_x)^2 - (\lambda f_y)^2} \right] \right\} \quad [6.44]$$

Finally, the complex amplitude of the object is obtained by multiplying by the complex conjugate of the spherical illumination wave, i.e.:

$$o_0(x_0,y_0) = O_0(x_0,y_0) \exp\left(-jk\frac{x_0^2 + y_0^2}{2(R_0 - d_0)} \right) \qquad [6.45]$$

Figure 6.16(f) shows the intensity of the reconstructed object field after the application of the entire process. Comparison with Figure 6.15(a) shows a very good agreement between the results.

6.4.1.2. *Experimental results*

Using the same setup to record the hologram of the same object, we obtain some experimental results. Applying the method described above, we reconstruct the object field. Figure 6.17 shows the results obtained experimentally, in a similar way to those presented in the simulation in Figure 6.16.

The inclination angle of the reference wave has not been set so that the spectrum of the object wave is situated in the first quadrant of the spectral plane, as it was in the numerical simulation (see Figure 6.17(c)). Nevertheless, comparison between the theoretical and the experimental results shows that the simulation based on the scalar theory of diffraction allows the correct prediction of all the experimental results.

In the case of digital Fresnel holography for which there are no optical elements between the object and the detector (apart from the cube), the reconstruction of the object field is faster and carried out by one single inverse diffraction calculation using the angular spectrum method.

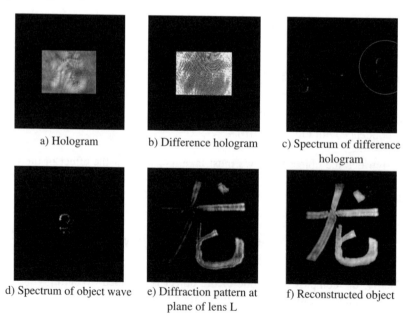

a) Hologram   b) Difference hologram   c) Spectrum of difference
                                                          hologram

d) Spectrum of object wave   e) Diffraction pattern at   f) Reconstructed object
                              plane of lens L

Figure 6.17. *Experimental results of the reconstruction of the object field*

6.4.2. *Reconstruction of the object wave in the object and image spaces*

In the previous sections, using Collins' formula and the angular spectrum method, we studied different methods allowing the reconstruction of a wavefront from its propagation through an optical system. From the Abbe and Rayleigh theory of diffraction, we may yet reconstruct the wavefront by two other methods:

– From Abbe's theory [GOO 72], the diffraction of light by a system is related to the diffraction from the input pupil of the system. If we consider the plane of the aperture diaphragm as that of the object, and carry out the reconstruction of the object image by a classical diffraction formula, the wavefront of the object may be obtained by the theoretical relation between the object and its image. This algorithm will be called "reconstruction in the image space".

– From the Rayleigh theory [GOO 72], the diffraction of light by a system is related to the diffraction from the exit pupil of the system. The process of reconstructing the image may be considered as that forming the image in the virtual object space. The outline of the detector matrix may be considered as the exit pupil of the system. Therefore, after forming the image of the detector in the object space, we may reconstruct the object field by a classical diffraction formula. This algorithm will be called "reconstruction in the object space".

For the result of the study to be general, we consider a spherical reference wave, and we include the theory of matrix optics to study both methods in the following section [LI 09d, LI 11c].

6.4.2.1. *Parameters*

Figure 6.18 represents an optical system, described by its transfer matrix $ABCD$, whose different planes are described by the following coordinates:

x_0y_0: the object plane;

x_cy_c: the CCD detector plane;

x_iy_i: the image plane of the object x_0y_0-plane in the image space;

$x_{0c}y_{0c}$: the image plane of the x_cy_c-plane in the object space;

x_ry_r: the plane of the point source producing the reference wave;

$x_{0r}y_{0r}$: image plane of the x_ry_r-plane in the object space.

The distances between the planes are indicated in Figure 6.18. We consider the object space to contain the object plane and the space containing the detector as the image space. Let us study the reconstruction algorithm in the image space, and then in the object space.

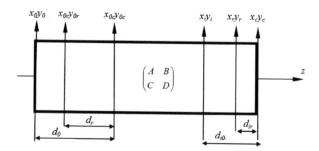

Figure 6.18. *Notation*

6.4.2.2. *Reconstruction in the image space*

From Figure 6.18, when the light propagates from the x_0y_0-plane to the x_iy_i-plane, the corresponding transfer matrix is

$$
\begin{bmatrix} A' & B' \\ C' & D' \end{bmatrix} = \begin{bmatrix} 1 & -d_{i0} \\ 0 & 1 \end{bmatrix} \begin{bmatrix} A & B \\ C & D \end{bmatrix}
$$
$$
= \begin{bmatrix} A - Cd_{i0} & B - Dd_{i0} \\ C & D \end{bmatrix}
$$

[6.46]

If the x_0y_0-plane and the x_iy_i-plane are both image planes of each other, the matrix element B' satisfies $B' = 0$, and we therefore have:

$$
d_{i0} = B / D
$$

[6.47]

In this case, the transverse magnification of the image in the object plane in the image space will be

$$
G_{yi} = A - Cd_{i0} = 1 / D
$$

[6.48]

Let us consider $U(x_c, y_c)$ to be the object field in the detector plane and the reference wave to be spherical, coming from the point with coordinates (x_r, y_r) in the $x_r y_r$-plane. If the image of the object is considered as the object in the image space and the reconstruction wave is spherical coming from the point $z = -d_{ir}$ on the optical axis, the previous chapters show that we may reconstruct the field of the object image, considering d_{i0} to be the reconstruction distance.

If L is the width of the matrix of $N \times N$ pixels and λ is the wavelength, then the width of the field reconstructed by the S-FFT method is [MAS 03, LI 07c]:

$$
L_{0i} = \lambda d_{i0} N / L
$$

[6.49]

Writing the field in the image plane as $U_i(x_i,y_i)$, then the relation between the object field $U_0(x_0,y_0)$ and the image field $U_i(x_i,y_i)$ is [LI 09a]:

$$U_i(x,y) = \frac{1}{G_{yi}} U_0\left(\frac{x}{G_{yi}}, \frac{y}{G_{yi}}\right) \exp\left(jk\left(1 - \frac{1}{G_{yi}}\right)\frac{(x^2 + y^2)}{2d_h}\right) \qquad [6.50]$$

where d_h is the distance between the plane of the exit pupil and the image plane in the image space.

Consequently, when the image field $U_i(x_i,y_i)$ has been determined, the object field may be obtained by relation [6.50].

6.4.2.3. Reconstruction in the object space

From Figure 6.18, when the object wave propagates from the $x_{0c}y_{0c}$-plane to the $x_c y_c$-plane, the optical system between these two planes is characterized by the following transfer matrix:

$$\begin{bmatrix} A'' & B'' \\ C'' & D'' \end{bmatrix} = \begin{bmatrix} A & B \\ C & D \end{bmatrix}\begin{bmatrix} 1 & -d_0 \\ 0 & 1 \end{bmatrix} = \begin{bmatrix} A & -Ad_0 + B \\ C & -Cd_0 + D \end{bmatrix} \qquad [6.51]$$

If the $x_{0c}y_{0c}$- and $x_c y_c$-planes are both image planes of each other, the matrix element B'' satisfies $B'' = 0$, and we therefore have:

$$d_0 = B/A \qquad [6.52]$$

In this case, the transverse magnification of the detector image in the object space will be [GER 75, KEA 02]:

$$G_{yc} = A \qquad [6.53]$$

When the wave propagates from the $x_{0r}y_{0r}$-plane to the $x_r y_r$-plane, the transfer matrix of the optical system characterizing these two planes is given by:

$$\begin{aligned}
\begin{bmatrix} A''' & B''' \\ C''' & D''' \end{bmatrix} &= \begin{bmatrix} 1 & -d_{ir} \\ 0 & 1 \end{bmatrix}\begin{bmatrix} A & B \\ C & D \end{bmatrix}\begin{bmatrix} 1 & -(d_0 - d_r) \\ 0 & 1 \end{bmatrix} \\
&= \begin{bmatrix} 1 & -d_{ir} \\ 0 & 1 \end{bmatrix}\begin{bmatrix} A & -A(d_0 - d_r) + B \\ C & -C(d_0 - d_r) + D \end{bmatrix} \\
&= \begin{bmatrix} A - Cd_{ir} & -(A - d_{ir}C)(d_0 - d_r) + B - d_{ir}D \\ C & -C(d_0 - d_r) + D \end{bmatrix}
\end{aligned} \qquad [6.54]$$

When both the $x_{0r}y_{0r}$-plane and the $x_{r}y_{r}$-plane are image planes of each other, we have $B''' = 0$, so $-(A - d_{ir}C)(d_0 - d_r) + B - d_{ir}D = 0$, and:

$$d_r = \frac{d_{ir}D - B}{A - d_{ir}C} + d_0 \qquad\qquad [6.55]$$

In Figure 6.18, d_r is the distance between the plane of the reference wave source and the $x_{0c}y_{0c}$-plane and d_0 is the distance between the object and the $x_{0c}y_{0c}$-plane. If L is the width of the sensor matrix of $N \times N$ pixels, the width of the hologram in the object space will be L/G_{yc}. Considering d_0 to be the reconstruction distance and the reconstruction wave to be spherical and coming from the point $z = -d_r$, we may reconstruct the object field. If the reconstruction is carried out by the S-FFT method, the width of the reconstructed field will be:

$$L_{00} = \lambda d_0 G_{yc} N / L \qquad\qquad [6.56]$$

From the previous discussion, it follows that:

$$L_{0i} / L_{00} = \frac{d_{i0}}{d_0 G_{yc}} = \frac{1}{D} = G_{yi} \qquad\qquad [6.57]$$

Since G_{yi} is the transverse magnification of the object image formed by the optical system, this relation shows that, in the reconstruction plane, the relative sizes of the images reconstructed by these two methods are identical.

6.4.2.4. *Experimental results*

We again use the setup shown in Figure 6.12 and the object is still mask of "the Monkey King" (height $D_0 = 65$ mm). It is illuminated by a green laser of wavelength $\lambda = 532$ nm. From [6.33], the four elements of the transfer matrix from the object plane to the detector plane are $A = 5.9788$, $B = 1713.5$ mm, $C = 0.091$ mm^{-1}, and $D = 2.7727$.

6.4.2.4.1. Reconstructing the wavefront in the image space

After substituting the parameters into [6.52] and [6.53], we obtain $d_{i0} = B/D = 617.99$ mm and $G_{yi} = 0.3607$. The reconstruction of the object field may be simplified by considering a simple equivalent case, such as that of the reconstruction of an object of height $G_{yi}D_0 \approx 16.23$ situated at a distance of 617.99 mm from the detector plane. Digitally illuminating the hologram with a plane wave, the intensity distribution of the image reconstructed by S-FFT is shown in Figure 6.19(a). With relation [6.49], the width of the reconstructed plane is $L_{0i} = 70.7$ mm.

6.4.2.4.2. Reconstructing the wavefront in the object space

Substituting the useful parameters into [6.52], [6.53], and [6.54], we obtain: d_0 = 286.61 mm, G_{yc} = 5.9788, and d_r = −18.398 mm. Figure 6.19(b) shows the intensity distribution of the object field reconstructed by the method. From [6.56], the reconstructed object plane now has a width of L_{00} = 196.0426 mm. Since L_{0i}/L_{00} = 0.2727 = G_y, relation [6.57] is confirmed experimentally.

Comparison of the two images in Figure 6.19 shows that, in the reconstruction plane, the relative sizes of the images calculated by these two methods are identical, and there are no notable differences.

a) Image space (70.7 mm × 70.7 mm)   b) Object space (196 mm × 196 mm)

Figure 6.19. *Image reconstructed in the image and object spaces*

6.5. Conclusion

This chapter has treated the case of wavefront reconstruction when an optical system is interposed between the object and detector planes. Collins' formula has been put to use for numerical calculations, both by S-FFT for monochromatic holograms and by D-FFT with and without adjustable magnification for digital color holograms. The theoretical aspects have been confirmed and validated by both numerical simulations and experimental results in the case of relatively simple systems. The matrix approach used to describe the optical system may be applied to more complex systems.

Chapter 7

Digital Holographic Interferometry and Its Applications

As the etymology of the word "holography" ("holo": whole and "graphein": writing) indicates, a holographic recording contains all the information about a given object: the *amplitude* of the object, which has been broadly discussed in previous chapters, and also the optical *phase* and, therefore, relief of the object. The optical phase contained in the reconstructed digital field is the key parameter in holographic interferometry and its numerous applications.

Classically, the interference fringes produced by the superposing of two holograms provides information about any displacement that the object is subjected to [SMI 94]. With digital holography, it is possible to directly obtain the optical phase and calculate its variations, which are related to the physical parameters of the medium. Thus, everything in nature which distorts is susceptible to holographic interferometric analysis: from the deformation of an eardrum under the effect of a supersonic boom to the deformation of a running motor [SMI 94], the density variations of the air around the profile of an airplane's wing, or even the analysis of the morphology and dynamics of neurons [PAV 11].

Holographic interferometry enables the analysis of physical phenomena in four dimensions (three spatial and one temporal) without contact, and with a high sensitivity and spatial resolution. In the 1970s, the use of high-resolution, low-sensitivity photosensitive media (such as photographic plates and films and thermoplastic films) presented a major hindrance, as they required lasers of sufficient energy and chemical processing that were prohibitive for a number of applications [SMI 94]. Photoreactive crystals brought about some industrial solutions during the 1990s [GEO 03, TIZ 82], but the development of digital holography gave new life to the methods of holographic interferometry, with the prospect of designing compact systems capable of providing efficient digital processing for applications requiring robustness and reliability.

Since 1970, holography has been the subject of a large number of studies and applications which cover a vast field of investigations: non-destructive testing [VAL 85], the study of fluids [SMI 94], the study of particles [STI 70], life sciences [DAN 75], etc. Holographic techniques are a key part of the domain of contactless, non-invasive measurement [JON 89, KRE 96, SMI 94, SMI 98, SMI 01]. It is possible to study micro- or macroscopic structures subjected to pneumatic, thermal, and mechanical stresses in the static, stationary, or transitional regime [JON 89, KRE 96, SMI 94]. Holography allows both a comprehensive and a qualitative evaluation by simply displaying the digital fringes' coding of the deformation, made quantitative by the arrangement, and scaling of these fringes. In recent years, digital Fresnel holography has been greatly developed and applied with success in a large number of domains. In fact, fascinating possibilities have been demonstrated: phase contrast digital holographic microscopy [ZHA 98, CUC 99a, CUC 99b, FER 06, PED 02, MAN 08, CHA 07, KUH 07], imaging across diffusive media [LEC 00], digital color holography [YAM 02, PIC 08b], measurement of surface profiles [YAM 01b], measurement of the parameters of microcomponents [SEE 01, CHA 06a], synthetic aperture imaging [BIN 02, LEC 00, JAC 01], compensation for lens aberrations [STA 00], mechanical measurement by spatial multiplexing [PIC 03a, PIC 04], and the phasing of laser beams [BEL 09, PAU 09]. Furthermore, the rise in robust and reliable high-energy dual-pulse lasers has permitted applications in vibration mechanics [PED 95]. Digital holography is also a promising technology for the recognition and comparison of three-dimensional (3D) objects as evidenced by recent works on the subject [JAV 00, OST 02].

Digital holographic interferometry exploits not only the amplitude of the object, but also its phase. This chapter presents an overview of the methods and applications of digital holographic interferometry. This review of the applications of digital Fresnel holography is not intended to be exhaustive, as it will focus on the methods that exploit the phase of the hologram for quantitative measurement. Since this chapter aims to describe digital holographic interferometry, applications of digital in-line holography will not be treated. The reason is that we focus here on methods that exploit the optical phase of the digital hologram. In many cases, in-line holography aims at reconstructing a particle in a measurement volume, but from an "amplitude" point of view. The bibliography includes papers that treat the problem of the reconstruction of particles. The reader may refer to references [ONU 92], [ONU 93], [HIN 02], [COE 02], [NIC 06], [NIC 07], [MAL 04], [DEN 06], [SIN 10], and [VER 10]. In-line holographic microscopy will not be discussed and it is suggested that the reader consider [GAR 06a] and [GAR 06b], as well as section 7.2 of this chapter.

This chapter first gives the basics of digital holographic interferometry, as well as its relationship to the disturbances experienced by an object. We will then explain the principles of digital holographic microscopy, two-wavelength profilometry, single and multiple wavelength photomechanics, time-averaged holography, special techniques for tracking high-amplitude vibrations, and three-color holography for fluid mechanics.

7.1. Basics of holographic interferometry

7.1.1. *Reconstructing the phase of the object field*

We recall that in Chapters 4 and 5, we studied the reconstruction of the object field encoded within an "analog" and then a "digital" hologram. In the context of digital holography, the object field is obtained using the S-FFT or D-FFT algorithms with or without adjustable magnification. The result of the digital calculation of the diffracted field gives access to the complex amplitude $O_0(x,y)$ sampled across a mesh corresponding to the number of reconstruction points of the algorithm. From this complex amplitude, we may access two quantities: the amplitude image (modulus) and the phase image (the argument of the field).

In this chapter, we will write the modulus of the reconstructed object as A_r, and its phase as ψ_r, i.e.

$$A_r(x,y) = |O_0(x,y)|$$

$$\psi_r(x,y) = \arg\{O_0(x,y)\} = \arctan\left\{\frac{\Im m[O_0(x,y)]}{\Re e[O_0(x,y)]}\right\} \quad \mathrm{mod}(2\pi) \qquad [7.1]$$

The phase of the field is calculated using the arctangent function, and as a consequence, the result will be contained within the interval $]-\pi,+\pi]$, i.e. modulo 2π. This phase is random in most cases, as it is related to the roughness of the object's surface. The reconstructed object is therefore marred with speckles [DAI 84]. The estimation of the optical phase of the reconstructed field is key to a large number of applications in digital holography.

Figure 7.1 shows a real digital hologram, as well as an expansion of one region. In the expanded view, we observe the speckle pattern, as well as the interference microfringes, which encode the object.

Note that the phase is similar to an unknown constant. Thus the absolute phase cannot be obtained with a single wavelength. For the same reason, the notion of relief in digital holography is very different to that in analog holography. It is considered that digital holography, using a single hologram, is only reconstructing a "2.5D" volume [KOU 07].

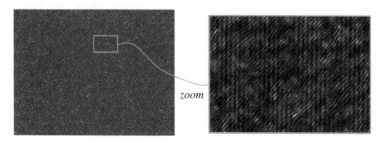

zoom

Figure 7.1. *Digital hologram and its speckle pattern*

7.1.2. *Optical phase variations and the sensitivity vector*

Non-contact measurements using holographic methods are based on the variation of the optical phase of the reconstructed object when it is subjected to a stress. This stress may be of a biological, electronic, pneumatic, thermal, acoustic, or mechanical nature. When subjected to a stress of any kind, the object is deformed, and thus the optical path along the *source-object-hologram* trajectory will vary. Let us imagine a point A at the light source and a point B attached to the object. When the object is slightly deformed by a stress, the point B attached to the object undergoes a 3D change, the displacement vector $\mathbf{D}(D_x, D_y, D_z)$ which generates variations in the optical path from A to B and from B to C (see Figure 7.2). These variations are much smaller than the absolute values of these path lengths and have moduli on the order of tens or hundreds of wavelengths of the light used. We write $\mathbf{K_e}$ the "illumination" vector of the object, $\mathbf{K_o}$ the "observation" vector of the object, and n the refractive index around the object. The variation of optical path length is [KRE 96]:

$$\delta_{\text{opt}}(\text{ABC}) = n\mathbf{K_e}.\mathbf{D} - n\mathbf{K_o}.\mathbf{D} = n\mathbf{D}.(\mathbf{K_e} - \mathbf{K_o}) \qquad [7.2]$$

The observation vector is related to the direction of observation from the object toward the hologram. The illumination vector represents the direction of illumination of the studied object. We pose:

$$\mathbf{S} = \mathbf{K_e} - \mathbf{K_o} \qquad [7.3]$$

This vector is called the *sensitivity vector*. The sensitivity vector corresponds to the bisector of the illumination and the observation vectors of the object. The sensitivity vector indicates the displacement direction in which the sensitivity of the apparatus is optimal. Knowledge of the coordinates of this vector is essential for the precise analysis of the amplitude of the displacements. The variation in optical phase induced by the variation in *source-object-hologram* optical path length is given by the following relation [JON 89, KRE 96, SMI 94]:

$$\Delta\varphi = \frac{2\pi}{\lambda}\delta_{opt}(ABC) = \frac{2n\pi}{\lambda}\mathbf{D}.(\mathbf{K_e} - \mathbf{K_o})$$ [7.4]

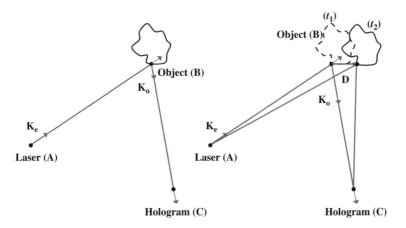

Figure 7.2. *Variation of the source-object-hologram path length*

When the object is displaced along the displacement vector **D**, this leads to a variation of the phase, which is itself due to the variation in optical path.

7.1.3. *Phase difference method*

The measurement of the optical phase variations generated by the object requires the recording and the reconstruction of at least two holograms (the double exposure principle). The first corresponds to a reference hologram, and the second corresponds to a hologram of the object having been subjected to the change. Consequently, the phase variation of equation [7.4] may be evaluated by calculating the difference in optical phase between the two holograms. Let ψ_{r1} and ψ_{r2} be the optical phases of the first and the second holograms, respectively. We then have:

$$\Delta\varphi = \psi_{r2} - \psi_{r1} \quad \mathrm{mod}(2\pi)$$ [7.5]

This phase variation will produce digital interference fringes, modulo 2π, which lets us quantify the displacement of the object between the two states. The variation in optical path seen in holographic interferometry therefore corresponds to the variation in the position of the object projected onto the sensitivity vector. Note that for a large number of applications, the refractive index of the medium in which the studied object is placed often equals one (air).

As an illustration, Figure 7.3 shows the two phases ψ_{r1} and ψ_{r2} of the first and the second holograms, respectively, as well as the phase difference calculated modulo 2π. The two phases are random and uniformly distributed across $]-\pi,+\pi]$. The phase difference is also obtained in $]-\pi,+\pi]$. We observe digital interference fringes that represent phase jumps each time that $\Delta\varphi$ passes $-\pi$ or $+\pi$. We also observe that the result is noisy, which is translated by the appearance of a "salt-and-pepper" texture in the image. This noise is due to the decorrelation of the speckle pattern, which exists more or less for each movement of the object [DAI 84, SLA 11].

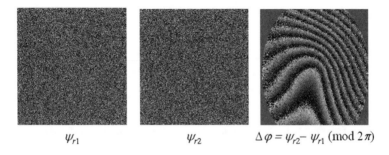

ψ_{r1} $\qquad\qquad\qquad$ ψ_{r2} $\qquad\qquad\qquad$ $\Delta\varphi = \psi_{r2} - \psi_{r1} \;(\mathrm{mod}\; 2\pi)$

Figure 7.3. *Illustration of the phase-subtraction method*

Such results lead to two conclusions:

– It is necessary to spatially filter the result to reduce the level of noise.

– It is necessary to reconstruct the continuity of the phase variation, which is destroyed by calculation using the arctangent function.

7.1.4. *Spatial filtering of the phase*

The filtering procedure must delete the noise without degrading the phase jumps, which are necessary to determine the continuity of the result. The most widely used method is sine/cosine phase filtering (simple or iterative) [AEB 99].

We calculate $\cos(\Delta\varphi)$ and $\sin(\Delta\varphi)$. Then, from a filter kernel of $n \times n$ points, we apply a linear "moving average" or "moving median" filter to the cosine and the sine. The obtained results are generally very close together, within a constant n. The choice of n is imposed by the spatial frequency of the digital fringes. The closer together they are, the smaller n is. Generally, we treat the image with odd values of n: 3×3, 5×5, 7×7, or 9×9. As a consequence of the filtering, there is a $2n$-pixel degradation of the spatial resolution.

7.1.5. *Phase unwrapping*

This operation consists of reconstructing the physical continuity of the phase map. Of course, this continuity may only be reconstructed within a phase constant, unless we know at which points of the mapping the phase is strictly zero. Figure 7.4 represents an illustration of this operation on a line of a result obtained after the subtraction of two phases.

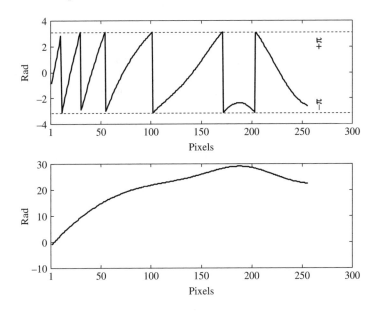

Figure 7.4. *Illustration of the "unwrapping" procedure*

The unwrapping algorithm starts at pixel N°1, and then searches for the phase jumps; at each one detected, -2π or $+2\pi$, it adds $+2\pi$ or -2π so that the phase of two neighboring points is continuous.

This section presents an introduction to phase unwrapping, but will not describe in detail the different types of algorithm. Phase unwrapping techniques have become more sophisticated in recent years with the appearance of powerful algorithms whose implementation is not always straightforward. For a complete description, the reader should refer to reference [GHI 98] in the bibliography. The unwrapping operation is relatively straightforward to carry out in the case where the number of pixels per interference fringe is sufficiently large, and when the signal-to-noise ratio of the interferogram is high. The scanning of the phase map may be conducted vertically or horizontally. These ideal conditions are not usually the case in practice, as the noise level may be high (see Figure 7.3). The procedure then becomes drastically more complicated. In general, the algorithms unwrap the phase by defining a criterion for the identification of discontinuities. The algorithms may be classed into two categories [GHI 98]:

– Those independent of the path taken through the phase map or "global" algorithms; they proceed at once by identifying, isolating, and excluding the zones of $\Delta\varphi$ which may lead to an error in the identification of discontinuities. The unwrapping process is carried out following an arbitrary path through the phase map.

– Those which depend on the path taken or "local" algorithms; these give the continuous phase, point by point, following a defined path.

Recently developed algorithms efficiently unwrap the phase even when the level of noise is comparable to the phase value, when the phase features abrupt jumps due to a discontinuity in the object being measured, or even when the density of pixels per fringe is low. The algorithms are distinguished according to their calculation time, their sensitivity to the propagation of errors during unwrapping, and their robustness with respect to the items mentioned previously. Despite the great progress made to date [GHI 98], we must point out that none of the algorithms may positively respond to the simultaneous accumulation of signal problems. Each is only efficient for a particular problem, and may only work completely when provided with supplementary information. Because of this, there are currently no entirely automatic algorithms.

As an example, one possible strategy for the algorithm to be insensitive to noise consists of comparing the currently treated point with a neighborhood which has already been unwrapped. To be insensitive to spikes in noise, a comparison may be carried out after the low-pass filtering of the neighborhood considered (by moving average filtering or median filtering, for example). Then, we move on to the next point, either using the same neighborhood, or slightly modifying it, and so on: we therefore propagate this algorithm through the whole image. To begin unwrapping, the algorithm therefore needs to know a zone in which there are no phase jumps. This area may be randomly chosen in the image, but it may also be chosen by an intervening experimenter, who will identify an area with a low fringe density. This strategy gives access to a complete immunity to noise. On the other hand, it is very sensitive to fringe openings (a loss of continuity in the $\pm\pi$ contour lines) and will propagate errors across the whole phase map. Nevertheless, it is always possible to "retouch" the relevant areas by the intervention of the experimenter.

An example of phase unwrapping is given in Figure 7.5 with the result illustrated in Figure 7.3. The algorithm has been applied on the smoothed result.

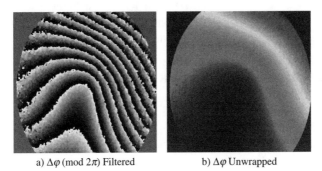

a) $\Delta\varphi$ (mod 2π) Filtered   b) $\Delta\varphi$ Unwrapped

Figure 7.5. *Phase difference: (a) filtered and (b) unwrapped (for a color version of this figure, see www.iste.co.uk/picart/digiholog.zip)*

7.1.6. *Out-of-plane sensitivity*

The phase variation is "sensitive" to the components of the displacement field of the object. The out-of-plane sensitivity is obtained for collinear illumination and observation vectors, as illustrated in Figure 7.6. In the frame of reference tied to the object, we simply have $\mathbf{K_e} = -\mathbf{k}$ and $\mathbf{K_o} = \mathbf{k}$, leading to $\mathbf{S} = -2\mathbf{k}$ and $\Delta\varphi = -4\pi D_z/\lambda$, from which it is possible to estimate the out-of-plane component by:

$$D_z = -\frac{\lambda}{4\pi}\Delta\varphi \qquad\qquad [7.6]$$

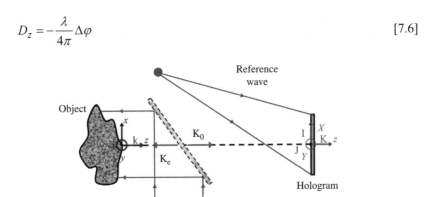

Figure 7.6. *Illumination and observation for out-of-plane sensitivity*

7.1.7. *In-plane sensitivity*

The in-plane sensitivity is obtained by illuminating the object symmetrically with two beams, and observing perpendicular to the face of the object. Figure 7.7 illustrates the geometry of the setup. In the frame of reference tied to the object, we now have $\mathbf{K_o} = \mathbf{k}$, $\mathbf{K_{e1}} = \sin\theta\,\mathbf{i} - \cos\theta\,\mathbf{k}$, and $\mathbf{K_{e2}} = -\sin\theta\,\mathbf{i} - \cos\theta\,\mathbf{k}$, leading to two sensitivity vectors $\mathbf{S_1}$ and $\mathbf{S_2}$. The difference in the optical phase variations seen at these two sensitivities provides access to the in-plane component. Indeed, we have:

$$\Delta\varphi_{IP} = \Delta\varphi_1 - \Delta\varphi_2 = \frac{2\pi}{\lambda}\mathbf{D}.(\mathbf{K_{e1}} - \mathbf{K_{e2}}) = \frac{4\pi}{\lambda}\sin\theta\,D_x \qquad [7.7]$$

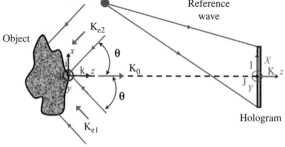

Figure 7.7. *Illuminations and observations for in-plane sensitivity*

7.1.8. *3D sensitivity*

In the case where the object has a displacement vector with three components, it may be of interest to develop an illumination architecture that allows the simultaneous detection of phase variations containing the projections of the displacement along three sensitivity vectors.

Figure 7.8 shows the illumination vector for a given sensitivity vector, the observation vector still being considered perpendicular to the surface of the object. Simultaneous 3D measurement is possible by three-color digital holography. Let us consider three wavelengths and three illumination vectors along three different directions. Each illumination vector is written as (angles are oriented):

$$\mathbf{K_e^\lambda} = -\cos\theta_z^\lambda \sin\theta_{xz}^\lambda\,\mathbf{i} - \sin\theta_z^\lambda\,\mathbf{j} - \cos\theta_z^\lambda \cos\theta_{xz}^\lambda\,\mathbf{k} \qquad [7.8]$$

and $\mathbf{K_o} \cong \mathbf{k}$ is the observation vector.

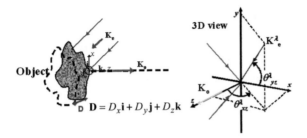

Figure 7.8. *3D measurement*

Thus, the 3D displacement field of the object, $\{D_x, D_y, D_z\}$ may be calculated from equation [7.9]:

$$\begin{bmatrix} D_x \\ D_y \\ D_z \end{bmatrix} = \frac{1}{2\pi\gamma} M_\theta \times \begin{bmatrix} \lambda_R \Delta\varphi_R \\ \lambda_G \Delta\varphi_G \\ \lambda_B \Delta\varphi_B \end{bmatrix} \qquad [7.9]$$

where

$$\begin{aligned} \gamma = & \cos\theta^R_{yz} \sin\theta^R_{xz} \left(\sin\theta^G_{yz}(1+\cos\theta^B_{yz}\cos\theta^B_{xz}) - \sin\theta^B_{yz}(1+\cos\theta^G_{yz}\cos\theta^G_{xz}) \right) \\ & - \sin\theta^R_{yz} \left(\cos\theta^G_{yz}\sin\theta^G_{xz}(1+\cos\theta^B_{yz}\cos\theta^B_{xz}) - \cos\theta^B_{yz}\sin\theta^B_{xz}(1+\cos\theta^G_{yz}\cos\theta^G_{xz}) \right) \\ & + (1+\cos\theta^R_{yz}\cos\theta^R_{xz})\left(\cos\theta^G_{yz}\sin\theta^G_{xz}\sin\theta^B_{yz} - \cos\theta^B_{yz}\sin\theta^B_{xz}\sin\theta^G_{yz} \right) \end{aligned} \qquad [7.10]$$

and

$$M_\theta = \begin{bmatrix} \begin{aligned} & \sin\theta^G_{yz}(1+\cos\theta^G_{yz}\cos\theta^G_{xz}) \\ & -\sin\theta^B_{yz}(1+\cos\theta^G_{yz}\cos\theta^G_{xz}) \end{aligned} & \begin{aligned} & -\sin\theta^B_{yz}(1+\cos\theta^B_{yz}\cos\theta^B_{xz}) \\ & +\sin\theta^B_{yz}(1+\cos\theta^R_{yz}\cos\theta^R_{xz}) \end{aligned} & \begin{aligned} & \sin\theta^R_{yz}(1+\cos\theta^R_{yz}\cos\theta^R_{xz}) \\ & -\sin\theta^G_{yz}(1+\cos\theta^R_{yz}\cos\theta^R_{xz}) \end{aligned} \\[2em] \begin{aligned} & -\cos\theta^G_{yz}\sin\theta^G_{xz}(1+\cos\theta^B_{yz}\cos\theta^B_{xz}) \\ & +\cos\theta^B_{yz}\sin\theta^B_{xz}(1+\cos\theta^G_{yz}\cos\theta^G_{xz}) \end{aligned} & \begin{aligned} & \cos\theta^R_{yz}\sin\theta^R_{xz}(1+\cos\theta^B_{yz}\cos\theta^B_{xz}) \\ & -\cos\theta^B_{yz}\sin\theta^B_{xz}(1+\cos\theta^R_{yz}\cos\theta^R_{xz}) \end{aligned} & \begin{aligned} & -\cos\theta^R_{yz}\sin\theta^R_{xz}(1+\cos\theta^G_{yz}\cos\theta^G_{xz}) \\ & +\cos\theta^G_{yz}\sin\theta^G_{xz}(1+\cos\theta^R_{yz}\cos\theta^R_{xz}) \end{aligned} \\[2em] \begin{aligned} & \cos\theta^G_{yz}\sin\theta^G_{xz}\sin\theta^B_{yz} \\ & -\cos\theta^B_{yz}\sin\theta^B_{xz}\sin\theta^G_{yz} \end{aligned} & \begin{aligned} & -\cos\theta^R_{yz}\sin\theta^R_{xz}\sin\theta^B_{yz} \\ & +\cos\theta^B_{yz}\sin\theta^B_{xz}\sin\theta^R_{yz} \end{aligned} & \begin{aligned} & \cos\theta^R_{yz}\sin\theta^R_{xz}\sin\theta^G_{yz} \\ & -\cos\theta^G_{yz}\sin\theta^G_{xz}\sin\theta^R_{yz} \end{aligned} \end{bmatrix} \qquad [7.11]$$

In [7.9], $\Delta\varphi_R$, $\Delta\varphi_G$, and $\Delta\varphi_B$ are the phase variations between two states of the object, which are obtained from the R(red), G(green), and B(blue) laser beams, respectively.

7.1.9. *Sensitivity variation across the field of view*

Note that the in-plane sensitivity (see Figure 7.7) is related to the difference of the illumination vectors of the object. If the illumination is collimated, that is if we illuminate with parallel beams, the vectors K_{e1} and K_{e2} are constant in the object plane. Thus, the in-plane sensitivity does not *a priori* depend on the object plane coordinates. On the other hand, in the case of 3D sensitivity or out-of-plane sensitivity, the sensitivity vector depends on the observation vector K_o, as shown in Figure 7.9. Thus, the variation of the observation vector in the object plane leads to a variation in the out-of-plane sensitivity as a function of the spatial coordinates in the plane of the object.

Figure 7.9. *Sensitivity variation in the field*

These variations increase when the aperture angle α under which we observe the object increases (i.e. a large object observed at close distance). In this case, the phase variation no longer exclusively contains the out-of-plane component, but a mix of the three displacement components. It is then necessary to take into account these variations by calibrating the sensitivity vector in advance. In the case of a small aperture angle (i.e. a small object observed at long distance), the mixing percentage of the two planar components is low and, depending on the stress applied to the object, the contributions may be neglected.

7.2. Digital holographic microscopy

7.2.1. *Principles and advantages*

Digital holographic microscopy (DHM) is the application of digital holography to microscopy. DHM is distinguished from other methods of microscopy by the fact that it does not require the focused recording of an image projected from the object onto the detector plane. The object wave is simply projected by the objective of the microscope toward the detector plane. Since we are recording a digital hologram, we may reconstruct the object with a focus which will be digitally adjusted during the reconstruction process. There exist other, very similar, techniques of microscopy which differ in name, such as interferential microscopy, optical coherence tomography, and diffraction phase microscopy. These methods each have in common, the use of the coherent combination of an object and a reference wave, allowing the ultimate obtainment of an amplitude image and a phase image of the object. In traditional microscopy, the image of the object is projected onto the detector, and since there is no reference wave, the essential phase information is lost.

Transparent objects, such as living biological cells, are observed with a phase contrast microscope or a differential interferometric microscope. These methods show the phase of the object by distorting the bright background of the image. In the case of DHM, we directly reconstruct a phase image and an amplitude image without creating a phase shift between the background and object images. Thus, a phase object is directly accessible and we may also quantify the measurement knowing the illumination and the observation conditions. This is why DHM allows us to carry out what is known as "quantitative phase microscopy".

The digital reconstruction of the object field provides access to 2.5D information [KOU 07]. In other words, by carrying out the calculation for different reconstruction distances, we obtain an image stack that allows us to visualize the scene in pseudo-3D. If we apply an angular scan to the object, we gain access to tomographic information [CHA 06b].

On a classical microscope, image focusing is carried out manually by modifying the physical position of the object relative to the objective of the microscope. With holographic reconstruction, we may define a digital focusing criterion so as to automatically determine the best image plane [FER 05, DUB 06, LIU 09].

The fact that DHM gives access to the optical phase of the field diffracted across the objective of the microscope allows us to envisage the correction for geometric aberrations in the optical system by taking into account the optical phase of the aberrations in the measured phase [COL 06a, COL 06b, STA 00].

7.2.2. *Architectures*

Principally, there exist two architectures, using transmission and using reflection. Figures 7.10(a) and (b) describe the transmission and reflection configurations, respectively [CUC 99a]. The beams are shaped in both arms using collimators and spatial filters. The objective is represented by its lenses and aperture diaphragm (AD). In the transmission configuration, the object is illuminated by a collimated beam, and diffracts the light toward the aperture cone of the microscope objective.

In the reflection configuration, the object is illuminated by a collimated beam which first passes through the microscope objective, and then diffracts/reflects the light toward the aperture cone of the microscope objective. The light therefore crosses the microscope objective twice.

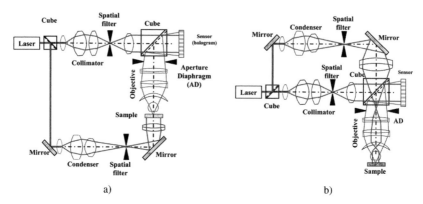

Figure 7.10. *(a) Transmission configuration and (b) reflection configuration*

In both cases, the hologram is in an off-axis configuration and the object is reconstructed after filtering in the Fourier plane, as indicated for the D-FFT methods in Chapter 5. Note that heterodyne techniques may also be implemented and combined with the off-axis method. In this case, they aid in the suppression of parasitic orders (the zero order and conjugate image). We will not describe these methods in detail here. We recommend reader to consult references [ATL 07], [ATL 08], [GRO 08], [GRO 07], and [YAM 97].

The spatial resolution of these methods is related to the digital aperture of the objective. Classically, when the system is diffraction-limited, we have:

$$\rho_x = \rho_y = 0{,}61 \frac{\lambda}{n \sin \alpha} \tag{7.12}$$

where $n \sin \alpha$ is the numerical aperture of the objective. The ultimate resolution limit is therefore $\lambda/2$.

On the other hand, and herein lies the interest of DHM, the measurement of the optical phase has nanometer-scale sensitivity, meaning that the microscope is capable of measuring variations in optical path of less than one nanometer [MAR 05].

In the reflection configuration, illumination and observation are collinear, and in opposite directions. We measure every variation in the height of the object surface, between two holograms, using the following relation (see Figure 7.6):

$$D_z = -\frac{\lambda}{4\pi} \Delta\varphi \qquad [7.13]$$

For the transmission configuration, illuminated along the optical axis, the object is transparent. The reconstructed optical phase of the object is:

$$\psi_r(x,y) = \frac{2\pi}{\lambda} \int_0^{h(x,y)} n(x,y,z)dz \qquad [7.14]$$

In [7.14], $h(x, y)$ is the thickness of the object. If we suppose as a first approximation that the refractive index is constant along the z-axis, $n(x, y, z) = n(x, y)$, then the variation in optical phase is given by:

$$\Delta\varphi(x,y) = \frac{2\pi}{\lambda} \left[h(x,y)\Delta n(x,y) + n(x,y)\Delta h(x,y) \right] \qquad [7.15]$$

where $\Delta n(x, y)$ is the variation of the index and $\Delta h(x, y)$ is the variation in thickness, between the first and the second holograms. This relation shows that for a configuration with a transparent object, it is not possible, from a single measurement, to know *a priori* each of the contributions to the phase variation.

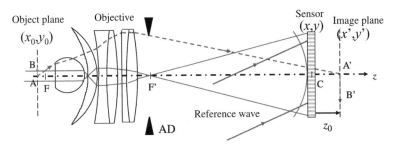

Figure 7.11. *Imaging across the microscope*

7.2.3. *Reconstruction of the object field*

The basics of the reconstruction of the object field using the S-FFT and the D-FFT methods have already been exhaustively discussed in Chapters 5 and 6. However, there remain some peculiarities owing to the imaging configuration, which must be taken into account to obtain a quantitative measurement of the phase contrast. Figure 7.11 shows this configuration in detail. The beam marked with a dashed line shows the optical path across the objective, toward the image plane, which is not necessarily the detector plane, forming an image of the object. The beam marked with a solid line shows the effective path followed by the illumination light, which is collimated. The beam leaving the objective converges at its focus, which is also the plane of the exit pupil.

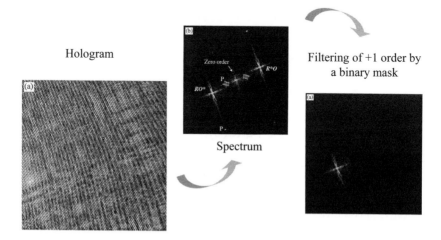

Hologram

Filtering of +1 order by
a binary mask

Spectrum

Figure 7.12. *Reconstruction procedure for a digital hologram
from a microscope (from [CUC 00])*

In the detector plane, the emergent wave has a curvature of radius $z_C = F'C$ (part of the full line, where C is the position of the detector). This curvature of the wave gives a contribution of $\pi\lambda/2z_C(x^2+y^2)$ to the measured optical phase for each hologram [FER 03]. It must consequently be eliminated if we wish to have access to an unbiased phase image of the object. This calculation is carried out by simply multiplying the reconstructed complex field by the term $\exp(-j\pi\lambda/2z_C(x^2+y^2))$. The reconstruction therefore follows the following steps:

Step 1: Apply the S-FFT or the D-FFT numerical treatment methods (see Chapter 5).

Step 2: Compensate for the curvature by multiplying by $\exp(-j\pi\lambda/2z_C(x^2+y^2))$.

Step 3: Re-propagate the field in the detector plane toward the object or the image (see Chapter 6).

Step 4: Calculate the amplitude and phase images of the reconstructed object.

As an illustration, Figure 7.12 shows the procedure for reconstructing the hologram of a 1951 USAF test chart (from [CUC 00]).

The setup is a reflection configuration with $\lambda = 632.8$ nm, and the object-detector distance is $z_0 = 285$ mm. The detector has 512×512 pixels with an interval of $\Delta x \times \Delta y = 9.4 \times 9.4$ μm.

Figure 7.13 shows that the image may be reconstructed in different planes (from [CUC 00]).

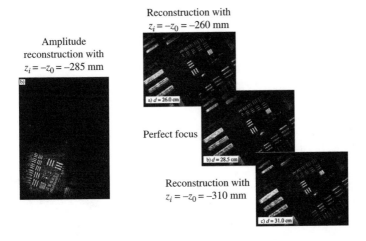

Amplitude reconstruction with $z_i = -z_0 = -285$ mm

Reconstruction with $z_i = -z_0 = -260$ mm

a) $d = 26.0$ cm

Perfect focus

b) $d = 28.5$ cm

Reconstruction with $z_i = -z_0 = -310$ mm

c) $d = 31.0$ cm

Figure 7.13. *Refocusing the image of the test pattern (from [CUC 00])*

7.2.4. *Phase contrast*

The phase of the optical field obtained in the reconstruction process gives a quantitative phase image, often called "phase-contrast image". However, as is pointed out in the previous section, we must compensate for all the parasitic phase terms in the image: curvature, parasitic plane, aberrations, etc.   [COL 06a, COL 06b]. The residual phase plane and the curvature are compensated for by multiplying the complex field by the term $\exp(-2j\pi(f_{x0}x+f_{y0}y) - j\pi\lambda/2z_c(x^2+y^2))$, where (f_{x0},f_{y0}) are the slopes of the phase plane along the x and y directions. Figure 7.14 illustrates the phase image of an epithelial cell obtained using a reflection configuration, with $\lambda = 632.8$ nm and a 40× objective lens and with $n\sin\alpha = 0.65$. Figure 7.14(a) shows the phase image of the object, having neither compensated for the curvature nor the plane. Figure 7.14(b) shows the image having compensated for the curvature but not the plane. There are still parallel fringes, which show the presence of a plane whose slope in x and y is non-zero.

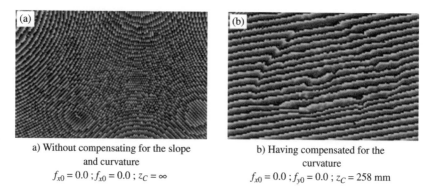

a) Without compensating for the slope
and curvature
$f_{x0} = 0.0$; $f_{x0} = 0.0$; $z_C = \infty$

b) Having compensated for the
curvature
$f_{x0} = 0.0$; $f_{y0} = 0.0$; $z_C = 258$ mm

Figure 7.14. *Phase contrast with compensation for the curvature (from [CUC 00])*

Figure 7.14 illustrates the procedure when the compensation is partial. Figure 7.15(a) shows the image with compensation for the curvature but not the slope, Figure 7.15(b) shows the image without compensation for the curvature, and Figure 7.15(c) shows the phase image having compensated completely for the parasitic terms [CUC 00].

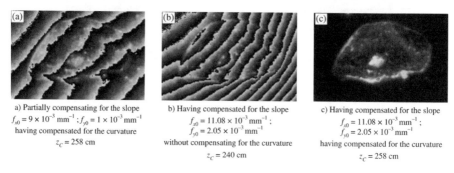

a) Partially compensating for the slope
$f_{x0} = 9 \times 10^{-3}$ mm^{-1} ; $f_{y0} = 1 \times 10^{-3}$ mm^{-1}
having compensated for the curvature
$z_C = 258$ cm

b) Having compensated for the slope
$f_{x0} = 11.08 \times 10^{-3}$ mm^{-1} ;
$f_{y0} = 2.05 \times 10^{-3}$ mm^{-1}
without compensating for the curvature
$z_C = 240$ cm

c) Having compensated for the slope
$f_{x0} = 11.08 \times 10^{-3}$ mm^{-1} ;
$f_{y0} = 2.05 \times 10^{-3}$ mm^{-1}
having compensated for the curvature
$z_C = 258$ cm

Figure 7.15. *Phase contrast having compensated for the parasitic terms (from [CUC 00])*

7.3. Two-wavelength profilometry

7.3.1. *Principle*

We saw in previous sections that the optical phase has determined modulo 2π to within a phase constant. In terms of physical scale, the result is "wrapped" with a period corresponding to $\lambda/2$. This means that if an object presents a step (discontinuity) of height greater than $\lambda/2$, it is not possible to precisely know this height (indeterminacy to within a multiple of $\lambda/2$). One solution consists of illuminating the object with two different wavelengths. Suppose a reflecting object has a z-profile of $h(x,y)$ with respect to the reference plane. Relative to this reference, the estimated optical phase in the reconstructed object field is:

$$\psi_r(x,y) = \frac{2\pi}{\lambda} h(x,y) \qquad [7.16]$$

If we illuminate the object with two wavelengths λ_1 and λ_2 ($\lambda_1 > \lambda_2$), the two phases measured are:

$$\psi_{r1}(x,y) = \frac{2\pi}{\lambda_1} h(x,y)$$

$$\psi_{r2}(x,y) = \frac{2\pi}{\lambda_2} h(x,y) \qquad [7.17]$$

We can then determine the height $h(x, y)$ by calculating the difference:

$$\psi_{r2}(x,y) - \psi_{r1}(x,y) = 2\pi \left(\frac{1}{\lambda_2} - \frac{1}{\lambda_1} \right) h(x,y)$$

$$= \frac{2\pi}{\Lambda} h(x,y) \qquad [7.18]$$

where $\Lambda = \lambda_1 \lambda_2/(\lambda_1 - \lambda_2)$ is the effective wavelength obtained in the measurement. Thus, when λ_1 and λ_2 are close, the effective wavelength Λ increases and becomes much greater than λ_1 or λ_2. Henceforth, the ambiguity in the determination of the step height no longer has a limit of $\lambda_1/2$, but instead $\Lambda/2$ and can be resolved.

7.3.2. Two-wavelength profilometry with spatio-chromatic multiplexing

There are multiple ways to proceed with the measurement [ZOU 96, KAN 04], such as using two distinct lasers to illuminate the object sequentially and then calculating the phase differences, or using a tunable diode laser and recording two interferograms sequentially with a slight shift in the wavelength. One elegant method consists of recording a single, two-color hologram, the two monochromatic holograms being spatially multiplexed. Figure 7.16 illustrates the architecture of a two-wavelength microscope [KUH 07]. The object is illuminated by two radiations simultaneously. The reference waves each have their own spatial filter, and we may adjust their spatial frequencies separately. These waves are inclined at different angles, leading to a spatial multiplexing of the holograms, each hologram being an image of the object at a given wavelength. This principle was already invoked in Chapter 5 (see Figure 5.21).

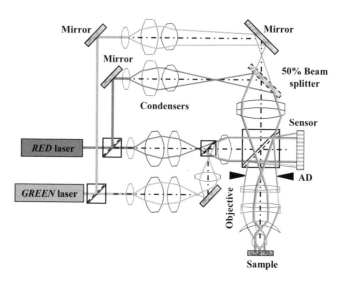

Figure 7.16. *Holographic microscope for two-wavelength profilometry (for a color version of this figure, see www.iste.co.uk/picart/digiholog.zip)*

One example of usage regards the determination of a staircase motif on a silicon slide [KUH 07]. The wavelengths are λ_1 = 760 nm and λ_2 = 680 nm and are much less than the height of the profile. With these parameters, the effective wavelength is Λ = 6.428 µm which is greater than the height of the profile. Figure 7.17(a) shows the digital two-color hologram recorded with the monochromatic detector. Zooming in to the center allows us to see the color microfringes (one direction per color). Figure 7.17(b) shows the spectrum of the hologram. We see the four complex conjugate orders two by two (two per color). The circles indicate the bandwidths conserved for the reconstruction of each color [KUH 07].

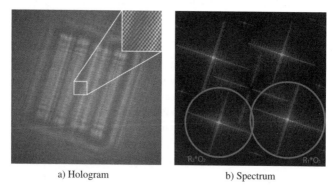

a) Hologram   b) Spectrum

Figure 7.17. *Two-color hologram and its spectrum (from [KUH 07]) (for a color version of this figure, see www.iste.co.uk/picart/digiholog.zip)*

Once the phases have been calculated and their difference obtained, we obtain a reconstruction of the object's profile. Figure 7.18(a) shows a scale model of the object and Figure 7.18(b) shows the result obtained by the method. Figure 7.18(c) shows a comparison of this measurement with a result obtained by white light profilometry [KUH 07].

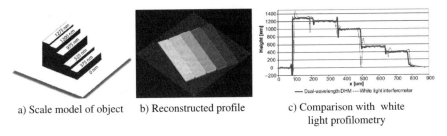

a) Scale model of object   b) Reconstructed profile   c) Comparison with white light profilometry

Figure 7.18. *Application of the microscope to the measurement of surface profiles (from [KUH 07])*

7.4. Digital holographic photomechanics

7.4.1. *Introduction*

The validation of the code used for finite element calculations often requires a comparison with experimental investigations. In mechanics, it is common practice to measure multiple components of the displacement field of an object subjected to a load. Classically, the components are measured sequentially, that is one after another, which does not isolate the measurement from any deviations and fluctuations of the loading device. Digital holography brings a major contribution to photomechanics, as it allows the simultaneous (i.e. real time) measurement of two or three components of the displacement vector. So as to simultaneously measure multiple components of the displacement field, it is necessary to make use of two (for two components) or three (for three components) illumination directions combined at one observation direction (see section 7.1.8). Depending on the orientation of the sensitivity vector of the interferometer, we will measure either a weighted composition of the components or simply the out-of-plane component. The flexibility of digital holography enables the easy measurement of two components simultaneously. To do this, we must spatially multiplex digital holograms corresponding to two reference waves having very different spatial frequencies (see Figure 5.2). There are two ways to proceed: either by using a single laser and multiplexing holograms which have been rendered incoherent, or by using two or three wavelengths and recording digital color holograms [TAN 11, TAN 10b]. This section illustrates these methods, dealing with monochromatic multiplexing, spatio-chromatic multiplexing, and 3D measurement by three-color digital holography.

7.4.2. *Twin-sensitivity measurement with monochromatic multiplexing*

7.4.2.1. *Principle*

Figure 7.19 illustrates the experimental setup [PIC 03a, PIC 04, PIC 05b]. Spatial multiplexing is based on the incoherent mixture of 2×2 coherent waves. Each coherent duplet is composed of a smooth plane reference wave, and of the wave diffracted by the object. The incoherent mixing is carried out by crossing the polarization of the fields. We may also use a delay line if the object depolarizes light. The two reference waves must have incidence angles such that there is no overlap between the holograms and between each hologram and their associated parasitic orders. Owing to the incoherent addition of the beams coming from each interferometer, the light intensity recorded at the detector is written as the sum of the intensities of the two holograms.

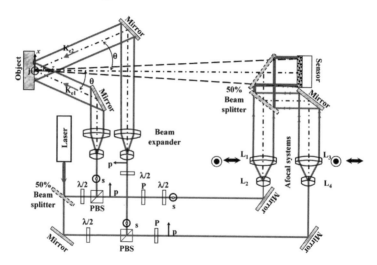

Figure 7.19. *Recording with double reference beams and spatial multiplexing (PBS: polarizing beam splitter cube)*

The independent orientation of the incident angles is realized by displacing the collimating lenses L_1 and L_3 perpendicularly to their optical axes, along the x and y directions, respectively (see section 5.2). As an illustration of the spatial multiplexing technique, we place an aluminum washer of diameter 24 mm × 995 mm in front of the detector ($M \times N = 1,360 \times 1,024$ pixels, pitch: $\Delta x = \Delta y = 4.65$ μm). Figure 7.20(a) shows the two multiplexed holograms. The higher one corresponds to interferometer N°2 (illumination K_{e2}) and the one on the right to N°1 (illumination K_{e1}).

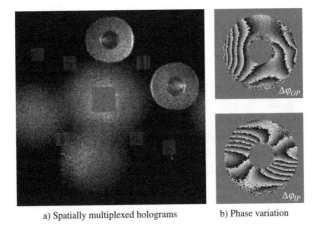

a) Spatially multiplexed holograms   b) Phase variation

Figure 7.20. *Reconstructed spatially multiplexed holograms and simultaneous twin sensitivity measurement*

The simultaneous measurement of two of the three displacement components is related to the sensitivity vectors produced by the two illuminations and the observation direction associated with the recording. The in-plane, along $\mathbf{i}$, and out-of-plane components, along $\mathbf{k}$, of the displacement fields will be obtained, respectively, by addition and subtraction, and from the optical phase variations, $\Delta\varphi_1$ and $\Delta\varphi_2$, given by the first and the second interferometers when the object is subjected to a constraint. In effect, we have [PIC 03a]:

$$\Delta\varphi_{OP} = \Delta\varphi_1 + \Delta\varphi_2 = \frac{2\pi}{\lambda}\mathbf{D}.(\mathbf{K_{e1}} - \mathbf{K_{e2}} - 2\mathbf{K_o}) = \frac{4\pi}{\lambda}(1 + \cos\theta)D_z$$

$$\Delta\varphi_{IP} = \Delta\varphi_1 - \Delta\varphi_2 = \frac{2\pi}{\lambda}\mathbf{D}.(\mathbf{K_{e1}} - \mathbf{K_{e2}}) = \frac{4\pi}{\lambda}\sin\theta\, D_x \qquad [7.19]$$

Figure 7.20(b) illustrates the procedure and shows the results obtained for the phase variations $\Delta\varphi_{OP}$ ($OP\equiv$out-of-plane) and $\Delta\varphi_{IP}$ modulo 2π ($IP\equiv$in-plane).

7.4.2.2. *Application: polymer concrete in a three-point bending test*

In this section, we describe the material and test. The three-point flexural test beam is placed 1,045 mm in front of the detector and illuminated at 45°. The test sample consists of a synthetic concrete composed of an aggregate matrix whose volume fractions are 70% and 30%. The matrix of the material is composed of 43% epoxy resin and 57% fine sand whose mean diameter is 0.4 mm. The aggregate is a sand of large grains whose mean diameter is 2 mm. The samples have the dimensions $95 \times 15 \times 8$ mm^3 and the radius of the loading pin is 9 mm. During the test, the supporting pins are mobile and the central pin is fixed. The mechanical configuration is shown in Figure 7.21 [PIC 04].

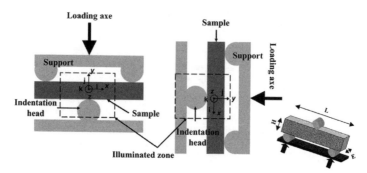

Figure 7.21. *Experimental setup for stress-testing the polymer concrete*

Only the central part marked by the dotted lines is observed. The test proceeds in the following manner: we acquire the first hologram of the object after it has been placed in the stress-machine; then we incrementally displace the external supports so as to make fringes appear on the sample during the digital reconstruction. We limit our analysis to a small number of fringes so as to maintain compatibility with the spatial resolution in the image of the beam. At each increment, we record a hologram of the current state, and each hologram serves as a reference for the next state. The test is continued until the material breaks.

7.4.2.3. Experimental results

The material breaks at a deflection of around 400 μm for the sample described above, after recording 125 holograms. Figure 7.22 is obtained with two tests of the same concrete, the bending head having been turned by 90° between the tests (Figure 7.21). It appears that the cracks do not appear in the same place for each test. Nevertheless, the normal component, which is systematically measured, exhibits a similar behavior and the cracks and ruptures of the samples appear at the same stresses (Figure 7.23a). The results are therefore reported for three estimated components with two different samples, the curve in Figure 7.23(a) being invariant from one sample to the other. In Figure 7.22, the displacement fields are represented as contour lines, modulo an arbitrary spatial wavelength equal to 1/60th of the peak-to-peak value of the displacement fields accumulated from the beginning of the test to the current point indicated on Figure 7.23(a). From the start of the test, linear behavior is exhibited in the first 30 holograms (red point n°1). These results show a good symmetry in their amplitudes as well as a perfect linearity of the behavior from the first to the 65th hologram (red point n°2). When a fissure appears, we observe a change in the direction of the fringes. After its initiation, the crack does not immediately propagate across the width of the beam (red point n°2). Then, the crack propagates across the width until the breaking point of the sample (red points n°3 and n°4). During this phase, the evolution of the displacement field along the *y*-direction does not show any modification. On the other hand, for both of the other directions, the appearance of the fissure prompts the appearance of a strong gradient which is perfectly visible in the off-plane component. Observation of the displacement maps allows us to estimate the position of the crack tip, leading to the progression represented in Figure 7.23(a) [PIC 04].

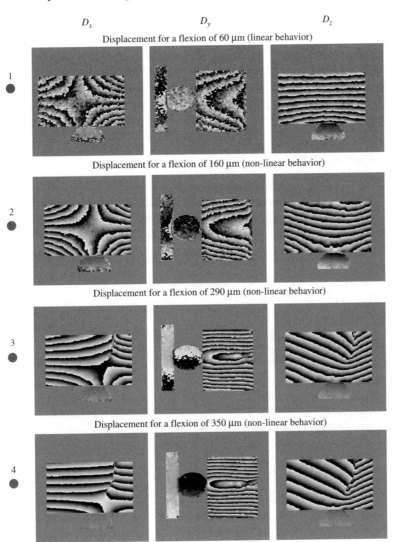

Figure 7.22. *Displacement field measured by twin-sensitivity digital holography*

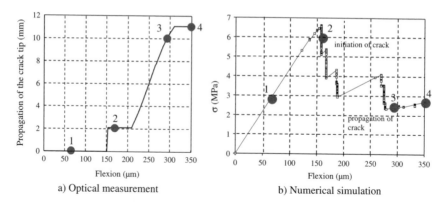

a) Optical measurement   b) Numerical simulation

Figure 7.23. *Propagation of the crack during the test and load-deflection curve obtained by finite elements*

7.4.2.4. *Comparison with finite element modeling*

The fracturing process in synthetic concretes is 3D, and a 3D model is therefore necessary to study the evolution of cracks. This chapter not being dedicated to modeling in solid mechanics, we refer the reader to references [LIL 03] and [BER 04]. Numerical modeling allows the obtainment of a *load-deflection* graph of the sample (Figure 7.23b).

On the curve in Figure 7.23(b), we observe two tendencies before the maximum load: before point 1, the structure exhibits linear behavior, and the number of damaged elements is low; between points 1 and 2, we notice nonlinear behavior associated with a decrease in rigidity of the structure; this is the cause of the apparition and the propagation of the microcracks. The results presented in Figure 7.23(a) agree with those from the simulation: the first microcracks appear in the vicinity of 150 µm on both curves. Beyond point 2, the coalescence of the microcracks gives rise to a macrocrack which leads to the destruction of the sample. Figure 7.24 shows the evolution of the damage across the sample, obtained by simulation. Owing to the gradient of the stress field in the sample, the crack is initiated in the area opposite the load, since the latter consists of fibers under tension whereas the area between the neutral axis and the central pin is under compression. The numerical simulation and the results of the optical measurement are therefore in good agreement, which validates the numerical model.

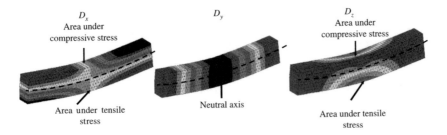

Figure 7.24. *3D displacement fields obtained by finite element simulation (for a color version of this figure, see www.iste.co.uk/picart/digiholog.zip)*

7.4.3. *Twin-sensitivity measurement with spatio-chromatic multiplexing*

7.4.3.1. *Principle*

The principle of spatio-chromatic multiplexing has been discussed in Chapter 5, section 5.7. Figure 5.21 illustrates the experimental setup.

7.4.3.2. *Application to crack detection in electrical components*

One example of an industrial application concerns the study of the mechanical causes of the cracking of one component in a PCB (Printed Circuit Board) card from a detector used in the automobile industry. The component cracks during the embedding of the electronic card in its casing. Figure 7.25(a) shows the PCB component and the examined area, whose diameter is 15 mm, containing the card attachment. Figure 7.25(b) shows the geometry of the illumination of the object (see also Figure 5.21) [TAN 11].

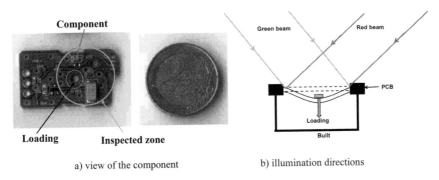

a) view of the component   b) illumination directions

Figure 7.25. *(a) View of the component and (b) illumination geometry*

The object illumination beams are symmetrical, thus simultaneously giving a double 2D sensitivity (in- and out-of-plane). Let us consider the red interferometer. From section 7.1.7, the phase variation along the red light is given by:

$$\Delta\varphi_R = +\frac{2\pi}{\lambda_R}\sin(\theta_R)D_x - \frac{2\pi}{\lambda_R}(1+\cos(\theta_R))D_z \qquad [7.20]$$

and for the green ray, we have:

$$\Delta\varphi_G = -\frac{2\pi}{\lambda_G}\sin(\theta_G)D_x - \frac{2\pi}{\lambda_G}(1+\cos(\theta_G))D_z \qquad [7.21]$$

With $\theta_R = \theta_G = \theta = 45°$, then:

$$D_x = \frac{1}{4\pi\sin(\theta)}(\lambda_R\Delta\varphi_R - \lambda_G\Delta\varphi_G)$$

$$D_z = -\frac{1}{4\pi(1+\cos(\theta))}(\lambda_R\Delta\varphi_R + \lambda_G\Delta\varphi_G) \qquad [7.22]$$

The in-plane, along **i**, and out-of-plane, along **k**, components of the displacement field will be obtained by the respective subtraction and addition of the optical phase variations, $\Delta\varphi_R$ and $\Delta\varphi_G$, weighted by their respective wavelengths. The optical phase variations between two loads may be determined and the differences/sums of the R and G phases may be calculated, as the reconstruction horizons are conserved by the Fresnel transform algorithm with wavelength-dependant zero-padding (see section 5.7.3). Of course, reconstruction with an adjustable magnification can also be applied [TAN 10b].

Figure 7.26 shows the out-of-plane/in-plane displacements obtained after the reconstruction of the holograms recorded during the test. Figure 7.26(b) shows that the component is situated in the region of maximum deflection.

After treating the experimental results, Figure 7.27 shows the region of the component that exhibits large, non-uniform deformations. These non-uniform deformations are indubitably the cause of the cracking of the component. The global curvatures of the displacement fields have been suppressed. Figure 7.27 shows the displacement fields after suppressing the curvatures and zooming in on the component region.

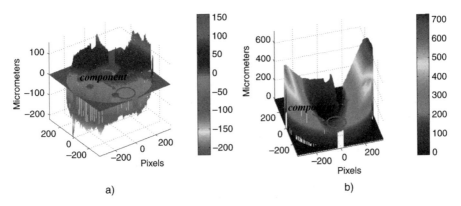

Figure 7.26. *Real-time color twin-sensitivity measurement: (a) in-plane displacements and (b) out-of-plane displacements (for a color version of this figure, see www.iste.co.uk/picart/digiholog.zip)*

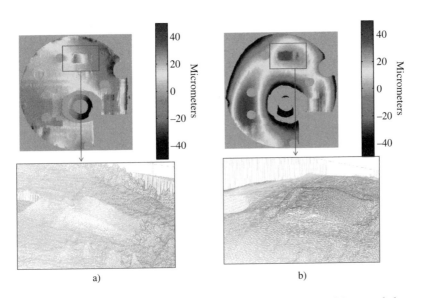

Figure 7.27. *(a) Zoom of the in-plane displacements and (b) zoom of the out-of-plane displacements (for a color version of this figure, see www.iste.co.uk/picart/digiholog.zip)*

7.4.4. *3D measurement by three-color digital holography*

7.4.4.1. *Principle*

This section illustrates the possibility of measuring in real time, i.e. simultaneously, the three components (3D measurement) of the displacement field of a mechanical structure subjected to a load. The experimental method is based on three-color digital holography, with the recording carried out by an image detector arranged as a stack of photodiodes (see Figure 5.20). This method offers an alternative to the methods using monochromatic radiation, which suffer from the complexity of their implementation [SCH 99, PIC 03a]. Indeed, the simultaneous recording of the three-color digital holograms at every detector pixel allows for a considerable simplification of the apparatus, as there is a single reference beam. Thus, it is not necessary to independently adjust the spatial frequencies of each monochromatic duplet [SCH 99, SAU 06]. In such a device, the three reference beams have an identical incidence angle to the detector, and the spatial frequencies depend on the wavelength. Compliance with Shannon's theorem for digital holography imposes that recording be optimized for blue light (here 457 nm). Thus, Shannon's conditions are automatically satisfied for red (here 671 nm) and green light (here 532 nm). The detector is a stack of photodiodes with 8 bits per channel and $(M,N) = (1,060,1,420)$ pixels whose pitch is $\Delta x = \Delta y = 5$ μm. The figure shows the geometry of the apparatus. Note that this figure is similar to Figure 5.26 in Chapter 5, except that the object is illuminated according to the geometry described in Figure 7.8, section 7.1.8.

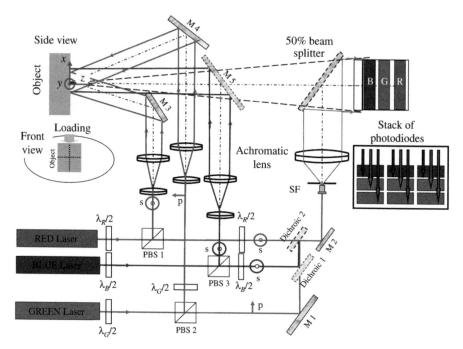

Figure 7.28. *Three-color setup for real-time 3D measurement (for a color version of this figure, see www.iste.co.uk/picart/digiholog.zip)*

7.4.4.2. *Illustration*

The apparatus is applied to a mechanical object of size 25×35 mm² subjected to a mechanical load (see Figure 7.28). The photodiode stack allows the simultaneous recording of the three-color digital holograms at every pixel of the detector. The reconstruction of the monochromatic holograms by S-FFT is shown in Figure 7.29. As mentioned in Chapter 5, the size of the image depends on the wavelength. Applying the D-FFT method with a magnification of $G_y = 0.2$, we reconstruct all three images with an identical size. From the complex field obtained for each wavelength, we extract the phase, and then calculate the phase difference. Figure 7.30 shows the results obtained for the R, G, and B phase differences [TAN 10a].

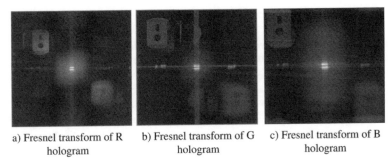

a) Fresnel transform of R   b) Fresnel transform of G   c) Fresnel transform of B
      hologram   hologram   hologram

Figure 7.29. *Reconstruction of the object by Fresnel transform*

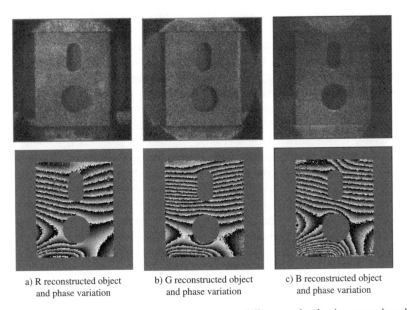

a) R reconstructed object   b) G reconstructed object   c) B reconstructed object
  and phase variation   and phase variation   and phase variation

Figure 7.30. *Reconstruction of the object and phase differences for the three wavelengths*

Let us consider equation [7.11] with $\theta^B{}_{xz} = 45°$, $\theta^G{}_{xz} = -31°$, $\theta^R{}_{xz} = 2{,}75°$ and $\theta^R{}_{yz} = -31°$, $\theta^B{}_{yz} = \theta^G{}_{yz} = 0$, and the phase variations from Figure 7.30 after unwrapping. Figure 7.31 shows the results obtained for the measurement of $\{D_x, D_y, D_z\}$ with the tricolor holograms.

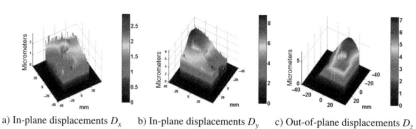

a) In-plane displacements D_x b) In-plane displacements D_y c) Out-of-plane displacements D_z

Figure 7.31. *3D displacement fields measured simultaneously by three-color digital holography (for a color version of this figure, see www.iste.co.uk/picart/digiholog.zip)*

The potential applications of this type of method are numerous in solid, vibrational, and structural mechanics, and in particular in the dynamics of non-condensed matter for which the movements are complex and the displacement fields must be measured simultaneously.

7.4.4.3. *Application to the study of the mechanical behavior of composite materials*

During recent decades, composite materials have dominated numerous high-tech domains, such as aeronautics, sport, and automobiles. The reasons for such success may be attributed to their specific mechanical properties. However, as with every other material, composites are subject to deteriorations of their mechanical properties leading to their breakdown, as they are stressed in regular ways through their use, or even at rest. It is for this reason that the control of the state of these materials during their use is a necessity. Recently, acoustic emission methods have been implemented in order to characterize composite structures *in situ* [JOH 00]. This method uses embedded piezoelectric transducers (PZT): small chips which provide information on acoustic emission inside the structure. However, the influence of the embedded component on the mechanical behavior of the structure is not established. Thus, three-color digital holographic method has a prominent place in the study of the behavior of these materials with or without embedded PZT. The composite material is subjected to a three-point bending test and the samples are unidirectional fiberglass laminates combined with epoxy resin, with PZT chips incorporated (EPZT or NEPZT). Figure 7.32 illustrates some measured values of $\{D_x, D_y, D_z\}$ obtained by EPZT and NEPZT chips. The displacement maps are realigned to compensate for the movement of the rigid body of the sample, which is inevitable at these scales of measurement. Detailed analysis of the x and y displacement components reveals a difference in rigidity: the chip locally rigidifies the sample in the downstream part. The z-component reveals a behavior particular to one quarter of the sample, which is probably due to the influence of the presence of the piezoelectric chip. This result demonstrates that, for the load presented in Figure 7.32, the sample has not undergone any interlaminar delamination [KAR 11].

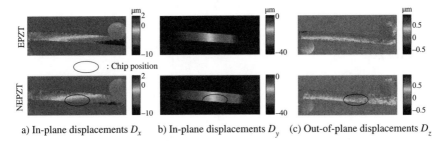

a) In-plane displacements D_x b) In-plane displacements D_y (c) Out-of-plane displacements D_z

Figure 7.32. *Applications to the study of laminated materials with incorporated piezoelectric transducers (for a color version of this figure, see www.iste.co.uk/picart/digiholog.zip)*

7.5. Time-averaged digital holography

7.5.1. *Principle*

This method is classically dedicated to the vibration analysis of structures and non-destructive testing methods [SMI 94]. The principle is simple: in a holographic interferometer, we record the hologram of the object under sinusoidal excitation with a very long exposure time compared with the period of the vibration [PIC 03b, PIC 05a, POW 65, SMI 94]. This method allows the visualization of the amplitude of the object undergoing periodic vibration, as well as its nodal lines.

The hologram is recorded when the object is harmonically excited. Let us consider the object to be excited in a purely sinusoidal regime. The displacement vector of the object is of the form:

$$\mathbf{D}(t) = \mathbf{D}_0 \sin(\omega_0 t + \varphi_0),\qquad\qquad [7.23]$$

and the instantaneous phase variation is written $\Delta\varphi(t) = \Delta\varphi_0 \sin(\omega_0 t + \varphi_0)$ with $\Delta\varphi_0 = 2\pi\mathbf{D}_0.\mathbf{S}/\lambda$. The energy received on the sensor during exposure $\Delta t >> 2\pi/\omega_0$ is thus:

$$I_{H\Delta t} = \int_{t_1}^{t_1+\Delta t} I_H(t)dt$$

$$= \Delta t |R|^2 + \int_{t_1}^{t_1+\Delta t} |O(t)|^2 dt + R \int_{t_1}^{t_1+\Delta t} O^*(t)dt + R^* \int_{t_1}^{t_1+\Delta t} O(t)dt \qquad [7.24]$$

The last term forms the virtual image during the digital reconstruction process. Taking into account the elements given previously on image formation, the diffracted amplitude is written as (omitting the spatial (x,y) dependence):

$$O_0 \propto \Delta t R_0 A_r \exp(j\psi_r) \int_{t_1}^{t_1+\Delta t} \exp(j\Delta\varphi_0 \sin(\omega_0 t + \varphi_0)) dt \qquad [7.25]$$

Since the recording time of the hologram is such that $\omega_0\Delta t \gg 1$, it may be shown that [POW 65]:

$$\int_{t_1}^{t_1+\Delta t} \exp(j\Delta\varphi_0 \sin(\omega_0 t + \varphi_0)) dt \approx \Delta t J_0(\Delta\varphi_0) \qquad [7.26]$$

The reconstructed image is therefore modulated by the Bessel function J_0. The value taken by the Bessel function depends on the amplitude of the object's vibration, via the optical phase $\Delta\varphi_0$. The modulating function is maximal for $\Delta\varphi_0 = 0$, which corresponds to the areas of the object which are immobile during the sinusoidal oscillation. Thus, the bright fringes correspond to the nodal lines of the object. When the amplitude of the vibration increases, the Bessel function decreases. It is zero for certain values, and we observe a dark fringe, since the image presents a minimum of zero. The secondary oscillations of the Bessel function have an amplitude which progressively decreases, so the dark fringes become less and less contrasted. Note that the phase information of the mechanical vibration φ_0 is not included in the reconstructed object field. Because of this fact, the time-averaged technique only gives information about the amplitude of the object's displacements.

7.5.2. Applications

7.5.2.1. Modal analysis

The principal application of time-averaging concerns the modal analysis of structures. The first proposed example concerns the vibrational behavior of an excited clarinet reed driven by an acoustic wave emitted by a loudspeaker placed behind it [PIC 06]. The examined area is 35 mm × 11 mm in size, and the distance is $d_0 = 1,030$ mm with an illumination angle of $\theta = 30°$, the setup being similar to that shown in Figure 5.2. The laser power is adjusted so that $\Delta t = 1$s, assuring that the condition $\Delta t \gg 1/\omega_0$ is satisfied for frequencies greater than 100 Hz. Figure 7.33 shows the time-averaged images, i.e. $|O_0(x,y)|$, in the range 1–10 kHz. At certain frequencies, the amplitude becomes sufficiently large to consider these frequencies as natural frequencies of the reed. Thus, at 1,880 Hz, we observe the first bending mode. 3,260 Hz corresponds to the resonance of the first twisting mode superposed with the first bending mode. The mode at 4,500 Hz may be interpreted as the second bending mode, even though the image does not completely correspond to a pure bend. The other frequencies correspond to modes combining the longitudinal and transverse properties of the reed. At high frequencies, especially at 8,480 Hz, it is clear that the reed is an orthotropic material in which the transverse Young's modulus is smaller than the longitudinal one. Such a study is fundamental, as it allows a comparison with numerical simulations: the measurements may be used to find the mechanical properties of the reed, such as Young's moduli and other parameters, by comparing simulations with measurements.

1,880 HZ   3,260 HZ   4,500 HZ   4,940 HZ   8,480 HZ

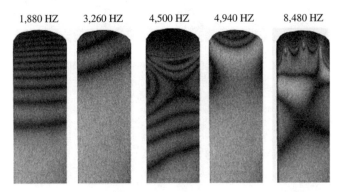

Figure 7.33. *Bessel fringes in the vibrations of a clarinet reed*

The second example, shown in Figure 7.34, concerns the detection of defects in the high-end resonance modes of the dome of a loudspeaker [PIC 06]. The loudspeaker, which has a diameter of 60 mm, is placed 1,186 mm from the detector. The dome mode at 15,700 Hz presents a dissymmetry when the excitation frequency is close to the resonance, whereas for a slightly lower frequency, 15,620 Hz, the mode is perfectly symmetric. In the same way, the resonant frequencies 17,600 HZ and 18,500 Hz present dissymmetries which the numerical model does not take into account. These modal dissymmetries are due to defects in the dome clamping.

7.5.2.2. *Analog/digital comparison*

As was mentioned in Chapters 4 and 5, the difference between results obtained with digital holography and analog holography essentially lies in the spatial resolution. To better appreciate this difference, Figure 7.35 shows a loudspeaker of diameter 60 mm excited at 3,700 Hz and placed 1,385 mm from the photosensitive support, which is either a holographic plate or a CCD-type detector.

The illumination conditions of the object are identical to those in the digital holographic apparatus. Note the very good agreement between the analog and digital fringes.

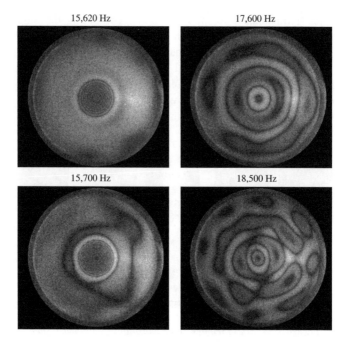

Figure 7.34. *Defects in a loudspeaker dome*

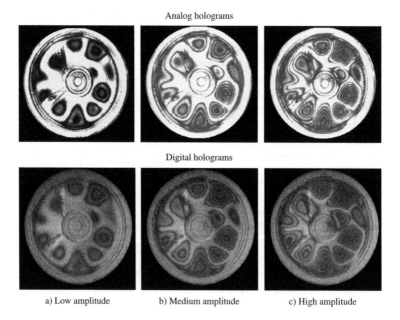

Figure 7.35. *Comparison between analog and digital time-averaging*

The difference in resolution between classical and analog holography is remarkable. The analog recording support is composed of dichromatic gelatin with a resolution of 5,000 mm^{-1} with grains of 15 nm for a sensitivity of 85 μJ/cm^2. The dimensions of the plate are 10 × 12 cm^2 [GEN 08]. The resolution is therefore up to 20 times better, in the larger dimension, in analog holography. The slight differences between the fringe images come from the hygrometry and the temperature, which were not rigorously identical during the digital and analog recordings. The images obtained in classical holography correspond to the square modulus of the diffracted field, which is not the case in digital holography, given that the calculation provides access to the complex image. It is for this reason that the use of the time-averaged phase is possible in digital holography [PIC 05a] and impossible in analog holography, but this is compensated for by a much higher resolution.

7.5.2.3. Time-averaged phase

From equations [7.25] and [7.26], it follows that the time-averaged phase is expressed by:

$$\psi_{av} = \arg(O_0) = \psi_r + \varphi_J \qquad [7.27]$$

The phase term φ_J is introduced, defined as:

$$\varphi_J = \begin{cases} 0 & \text{if } J_0(\Delta\varphi_0) > 0 \\ \pm\pi & \text{if } J_0(\Delta\varphi_0) < 0 \end{cases} \qquad [7.28]$$

The phase φ_J takes the values, 0 or $\pm\pi$, and thus exhibits phase jumps when the J_0 Bessel function crosses 0 and then changes its sign. Thus, the phase φ_J is called the "zero-crossing phase" of the object modulation. Because of the restricted values of φ_J, the determination of its phase jumps enables the precise determination of the contour lines associated with the zero-crossing of the Bessel function with a very high contrast. The zero-crossing phase can be evaluated from two acquired digital holograms, first when the object is in a static state, and second in a time-averaged state. Figures 7.36 shows the zero-crossing phase extracted from the time-averaged phase and the static reference phase, for three amplitudes of the excitation; the phase φ_J (modulo 2π) can be visualized; it exhibits highly contrasted phase jumps located at the zero crossing of the J_0 function. The determination of the phase jumps of φ_J is a way to precisely determine the contour lines associated with the zero-crossing of the Bessel function. The zeros of J_0, noted here as ω_n, are related to the amplitude of the vibration and to the sensitivity vector of the recording setup according to (see Figure 5.2, θ: illuminating angle):

$$D_z(x,y) = \frac{\lambda}{2\pi}\frac{1}{1+\cos\theta}\omega_n(x,y) \qquad [7.29]$$

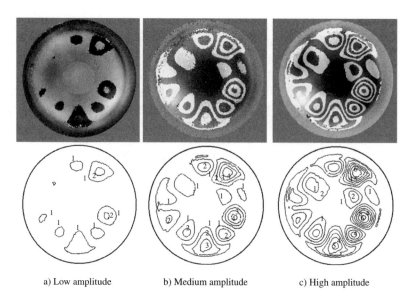

a) Low amplitude   b) Medium amplitude   c) High amplitude

Figure 7.36. *Zero-crossing phase, modulo* 2π*, at contour lines of the amplitude map*

In equation [7.29], the loudspeaker is considered to move in a pure out-of-plane displacement. Figures 7.36 shows the contour lines extracted from the zero-crossing phase maps using edge detection and image processing. These lines are related to the amplitude of the vibration.

n	ω_n (rad)	D_z (μm)
1	2.4048	0.131
2	5.5201	0.301
3	8.6537	0.472
4	11.7915	0.643
5	14.9309	0.814
6	18.0711	0.986

Table 7.1. *Altitude of vibration contour lines (*$\lambda = 0.6328$ *mm,* $\theta = 35°$*)*

Note that presence of the static phase ψ_r in the time-averaged phase is also a useful way of studying drifts of the system under sinusoidal excitation. Indeed, when vibration exhibits an offset drift which varies very slowly compared to the vibration period and the exposure time, then subtraction of time-averaged phases obtained at different instants allows its variation to be studied. Thus, this gives one possibility for the study of drifts, which is a feature offered by time-averaged digital Fresnel holography. Figure 7.37 shows the phase map of the drift obtained from time-averaged phases which are estimated from recordings every 2 min over a total lapse of time of 30 min. Some regions within, which, the drift is significant can be seen. This is due to a temperature change in the electrodes of the loudspeaker.

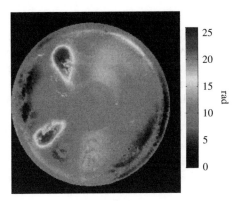

Figure 7.37. *Phase map of the drift over 30 min (for a color version of this figure, see www.iste.co.uk/picart/digiholog.zip)*

7.6. Tracking high-amplitude vibrations

7.6.1. *Introduction*

For the analysis of vibrations, we must distinguish between auto and forced oscillations. In the forced oscillation regime, the amplitude of vibrations can be controlled by the excitation source, whereas in the auto-oscillation regime the object imposes its own rule to the observer. So, the digital holographic setup must be configured according to the nature and the amplitude of the oscillation. In the time-averaging regime, one peculiarity of the setup is that the vibration is under a monochromatic excitation. This means that the maximum amplitude of oscillation to be measured can be controlled and chosen so that the fringes due to the Bessel modulation in reconstructed holograms are spatially resolved (Figures 7.35 and 7.36). This way of analyzing vibrations is quite simple and does not need a complicated setup although the experimental results are partial because of the disappearing of the vibration phase φ_0 in the reconstructed object [PIC 03b, PIC 05a]. Nevertheless, as a general rule, acoustic engineers are often confronted with auto oscillations which are multichromatic and have high amplitude with respect to the optical wavelength. This kind of vibration is generally not controlled since it is often initiated with nonlinear phenomena leading to an auto-oscillation phenomenon. The study of such oscillations needs a strategy more elaborate than that used for forced oscillations. Indeed, the oscillation must be finely temporally sampled with a temporal resolution allowing fringe resolution in the phase data, especially if the amplitude is high. The full movement of the object can then be reconstructed by adding all the partial results obtained with the temporal sampling. Note that greater the oscillation amplitude is, greater must be the number of recorded holograms.

An example of such vibrations is found in a single-reed woodwind musical instrument. The clarinet is typically such an instrument. Its reed is a small slice of natural cane or synthetic material put into vibration when the musician blows air into the instrument. The clarinet is usually considered as the association of a linear resonator, the pipe, and a nonlinear exciter, the reed, subject to the air flow from the mouth. The understanding of the physical mechanisms that lead to the production of sound in the clarinet needs an in-depth investigation of the reed oscillation under the auto-oscillation regime.

The experimental investigation of the clarinet reed behavior can be performed with pulsed digital holograms.

7.6.2. *Principle*

The case of auto oscillations for the clarinet reed corresponds to playing conditions, i.e. when the clarinet reed is in the auto-oscillation regime. In order to produce suitable oscillation conditions, the clarinet reed must be placed in an artificial mouth modeling that of a musician playing clarinet [PIC 10]. This artificial mouth is constituted mainly with an air-proof caisson and an artificial lip modeling the tight-lipped going of the musician. The schematic diagram of the artificial mouth is depicted in Figure 7.38. The artificial lip is made with a rubber membrane filled with water such that it has quite the same consistency as the real musician's lip. The mouth includes an optical window which allows illumination of the reed. To initiate auto-oscillation of the reed, flow is blown through the mouth. The over-pressure in the mouth is of the order of 60 hPa. It induces a flexure of the reed and introduces an air flow in the instrument. After a threshold pressure, the equilibrium position of the reed becomes unstable and the reed oscillates at a frequency inversely proportional to the effective length of the clarinet. The sound generated by this oscillation is periodic but multichromatic, and in this setup the fundamental frequency is about 162 Hz.

The peculiarity of the observed auto-oscillation regime is that the amplitude is imposed by the characteristics of the mouthpiece. This amplitude can vary from a few tenths of a millimeter to one millimeter. A pressure sensor made with piezo-resistive gages (as in a microphone) is placed in the mouthpiece of the clarinet, as indicated in Figure 7.38 (top view). This sensor measures the pressure fluctuations induced by the mechanical vibration of the reed. The pressure signal delivered by the mouth is of primary use in the optical setup described in Figure 7.39. The laser beam is issued from the double-frequency pulsed NdYAG laser with a pulse width of 20 ns and pulse energy about 7 mJ. The inspected zone is a rectangular region of about 9 mm × 5 mm and the recording distance is $z_0 = 315$ mm (illumination angle $\theta = 2°$).

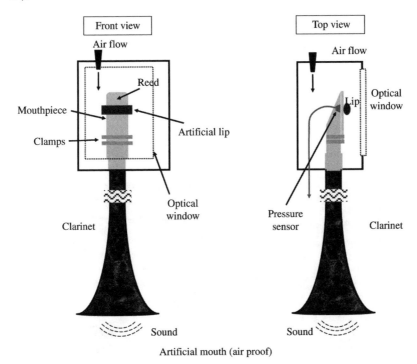

Figure 7.38. *Artificial mouth*

Figure 7.40 shows a photograph of the artificial mouth illuminated by the pulsed laser. Considering that the amplitude can reach several hundredths of microns, the study of the vibrating field must be performed according to a stroboscopic strategy. The laser fire is adjusted such that the movement is finely sampled giving resolved fringes in the field of view. Thus, the pressure sensor included in the beak gives a reference signal which is used to synchronize the laser fire and the digital recording. The reference instant is the zero-crossing of the pressure signal, and then the laser fire is temporally shifted relative to the pressure signal. The recording of 3,150 digital holograms was performed to fully reconstruct the movement of the reed during one oscillatory period.

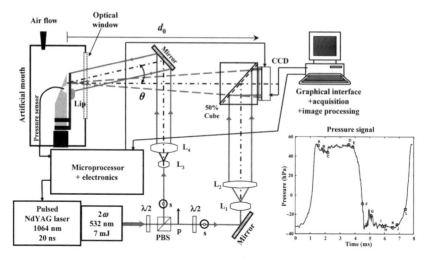

Figure 7.39. *Experimental setup*

Figure 7.40. *Photograph of the artificial mouth illuminated by the laser*

Figure 7.41 represents experimental results for the reed motion at six time intervals, indicated in the pressure signal shown in Figure 7.39 by points {A,B,C,D,E,F,G,H,I,J,K,L}. Each picture in Figure 7.41 is obtained by summing up deformation maps between each pair of considered points in Figure 7.39. The first part (A–E) corresponds to the time during which the reed channel is open: the total pressure on the reed is close to zero, the pressure in the mouth being almost equal to the pressure in the mouthpiece. Then, what is observed in this part is the quasi-free oscillation of the reed which is rapidly damped in the present example (points ABC). At the end of this part, the reed is at rest waiting for the depression wave which provokes the closing of the reed (points E–F approximately). The reed then violently closes the reed channel which provokes a bounce which is clearly visible both on the reed displacement (GHIJ) and on the pressure signal (Figure 7.38, around point G). The shock excites higher modes of the reed in a complex manner. Moreover, it seems that the local characteristics of the reed are more important than its global characteristics. As for the open episode, the motion of the reed stops rapidly and the reed waits for the overpressure wave which tends to open the reed channel again (J–A). Movies of the reed movement are visible in reference [PIC 07].

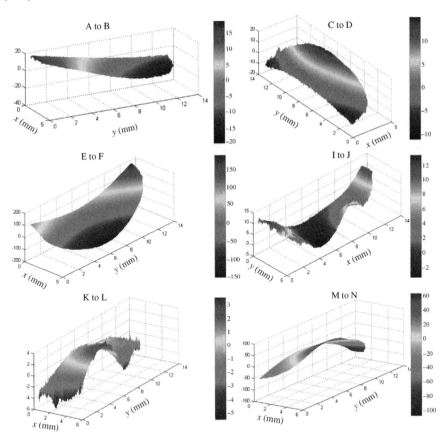

Figure 7.41. *Reed deformation for different parts of the movement (units: micrometers) (for a color version of this figure, see www.iste.co.uk/picart/digiholog.zip)*

7.7. Three-color digital holographic interferometry for fluid mechanics

7.7.1. *Principle*

The analysis of complex flows in the domain of fluid mechanics necessitates the development of metrological tools to provide access to finer and finer quantities of flow. Three-wavelength, "real-time", holographic interferometry techniques were developed in the past to analyze unsteady aerodynamic flows [DES 02]. The method requires the recording, with three wavelengths simultaneously, of a reference hologram and the placement of this in the optical setup after its development [SMI 94]. Panchromatic holographic plates are used in a transmission configuration in the absence of the phenomenon in the flow tube, and it is essential that the hologram has a diffraction efficiency of around 50% for the three wavelengths used [DES 09]. The use of three wavelengths lets us determine the location of the single, white, central fringe in the observation field, directly displaying the zero order of the difference in optical path lengths of the studied phenomenon. However, it is necessary to perfectly control the thickness of the gelatin of the hologram during chemical treatment (the development and bleaching phases). In the case of three-wavelength digital holographic interferometry, to overcome the difficulties associated with panchromatic holograms, a three-CCD detector records the interference pattern between three reference waves and three measurement waves which cross the flow tube in a round trip. Figure 7.42 illustrates the setup.

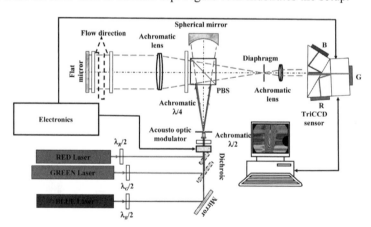

Figure 7.42. *Three-color digital holographic interferometer for the study of fluid flow (for a color version of this figure, see www.iste.co.uk/picart/digiholog.zip)*

The three lasers are combined using dichroic plates, and then separated into two paths using an achromatic polarization beam splitter cube to form the probe beam which crosses the flow tube in a round trip, and the reference beam which is reflected by the spherical mirror. The orientation of the spherical mirror allows the adjustment of the inclination angle of the reference waves to the detector to form the off-axis hologram. An optoacoustic modulator placed in front of the beam splitter cube allows the laser shot and the detector to be synchronized with the phenomenon to be studied, via the use of an electronic control unit. We may thus attain pulse durations of tens of nanoseconds without the use of pulsed lasers. Continuous 300 mW lasers are sufficient to carry out this kind of experiment.

Generally, we arrange matters so that the achromatic lenses form the image of the tube on the detector such that, during the reconstruction process, the angular spectrum may be used with a reconstruction distance of zero. In this case, the phase of the angular spectrum transfer function is uniform and equal to 1: we have a binary filter in the spectral plane.

Taking into account the illumination configuration, the optical phase of the reconstructed field, for the whole hologram recorded during the time Δt, is:

$$\psi_r(x, y) = \frac{4\pi}{\lambda} \frac{1}{\Delta t} \int_{t_1}^{t_1 + \Delta t} \int_0^e n(x, y, z, t) dz dt \qquad [7.30]$$

where e is the thickness of the tube and $n(x,y,z,t)$ is the refractive index at time t.

If we suppose that the first reference hologram is recorded without flow, with a refractive index equal to $n(x,y,z,t) = 1$ (air), and that the exposure time is sufficiently short that in the presence of flow, $n(x,y,z,t)$ is constant during Δt, and that the phenomenon is axisymmetric (along z), then the optical phase variation between these two holograms is given by:

$$\Delta\varphi = \frac{4\pi}{\lambda}(n-1)e \qquad [7.31]$$

In the case of non-axisymmetric flow, it is necessary to record from multiple perspectives and to proceed to a tomographic reconstruction [KRE 96]. The variation in refractive index generated by the flow depends on the density of the fluid according to the Gladstone–Dale relation:

$$(n-1) = K\rho_m \qquad [7.32]$$

In [7.32], K is the Gladstone–Dale constant, which depends on the refractivity of the medium, and ρ_m is the density of the traversed medium. This method therefore allows the measurement of density variations in the medium perturbed by the flow.

Calculation of the variation in optical phase for each wavelength allows the determination of a color image of the flow, and the visualization of the white fringe which determines, without ambiguity, the absolute position of the zero of the measurement.

As an illustration, Figure 7.43(a) shows a three-color hologram without flow in the tube, Figure 7.43(b) shows a hologram in the presence of flow, and Figure 7.43(c) is a magnification of the microfringes. We observe that the microfringes are deformed by the flow. Figure 7.43(d) shows the red spectral plane in which we observe the spectral spreading of the microfringes due to the flow [DES 08].

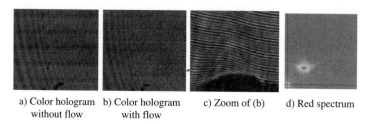

a) Color hologram   b) Color hologram   c) Zoom of (b)   d) Red spectrum
   without flow   with flow

Figure 7.43. *Illustration of the influence of the flow on the three-color hologram (for a color version of this figure, see www.iste.co.uk/picart/digiholog.zip)*

Figure 7.44 illustrates the determination of the white fringe in the case where the flow is produced by a candle flame. The reconstruction of the RGB image (Figure 7.44a) allows us to visualize the white fringe and identify the zero of the flow (Figure 7.44b). We can model the succession of color, precisely knowing the wavelengths, and we can compare the colors of the flow with the color reference table [DES 08].

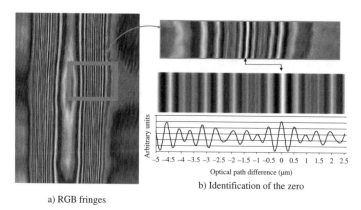

a) RGB fringes

b) Identification of the zero

Figure 7.44. *White fringe and determination of the absolute zero (for a color version of this figure, see www.iste.co.uk/picart/digiholog.zip)*

7.7.2. *Application to turbulent flows*

One example of application concerns a flow at Mach 0.45 around a cylinder. The configuration is axisymmetric. Figure 7.45 shows the phase difference maps extracted from the measurement. The flow propagates from the left to the right of the cylinder.

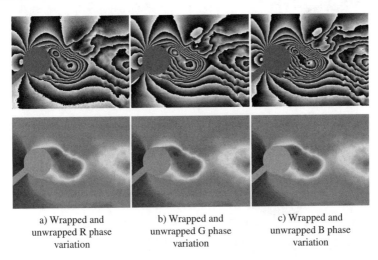

a) Wrapped and unwrapped R phase variation	b) Wrapped and unwrapped G phase variation	c) Wrapped and unwrapped B phase variation

Figure 7.45. *R, G, and B phase differences, and unwrapped phases (for a color version of this figure, see www.iste.co.uk/picart/digiholog.zip)*

Figure 7.46 shows the comparison of the RGB intensity maps obtained by analog (panchromatic) and digital holographic interferometry for Mach numbers very close to 0.45. We note that, even though the resolution of the panchromatic plates is much greater than that of the detector (~10000 mm^{-1} compared with ~200 mm^{-1}), the result obtained by the digital process is better than that obtained by the panchromatic process. The reason for this is that image in Figure 7.46(b) is obtained with a high-speed camera using plastic film, and it is necessary to rescan the images after recording to the film. The entire process therefore strongly degrades the final resolution, which is not higher than that given by three-color digital holography.

The density of the gas measured at the nose of the cylinder is particular, as it is equal to the stagnation density of the gas, regardless of the position of the vortex. This means that the color at this point must be constant and always white in each of the interferograms describing a vortex cycle. The color may therefore be compensated for, so as to impose $\delta = 0$ µm at this point, and we may then extract the density map from each image, and thus a map of the mean density during the flow. Figure 7.47 shows the obtained results [DES 11a]. Figure 7.47(a) shows the average

RGB fringes obtained during the flow cycle, and Figure 7.47(b) shows the average density measured during this cycle.

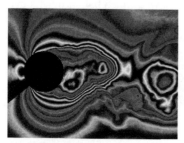

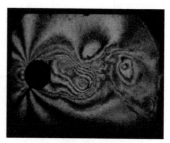

a) RGB digital holographic
fringes at Mach 0.45

b) RGB panchromatic
holographic fringes at Mach 0.45

Figure 7.46. *RGB fringes obtained by (a) digital and (b) analog holographic methods (image courtesy of Dr. J.M. Desse, ONERA, Lille, France (for a color version of this figure, see www.iste.co.uk/picart/digiholog.zip)*

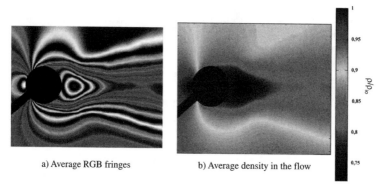

a) Average RGB fringes   b) Average density in the flow

Figure 7.47. *(a) Mean RGB fringes and (b) mean measured density (for a color version of this figure, see www.iste.co.uk/picart/digiholog.zip)*

7.8. Conclusion

This chapter has presented the methods of holographic interferometry for which the phase of the reconstructed field is the principal parameter. The exploitation of the phase gives versatility to digital holography: quantitative microscopy, phase contrast, profilometry, the measurement of displacement fields, vibrations, and of fluid mechanics. We have chosen to present a certain number of these methods which are based on the recording of multiple holograms or on time-averaging. Other methods exist in the literature, such as vibrometry [LEV 05, JOU 09]. For an exhaustive presentation of these holographic techniques and their domains of application, the reader is referred to the bibliography provided.

Appendix

Examples of Digital Hologram Reconstruction Programs

This appendix offers some programs for the calculation of diffraction and the reconstruction of digital holograms. These programs were written in the MATLAB language. This software allows scientific calculations to be carried out in a very straightforward way, considerably simplifying coding compared to other languages (such as VC++, VB, or DELPHI). The programs are organized into ".m" files. The programs have been validated in MATLAB 7.0. If a subsequent version is used, the reader will have to verify that the code is compatible.

The selected programs are the following:

– LIM1.m: diffraction calculation using the S-FFT algorithm;

– LIM2.m: diffraction calculation using the D-FFT algorithm;

– LIM3.m: theoretical simulation of a digital hologram;

– LIM4.m: reconstruction of a hologram using the S-FFT algorithm;

– LIM5.m: reconstruction of a hologram using the D-FFT algorithm;

A1.1. Diffraction calculation using the S-FFT algorithm

A1.1.1. *Code for the program: LIM1.m*

```
%------------------------LIM1------------------------
% Function: Diffraction calculation using the S-FFT algorithm
```

```
%
% Procedure: consider an image file as the amplitude distribution of
% the initial plane, then calculate the amplitude of the diffracted field,
% giving a wavelength and a diffraction distance.
%
% Variables:
% h : wavelength (mm);
% z0 : diffraction distance (mm);
% U0 : complex amplitude of the initial field;
% L0 : width of the initial field (mm);
% Uf : complex amplitude of the field in the observation plane;
% L : width of the observation plane (mm);
% In case of a rectangular image, it is padded with zeros to its larger dimension
%-------------------------------------------------------------
clear;close all;
chemin='C:\';
[nom,chemin]=uigetfile([chemin,'*.*'],['initial image'],100,100);
[XRGB,MAP]=imread([chemin,nom]);
X=XRGB(:,:,1); % conserve the first channel if the image is RGB
h=input('Wavelength (mm) : ');
L0=input('Maximum width of the initial plane L0 (mm) : ');
k=2*pi/h;
[M,N]=size(X);
K=max(M,N);
% Zeros-padding to get KxK image
Z1=zeros(K,(K-N)/2);
Z2=zeros((K-M)/2,N);
Xp=[Z1,[Z2;X;Z2],Z1];
zmin=L0^2/K/h;
disp(['Minimum distance to fullfill sampling theorem : ',num2str(zmin),' mm']);
```

```
z0=input(['Diffraction distance z0 (mm) (>',num2str(zmin),'mm) : ']);
U0=double(Xp);
figure(1),imagesc(Xp),colormap(gray);axis equal;axis tight;ylabel('pixels');
xlabel(['Width of the initial plane: ',num2str(L0),' mm']);
title('Amplitude of the initial field');
%---------------
n=1:K;m=1:K;
x=-L0/2+L0/K*(n-1);
y=-L0/2+L0/K*(m-1);
[xx,yy]=meshgrid(x,y);
Fresnel=exp(i*k/2/z0*(xx.^2+yy.^2));
f2=U0.*Fresnel;
Uf=fft2(f2,K,K);
Uf=fftshift(Uf);
L=h*abs(z0)*N/L0;
x=-L/2+L/K*(n-1);
y=-L/2+L/K*(m-1);
[xx,yy]=meshgrid(x,y);
phase=exp(i*k*z0)/(i*h*z0)*exp(i*k/2/z0*(xx.^2+yy.^2));
Uf=Uf.*phase;
%---------------
If=abs(Uf);% amplitude of the diffracted field
figure(2),imagesc(abs(Uf)),colormap(gray);axis equal;axis tight;ylabel('pixels');
xlabel(['Width of the observation plane: ',num2str(L),'x',num2str(L),' mm']);
title('Amplitude of the image diffracted by S-FFT');
```

A1.1.2. *Examples of diffraction calculations using LIM1.m*

The studied object is an image of $M \times N = 512 \times 512$ pixels that represents a section of the famous painting the "Mona Lisa" (see Figure A1.1(a)).

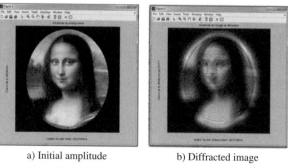

a) Initial amplitude   b) Diffracted image

$L0 = L = 20.2133$ mm, $N \times N = 512 \times 512$
$h = 532$ nm, $z0 = 1500$ mm

Figure A1.1. *Comparison between the initial and diffracted fields*

Considering the parameters of the program to be $h = 0.000532$ mm (wavelength), and $L0 = 20.2133$ mm (width of the initial plane), Figure A1.1(b) shows the distribution of the modulus of the diffracted field in the observation plane. The minimum distance is given by zmin $= L0^2/N/h = 1500$ mm; with a diffraction distance of $z0 = 1,500$ mm, the width of the observation plane L is equal to L0, satisfying relation [3.15]. The calculated field satisfies the sampling theorem. We note that after diffraction across a distance of 1,500 mm, the amplitude is strongly modified.

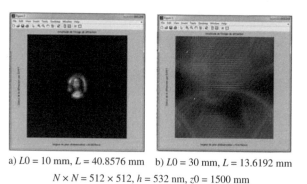

a) $L0 = 10$ mm, $L = 40.8576$ mm   b) $L0 = 30$ mm, $L = 13.6192$ mm

$N \times N = 512 \times 512$, $h = 532$ nm, $z0 = 1500$ mm

Figure A1.2. *Influence of L_0 on the diffraction calculation by S-FFT*

From the calculation of diffraction using S-FFT (see section 3.2.1), the physical width of the diffracted field varies with the wavelength, the diffraction distance and the number of samples. The numerical result must satisfy the sampling theorem. As an example, we consider $L0 = 10$ mm and $L0 = 30$ mm. Figures A1.2(a) and (b) show the respective results, calculated by LIM1.m. The result in Figure A1.2(a) satisfies the sampling condition. The width of the initial field is relatively small, and the width L calculated by L = h*z0*N/L0 is large (see section 3.2.1). In this case, the diffracted image is situated in a small zone at the center of the observation plane. This result is therefore not well optimized. In the case of Figure A1.2(b), the sampling condition is no longer satisfied. The width of the initial field is relatively large, and because of the phenomenon of spectral aliasing (see section 3.1.2), the result is incorrect and unusable.

The reader may exhaustively study the influence of the variation in the physical parameters on the obtained result using the program LIM1.m.

A1.2. Diffraction calculation by D-FFT

A1.2.1. *Code for the program: LIM2.m*

```
%------------------------LIM2-------------------------
% Function: Diffraction calculation using the D-FFT algorithm
% Procedure: consider an image file as the optical amplitude
% distribution of the initial plane, the calculate the amplitude of the
% diffracted field, giving a wavelength and a diffraction distance
%
% Variables :
% h : wavelength (mm);
% z0 : diffraction distance (mm);
% U0 : complex amplitude of the initial optical field;
% L0 : width of the initial optical field and observation plane (mm);
% In case of a rectangular image, it is padded with zeros to its larger dimension
%-------------------------------------------------------------
clear;close all;
chemin='C:\';
[nom,chemin]=uigetfile([chemin,'*.*'],['initial image'],100,100);
[XRGB,MAP]=imread([chemin,nom]);
X=XRGB(:,:,1);
```

```
h=input('Wavelength (mm) : ');
L0=input('Maximum width of the initial field L0 (mm) : ');
k=2*pi/h;
[M,N]=size(X);
X=double(X);
K=max(M,N);
% Zeros-padding to get KxK image
Z1=zeros(K,(K-N)/2);
Z2=zeros((K-M)/2,N);
Xp=[Z1,[Z2;X;Z2],Z1];
zmax=L0^2/K/h;
disp(['Maximum distance to fullfill sampling theorem : ',num2str(zmax),' mm']);
z0=input(['Diffraction distance z0 (mm) (<',num2str(zmax),'mm) : ']);
U0=Xp;
figure(1),imagesc(Xp),colormap(gray);ylabel('pixels');
axis equal;axis tight;
xlabel(['Width of the initial field =',num2str(L0),' mm']);title('Initial amplitude ');
%--------------Diffraction calculation by D-FFT
Uf=fft2(U0,K,K);
Uf=fftshift(Uf); % Spectrum of the initial field
fex=K/L0;fey=fex;% sampling of frequency plane
fx=[-fex/2:fex/K:fex/2-fex/K];
fy=[-fey/2:fey/K:fey/2-fey/K];
[FX,FY]=meshgrid(fx,fy);
G=exp(i*k*z0*sqrt(1-(h*FX).^2-(h*FY).^2)); % Angular spectrum transfer function
% Diffraction
result=Uf.*G;
Uf=ifft2(result,K,K);
%--------------End of D-FFT calculation
If=abs(Uf);
```

figure(2),imagesc(abs(Uf)),colormap(gray);ylabel('pixels');

axis equal;axis tight;

xlabel(['Diffraction distance = ',num2str(z0),' mm, largeur du plan= ',num2str(L0),'

mm']);title('Amplitude of field diffracted by D-FFT');

A1.2.2. *Examples of diffraction calculations using LIM2.m*

We again consider the "Mona Lisa" from Figure A1.1(a). With h = 0.532e-3 mm (wavelength), z0 = 1,500 mm (diffraction distance) and L0 = 20.2133 mm (width of the initial plane), Figure A1.3(a) shows the modulus of the amplitude of the diffracted field in the observation plane. From section 3.4.2, the width of the observation plane L is always equal to L0 and the calculated result satisfies the sampling theorem (see section 3.2.3).

If we now consider the width of the initial plane to be L0 = 10.10665 mm and keep the other parameters the same as in Figure A1.3(a), the obtained result is shown in Figure A1.3(b). In this case, the angular spectrum transfer function does not satisfy the sampling conditions. However, the spectrum of the image being very narrow and localized at the center of the spectrum, the result does not suffer from aliasing.

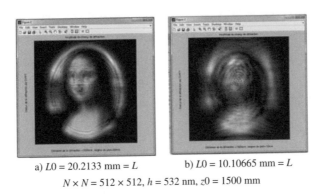

a) $L0 = 20.2133$ mm $= L$ b) $L0 = 10.10665$ mm $= L$

$N \times N = 512 \times 512$, $h = 532$ nm, $z0 = 1500$ mm

Figure A1.3. *Diffraction calculations using the D-FFT algorithm*

To solve a practical diffraction problem, we must therefore make a suitable choice between the S-FFT and D-FFT methods.

A1.3. Simulation of a digital hologram

A1.3.1. *Code for the program: LIM3.m*

```
%------------------------LIM3------------------------
% Function: simulate a hologram using an image whose width
% is less than a quarter of the initial plane.
% The simulated hologram will be saved with the name "Ih.tif".
%
% Procedure: (1) Read an image file
%            (2) Give the parameters asked for on the screen
% Variables :
%  h : wavelength (mm);
%  Ih : hologram;
%  L : width of the hologram (mm);
%  L0 : width of the diffracted object field (mm);
%  z0 : recording distance (mm);
% In case of a rectangular image, it is padded with zeros to its larger dimension
%------------------------------------------------------------
clear;close all;
chemin='C:\';
[nom,chemin]=uigetfile([chemin,'*.*'],['Choose an image file'],100,100);
[XRGB,MAP]=imread([chemin,nom]);
X=double(XRGB(:,:,1));% We recover the image of the red RGB
% band (channel 1)
[M,N]=size(X);
% Extended size to two times
K=2*max(N,M);
% Zeros-padding to get N×N image
```

```
Z1=zeros(K,(K-N)/2);
Z2=zeros((K-M)/2,N);
Obj=[Z1,[Z2;X;Z2],Z1];
% Parameters
h=input('Wavelength (mm) : ');
k=2*pi/h;
L=input('Maximum width of the object (mm) : ');
z0=input(['Recording distance z0 (mm) : ']);
pix=abs(z0)*h/L;
Lx=K*pix;
Ly=K*pix;
disp(['Pixel pitch to fullfill sampling conditions : ',num2str(pix),'mm']);
disp(['Width of the object field = ',num2str(Lx),'mm x ',num2str(Ly),'mm']);
% Object field
psi=2*pi*(rand(K,K)-0.5);% Random phase
Ao=Obj.*exp(i.*psi); % Complex field in the object plane
figure;imagesc(Obj);colormap(gray);
colormap(gray);ylabel('pixels');
axis equal;axis tight;
xlabel(['Width of the object field = ',num2str(Lx),'mm x ',num2str(Ly),'mm']);
title('Initial Object');
%--------------Calculation using S-FFT
% Complex factor in the integral
n=-K/2:K/2-1;m=-K/2:K/2-1;
x=n*pix;y=m*pix;
[xx,yy]=meshgrid(x,y);
Fresnel=exp(i*k/2/z0*(xx.^2+yy.^2));
```

```
f2=Ao.*Fresnel;
Uf=fft2(f2,K,K);% Zero padding at KxK
Uf=fftshift(Uf);
% Complex factor in front of the integral
% Pitch in sensor plane
ipix=h*abs(z0)/K/pix;
xi=n*ipix;
yi=m*ipix;
L0x=K*ipix;
L0y=K*ipix;
[xxi,yyi]=meshgrid(xi,yi);
phase=exp(i*k*z0)/(i*h*z0)*exp(i*k/2/z0*(xxi.^2+yyi.^2));
Uf=Uf.*phase;
%--------------End of S-FFT calculation
disp(['Width of the diffracted field = ',num2str(L0x),'mm x ',num2str(L0y),'mm']);
figure,imagesc(abs(Uf)),colormap(gray);ylabel('pixels');
axis equal;axis tight;
xlabel(['Width of the diffracted field = ',num2str(L0x),'mm x ',num2str(L0y),'mm']);
title('Diffracted field in the detector plane (modulus)');
% Reference wave
ur=Lx/8/h/z0; % Spatial frequencies
vr=ur;
Ar=max(max(abs(Uf)));% Amplitude of the reference wave
Ur=Ar*exp(2*i*pi*(ur*xx+vr*yy));% Reference wave
%--------------Calculation of the hologram
H=abs(Ur+Uf).^2;
% 8-bit digitization
Imax=max(max(H));
Ih=uint8(255*H/Imax);
```

nom='Ih.tif';

imwrite(Ih,nom);% Recording the hologram

disp(['Pixel pitch = ',num2str(ipix),' mm avec ',num2str(K),'X',num2str(K),' pixels']);

figure,imagesc(Ih),colormap(gray);ylabel('pixels');

xlabel(['Pixel pitch = ',num2str(ipix),' mm avec ',num2str(K),'X',num2str(K),'

pixels']);

title(['Digital hologram with the name : ',nom]);

A1.3.2. *Example of the calculation of a hologram with LIM3.m*

In this program, the object is an image file, and the diffraction is calculated using the S-FFT method. From Chapter 5 (see section 5.1.2), the width of the figure must be less than a quarter of the object plane so that the image reconstructed by S-FFT may be separated from the parasitic orders. The inclination of the reference wave is simulated so that the reconstructed image lies in the second quadrant of the reconstruction plane.

As an example, the image of the "Mona Lisa" is the object, and it is padded with zeros to form the object plane with $N \times N = 1,024 \times 1,024$ pixels (see Figure A1.4(a)). Letting the wavelength be h = 0.000532 mm, the pixel width of the hologram pix = 0.00465 mm and the recording distance z0 = 1,500 mm. The hologram of $1,024 \times 1,024$ pixels calculated by LIM3.m is displayed in Figure A1.4(b). This hologram may be reconstructed by the different methods described in Chapter 5.

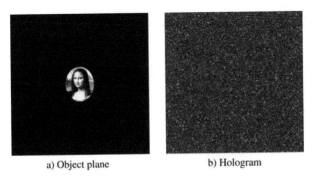

a) Object plane   b) Hologram

Figure A1.4. *Simulation of the digital hologram*

A1.4. Reconstruction of a hologram by S-FFT

A1.4.1. *Code for the program: LIM4.m*

```
%------------------------LIM4------------------------
% Function: the reconstruction of a hologram using the S-FFT
% algorithm
%
% Procedure: (1) Read an image file
%          (2) Give the parameters asked for on the screen
%
% Variables:
%  Ih : hologram;
%  h : wavelength (mm);
%  L : width of the hologram (mm);
%  L0 : width of the diffracted object field (mm);
%  z0 : reconstruction distance (mm);
%  U0 : complex amplitude in the reconstruction plane;
%------------------------------------------------------------
clear;clc;close all;
chemin='C:\';
[nom,chemin]=uigetfile([chemin,'*.*'],['Choose a hologram'],100,100);
I1=imread([chemin,nom]);
figure;imagesc(I1);colormap(gray);axis equal;axis tight;title('Digital hologram');
Ih1=double(I1)-mean2(double(I1));
[N1,N2]=size(Ih1);
N=min(N1,N2); % Restriction to NxN
Ih=Ih1(1:N,1:N);
pix=input('Pixel pitch (mm) : ');
h=input('Wavelength (mm) : ');
```

```
z0=input('Reconstruction distance z0 (+ for a real image, - for a virtual image)
(mm) : ');
L=pix*N;
%-----------------------Reconstruction by S-FFT
n=-N/2:N/2-1;
x=n*pix;y=x;
[xx,yy]=meshgrid(x,y);
k=2*pi/h;
Fresnel=exp(i*k/2/z0*(xx.^2+yy.^2));
f2=Ih.*Fresnel;
Uf=fft2(f2,N,N);
Uf=fftshift(Uf);
ipix=h*abs(z0)/N/pix;
x=n*ipix;
y=x;
[xx,yy]=meshgrid(x,y);
phase=exp(i*k*z0)/(i*h*z0)*exp(i*k/2/z0*(xx.^2+yy.^2));
U0=Uf.*phase;
%-----------------------End of S-FFT
If=abs(U0).^0.75;
Gmax=max(max(If));
Gmin=min(min(If));
L0=abs(h*z0*N/L);
disp(['Width of the reconstruction plane =',num2str(L0),' mm']);
figure;imagesc(If,[Gmin,Gmax]),colormap(gray);axis equal;axis
tight;ylabel('pixels');
xlabel(['Width of the reconstruction plane =',num2str(L),' mm']);
title('Image reconstructed by S-FFT');
p=input('Display parameter (>1) : ');
```

```
while isempty(p) == 0
  imagesc(If,[Gmin Gmax/p]),colormap(gray);axis equal;axis tight;ylabel('pixels');
  xlabel(['Width of the reconstruction plane =',num2str(L),' mm']);
  title(' Image reconstructed by S-FFT ');
  p=input('Display parameter (>1) (0=end) : ');
  if p==0,
    break
  end
end
```

A1.4.2. *Example of reconstruction with LIM4.m*

Using the hologram calculated previously by LIM3.m, Figure A1.5 shows the result of the reconstruction. We observe in Figure A1.5(a) a very intense central spot which corresponds to the Fresnel transform of the mean value of the hologram. It is therefore difficult to observe the virtual image. Capping the grayscale at 1/20 of the maximum reconstructed amplitude (consider p = 20 in the dialog box at the end of the program's execution), Figure A1.5(b) shows the reconstruction plane. We now clearly observe the image in the upper left part of the plane, the expanded zero order, and the twin image at the bottom right.

This program may be used for any experimental hologram.

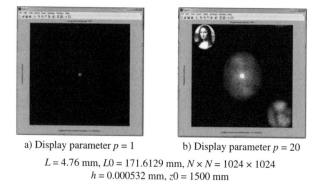

a) Display parameter $p = 1$ b) Display parameter $p = 20$

$L = 4.76$ mm, $L0 = 171.6129$ mm, $N \times N = 1024 \times 1024$
$h = 0.000532$ mm, $z0 = 1500$ mm

Figure A1.5. *Image reconstruction by S-FFT*

A1.5. Adjustable-magnification reconstruction by D-FFT

A1.5.1. *Code for the program: LIM5.m*

```
%------------------------LIM5-------------------------------
% Function: reconstruct an image with a adjustable magnification using
% the D-FFT algorithm.
% We may decrease the perturbation by the zero order by suppressing the
% mean value of the hologram.
%
% Procedure: (1) Read an image file
%                (2) Give the parameters asked for on the screen
%                (3) Calculate by D-FFT with adjustable magnification
%
% Variables:
%  Ih : hologram;
%  h : wavelength (mm);
%  L : width of the hologram (mm);
%  L0 : width of the diffracted object field (mm);
%  z0 : recording distance of the hologram (mm);
%  zi : reconstruction distance (mm);
%  zc : radius of the reconstruction wave's wavefront (mm);
%  U0 : complex amplitude in the reconstruction plane;
%  pix : pixel pitch of the hologram (mm);
%  ipix : pixel pitch in the reconstructed field using S-FFT;
%-------------------------------------------------------------
clear;close all;
chemin='C:\';
[nom,chemin]=uigetfile([chemin,'*.*'],['Choose the hologram to be
reconstructed'],100,100);
I1=imread([chemin,nom]);
```

```
Ih1=double(I1);
figure;imagesc(I1);colormap(gray);axis equal;axis tight;
title('Digital hologram');
pix=input('Pixel pitch (mm) : ');
h=input('Wavelength (mm) : ');
z0=input('Reconstruction distance z0 (+ for a real image, - for a virtual image) (mm)
: ');
k=2*pi/h;
[N1,N2]=size(Ih1);
N=min(N1,N2);
Ih=Ih1(1:N,1:N)-mean2(Ih1(1:N,1:N));% suppression of the mean value
L=pix*N;
disp(['Width of sensor : ',num2str(L),' mm']);
pg=input('Filter the 0 order of the hologram (1/0) ? ');
if pg==1,
    fm=filter2(fspecial('average',3),Ih); % see section 5.3.4.
    Ih=Ih-fm;
end
%--Reconstruction by S-FFT to find center/bandwidth of object
n=-N/2:N/2-1;
x=n*pix;y=x;
[xx,yy]=meshgrid(x,y);
Fresnel=exp(i*k/2/z0*(xx.^2+yy.^2));
f2=Ih.*Fresnel;
Uf=fft2(f2,N,N);
Uf=fftshift(Uf);
ipix=h*abs(z0)/N/pix;
xi=n*ipix;
yi=xi;
figure;imagesc(xi,yi,abs(Uf).^0.75);colormap(gray);axis equal;axis tight;
```

```
title('Click on the upper-left and lower-right corner of the object');
XY=ginput(2);
% Center and width of the object
xc=0.5*(XY(1,1)+XY(2,1));
yc=0.5*(XY(1,2)+XY(2,2));
DAX=abs(XY(1,1)-XY(2,1));
DAY=abs(XY(1,2)-XY(2,2));
%--Reconstruction with adjustable magnification
Gyi=min(L/DAX,L/DAY);
Gy=input(['Magnification factor for the reconstruction (ideal : ',num2str(Gyi),') : ']);
zi=-Gy*z0;
zc=1/(1/z0+1/zi);
% Spherical wave calculation
sphere=exp(i*k/2/zc*(xx.^2+yy.^2));
% Illumination of the hologram by a spherical wave
f=Ih.*sphere; % Spectrum of hologram multiplied by spherical wave
TFUf=fftshift(fft2(f,N,N));
% Fourier space
du=1/pix/N;dv=du;
fex=1/pix;fey=1/pix;
fx=[-fex/2:fex/N:fex/2-fex/N];
fy=[-fey/2:fey/N:fey/2-fey/N];
[FX,FY]=meshgrid(fx,fy);
% Spatial frequencies of reference wave
Ur=xc/h/abs(z0);
Vr=yc/h/abs(z0);
% Transfer function
Du=abs(Gy*DAX/h/zi);
Dv=abs(Gy*DAY/h/zi);
Gf=zeros(size(f));
```

```
Ir=find(abs(FX-Ur) < Du/2 & abs(FY-Vr) < Dv/2);
Gf(Ir)=exp(-i*k*zi*sqrt(1-(h*(FX(Ir)-Ur)).^2-(h*(FY(Ir)-Vr)).^2));
% Reconstruction
if sign(z0) == -1
  U0=fft2(TFUf.*Gf,N,N);
elseif sign(z0) == +1
  U0=ifft2(TFUf.*Gf,N,N);
end
Gmax=max(max(abs(U0).^0.75));
Gmin=min(min(abs(U0).^0.75));
figure;imagesc(abs(U0).^0.75,[Gmin,Gmax/1]);colormap(gray);
axis equal;axis tight;
xlabel(['Magnification : ',num2str(Gy)]);
title('Image reconstructed by D-FFT');
p=input('Display parameter (>1) : ');
while isempty(p) == 0
  imagesc(abs(U0).^0.75,[Gmin,Gmax/p]),colormap(gray);axis equal;axis
tight;ylabel('pixels');
  xlabel(['Width of the reconstruction plane =',num2str(L),' mm']);
  title(' Image reconstructed by D-FFT with adjustable magnification ');
  p=input('Display parameter (>1) (0=end) : ');
  if p==0,
    break
  end
end
```

A1.5.2. *Example of adjustable-magnification reconstruction with LIM5.m*

Using the hologram previously calculated by LIM3.m, Figure A1.6 shows the images reconstructed with magnifications of $G_y = 0.05$ and $G_y = 0.1$. During the execution of the program, we may diminish the perturbation by the zero order by deleting the hologram smoothed by a 3×3 moving average filter (see section 5.3.4). Furthermore, the display of the calculated image plane by S-FFT is considered as the reference determining the spectral position of the object wave and its bandwidth (see section 5.4.1.2). To clearly display the reconstructed image, as with LIM4.m, we may modify the value of the display parameter p.

a) Magnification $G_y = 0.05$ b) Magnification $G_y = 0.1$

($L = 4.76$ mm, $N \times N = 1024 \times 1024$, $h = 0.000532$ nm, $z0 = 1500$ mm)

Figure A1.6. *Reconstruction of the image using D-FFT*

This program may be used for any experimental hologram.

Note that LIM5.m supposes that the reference wave is a plane wave.

Bibliography

[AEB 99] AEBISCHER H.A., WALDNER S., "A simple and effective method for filtering speckle-interferometric phase fringe patterns", *Optics Communications*, vol. 162, pp. 205–210, 1999.

[ALF 06] ALFIERI D., COPPOLA G., DE NICOLA S., FERRARO P., FINIZIO A., PIERATTINI G., JAVIDI B., "Method for superposing reconstructed images from digital holograms of the same object recorded at different distance and wavelength", *Optics Communications*, vol. 260, pp. 113–116, 2006.

[ATL 07] ATLAN M., GROSS M., ABSIL E., "Accurate phase-shifting digital interferometry", *Optics Letters*, vol. 32, pp. 1456–1458, 2007.

[ATL 08] ATLAN M., GROSS M., DESBIOLLES P., ABSIL E., TESSIER G., COPPEY-MOISAN M., "Heterodyne holographic microscopy of gold particles", *Optics Letters*, vol. 33, pp. 500–502, 2008.

[BEL 00] BELLANGER M., AIGRAIN P.R., *Digital Processing of Signals: Theory and Practice*, 3rd Revised Edition, John Wiley & Sons Ltd., Chichester, 2000.

[BEL 09] BELLANGER C., BRIGNON A., COLINEAU J., HUIGNARD J.P, "Coherent fiber combining by digital holography", *Proceedings SPIE*, vol. 7195, pp. 71951N-, 2009.

[BER 04] BERTHELOT J.-M., FATMI L., "Statistical investigation of the fracture behaviour of inhomogeneous materials in tension and three-point bending", *Engineering Fracture Mechanics*, vol. 71, pp. 1535–1556, 2004.

[BIN 02] BINET R., COLINEAU J., LEHUREAU J.C., "Short-range synthetic aperture imaging at 633 nm by digital holography", *Applied Optics*, vol. 41, pp. 4775–4782, 2002.

[BJE 96] BJELKHAGEN H.I., JEONG T.H., VUKICEVIC D., "Color reflection holograms recorded in a panchromatic ultrahigh-resolution single-layer silver halide emulsion", *Journal of Imaging Science and Technology*, vol. 40, pp. 134–146, 1996.

[BOR 99] BORN M., WOLF E., *Principles of Optics*, 7th Edition, Cambridge University Press, 1999.

[BRA 56] BRACEWELL R.N., "Two-dimensionnal aerial smoothing in radio astronomy", *Australia Journal of Physics*, vol. 9, pp. 297–314, 1956.

[BRA 65] BRACEWELL, R.N., *The Fourier Transform and Its Application*, McGraw-Hill, New York, 1965.

[BRU 74] BRUNING J.H., HERRIOTT D.R., GALLAGHER J.E., ROSENFELD D.P., WHITE A.D., BRANGACCIO D.J., "Digital wavefront measuring interferometer for testing optical surfaces and lenses", *Applied Optics*, vol. 13, pp. 2693–2703, 1974.

[CAI 03] CAI L.Z., LIU Q., YANG X.L., "Phase-shift extraction and wave-front reconstruction in phase-shifting interferometry with arbitrary phase steps", *Optics Letters*, vol. 28, pp. 1808–1810, 2003.

[CAI 04] CAI L.Z., LIU Q., YANG X.L., "Generalized phase-shifting interferometry with arbitrary unknown phase steps for diffraction objects", *Optics Letters*, vol. 29, pp. 183–185, 2004.

[CHA 06a] CHARRIÈRE F., KÜHN J., COLOMB T., MONTFORT F., CUCHE E., EMERY Y., WEIBLE K., MARQUET P., DEPEURSINGE C., "Characterisation of micro lens by digital holographic microscopy", *Applied Optics*, vol. 45, pp. 829–835, 2006.

[CHA 06b] CHARRIÈRE F., MARIAN A., MONTFORT F., KUHN J., COLOMB T., CUCHE E., MARQUET P., DEPEURSINGE C., "Cell refractive index tomography by digital holographic microscopy", *Optics Letters*, vol. 31, pp. 178–180, 2006.

[CHA 07] CHALUT K., BROWN W., WAX A., "Quantitative phase microscopy with asynchronous digital holography", *Optics Express*, vol. 15, pp. 3047–3052, 2007.

[CHE 02] CHEN J.B, SU X.Y, *Optical Information Technique – Principles & Applications*, Higher Education Press, Beijing, 2002.

[CHE 07] CHEN G.L., LIN C.Y., KUO M.K., CHANG C.C., "Numerical suppression of zero-order image in digital holography", *Optics Express*, vol. 15, pp. 8851–8856, 2007.

[COE 02] COETMELLEC S., LEBRUN D., OSKUL C., "Application of the two-dimensional fractional-order Fourier transformation to particle field digital holography", *Journal of the Optical Society of America A*, vol. 19, pp. 1537–1546, 2002.

[COL 70] COLLINS S.A., "Laser-system diffraction integral written in terms of matrix optics", *Journal of the Optical Society of America*, vol. 60, p. 1168, 1970.

[COL 71] COLLIER R.J., BURCKHARDT C.B., LIN L.H., *Optical Holography*, Academic Press, New York, 1971.

[COL 06a] COLOMB T., MONTFORT F., KÜHN J., ASPERT N., CUCHE E., MARIAN A., CHARRIÈRE F., BOURQUIN S., MARQUET P., DEPEURSINGE C., "Numerical parametric lens for shifting, magnification and complete aberration compensation in digital holographic microscopy", *Journal of the Optical Society of America A*, vol. 23, pp. 3177–3190, 2006.

[COL 06b] COLOMB T., KÜHN J., CHARRIÈRE F., DEPEURSINGE C., MARQUET P., ASPERT N., "Total aberrations compensation in digital holographic microscopy with a reference conjugated hologram", *Optics Express*, vol. 14, pp. 4300–4306, 2006.

[COO 65] COOLEY J.W., TUKEY J.W., "An algorithm for the machine calculation of complex Fourier series", *Mathematics of Computation*, vol. 19, pp. 297–301, 1965.

[CRE 88] CREATH K., "Phase measurement interferometry techniques", in WOLF E. (ed.), *Progress in Optics*, North-Holland Publishing Company, vol. XXVI, pp. 349–393, 1988.

[CUC 99a] CUCHE E., MARQUET P., DEPEURSINGE C., "Simultaneous amplitude-contrast and quantitative phase-contrast microscopy by numerical reconstruction of Fresnel off-axis holograms", *Applied Optics*, vol. 38, pp. 6994–7001, 1999.

[CUC 99b] CUCHE E., BEVILACQUA F., DEPEURSINGE C., "Digital holography for quantitative phase contrast imaging", *Optics Letters*, vol. 24, pp. 291–293, 1999.

[CUC 00] CUCHE E., MARQUET P., DEPEURSINGE C., "Spatial filtering for zero-order and twin-image elimination in digital off-axis holography", *Applied Optics*, vol. 39, pp. 4070–7075, 2000.

[DAI 84] DAINTY J.C., *Laser Speckle and Related Phenomena*, Springer-Verlag, Berlin, 1984.

[DAN 75] DANCER A., FRANKE R., SMIGIELSKI P., ALBE F. FAGOT H, "Holographic interferometry applied to the investigation of tympanic membrane displacements in Guinea pigs ears subjected to acoustic impulses", *Journal of the Acoustical Society of America*, vol. 58, pp. 223–228, 1975.

[DEM 03a] DEMOLI N., VUKICEVIC D., TORZYNSKI M., "Dynamic digital holographic interferometry with three wavelengths", *Optics Express*, vol. 11, pp. 767–774, 2003.

[DEM 03b] DEMOLI N., MESTROVIC J., SOVIC I., "Subtraction digital holography", *Applied Optics*, vol. 42, pp. 798–804, 2003.

[DEN 06] DENIS L., FOURNIER C., FOURNEL T., DUCOTTET C., JEULIN D., "Direct extraction of the mean particle size from a digital hologram", *Applied Optics*, vol. 45, pp. 944–952, 2006.

[DEN 62] DENISYUK Y.N., "Manifestation of optical properties of an object in wave field of radiation in scatters", *Doklady Akademii nauk SSSR* , vol. 144, p. 1275, 1962.

[DEN 63] DENISYUK Y.N., "The reflexion of the optical properties of an object in the wave field of its scattered radiation", *Optika i Spektroskopiya*, vol. 15, pp. 522–532, 1963.

[DES 02] DESSE J.M., ALBE F., TRIBILLON J.L., "Real-time color holographic interferometry", *Applied Optics*, vol. 41, pp. 5326–5333, 2002.

[DES 06a] DESSE J.M., TRIBILLON J.L., "State of the art of color interferometry at ONERA", *Journal of Flow Visualization*, vol. 9, pp. 363–371, 2006.

[DES 06b] DESSE J.M., "Recent contribution in color interferometry and applications to high-speed flows", *Optics and Lasers in Engineering*, vol. 44, pp. 304–320, 2006.

[DES 08] DESSE J.M., PICART P., TANKAM P., "Digital three-color holographic interferometry for flow analysis", *Optics Express*, vol. 16, pp. 5471–5480, 2008.

[DES 09] DESSE J.M., TRIBILLON J.L., "Real-time three-color reflection holographic interferometer", *Applied Optics*, vol. 48, pp. 6870–6877, 2009.

[DES 11a] DESSE J.M., PICART P., TANKAM P., "Digital color holography applied to fluid mechanics and structure mechanics", *Optics and Lasers in Engineering*, vol. 50, pp. 18–28, 2011.

[DES 11b] DESSE J.M., PICART P., TANKAM P., "Sensor influence in digital 3λ holographic interferometry", *Measurement Science & Technology*, vol. 22, p. 064005, 2011.

[DOR 99] DORRIO B.V., FERNANDEZ J.L., "Phase evaluation methods in whole-field optical measurement techniques", *Measurement Science and Technology*, vol. 10, pp. 33–55, 1999.

[DOV 00] DOVAL A.F., "A systematic approach to TV holography", *Measurement Science and Technology*, vol. 11, pp. R1–R36, 2000.

[DUB 06] DUBOIS F., SCHOCKAERT C., CALLENS N., YOURASSOWSKY C., "Focus plane detection criteria in digital holography microscopy by amplitude analysis", *Optics Express*, vol. 14, pp. 5895–5908, 2006.

[FER 03] FERRARO P., DE NICOLA S., FINIZIO A., COPPOLA G., GRILLI S., MAGRO C., PIERATTINI G., "Compensation of the inherent wave front curvature in digital holographic coherent microscopy for quantitative phase-contrast imaging", *Applied Optics*, vol. 42, pp. 1938–1946, 2003.

[FER 04] FERRARO P., DE NICOLA S., COPPOLA G., FINIZIO A., ALFIERI D., PIERATTINI G., "Controlling image size as a function of distance and wavelength in Fresnel-transform reconstruction of digital holograms", *Optics Letters*, vol. 29, pp. 854–856, 2004.

[FER 05] FERRARO P., GRILLI S., ALFIERI D., DE NICOLA S., FINIZIO A., PIERATTINI G., JAVIDI B., COPPOLA G., STRIANO V., "Extended focused image in microscopy by digital Holography", *Optics Express*, vol. 13, pp. 6738–6749, 2005.

[FER 06] FERRARO P., ALFERI D., DE NICOLA S., DE PETROCELLIS L., FINIZIO A., PIERATTINI G., "Quantitative phase-contrast microscopy by a lateral shear approach to digital holographic image reconstruction", *Optics Letters*, vol. 31, pp. 1405–1407, 2006.

[FRA 74] FRANÇON M., *Holography*, Academic Press Inc., 1974.

[GAB 48] GABOR D., "A new microscopic principle", *Nature*, vol. 161, pp. 777–778, 1948.

[GAB 49] GABOR. D., "Microscopy by reconstructed wavefronts", *Proceedings of the Royal Society*, vol. A1947, p. 454, 1949.

[GAB 51] GABOR. D., "Microscopy by reconstructed wavefronts II", *Proceedings of the Physical Society*, vol. B64, p. 449, 1951.

[GAD 80] GADSHTEYN S., RYZHIK I.M., *Table of Integrals, Series, and Products*, Academic Press, New York, 1980.

[GAR 06a] GARCIA-SUCERQUIA J., XU W., JERICHO M.H., KREUZER H.J., "Immersion digital in-line holographic microscopy", *Optics Letters*, vol. 31, pp. 1211–1213, 2006.

[GAR 06b] GARCIA-SUCERQUIA J., XU W., JERICHO S.K., KLAGES P., JERICHO M.H., KREUZER H.J., "Digital in-line holographic microscopy", *Applied Optics*, vol. 45, pp. 836–850, 2006.

[GEN 00] GENTET Y., GENTET P., "Ultimate" emulsion and its applications: a laboratory-made silver halide emulsion of optimized quality for monochromatic pulsed and full color holography", *Proceedings SPIE*, vol. 4149, pp. 56–62, 2000.

[GEN 08] GENTET Y., http://www.ultimate-holography.com, 2008.

[GEO 03] GEORGES M., THIZY C., SCAUFLAIRE W., RYHON S., PAULIAT G., LEMAIRE P., ROOSEN G., "Dynamic holographic interferometry with photorefractive crystals: review of applications and advanced techniques", *Proceedings SPIE*, vol. 4933, pp. 250–255, 2003.

[GER 75] GERRAD A., BURCH J.M., *Introduction to Matrix Methods in Optics*, John Wiley & Sons, London, 1975.

[GHI 98] GHIGLIA D.C., Pritt M.D., *Two-dimensional Phase Unwrapping: Theory, Algorithms and Software*, Wiley, New York, 1998.

[GOO 67] GOODMAN J.W., LAWRENCE R.W., "Digital image formation from electronically detected holograms", *Applied Physics Letters*, vol. 11, pp. 77–79, 1967.

[GOO 72] GOODMAN J.W., *Introduction à l'optique de Fourier et à l'holographie*, Traduction Française par Christian Durou et José-Philippe Perez, Masson, Paris, 1972.

[GOO 85] GOODMAN J.W., *Statistical Optics*, Wiley, New York, 1985.

[GOO 05] GOODMAN J.W., *Introduction to Fourier Optics*, 3rd Edition, Roberts & Company Publishers, Greenwood Village, 2005.

[GOO 07] GOODMAN J.W., *Speckle Phenomena in Optics*, Ben Roberts and Co, Swansea, 2007.

[GRE 84] GREIVENKAMP J.E., "Generalized data reduction for heterodyne interferometry", *Optical Engineering*, vol. 23, pp. 350–352, 1984.

[GRO 07] GROSS, M., ATLAN M., "Digital holography with ultimate sensitivity", *Optics Letters*, vol. 32, pp. 909–911, 2007.

[GRO 08] GROSS M., ATLAN M., ABSIL E., "Noise and aliases in off-axis and phase-shifting holography", *Applied Optics*, vol. 47, pp. 1757–1766, 2008.

[HAR 02] HARIHARAN P., *Basics of Holography*, Cambridge University Press, New York, 2002.

[HAR 06] HARIHARAN P., *Basics of Interferomerty*, Academic Press, New York, 2006.

[HIN 02] HINSCH K.D., "Holographic particle image velocimetry", *Measurement Science & Technology*, vol. 13, pp. R61–R72, 2002.

[HUA 71] HUANG T.S., "Digital holography", *Proceedings of the IEEE*, vol. 159, pp. 1335–1346, 1971.

[HUB 91] HUBEL P.M., SOLYMAR L., "Color-refection holography – theory and experiment", *Applied Optics*, vol. 30, pp. 4190–4203, 1991.

[JAC 01] JACQUOT M., SANDOZ P., TRIBILLON G., "High resolution digital holography", *Optics Communications*, vol. 190, pp. 87–94, 2001.

[JAV 00] JAVIDI B., TAJAHUERCE E., "Three-dimensional object recognition by use of digital holography", *Optics Letters*, vol. 25, pp. 610–612, 2000.

[JAV 05] JAVIDI B., FERRARO P., HONG S., DE NICOLA S., FINIZIO A., ALFIERI D., PIERATTINI G., "Three-dimensional image fusion by use of multi-wavelength digital holography", *Optics Letters*, vol. 30, pp. 144–146, 2005.

[JOH 00] JOHNSON M., GUDMUNDSON P., "Broad-band transient recording and characterization of acoustic emission events in composite laminates", *Composites Science and Technology*, vol. 60, pp. 2803–2818, 2000.

[JON 89] JONES R., WYKES C., *Holographic and Speckle Interferometry*, Cambridge University Press, New York, 1989.

[JOU 09] JOUD F., LALOE F., ATLAN M., HARE J., GROSS M., "Imaging a vibrating object by sideband digital holography", *Optics Express*, vol. 17, pp. 2774–2779, 2009.

[KAN 04] KANDULLA J., KEMPER K., KNOCHE S., VON BALLY G., "Two-wavelength method for endoscopic shape measurement by spatial phase-shifting speckle-interferometry", *Applied Optics*, vol. 43, pp. 5429–5437, 2004.

[KAN 09] KANKA M., RIESENBERG R, KREUZER H.J., "Reconstruction of high-resolution holographic microscopic images", *Optics Letters*, vol. 34, pp. 1162–1164, 2009.

[KAR 11] KARRAY M., GARGOURI M., POILANE C., PICART P., "Étude du comportement mécanique de matériaux composites stratifiés par l'holographie numérique trichromatique", *Méthodes et Techniques Optiques pour l'Industrie*, Lille, France, 22–25 November 2011.

[KEA 02] KEATING M.P., *Geometric, Physical, and Visual Optics,* 2nd Revised edition, Butterworth-Heinemann Ltd., Boston, 2002.

[KHM 08] KHMALADZE A., MARTÍNEZ A.R., KIM M., CASTAÑEDA R., BLANDÓN A., "Simultaneous dual wavelength reflection digital holography applied to the study of the porous coal samples", *Applied Optics*, vol. 47, pp. 3203–3210, 2008.

[KOU 07] KOU S.S., SHEPPARD C.J., "Imaging in digital holographic microscopy", *Optics Express*, vol. 15, pp. 13640–13648, 2007.

[KRE 96] KREIS TH., *Holographic Interferometry – Principles and Methods*, Akademie Verlag Gmbh, Berlin, 1996.

[KRE 97a] KREIS TH., ADAMS M., JÜPTNER W., "Methods of digital holography: a comparison", *Proceedings SPIE*, vol. 3098, pp. 224–233, 1997.

[KRE 97b] KREIS TH., JÜPTNER W., "Suppression of the dc term in digital holography", *Optical Engineering*, vol. 36, pp. 2357–2360, 1997.

[KRE 02a] KREIS TH., "Frequency analysis of digital holography", *Optical Engineering*, vol. 41, pp. 771–778, 2002.

[KRE 02b] KREIS TH., "Frequency analysis of digital holography with reconstruction by convolution", *Optical Engineering*, vol. 41, pp. 1829–1839, 2002.

[KRE 04] KREIS TH., *Handbook of Holographic Interferometry Optical and Digital Methods*, Wiley-VCH, Weinheim, 2004.

[KRO 72] KRONROD M.A., MERZLYAKOV N.S., YAROSLAVSKII L.P., "Reconstruction of a hologram with a computer", *Soviet Physics Technical Physics*, vol. 17, pp. 333–334, 1972.

[KUH 07] KUHN J., COLOMB T., MONTFORT F., CHARRIERE F., EMERY Y., CUCHE E., P., MARQUET, DEPEURSINGE C., "Real-time dual-wavelength digital holographic microscopy with a single hologram acquisition", *Optics Express*, vol. 15, pp. 7231–7242, 2007.

[KUM 09] KUMAR U.P., BHADURI B., KOTHIYAL M.P., MOHAN N.K., "Two-wavelength microinterferometry for 3-D surface profiling", *Optics and Lasers in Engineering*, vol. 47, pp. 223–229, 2009.

[LAU 10] LAUTERBORN W., KURZ TH., *Coherent Optics: Fundamentals and Applications*, Springer-Verlag, Berlin, 2010.

[LEC 00] LE CLERC F., COLLOT L., GROSS M., "Numerical heterodyne holography with two-dimensional photodetector arrays", *Optics Letters*, vol. 25, pp. 716–718, 2000.

[LEI 61] LEITH E., UPATNIEKS J., "New technique in wavefront reconstruction", *Journal of the Optical Society of America*, vol. 51, pp. 1469, 1961.

[LEI 62] LEITH E., UPATNIEKS J., "Reconstructed wavefronts and communication theory", *Journal of the Optical Society of America*, vol. 52, pp. 1123–1130, 1962.

[LEV 05] LEVAL J., PICART P., BOILEAU J.-P., PASCAL J.C., "Full field vibrometry with digital Fresnel holography", *Applied Optics*, vol. 44, pp. 5763–5771, 2005.

[LI 00] LI J.C., XIONG B., ZHONG L., LU X., "Inverse calculation of diffraction and its application to the real-time holographic interferometry", *Proceedings SPIE*, vol. 4659, pp. 284–290, 2000.

[LI 02a] LI J.C., *Calcul de la diffraction du laser et des effets thermiques*, Science Press, Beijing, 2002.

[LI 02b] LI J.C., FAN Z., FU Y., "The FFT calculation for Fresnel diffraction and energy conservation criterion of sampling quality", *Proceedings SPIE*, vol. 4915, pp. 180–186, 2002.

[LI 07a] LI J.C., LI C., DELMAS C., "Calculation of diffraction patterns in spatial surface", *Journal of the Optical Society of America*, vol. 24, pp. 1950–1954, 2007.

[LI 07b] LI J.C., PENG Z., FU Y., "Diffraction transfer function and its calculation of classic diffraction formula", *Optics Communications*, vol. 280, pp. 243–248, 2007.

[LI 07c] LI J.C., PENG Z., "The S-FFT calculation of Collins formula and its application in digital holography", *Eur. Phys. J. D*, vol. 45, pp. 325–330, 2007.

[LI 08a] LI J.C., FAN Z., PENG Z., "Application research on digital holography zoom system", *Acta Photonica Sinica*, vol. 37, pp. 1420–1424, 2008.

[LI 08b] LI J.C., LI C., "Algorithm study of Collins formula and inverse Collins formula", *Applied Optics*, vol. 47, pp. A97–A102, 2008.

[LI 08c] LI J.C., GUO R.X., FAN Z.B., "A study on the digital real-time holography of non-planar reference wave", *Acta Photonica Sinica*, vol. 37, pp. 1156–1160, 2008.

[LI 09a] LI J.C., XIONG B., *Information Optics Theory and Computation*, Science Press, Pékin, 2009.

[LI 09b] LI J.C., TANKAM P., PENG Z., PICART P., "Digital holographic reconstruction of large objects using a convolution approach and adjustable magnification", *Optics Letters*, vol. 34, pp. 572–574, 2009.

[LI 09c] LI J.C., ZHANG Y.P., XU W., "High quality digital holographic wave-front reconstruction system", *Acta Physica Sinica*, vol. 58, pp. 5385–5391, 2009.

[LI 09d] LI J.C., "FFT computation of angular spectrum diffraction formula and its application in wavefront reconstruction of digital holography", *Acta Optica Sinica*, vol. 29, pp. 1163–1167, 2009.

[LI 10a] LI J.C., WU Y.M., LI Y., "Common diffraction integral calculation based on a Fast Fourier Transform algorithm", *Advances in Imaging and Electron Physics*, vol. 164, pp. 257–302, 2010.

[LI 10b] LI J.C., SONG Q., TANKAM P, PICART P., "Eliminating zero-order diffraction in the digital holography wavefront reconstruction with adjustable magnification", *Proceedings SPIE*, vol. 7848, pp. 78481Y-, 2010.

[LI 10c] LI J.C., PENG Z., TANKAM P., PICART P., "An optical system of scattered light digital color holography and its wave front reconstruction algorithm", *Acta Physica Sinica*, vol. 59, pp. 4646–4655, 2010.

[LI 10d] LI J.C., FAN Z.B., "Algorithm of the non interpolation wave front reconstruction of the color digital holography", *Acta Physica Sinica*, vol. 59, pp. 2457–2461, 2010.

[LI 11a] LI J.C., YUAN C., TANKAM P., PICART P., "The calculation research of classical diffraction formulas in convolution form", *Optics Communications*, vol. 284, pp. 3202–3206, 2011.

[LI 11b] LI J.C., PENG Z., TANKAM P., SONG Q., PICART P., "Digital holographic reconstruction of local object field using an adjustable magnification", *Journal of the Optical Society of America A*, vol. 28, pp. 1291–1296, 2011.

[LI 11c] LI J.C., PENG Z., FU Y.C., "Research of digital holographic object wave field reconstruction in image and object space", *Chinese Physics Letters*, vol. 28, p. 064201, 2011.

[LIE 03] LIEBLING M, BLU T., UNSER M., "Fresnelets: New multiresolution wavelet bases for digital holography", *IEEE Transactions on Image Processing*, vol. 12, pp. 29–43, 2003.

[LIE 04a] LIEBLING M., On Fresnelets, interferences fringes, and digital holography, PhD Thesis, No. 2977, Ecole Polytechnique Fédérale de Lausanne, Switzerland, 2004.

[LIE 04b] LIEBLING M, BLU T., UNSER M., "Complex-wave retrieval from a single off-axis hologram", *JOSA A*, vol. 21, pp. 367–377, 2004.

[LIG 60] LIGHTHILL, M.J., *Introduction to Fourier Analysis and Generalized Functions*, Cambridge University Press, New York, 1960.

[LIL 03] LILLIU G., VAN MIER J.G.M., "3D lattice type fracture model for concrete", *Engineering Fracture Mechanics*, vol. 70, pp. 927–941, 2003.

[LIN 59] LINDEN D.A., "Discussion of sampling theorems", *Proceedings IRE*, vol. 47, p. 1219, 1959.

[LIN 88] LIN Q., LU X., WANG S., "ABCD law for non-symmetric optical systems", *Acta Optica Sinica*, vol. 8, pp. 658–662, 1988.

[LIU 02] LIU C., LI Y.Z., CHENG X.T., LIU Z.G., BO F., ZHU J.Q., "Elimination of zero-order diffraction in digital holography", *Optical Engineering*, vol. 41, pp. 2434–2437, 2002.

[LIU 09] LIU J., SONG X., HAN R., WANG H., "Autofocus method in digital holographic microscopy", *Proceedings SPIE*, vol. 7283, p. 72833Q-6, 2009.

[LOU 10] LOU Y., LI J.C., ZHANG Y., GUI J., LI C., FAN Z., "Optimization research for digital hologram recording system of big objects". *Proceedings SPIE*, vol. 7600, p. 76001Q, 2010.

[LYN 11] LYNCÉE TEC, http://www.lynceetec.com/.

[LYO 04] LYONS R.G., *Understanding Digital Signal Processing*, Prentice Hall, 2004.

[MAL 04] MALEK M., ALLANO D., COËTMELLEC S., LEBRUN D., "Digital in-line holography: influence of the shadow density on particle field extraction", *Optics Express*, vol. 12, pp. 2270–2279, 2004.

[MAN 05] MANN C., YU L., CHUN-MIN L., KIM M.Y., "High-resolution quantitative phase-contrast microscopy by digital holography", *Optics Express*, vol. 13, pp. 8693–8698, 2005.

[MAN 08] MANN C.J., BINGHAM P.R., PAQUIT V.C., TOBIN K.W., "Quantitative phase imaging by three wavelength digital holography", *Optics Express*, vol. 16, pp. 9753–9764, 2008.

[MAR 96] MARVEN C., EWERS G., *A Simple Approach to Digital Signal Processing*, John Wiley & Sons, Chichester, 1996.

[MAR 05] MARQUET P., RAPPAZ B., MAGISTRETTI P., CUCHE E., EMERY Y., COLOMB T., DEPEURSINGE C., "Digital holographic microscopy: a noninvasive contrast imaging technique allowing quantitative visualization of living cells with sub-wavelength axial accuracy", *Optics Letters*, vol. 30, pp. 468–470, 2005.

[MAS 02] MASSIG J.H., "Digital off-axis holography with a synthetic aperture", *Optics Letters*, vol. 27, pp. 2179–2181, 2002.

[MAS 03] MAS D., PEREZ J., HERNANDEZ C., VAZQUEZ C., MIRET J.J., ILLUECA C., "Fast numerical calculation of Fresnel patterns in convergent systems", *Optics Communications*, vol. 227, pp. 245–258, 2003.

[MAS 99] MAS D., GARCIA J., FERREIRA C., BERNARDO L.M., MARINHO F., "Fast algorithms for free-space diffraction patterns calculation", *Optics Communications*, vol. 164, pp. 233–245, 1999.

[MAY 96] MAY M., CAZABAT, A.M., *Optique*, Dunod, Paris, 1996.

[MEI 96] MEIWEN Y., *Optical Holography and its Applications*, Beijing Institute of Technology Press, Pékin, 1996.

[NIC 06] NICOLAS F., COETMELLEC S., BRUNEL M., LEBRUN D., "Digital in-line holography with a sub-picosecond laser beam", *Optics Communication*, vol. 268, pp. 27–33, 2006.

[NIC 07] NICOLAS F., COETMELLEC S., BRUNEL M., LEBRUN D., "Suppression of the Moiré effect in sub-picosecond digital in-line holography", *Optics Express*, vol. 15, pp. 887–895, 2007.

[ONU 92] ONURAL L., OZGEN M.T., "Extraction of three-dimensional object-location Information directly from in-line holograms using Wigner analysis", *Journal of the Optical Society of America A*, vol. 9, pp. 252–260, 1992.

[ONU 93] ONURAL L., "Diffraction from a wavelet point of view", *Optics Letters*, vol. 18, pp. 846–848, 1993.

[OPP 89] OPPENHEIM A.V., SCHAFER R.W., *Discrete-time Signal Processing*, Pearson Education, 1989.

[OPT 11] OPTRION, Optics and Metrology, http://www.optrion-tech.com/intro.html.

[OST 02] OSTEN W., BAUMBACH T., JUPTNER W., "Comparative digital holography", *Optics Letters*, vol. 27, pp. 1764–1766, 2002.

[PAU 09] PAURISSE M., HANNA M., DRUON F., GEORGES P., BELLANGER C, BRIGNON A., HUIGNARD J.P., "Phase and amplitude control of a multimode LMA fiber beam by use of digital holography", *Optics Express*, vol. 17, pp. 13000–13008, 2009.

[PAV 09] PAVILLON N., SEELAMANTULA C.S., KÜHN J., UNSER M., DEPEURSINGE C., "Suppression of the zero-order in off-axis digital holography through nonlinear filtering", *Applied Optics*, vol. 48, pp. H186–H195, 2009.

[PAV 10] PAVILLON N., ARFIRE C., BERGOËND I., DEPEURSINGE C., "Iterative method for zero-order suppression in off-axis digital holography", *Optics Express*, vol. 18, pp. 15318–15331, 2010.

[PAV 11] PAVILLON N., Cellular dynamics and three-dimensional refractive index distribution studied with quantitative phase imaging, PhD Thesis, EPFL, 2011.

[PED 95] PEDRINI G., TIZIANI H.J., "Digital double pulse holographic interferometry using Fresnel and image plane holograms", *Measurement*, vol. 18, pp. 251–260, 1995.

[PED 02] PEDRINI G., TIZIANI H.J., "Short-coherence digital microscopy by use of a lens less holographic imaging system", *Applied Optics*, vol. 41, pp. 4489–4496, 2002.

[PET 62] PETERSON D.P., MIDDLEDON D., "Sampling and reconstruction of wave-number-limited functions in N-dimensional Euclidean spaces", *Information and Control*, vol. 5, pp. 279–283, 1962.

[PIC 03a] PICART P., MOISSON E., MOUNIER D., "Twin sensitivity measurement by spatial multiplexing of digitally recorded holograms", *Applied Optics*, vol. 42, pp. 1947–1957, 2003.

[PIC 03b] PICART P., LEVAL J., MOUNIER D., GOUGEON S., "Time-averaged digital holography", *Optics Letters*, vol. 28, pp. 1900–1902, 2003.

[PIC 04] PICART P., DIOUF B., BERTHELOT J.-M., "Investigation of fracture mechanisms in resin concrete using spatially multiplexed digital Fresnel holograms", *Optical Engineering*, vol. 43, pp. 1169–1176, 2004.

[PIC 05a] PICART P., LEVAL J., MOUNIER D., GOUGEON S., "Some opportunities for vibration analysis with time averaging in digital Fresnel holography", *Applied Optics*, vol. 44, pp. 337–343, 2005.

[PIC 05b] PICART P., LEVAL J., GRILL M., BOILEAU J.P., PASCAL J.C., BRETEAU J.M., GAUTIER B., GILLET S., "2D full field vibration analysis with multiplexed digital holograms", *Optics Express*, vol. 13, pp. 8882–8892, 2005.

[PIC 06] PICART P., LEVAL J., BOILEAU J.P., PASCAL J.-C., DALMONT J.-P., "Use of digital wave front reconstruction for vibration analysis", *Proceedings SPIE*, vol. 6341, pp. 634113.1–634113.6, 2006.

[PIC 07] PICART P., LEVAL J., PIQUET F., BOILEAU J.P., GUIMEZANES T., DALMONT J.P., "Tracking high amplitude auto-oscillations with digital Fresnel holograms" *Optics Express*, vol. 15, pp. 8263–8274, 2007.

[PIC 08a] PICART P., LEVAL J., "General theoretical formulation of image formation in digital Fresnel holography", *Journal of the Optical Society of America A*, vol. 25, pp. 1744–1761, 2008.

[PIC 08b] PICART P., MOUNIER D., DESSE J.M., "High resolution digital two-color holographic metrology", *Optics Letters*, vol. 33, pp. 276–278, 2008.

[PIC 09] PICART P., TANKAM P., MOUNIER D., PENG Z., LI J.C., "Spatial bandwidth extended reconstruction for digital color Fresnel holograms", *Optics Express*, vol. 17, pp. 9145–9156, 2009.

[PIC 10] PICART P., LEVAL J., PIQUET F., BOILEAU J.-P., GUIMEZANES TH., DALMONT J.-P., "Study of the mechanical behavior of a clarinet reed under forced and auto-oscillations with digital Fresnel holography", *Strain*, vol. 46, pp. 89–100, 2010.

[POW 65] POWELL R.L., STETSON K.A., "Interferometric analysis by wavefront reconstruction", *Journal of the Optical Society of America*, vol. 12, pp. 1593–1598, 1965.

[PRO 96] PROAKIS J.G., MANOLAKIS D.G., *Digital Signal Processing: Principles, Algorithms and Applications*, Prentice Hall, Upper Saddle River, 1996.

[QIA 01] QIAN K.-M., XU B.Q., WU X.P., "Phase measurement methods in optical interferometry", *Journal of Experimental Mechanics*, vol. 16, pp. 239–245, 2001.

[RAM 07] RAMIREZ J., GARCIA-SUCERQUIA J., "Digital off-axis holography without zero-order diffraction via phase manipulation", *Optics Communications*, vol. 277, pp. 259–263, 2007.

[RAS 94] RASTOGI P.K., *Holographic Interferometry – Principles and Methods*, Springer-Verlag, Berlin, 1994.

[SAU 06] SAUCEDO A., MENDOZA SANTOYO F., DE LA TORRE-IBARRA M., PEDRINI G., OSTEN W., "Endoscopic pulsed digital holography for 3D measurements", *Optics Express*, vol. 14, pp. 1468–1475, 2006.

[SCH 94] SCHNARS U., JÜPTNER W., "Direct recording of holograms by a CCD target and numerical reconstruction", *Applied Optics*, vol. 33, pp. 179–181, 1994.

[SCH 99] SCHEDIN S., PEDRINI G., TIZIANI H.J., SANTOYO F.M., "Simultaneous three-dimensional dynamic deformation measurements with pulsed digital holography", *Applied Optics*, vol. 38, pp. 7056–7062, 1999.

[SCH 05] SCHNARS U., JUEPTNER W., *Digital Holography – Digital Hologram Recording, Numerical Reconstruction, and Related Techniques*, Springer, Berlin, 2005.

[SEE 01] SEEBACHER S., OSTEN W., BAUMBACH T., JUPTNER W., "The determination of material parameters of microcomponents using digital holography", *Optics and Lasers in Engineering*, vol. 36, pp. 103–126, 2001.

[SHA 49] SHANNON C.E., "Communication in the presence of noise", *Proceedings IRE*, vol. 37, pp. 10–21, 1949.

[SIE 86] SIEGMAN A.E., *Laser*, University Science Books, Sausalito, CA, 1986.

[SIN 10] SINGH D.K., PANIGRAHI P.K., "Improved digital holographic reconstruction algorithm for depth error reduction and elimination of out-of-focus particles", *Optics Express*, vol. 18, pp. 2426–2448, 2010.

[SLA 11] SLANGEN P.R.L., KARRAY M., PICART P., "Some figures of merit so as to compare digital Fresnel holography and speckle interferometry", *Proceedings SPIE*, vol. 8082, pp. 808205-1-808205-13, 2011.

[SMI 94] SMIGIELSKI P., *Holographie Industrielle*, Teknéa, Toulouse, 1994.

[SMI 98] SMIGIELSKI P., *Holographique Optique – Principes*, Traité Sciences fondamentales, Article AF 3345, Techniques de l'Ingénieur, Paris, 1998.

[SMI 01] SMIGIELSKI P., *Holographique Optique – Interférométrie holographique*, Traité Mesures et contrôle, Article R 6330, Techniques de l'Ingénieur, Paris, 2001.

[STA 00] STADELMAIER A., MASSIG J.H., "Compensation of lens aberration in digital holography", *Optics Letters*, vol. 25, pp. 1630–1632, 2000.

[STI 70] STIGLIANI D.J., MITTRA R., SEMONIN R.G., DANIEL J.S., "Particle-size measurement using forward-scatter holography", *Journal of the Optical Society of America A*, vol. 60, pp. 1059–1067, 1970.

[TAL 36] TALBOT H.F., "Facts relating to optical science", *Philosophical Magazine*, vol. IV, p. 9, 1836.

[TAN 10a] TANKAM P., SONG Q., KARRAY M., LI J.C., DESSE J.M., PICART P., "Real-time three-sensitivity measurements based on three-color digital Fresnel holographic interferometry", *Optics Letters*, vol. 35, pp. 2055–2057, 2010.

[TAN 10b] TANKAM P., PICART P., MOUNIER D., DESSE J.M., LI J.C., "Method of digital holographic recording and reconstruction using a stacked color image sensor", *Applied Optics*, vol. 49, pp. 320–328, 2010.

[TAN 11] TANKAM P., PICART P., "Use of digital color holography for crack investigation in electronic components", *Optics and Lasers in Engineering*, vol. 49, no. 11, pp. 1335–1342, 2011.

[TAR 85] TARASSOV L., *Physique des processus dans les générateurs de rayonnement optique cohérent*, Editions MIR, translated from Russian by V. Kolimeev, Moscow, 1985.

[TIZ 82] TIZIANI H.J., "Real time metrology with BSO cristals", *Optica Acta*, vol. 29, pp. 463–470, 1982.

[VAL 85] VALLAT M.F., SMIGIELSKI P., MARTZ P., SCHULTZ J., "The appplication of coherent optics to the study of adhesive joints 2 – holographic interferometry", *Journal of Applied Polymer Science*, vol. 30, pp. 3853–3959, 1985.

[VER 10] VERRIER N., REMACHA C., BRUNEL M., LEBRUN D., COËTMELLEC S., "Micropipe flow visualization using digital in-line holographic microscopy", *Optics Express*, vol. 18, pp. 7807–7819, 2010.

[WHI 15] WHITTAKER, E.T., "On the functions which are represented by the expansions of the interpolation theory", *Proceedings Royal Society Edinburgh*, vol. 35, pp. 181–194, 1915.

[WYA 75] WYANT J.C., "Use of an ac heterodyne lateral shear interferometer with real-time wavefront correction systems", *Applied Optics*, vol. 14, pp. 2622–2626, 1975.

[XIO 09] XIONG B., LI J.C., *Holographic Interference Measurements – Principles & Methods*, Science Press, Pékin, 2009.

[XU 06] XU X.F., CAI L.Z., MENG X.F., DONG G.Y., SHEN X.X., "Fast blind extraction of arbitrary unknown phase shifts by an iterative tangent approach in generalized phase-shifting interferometry", *Optics Letters*, vol. 31, pp. 1966–1968, 2006.

[YAM 97] YAMAGUCHI I., ZHANG T., "Phase-shifting digital holography", *Optics Letters*, vol. 22, pp. 1268–1270, 1997

[YAM 01a] YAMAGUCHI I., KATO J., OHTA S., MIZUNO J., "Image formation in phase shifting digital holography and application to microscopy", *Applied Optics*, vol. 40, pp. 6177–6186, 2001.

[YAM 01b] YAMAGUCHI I., KATO J., OHTA S., "Surface shape measurement by phase shifting digital holography", *Optical Review*, vol. 8, pp. 85–89, 2001.

[YAM 02] YAMAGUCHI I., MATSUMURA T., KATO J., "Phase shifting color digital holography", *Optics Letters*, vol. 27, pp. 1108–1110, 2002.

[YAN 06] YANG G.-G., "Commemorate a forerunner of holography – Professor Emmett Leith", *Physics*, vol. 35, p. 611, 2006.

[YAR 85] YARIV A., *Optical Electronics*, Holt, Rinehart and Winston, New York, 1985.

[YIN 05] YING C.F., MA L.H., WANG H., "Digital holograms with large viewing angle", *Chinese Journal of Lasers*, vol. 32, pp. 87–90, 2005.

[YU 05] YU L., KIM M.K., "Wavelength-scanning digital interference holography for tomographic three-dimensional imaging by use of the angular spectrum method", *Optics Letters*, vol. 30, pp. 2092–2094, 2005.

[ZHA 04a] ZHANG Y., LÜ Q., GE B., "Elimination of zero-order diffraction in digital off-axis holography", *Optics Communication*, vol. 240, pp. 261–267, 2004.

[ZHA 04b] ZHANG F., YAMAGUCHI I., "Algorithm for reconstruction of digital holograms with adjustable magnification", *Optics Letters*, vol. 29, pp. 1668–1670, 2004.

[ZHA 08] ZHAO J., JIANG H., DI J., "Recording and reconstruction of a color holographic image by using digital lensless Fourier transform holography", *Optics Express*, vol. 16, pp. 2514–2519, 2008.

[ZHA 98] ZHANG T., YAMAGUCHI I., "Three-dimensional microscopy with phase shifting digital holography", *Optics Letters*, vol. 23, pp. 1221–1223, 1998.

[ZOU 96] ZOU Y., PEDRINI G., TIZIANI H.J., "Surface contouring in a video frame by changing the wavelength of a diode laser", *Optical Engineering*, vol. 35, pp. 1074–1079, 1996.

Index